Fromm

Montréal & Québec City

by Herbert Bailey Livesey

Macmillan • USA

ABOUT THE AUTHOR

Herbert Bailey Livesey has written about travel and food for many magazines, including *Travel & Leisure, Food & Wine,* and *Playboy,* and is the author or co-author of several guidebooks, including *Frommer's Walking Tours: Spain's Favorite Cities.*

MACMILLAN TRAVEL

A Simon & Schuster/Macmillan Company
1633 Broadway
New York, NY 10019
Find us online at **http://www.mcp.com/mgr/travel** or
on America Online at Keyword: **SuperLibrary.**

ISBN 0-02-860865-8
ISSN 0899-3165

Editor: Erica Spaberg
Production Editor: Kathleen Varanese
Design by Michele Laseau
Digital Cartography by John Decamillas and Ortelius Design

SPECIAL SALES

Bulk purchases (10+ copies) of Frommer's Travel Guides are available to corporations at special discounts. The Special Sales Department can produce custom editions to be used as premiums and/or for sales promotion to suit individual needs. Existing editions can be produced with custom cover imprints such as corporate logos. For more information, write to: Special Sales, Macmillan Publishing USA, 1633 Broadway, 8th floor, New York, NY 10019.

Manufactured in the United States of America

Contents

1 Introducing Montréal & Québec City 1

1 Frommer's Favorite Montréal & Québec City
   Experiences 2

2 A Look at the Past 3

★ *Dateline* 3

3 Famous Quebecers 10

4 The Politics of Language 13

5 Cuisine Haute, Cuisine Bas: Smoked Meat,
   Fiddleheads & Caribou 15

6 Recommended Books, Films & Recordings 16

2 Planning a Trip to Montréal & Québec City 18

1 Information, Entry Requirements & Money 18

★ *What Things Cost in Montréal* 22

★ *What Things Cost in Québec City* 23

2 When to Go 23

★ *Montréal & Québec City Calendar of Events* 24

3 Tips for Special Travelers 27

4 Getting There 29

3 Getting to Know Montréal 34

1 Orientation 34

2 Getting Around 41

★ *Fast Facts: Montréal* 43

3 Networks & Resources 48

4 Montréal Accommodations 49

1 Best Bets 50

2 Downtown 52

★ *Family-Friendly Accommodations* 61

3 Vieux-Montréal 62

4 Plateau Mont-Royal 64

5   Montréal Dining 65

1 Best Bets 67

2 Restaurants by Cuisine 69

3 Downtown 70

4 Vieux-Montréal 76

★ *Family-Friendly Restaurants* 78

5 Plateau Mont-Royal 79

6 Early-Morning & Late-Night Bites 84

7 Picnic Fare & Where to Eat It 86

6   What to See & Do in Montréal 87

1 Suggested Itineraries 87

2 The Top Attractions 89

3 More Attractions 97

4 Especially for Kids 103

5 Special-Interest Sightseeing 104

6 Organized Tours 106

7 Spectator Sports 108

8 Outdoor Activities 109

★ *Did You Know?* 110

7   Montréal Strolls 111

Walking Tour 1—Vieux-Montréal 111

Walking Tout 2—Downtown 118

Walking Tour 3—Plateau Mont-Royal 124

Walking Tour 4—Mont-Royal 127

8   Montréal Shopping 132

1 The Shopping Scene 132

2 Shopping A to Z 134

9   Montréal Nights 141

1 The Performing Arts 142

2 The Club & Music Scene 146

3 The Bar & Café Scene 150

4 Gay & Lesbian Bars & Clubs 152

5 More Entertainment 153

10   Excursions from Montréal   154

  1 The Laurentides (The Laurentians)   154

  2 The Estrie Region   177

  ★ *The Estrie Wine Country?*   182

11   Getting to Know Québec City   190

  1 Orientation   190

  2 Getting Around   194

  ★ *March of the Tonque Troopers*   194

  ★ *Fast Facts: Quebéc City*   196

  3 Networks & Resources   198

12   Québec City Accommodations   200

  1 Best Bets   201

  2 Upper Town   202

  ★ *Family-Friendly Hotels*   203

  3 On or Near the Grande-Allée   207

  4 Lower Town   210

13   Québec City Dining   212

  1 Best Bets   213

  2 Restaurants by Cuisine   214

  3 Upper Town   215

  ★ *It Helps to Be Born Here*   217

  4 On or Near the Grande-Allée   218

  ★ *Family-Friendly Restaurants*   220

  5 Lower Town   220

  6 Picnic Fare & Where to Eat It   223

14   What to See & Do in Québec City   224

  1 Suggested Itineraries   224

  2 The Top Attractions   225

  3 More Attractions   229

  ★ *Did You Know?*   232

  4 Especially for Kids   233

  5 Organized Tours   234

  6 Spectator Sports   235

  7 Outdoor Activities   236

15   Québec City Strolls   237

Walking Tour 1—Upper Town   237
Walking Tour 2—Lower Town   245

16   Québec City Shopping   251

1   The Shopping Scene   251
2   Shopping A to Z   253

17   Québec City After Dark   257

1   The Performing Arts   257
2   The Club & Music Scene   258
3   The Bar & Café Scene   260
★   *The Major Concert & Performance Halls*   261
4   More Entertainment   262

18   Excursions from Québec City   263

1   Île d'Orléans   263
2   Montmorency Falls   269
3   Ste-Anne-de-Beaupré   270
4   Mont Ste-Anne   272
5   Charlevoix   273
6   The Southern Bank   278
★   *Flight of the Bone-Headed Goose*   283

Index   284

List of Maps

Eastern Canada   9

Montréal

Montréal Métro   42

Montréal Downtown
   Accommodations
   54

Vieux-Montréal
   Accommodations &
   Attractions   63

Montréal Downtown
   Attractions   90

Walking Tour—
   Vieux-Montréal
   113

Walking Tour—
   Downtown   120

Walking Tour—
   Plateau Mont-Royal
   125

Walking Tour—
   Mont-Royal   129

The Laurentides
   (The Laurentians)
   157

Québec City

Québec City
   Accommodations   204

Québec City Attractions
   226

Walking Tour—
   Upper Town   240

Walking Tour—
   Lower Town   247

Excursions from Québec
   City   265

For Joanne
The Best One.

ACKNOWLEDGMENTS

For their generous assistance and welcome advice, the author particularly wants to express his gratitude to Gilles Bengle of the Greater Montréal Convention and Tourism Bureau, Pierre Tougas of the Government of Québec Ministry of Tourism in Montréal, and Michael Gagnon of the Greater Québec Area Tourism and Convention Bureau in Quebec.

And for her patience and gentle guidance, he wishes to thank his editor, Erica Spaberg.

AN INVITATION TO THE READER

In researching this book, I discovered many wonderful places—hotels, restaurants, shops, and more. I'm sure you'll find others. Please tell us about them, so we can share the information with your fellow travelers in upcoming editions. If you were disappointed with a recommendation, we'd love to know that, too. Please write to:

Herbert Livesey
Frommer's Montréal & Québec City, 8th Edition
Macmillan Travel
1633 Broadway
New York, NY 10019

AN ADDITIONAL NOTE

Please be advised that travel information is subject to change at any time—and this is especially true of prices. We therefore suggest that you write or call ahead for confirmation when making your travel plans. The authors, editors, and publisher cannot be held responsible for the experiences of readers while traveling. Your safety is important to us, however, so we encourage you to stay alert and be aware of your surroundings. Keep a close eye on cameras, purses, and wallets, all favorite targets of pickpockets.

WHAT THE SYMBOLS MEAN

✪ Frommer's Favorites

Hotels, restaurants, attractions, and entertainment you should not miss.

⑤ Super-Special Values

Hotels and restaurants that offer great value for your money.

The following abbreviations are used for credit cards:

AE	American Express	ER	enRoute
CB	Carte Blanche	JCB	Japan Credit Bank
DC	Diners Club	MC	MasterCard
DISC	Discover	V	Visa
ER	enRoute		

Introducing Montréal & Québec City

The duality of Canadian life has been called the "Twin Solitudes." One, English and Calvinist in origin, tends to be staid, smug, and work-obsessed. The other, French and Catholic, is more creative, lighthearted, and inclined to see pleasure as the end-purpose of labor. That shifting set of relationships applies to Québec and the nine provinces of English Canada, but also to its largest city, Montréal, if in reverse. French speakers, known as Francophones, constitute 66% of the population, while most of the rest are speakers of English—Anglophones. Those few residents who speak neither, or who have another primary tongue, are called Allophones. While all are decidedly North American, the contending groups are as much alike as the British and the French.

Montréal is a contemporary city in nearly every regard. Its downtown bristles with skyscrapers, but these are playful, almost perky, in unexpected shapes and even shades of uncorporate colors. The city above is mirrored by another one below, where an entire winter can be avoided in coatless comfort. To the west and north of downtown are Anglo commercial and residential neighborhoods, centered around Westmount. To the east and north are Francophone *quartiers*, centered on Outremount. In between are the many dialects and skin tones of the immigrant rainbow, roiled by social conflicts and pressured to choose sides.

There is an impression, buttressed by a recent rash of *Vente*—FOR SALE—signs, that Montréal is in steep decline. American expatriates I know report a pervasive sadness in the citizenry, driven by lingering recession and uncertainty over the future. There is a large measure of truth in that. After all, it remains possible that Québec will yet choose to fling itself into an unknown independence, despite the razor thin margin by which pro-unity forces won the 1995 referendum on sovereignty. That would be a seismic event accompanied by Anglo flight, loss of federal subsidies, and a baleful of economic uncertainty.

But to many American city dwellers, Montréal might well seem an urban paradise. The subway system, called the *métro*, is modern and swift. Streets are clean and safe. There were only 52 homicides in Montréal in 1994, compared to the hundreds of murders annually in every American city of comparable or greater size. In the same year, police of the greater metropolitan region discharged their weapons exactly 16 times. Montréal's best restaurants are the equal of their south-of-the-border compatriots in almost every way, yet they are as much as 30 to 40% cheaper. And, the government gives visitors back most of the taxes they collect.

Québec City is less sophisticated, more conservative, and more French. With its splendid location above the St. Lawrence River and its virtually umblemished Old Town of 18th- and 19th-century houses, it even looks French. Probably 95% of its residents speak the mother tongue, and far fewer of them are bilingual, as most Montréalers are. (In the province as a whole, about 81% are Francophone.) With that homogeneity and its status as the putative capital of a future independent nation, citizens seem to suffer less angst over what might happen down the road. They are also aware that a critical part of their economy is based on tourism, and they are far less likely to vent the open hostility toward visitors that Americans can experience in other parts of the world, including English Canada.

That determination was tempered by 1995 by the election of federalist Liberals in important by-elections, suggesting a contrary sentiment in at least a segment of the populace. When the sovereignty referendum was finally set for October 1995, early polls asserted that Québec's voters would again choose overwhelmingly to remain a part of Canada. But as election day neared, the gap was closed, making the outcome too close to call. The federalists won, by a scant one percent. The next day, Québec's Prime Minister Jacques Parizeau resigned, and other separatist leaders vowed to hold yet another referendum as soom as practicable.

1 Frommer's Favorite Montréal & Québec City Experiences

MONTRÉAL

- **Exploring Old Montréal:** Wander place Jacques-Cartier, the most engaging of the old city's squares, explore museums and the stunning architecture of churches, and stroll along the waterfront.
- **Listening to Jazz:** Downtown, Old Town, all over, this is a favorite activity of locals and visitors alike, especially in June during the Montréal Jazz Festival.
- **Shopping:** Browse the shops of world-class domestic designers, from the up-and-coming to the well-established, search for Inuit (Eskimo) sculptures of the highest order, with prices to match, and take in the eclectic antiques shops on the two blocks along rue Notre-Dame between Rue Guy and rue des Seigneurs.
- **Dining:** Savor French cuisine in all its permutations *haute,* bistro, original Québécois, and Cal-Asian hybrids and sample the offerings of the city's many good ethnic restaurants representing dozens of foreign cuisines, notably Thai, Chinese, Polish, and Indian.

QUÉBEC CITY

- **Strolling and Sitting on the terrasse Dufferin:** Captivating Québec is at its best here, with the copper-spired Château Frontenac rearing up behind, the lower town below, and ferries, freighters, and pleasure craft moving on the broad, silvered river.
- **Lingering at an Outdoor Café:** They set out tables at place d'Armes, in the Quartier du Petit-Champlain, and along the Grande-Allée, a quality-of-life invention the French and their Québécois brethren have perfected.
- **Hanging out in Battlefields Park:** The park is beautifully situated, overlooking the St. Lawrence River, and is particularly lively on weekends, when families and lovers come here to picnic and play.
- **Taking the Funicular:** Even those who prefer to walk most of the time, should take it at least once for the ride and the view.
- **Admiring the Skyline from the Lévis Ferry:** This provides quite a view for very little money, and passengers can turn around and come right back without disembarking.
- **Taking Advantage of Table d'Hôte Specials:** Indulge in three or four courses for a fixed price that is about the same or slightly more than the cost of an à la carte main course alone. Most full-service restaurants offer the table d'hôte, if only at midday.

2 A Look at the Past

Québec is immense, encompassing almost 600,000 square miles—two times the size of Texas—stretching from the northern borders of New York, Vermont, and New Hampshire almost to the Arctic Circle. To the east of it are Maine and the province of New Brunswick, and to the west, the province of Ontario and the Hudson Bay. Québec is the largest province in the second-largest country in the world (after Russia) and more than three times as large as France. (It would be even larger had Labrador not been awarded to Newfoundland in 1927, still a point of contention to Quebecers.) Its natural resources include 16% of the world's supply of fresh water. Most of the province's population lives in its lower regions—the St. Lawrence lowlands and parts of the Appalachians and the Laurentians. More than 80% of its almost seven million residents live within an area 200 miles long and 60 miles wide, one of the highest concentrations of population in Canada.

Montréal, home to a third of the province's population, occupies about one-third (60 square miles) of the island of Montréal, which is part of

Dateline

- **1534** Jacques Cartier sails up the St. Lawrence, claiming the territory for France and marking the first European discovery of Canada.
- **1608** Samuel de Champlain founds a settlement at Kebec, at the foot of Cape Diamond. It will become Québec City.
- **1642** Paul de Chomedey, sieur de Maisonneuve,

continues

establishes a colony called Ville-Marie that will become Montréal.

- **1668** Québec Seminary is founded in Québec City, later to become Laval University in 1852.

- **1759** British General Wolfe defeats French General Montcalm on the Plains of Abraham in Québec City.

- **1760** Montréal falls to the British.

- **1763** The king of France cedes all of Canada to the king of England in the Treaty of Paris.

- **1775** Montréal is occupied by American Revolutionary forces, who withdraw after a few months, when an attempted siege of Québec City by Benedict Arnold fails.

- **1821** English-speaking McGill University is founded in Montréal.

- **1867** The British North America Act creates the federation of the

continues

the Hochelaga Archipelago. The island is situated in the St. Lawrence River near where it joins the Ottawa River. At the city's center is a 764-foot hill the natives like to think of as a mountain called Mont-Royal, and from which the city takes its name. Nearby rise more mountains, the Laurentides (the Laurentians), the oldest mountain range in the world and the playground of the Québécois. The foothills of the Appalachian mountains separate Québec from the United States; they add to the beauty of Estrie, the hill country on the opposite side of the St. Lawrence once known as the Eastern Townships, where many Montréalers have country homes. The capital city of Québec, 166 miles northeast of Montréal, commands a stunning location high atop Cape Diamond, overlooking the St. Lawrence River at its narrowest point here, 1,969 feet across.

THE EUROPEANS ARRIVE   The Vikings landed in Canada over 1,000 years ago, probably followed by Irish and Basque fishermen. English explorer John Cabot stepped ashore briefly on the east coast in 1497, but it was the French who managed the first meaningful European toehold in the country. When Jacques Cartier sailed up the St. Lawrence in 1535, he recognized at once the tremendous strategic potential of Cape Diamond, "the Gibraltar of the North." But he was exploring, not empire building, and after stepping ashore he reembarked for the trip upriver.

Samuel de Champlain arrived 73 years later, in 1608, determined to settle at Québec, a year after the Virginia Company founded a fledgling colony called Jamestown, hundreds of miles to the south. The British and French struggle for dominance in the new continent focused on their explorations, and there the French outdid the English. Their far-ranging fur traders, navigators, soldiers, and missionaries opened up not only Canada but also most of the United States, moving all the way south to the future New Orleans and claiming most of the territory to the west. This vast region later comprised the Louisiana Purchase. At least 35 of the subsequent 50 states were discovered, mapped, or settled by Frenchmen, who left behind some 4,000 place names to prove it, among them Detroit, St. Louis, New Orleans, Duluth, and Des Moines.

Champlain's first settlement, or "Habitation," grew to become Québec's Lower Town, down on the flat riverbank beneath the cliffs of Cape Diamond. But almost from the beginning there were attacks, first by the Iroquois, then the English, and later by the Americans. To better defend themselves, the Québécois constructed a fortress atop the cape, and gradually the center of urban life moved to the top of the cliffs.

In the 1750s the struggle between Britain and France had escalated, after a series of conflicts that had embroiled both Europe and the New World. The latest episode was known as the French and Indian War in North America, an extension of Europe's Seven Years' War. Strategic Québec became a valued prize. The French sent Louis Joseph, marquis de Montcalm, to command their forces in the town. The British sent an expedition of 4,500 men in a fleet under the command of a 32-year-old general named James Wolfe. The ensuing battle for Québec, fought on the Plains of Abraham southwest of the city on September 13, 1759, is one of the most famous in North American history, since it also resulted in a continent that was thus transferred to British culture and influence for centuries to come. Wolfe and his forces rowed upriver to a cove behind the city. Then they silently climbed the towering cliff face in darkness through a narrow but undefended ravine.

Both generals perished as a result of the 20-minute battle. Wolfe lived just long enough to hear that he had won. Montcalm died a few hours later. Told that he was mortally wounded, he replied, "All the better. I will not see the English in Québec." Today a memorial to both men overlooks terrasse Dufferin in Québec City, the only statue in the world commemorating both victor and vanquished of the same battle. The inscription, in neither French nor English but Latin, says simply, "Courage was fatal to them."

THE U.S. INVASION   The capture of Québec determined the course of the war, and the Treaty of Paris in 1763 ceded all of French Canada to England. In a sense, this victory led to Britain's worst defeat. If the French had held Canada, the British government might have been more tactful in its treatment of the American colonists. As it was, the British decided to make the colonists

- provinces of Québec, Ontario, Nova Scotia, and New Brunswick.
- **1883** "Je me souviens" becomes the motto of Québec—an ominous "I remember."
- **1900–1910** 325,000 French Canadians immigrate to the United States.
- **1922** Armand Bombardier invents the prototype for the Ski-Doo, the first snowmobile, which will make him famous and wealthy in the late 1950s.
- **1925** The Seagram Company is founded in Montréal.
- **1940** Women obtain the right to vote in provincial elections in Québec, having obtained that right in federal elections in 1917.
- **1948** The Québec flag, bearing four fleurs-de-lis, is adopted.
- **1962** Montréal's Underground City is born, with the construction of place Ville-Marie.
- **1967** Montréal hosts Expo '67.

continues

- **1968** The Parti Québécois is founded by René Lévesque, and the separatist movement begins.

- Québécois Pierre Elliott Trudeau is elected prime minister of Canada, and holds that office for most of the following 18 years.

- **1976** The Parti Québécois comes to power in Québec and remains in office until 1985, when the Liberal Party supersedes it. Montréal hosts the Olympics.

- **1984** Québécois Brian Mulroney becomes prime minister of Canada.

- **1989** The Canada-U.S. Free-Trade Agreement goes into effect, gradually removing all tariffs on goods of national origin moving between the two countries.

- **1990** The Meech Lake Accord, recognizing Québec as a "distinct society" within Canada, is voted down, and separatist agitation increases.

continues

pay the costs of the French and Indian War, on the principle that it was their homes being defended. They slapped so many taxes on all imports that the infuriated colonists openly rebelled against the Crown.

But if the British misjudged the temper of the colonists, the Americans were equally wrong about the mood of the Canadians. George Washington felt sure that French Canadians would want to join the Revolution, or at least be supportive. He was mistaken on both counts. Even the arguments of Benjamin Franklin, who was sent to Montréal to argue the case, could not convince them. The Québécois were at best ambivalent about the American cause, in part because of the virulent antimonarchist tenor of the rebels. They detested their British conquerors, but they were also staunch Royalists and devout Catholics, and saw their contentious neighbors as godless Republicans. Only a handful supported the Americans, as often as not to sell them supplies, and three of Washington's most competent commanders came to grief in attacks against Québec. Vermonter Ethan Allen and his Green Mountain Boys were taken prisoner at Montréal, and Montgomery fell before Québec, where the ambitious Benedict Arnold was also driven back in defeat, possibly fueling his eventual perfidy.

Thirty-eight years later, in the War of 1812, another U.S. army marched up the banks of the Richelieu River where it flows from Lake Champlain to the St. Lawrence. And once again the French Canadians stuck by the British and drove back the invaders. The war ended essentially in a draw, but had at least one encouraging result. Britain and the young United States agreed to demilitarize the Great Lakes and to extend their mutual border along the 49th parallel to the Rockies.

MONTRÉAL Jacques Cartier sailed up the broad St. Lawrence River, past the spot that would become Québec City under Champlain, to what was then a large island with a small Native American settlement. Cartier, as usual, did not linger, but pushed onward in his search for the sea route to China. His progress was halted by the fierce rapids just west of the island. In a demonstration of mingled optimism and frustration, he dubbed the rapids La Chine on the assumption that China was just the other side of them. He then decided to check out the large island after all, landing at a spot in what is now Old Montréal, and paid his respects to the native people before moving on.

That was the extent of Cartier's contribution to the future city. Over 100 years later, Paul de Chomedey, sieur de Maisonneuve, arrived (1642) to establish a colony and to plant a crucifix atop the hill he called Mont-Royal. He and his band of settlers came ashore and founded Ville-Marie, dedicated to the Virgin Mary, at the spot now marked by place Royale. They built a fort, a chapel, stores, and houses, and the energetic Jeanne Mance made her indelible mark by founding the hospital named Hôtel-Dieu-de-Montréal, which still exists today.

Life was not easy. Unlike the friendly Algonquins who lived in nearby regions, the Iroquois in Montréal had no intention of living in peace with the new settlers. Maisonneuve had said he would settle at Montréal "even if the very trees of the island turn to Iroquois," and it must have seemed to the handful of inhabitants of Ville-Marie that the trees had done just that. Fierce battles raged for years, and the settlers were lucky that their numbers included such undauntable souls as la Salle, du Luth, de la Mothe Cadillac, and the brothers Lemoyne, all of whom later left their names on territories in the Great Lakes and Mississippi.

At place d'Armes stands a statue of Maisonneuve, marking the spot where the settlers defeated the Iroquois in bloody hand-to-hand fighting, with Maisonneuve himself locked in mortal combat with the Iroquois chief. Maisonneuve won.

From that time the settlement prospered, though in 1760 it fell to the British, the year after Wolfe defeated Montcalm on the Plains of Abraham in Québec. Until the 1800s the city was contained in the area known today as Old Montréal. Its ancient walls no longer stand, but half of its long and colorful past is preserved in the streets, houses, and churches of the Old City.

Québec City seems to have changed little with time, the ancient walls that protected it over the centuries still in place today, preserving for posterity the heart of New France. Montréal, though, has gone through a metamorphosis. The

- **1992** Montréal celebrates its 350th birthday. The Charlottetown Accord, a reworking of Meech Lake, is defeated at the polls.
- **1993** Mulroney resigns with public approval ratings in the single digits. He is succeeded by Kim Campbell, the first woman to head the Progressive Conservative Party and the first female prime minister. She and the Tories are soundly defeated by Jean Chrétien and the Liberals in October.
- **1994** Québec's separatist Parti Québécois wins provincial elections, ending nine years of Liberal rule.
- **1995** Despite a seemingly unstoppable momentum toward independence, federalist politicians defeat separatists in important by-elections in Québec. Referendum on separation from

continues

the rest of Canada defeated. A conflict with Spain over fishing rights brings threats of retaliation from the European Union.

city's recent history is almost as fascinating as its early days, for it was "wet" when the United States was "dry" due to Prohibition. Bootleggers, hard drinkers, prostitutes, and the rest flocked to this large city so well situated close to the American border, and mixed with the rowdy elements from the port, much to the distress of Montréal's mainly upstanding citizenry. For half a century the city's image was off-color, but in the 1950s the cleanup began, with a boom in high-rise construction and eventual restoration of much of the derelict Old Town. In 1967 Montréal welcomed the world to Expo. The great gleaming skyscrapers and towering hotels, the suberb metro system, and the highly practical Underground City, so much a part of this modern city, date mostly from the last 30 years.

All this activity helped to fuel a phenomenon later labeled the "Quiet Revolution." It was to transform the largely rural, agricultural province into an urbanized, industrial entity with a pronounced secular outlook. French Canadians, long confined to secondary careers well removed from the control rooms of the economy by what amounted to the linguistic racism of the ruling Anglophones, started to insist upon equal opportunity with the powerful minority. Inevitably, perhaps, a fringe radical movement of separatists emerged, signaling its intentions by bombing Anglophone businesses. The FLQ, as it was known, was behind most of the terrorist attacks, reaching its nadir with the kidnapping-murder of a cabinet minister, Pierre Laporte.

Most Québécois separatists were not violent, and most Québécois were not even separatists. Pierre Trudeau, a bilingual Québécois, became prime minister in 1968. As flamboyant, eccentric, and brilliant as any Canadian who ever held the post, he necessarily devoted much of his time trying to placate both sides of the issue. In 1969, the Official Languages Act mandated that all federal agencies provide services in both French and English. Yet by 1980, a provincial referendum on separation from the confederation was only defeated by 60% of the vote. Subsequent attempts to assuage the chafed sensibilities of French Québecers failed again and again, as often at the hands of other provincial premiers as by the Québécois, hounding at least three prime ministers from office.

In 1993, the governing Tories were defeated by the opposition Liberals. The new prime minister, Jean Chrétien, a federalist, is not aided in his task of national reconciliation by representation in the House of Commons of the militantly separatist Bloc Québécois. And in Québec

Impressions

Being ourselves is essentially a matter of keeping and developing a personality that has survived for three and a half centuries.

—René Lévesque, founder of the Parti Québécois (1968)

Eastern Canada

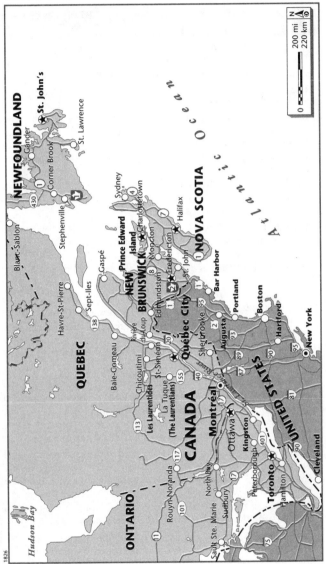

the following year, the Parti Québécois won provincial elections to end nine years of Liberal control. The new premier, Jacques Parizeau, vowed to hold an early referendum on sovereignty, which was held in late October 1995 and was narrowly defeated. Porizeau resigned the day after, amid vows from other separatist leaders to hold another referendum soon after.

3 Famous Quebecers

Joseph-Armand Bombardier (1907–64)   The inventor of the Ski-Doo snowmobile in the late 1950s lived in Estrie, across the river from Montréal, where his devices have their own museum.

Edgar M. Bronfman, Jr. (b. 1955)   Chairman and CEO of the Seagram Company Ltd. (Montréal) and Joseph E. Seagram & Sons Inc. (the U.S. subsidiary, in New York) since 1994. His grandfather and great-uncle founded the company in 1925, and his father, Edgar Bronfman, served as its chairman and CEO from 1975 to 1994. The Seagram Company produces Seagram and Chivas Regal whisky, Sterling wines, and Tropicana orange juice and recently took over Universal Pictures and the MCA entertainment conglomerate. Although the Bronfman family is the largest private landowner in Canada, he and his father are U.S. citizens.

Geneviève Bujold (b. 1942)   An actress who studied at the Montréal Drama Conservancy, she is best known for the films *La Guerre est Finie* (1966), *King of Hearts* (1967), *Anne of a Thousand Days* (1970), *Coma* (1978), with Michael Douglas, and *Tightrope* (1984), with Clint Eastwood.

Jean Chrétien (b. 1934)   Elected in 1963 as the prime minister of Canada, Chrétien studied law at Laval University and was elected to the House of Commons first in 1963. He resigned from the House of Commons in 1986 and practiced law privately until 1990, when he was elected leader of the Liberal Party of Canada. A bilingual Québécois, he is a committed federalist.

Leonard Cohen (b. 1934)   A singer and songwriter who gained a reputation in the sixties and seventies for his melancholy, mournful songs, delivered in a "distinctive drone." Perhaps his best-known song is "Suzanne," made especially popular by singer Judy Collins. His novel *Beautiful Losers* won the Québec Prize for Literature in 1964.

Céline Dion (b. 1968)   This singer gained recognition in the United States with the recording of the Grammy Award–winning "Beauty and the Beast," from the Walt Disney animated film. Her duet with Clive Griffin, "When I Fall in Love," was the signature song on the soundtrack of the movie *Sleepless in Seattle.* Dion has won numerous Juno Awards, the Canadian equivalent to the American Grammys.

Glenn Ford (b. 1916)   His long career in film began in 1939 with *Heaven with a Barbed Wire Fence* for Twentieth Century-Fox, and went on to include starring roles in many films over more than five decades, among them *Blackboard Jungle* (1955), *The Teahouse of the August Moon* (1956), *The Four Horsemen of the Apocalypse* (1961), *The Courtship of Eddie's Father* (1963), *Midway* (1976), and *Superman* (1978).

Oliver Jones (b. 1934)   The son of immigrants from Barbados, Jones studied classical piano and eased into jazz in the early 1980s. He has recorded extensively; his work has been influenced greatly by Art Tatum.

Impressions

*I expected to find a contest between a government and a people: I found
two nations warring in the bosom of a single state: I found a struggle, not
of principles, but of races . . .*

—Lord Durham, Report on the Affairs of
British North America (1839)

Guy Lafleur (b. 1951)   A hockey star with the Montréal Canadiens
from 1971 to 1985, he scored more than 50 goals and more than 100
points in six consecutive seasons and claimed 560 goals and 739 assists
in his career. He played for Montréal with five Stanley Cup teams.

Phyllis Lambert (b. 1927)   Director and founder of the Canadian
Centre for Architecture, founding president of Heritage Montréal, and
current president of Société du Patrimoine Urbain de Montréal, she has
long been a champion of architectural preservation in Montréal.

Antoine Lamet de la Mothe Cadillac (1658–1730)   Born in Gas-
cony, he later lived much of his life in Montréal, in a house marked by
a plaque on rue Notre-Dame. In 1701 he founded Detroit, Michigan,
and he was a governor of Louisiana from 1711 to 1716.

René Lévesque (1922–87)   The father of the mainstream separatist
movement in Québec and a founder of the Parti Québécois in 1968,
he worked as a radio and television journalist before becoming involved
in politics. Lévesque dreamed of a Québec under a Swedish-style social system, with nationalized essential industries, guaranteed income,
and socialized medicine, and an American-style government with a
president and a supreme court, which he described in the book *An
Option for Québec* (McClelland, 1968). He was premier of Québec
from 1976 to 1985.

Louis Lortie (b. 1959)   The award-winning pianist made his debut
in Toronto in 1978 at the age of 19. Soon afterward, he accompanied
the Toronto Symphony on tours of Japan and China, and returned to
China to great acclaim in 1983. Lortie has given recitals in New York,
Chicago, Los Angeles, San Francisco, Washington, and through-
out Europe. He has appeared with the Philadelphia and Cleveland
Orchestras, and the Boston, San Francisco, and Montréal Symphony
Orchestras.

John Molson (1763–1836)   In 1786, at the age of 23, he founded
Molson Breweries, the oldest continuously active brewery operating in
North America. Molson's business enterprises extended beyond beer to
include steamboat and railway building. He was a founder of the
Montréal General Hospital and served as chairman of the board for the
Bank of Montréal.

Brian Mulroney (b. 1939)   A Conservative Party leader, he was
prime minister from September 1984 to February 1993. Among the
issues he had to grapple with were the free-trade agreement with the
U.S. in 1989, the institution of a federal goods-and-services tax of 7%,
put into effect in 1991, and the question of Québec's secession from

Canada. Mulroney supported a degree of autonomy for his native province of Québec, but was opposed to secession. He resigned from office with the lowest approval rating of any prime minister in this century.

Oscar Peterson (b. 1925)   The jazz great and prolific recording artist made magic on the keyboard with his trio and with other artists from the early fifties to the seventies, when he went solo. His *Canadiana Suite* was nominated as one of the best jazz compositions in 1965 by the National Academy of Recording Artists and Scientists.

Henri Richard (b. 1936)   Known as the "Pocket Rocket," a reference to his hockey-star older brother, he played on 11 Stanley Cup teams for Montréal, and was named an All Star four times. His 20-year career spanned from 1955 to 1975.

Maurice Richard (b. 1921)   "The Rocket," he scored 544 goals in his hockey career, from 1942 to 1959, and thrilled fans by making 50 goals in one season (1945) and 5 goals in a single game. He played on eight Stanley Cup championship teams and was named an All Star eight times.

Mordecai Richler (b. 1931)   Well known in the United States, the novelist, essayist, screenwriter, and cultural critic was born in Montréal, lived in London from 1954 to 1972, but returned to his hometown frequently. His fictional characters are Jewish-Canadians at odds with society, as in *Joshua Then and Now* and *The Apprenticeship of Duddy Kravitz*, the latter produced as a movie. His frequent essays decrying Québécois separatism and what he has called the "tongue troopers" have infuriated many French Canadians.

Jean-Paul Riopelle (b. 1923)   Painter, sculptor, printmaker, Riopelle is one of Canada's leading abstract expressionists. His works have been exhibited internationally and his *Don Quixote* (1961) stands in the Hirshhorn Museum & Sculpture Garden in Washington, D.C. He has lived primarily in Paris since 1946, once described as "He looks like Chico Marx–acts rather like him, too."

Gabrielle Roy (1909–83)   Writing books and stories about her French-Canadian upbringing and experiences as a teacher in one-room schools, Roy's most honored work was *The Tin Flute*. The film version of the book premiered at the Moscow Film Festival.

Moshe Safdie (b. 1938)   Born in Israel and raised on a kibbutz until he was 16, Safdie then moved to Montréal with his family and studied architecture at McGill University. Since then, he has done much to change the cityscapes of Montréal and Québec City, as well as the United States. In 1963 Safdie designed the general plan for Expo '67, including Habitat 67, based on concepts in his McGill thesis and consisting of 354 prefabricated concrete boxes that form 158 dwellings stacked into three pyramids. At that time, the 29-year-old Safdie was heralded by the London *Sunday Times* as the "heir to Le Corbusier." In 1991, Safdie completed the annex for the Museum of Fine Arts in Montréal. He also designed the Museum of Civilization in Québec City. Safdie, now based in Boston, Mass., has taught at Harvard and Yale.

William Shatner (b. 1931)   Born in Montréal, Shatner is best known as Capt. James T. Kirk on the television series "Star Trek" (1966-69), and the subsequent theatrical films.

Norma Shearer (1904–83)   A film actress, she won an Academy Award for *The Divorcee* (1930), and was nominated for an award for *Their Own Desire* (1930), *A Free Soul* (1931), *The Barretts of Wimpole Street* (1934), *Romeo and Juliet* (1936), and *Marie Antoinette* (1938). Shearer was married to Irving Thalberg.

Michel Tremblay (b. 1942)   A playwright, novelist, and screenwriter whose works have been widely translated, Tremblay often addresses the social and cultural problems of French-Canadian life. His semiautobiographical novels, *The Fat Woman Next Door Is Pregnant* and *Thérèse and Pierette and the Little Hanging Angel*, have been translated into English.

Pierre Trudeau (b. 1919)   Prime minister of Canada from 1968 to 1979 and 1980 to 1984, he is a federalist and a liberal who was described during his tenures as a "cautious darer." Trudeau was a founder of the Montréal Civil Liberties Union and has a master's degree from Harvard.

4 The Politics of Language

The defining dialectic of Canadian life is language, the thorny issue that might yet tear the country apart. It manifests itself in the assumption of many Québécois that a separate independent state is the only way to maintain their culture in the face of the Anglophone ocean that surrounds them. The role of Québec within the Canadian federation is the most debated and volatile issue in Canadian politics—and it will not be easily resolved in the predictable future.

One attempt was made in 1969, when federal legislation stipulated that all services were henceforth to be offered in both English and French, in effect declaring the nation bilingual. That didn't long assuage militant Québécois. Having made the two languages equal in the rest of the country, they undertook to guarantee the primacy of French in their own province. Bill 101 was passed in 1977, which all but banned the use of English on public signage. Ogilvy's and Eaton's department stores were made to drop their offensive Anglo apostrophes, STOP signs now read ARRÊT, and "Going Out of Business" posters were taken down. The bill funded establishment of enforcement units, virtual language police who let no nit go unpicked.

And that was not enough. In a 1980 referendum, Québec's citizens voted on whether they favored maintaining the political status quo or wished to seek a "sovereignty-association" with the Canadian government. In sovereignty-association, they would have had political autonomy while retaining economic links with Canada. Though the latter proposition was narrowly defeated, the whole separatist issue was hardly put to rest. Two years later a new national constitution was adopted, though never endorsed by Québec, whose constituency felt it did not adequately protect the province's distinct linguistic and cultural heritage.

As a result of this backlash, Canadian prime minister Brian Mulroney met with the 10 provincial premiers in April 1987 at a retreat at Québec's Meech Lake to cobble together a group of constitutional reforms. The Meech Lake Accord, as it came to be known, addressed a variety of issues, but most important to the Québécois, it recognized Québec as a "distinct society" within the federation. In the end, however, Manitoba and Newfoundland failed to ratify the accord by the June 23, 1990, deadline. As a result, support for the secessionist cause has burgeoned in Québec, and the separatist Parti Québécois, now controls the provincial government. A referendum held in 1995 was narrowly won by those Quebecers who favored staying within the union, but the vote settled nothing. The issue continues to divide families and dominate all political discourse.

People talk about separation in Québec as often as those elsewhere discuss the weather, though there are times, due to sheer exhaustion with the subject, that it seems to be the last thing anyone wants to discuss. In bars, restaurants, hair salons, and around kitchen tables, the same questions continue to be uttered, over and over. Would a politically independent Québec continue to share a common currency, a common central bank, and a tariff-free relationship with the rest of Canada? Would the Canadian-U.S. Free-Trade Agreement be extended to an independent Québec? Would the Atlantic provinces, cut off from the rest of Canada, apply to the United States for statehood? Would Seagram's Canadian whiskies become Québec whiskies?

In the midst of the unshakable fray, Québec remains committed to ensuring, one way or another, the survival of the province's unique culture and French language, its bedrock loyalty to its Gallic roots. France may have relinquished control of Québec in 1763, but its influence, after a century and a half of rule, remains powerful to this day. The Québécois continue to look across the Atlantic for inspiration in fashion, food, and the arts. Culturally and linguistically, it is that tenacious French connection that gives the province its special character, which is a source of great regional pride, if considerable national controversy.

There are reasons for the festering intransigence of the Québécois, about 220 years' worth. After what they unfailingly call "The Conquest," their English rulers made a few concessions to French-Canadian pride, including allowing them a Gallic version of jurisprudence. But a kind of linguistic racism prevailed, with wealthy Scottish and English bankers and merchants ensuring that French Canadians were repeatedly denied access to the higher levels of business and government. Intentionally, or simply thoughtlessly, Anglophones lowered an opaque ceiling on Francophone advancement. The present strife, and the frequent foolishness and small-mindedness that attends it on both sides, is as much revenge as it is pride in the French heritage.

Impressions

Je me souviens. "I remember."—Motto for Québec province, seen on automobile license plates.

None of this should deter potential visitors. The Québécois are gracious hosts. While Montréal may be the largest French-speaking city outside Paris, most Montréalers grow up speaking both French and English, switching effortlessly from one language to the other as the situation dictates.

Telephone operators go from French to English the instant they hear an English word out of the other party, as do most store clerks, waiters, and hotel staff. This is less so in country villages and in Québec City, but there is virtually no problem that can't be solved with a few French words, some expressive gestures, and a little goodwill.

5 Cuisine Haute, Cuisine Bas: Smoked Meat, Fiddleheads & Caribou

French cuisine, in its several permutations, has prevailed since the arrival of Québec's earliest white settlers. Called Québécois, it was originally the country cooking of the motherland adapted to the ingredients found in New France (root vegetables, dried legimes, apples, whatever catchable fish and game were available, and maple sugar). Dishes native to the region evolved, many of them still savored by the Québécois today. Among these are a meat pie called *tourtière,* beans and pork baked in maple syrup, and maple sugar pie (*tarte au sucre*). As time passed and food became more than sustenance, the gastronomic fervor of the old country was imported to Québec, and replications of Parisian bistros and the manifestations of the epicurean teachings of Brillat-Savarin arrived and multiplied. The entire range of Gallic cuisines were then available, from lowbrow to upper-crust. They persist in the cities and in several excellent restaurants in the country. Game is still highly popular, with wild boar, venison, pheasant, quail, hare, and even caribou appearing frequently on menus. Oddly, for a region whose identity is shaped in large part by the great river that runs through it, fish is seen much less often. When it is, it is almost always salmon. Extremely popular shellfish are mussels, served in the Belgian manner with thin *frites* (french fries)—and usually refilled for free—and lobster, which comes at remarkable bargain prices during the customary summer *festival* celebrating its availability.

There it stood, until quite recently. There was French food and there was everything else, which was foreign. Ethnic eateries existed, serving mostly the immigrant groups from whence they sprang. The biggest, priciest, and longest-lived restaurants remained the French ones. The culinary revolution that rolled across the continent from California in the 1980s swallowed up Vancouver, Toronto, Chicago, and New York, but it barely touched Montréal, and Québec City not at all. That is changing, quite dramatically, in the nineties. Cal-Ital and Fusion have arrived, and are taking their place at the head of the table. Of the five or six top restaurants in the province, three are making their own rules, improvising, inventing new combinations of textures, tastes, and ingredients. The traditional kitchens remain, but they are lightening their sauces, rethinking their assumptions, and even tossing out old recipes. More Italian, Mediterranean, and Asian restaurants are opening every year. Already, cosmopolitan Québec has become more sophisticated.

A little knowledge of local restaurant terminology will help avoid confusion when dining in Québec. An *entrée* is an appetizer, not the main course, which is *le plat*. In fancier places, where a pre-appetizer nibble is proffered, it is an *amuse-gueule,* and the little plate of cookies and sweets that comes with coffee contains *les mignardises.* A tip left at the end of a meal is a *pourboire.*

The Québécois enjoy their lowbrow treats as much as anyone. In Montréal, these include smoked meat, a maddeningly tasty sandwich component that hovers somewhere in the neighborhood of pastrami and corned beef but is somehow different. And the Montréal rendition of the bagel is thinner, chewier, and better than the more famous New York prototype. Take it from someone born in *Le* Bronx.

Many lower-priced restaurants in Montréal allow patrons to bring their own wine, indicated by signs in the window that show a red hand holding a bottle or carry the words APPORTEZ VOTRE VIN. To buy wine or spirits outside a bar or restaurant, go to an outlet of the Québec Société des Alcools, the governmental monopoly that holds the exclusive right to sell all strong liquor in the province. Licensed grocery stores may sell wine, beer, and alcoholic cider, but the Société des Alcools stores have the largest selections of wines. A subcategory of stores, "Maisons des Vins," also carry old, rare, and special wines. Imported wines and spirits are very expensive, encouraging experimentation with Canadian efforts with the grape. Some are appallingly bad, a few are . . . not bad. Excellent Québec beers include Belle Gueule, Boréal, and the darker St-Amboise.

6   Recommended Books, Films & Recordings

BOOKS

Writing from the perspective of a minority within a minority, Mordecai Richler has inveighed against the excesses of Québec's separatists and language zealots in a barrage of books and critical essays in newspapers and magazines. His outrage and mordant wit can be sampled in his *Oh Canada! Oh Québec!* (Knopf, 1992) and *Home Sweet Home: My Canadian Album* (Knopf, 1984; paperback, Penguin, 1985). An amusing, less caustic look at the Anglophone-Francophone conflict is provided by *The Anglo Guide to Survival in Québec* (Eden Press, 1983). A serious, relatively balanced view—with a slight lean to the French-Canadian side of the issue—is given by Brian Young and John A. Dickinson in *A Short History of Québec: A Socio-Economic Perspective* (Copp Clark Pitman Ltd., 1988). One of the authors taught at McGill University, the other at the Université de Montréal.

FILMS

Due to lower production costs and the presence of a large and capable cadre of filmmakers, Montréal has often served as a setting for Hollywood theatrical and TV productions, not infrequently as a stand-in for an American city. Among the more notable have been *Agnes of God*

(1985) starring Anne Bancroft and Jane Fonda and *Dead Ringers* with Jeremy Irons. But films made in the province have also attempted to illuminate the Québécois experience, as in the film version of Richler's *The Apprenticeship of Duddy Kravitz* (1974), which starred Richard Dreyfuss and Randy Quaid; *Black Robe* (1991), which dealt with the challenges faced by missionaries in the early years of New France; and *Jesus of Montréal* (1989), directed by Denys Arcand, and set in contemporary Montréal. Québec City has occasionally been utilized for fictional film, too, as when Alfred Hitchcock shot much of *I Confess*, a 1953 release with Montgomery Clift and Karl Malden, at the Château Frontenac.

RECORDINGS

The Montréal Symphony Orchestra has garnered its full share of accolades over the years, and it has produced an extensive, near-comprehensive library of classical recordings, from Bartók and Berlioz to Shostakovitch and Stravinsky, with detours to Janácek and Scarlatti. Native son Oscar Peterson has stayed a key figure on the international jazz scene for decades. His teaming with the great Dizzy Gillespie on their 1974 recording should be in every aficionado's collection. On the pop side, Céline Dion has made her mark with her singing for the soundtrack of *Beauty and the Beast* and her later album, *The Colour of My Love.*

2

Planning a Trip to Montréal & Québec City

Montréal and Québec City have more of a foreign flavor than other cities in North America, and the residents speak French. But once you decide to go, pulling together information on ways to get there, border formalities, exchanging money, climate, lodging possibilities, and related details is almost as easy as getting from Illinois to Florida. The information below and in the subsequent "Fast Facts" sections should help speed the process along.

1 Information, Entry Requirements & Money

VISITOR INFORMATION

Québec tourism authorities produce volumes of detailed and highly useful publications, and they're easy to obtain by mail, phone, or in person. To contact Tourisme Québec, write C.P. 979, Montréal, PQ H3C 2W3 or call ☎ **800/363-7777,** operator 806 (within the Montréal area, call ☎ **514/873-2015**). General information on travel in Canada can be obtained from the following offices:

Atlanta: Canadian Consulate General, 400 South Tower, One CNN Center, Atlanta, GA 30303-2705 (☎ 404/577-6810).

Boston: Canadian Consulate General, 3 Copley Place, Suite 400, Boston, MA 02116 (☎ 617/262-3760).

Chicago: Consulate General, 2 Prudential Plaza, 180 N. Stetson Ave., Suite 2400, Chicago, IL 60601-6710 (☎ 312/616-1860).

Dallas: Canadian Consulate General, 750 N. St. Paul, Suite 1700, Dallas, TX 75201 (☎ 214/922-9806).

Detroit: Canadian Consulate General, 600 Renaissance Center, Suite 1100, Detroit, MI 48243-1704 (☎ 313/567-2340).

Los Angeles: Canadian Consulate General, 300 S. Grand Ave., Suite 1000, Los Angeles, CA 90071 (☎ 213/687-7432).

Minneapolis: Canadian Consulate General, 701 Fourth Ave. S, Suite 900, Minneapolis, MN 55415-1899 (☎ 612/333-4641).

New York: Canadian Consulate General, 1251 Ave. of the Americas, 16th floor, New York, NY 10020-1175 (☎ 212/596-1600).

San Francisco: Canadian Consulate General, 50 Fremont St., Suite 2100, San Francisco, CA 94105 (☎ 415/543-2550).

Seattle: Canadian Consulate General, 412 Plaza 600, Sixth and Stewart, Seattle, WA 98101-1286 (☎ 206/443-1777).

Washington, D.C.: Canadian Embassy, Tourism Section, 501 Pennsylvania Ave. NW, Washington, DC 20001 (☎ 202/682-1740).

In addition, the Québec government maintains a number of offices in the United States and abroad, which can provide specific tourism information about the province:

Boston: Délégation du Québec, Exchange Place, State and Congress Sts., 19th floor, Boston, MA 02109 (☎ 617/723-3366).

Chicago: Délégation du Québec, 2 Prudential Plaza, Suite 4300, 180 N. Stetson Ave., Chicago, IL 60601 (☎ 312/856-0655).

New York: Délégation du Québec, Rockefeller Plaza, 26th floor, New York, NY 10020-2201 (☎ 212/397-0200).

Worldwide, there are offices ready to answer travelers' questions and provide literature:

Düsseldorf: Délégation du Québec, Immermannstrasse 65d, Immermannhof, 40210 Düsseldorf 1, Germany (☎ 211/320-816).

London: Délégation du Québec, 59 Pall Mall, London SW1Y 5JH, England (☎ 071/930-8314); High Commission of Canada, Canada House, Cockspur St., Trafalgar Square, London SW1Y, England 5BJ (☎ 071/258-6600).

Paris: Délégation du Québec, 4 av. Victor-Hugo, 75116 Paris, France (☎ 144/17-32-40); Canadian Embassy, 35 av. Montaigne, 75008 Paris, France (☎ 14/143-2900).

Rome: Délégation du Québec, Via XX Settembre 4, 00187 Rome, Italy (☎ 6/488-4183).

Besides these offices outside Québec, the province has a large office in Montréal, and there are convenient regional offices in Montréal and Québec City as well.

ENTRY REQUIREMENTS

DOCUMENTS   U.S. citizens or permanent residents of the United States require neither passports nor visas, but will need some identification, such as a birth, baptismal, or voter's certificate as proof of citizenship, both to enter Canada and to reenter the United States. An ID with photo is best, which makes a passport the logical document, even though it isn't specifically required. Permanent U.S. residents who are not citizens must have their Alien Registration Cards (green cards) with them. If you plan to drive into Canada, be sure to have your car's registration handy.

An important point for teenage travelers: Any person under 19 requires a letter from a parent or guardian granting them permission to travel to Canada. The letter must state the traveler's name and the duration of trip. It is therefore essential that teenagers carry proof of identity. Otherwise, the letter from Mom and Dad is useless at the border.

Citizens of Australia, New Zealand, the United Kingdom, and Ireland need only carry a valid passport. Citizens of many other countries must have visas, applied for well in advance at their local Canadian embassy or consulate.

Canadian & U.S. Dollar Equivalents

Can. $	U.S. $	Can. $	U.S. $	Can. $	U.S. $
0.10	.08	1	.75	25	18.75
–	–	2	1.50	50	37.50
0.20	.15	3	2.25	75	56.25
–	–	4	3.00	100	75.00
0.30	.23	5	3.75	125	93.75
–	–	6	4.50	150	112.50
0.40	.30	7	5.25	175	131.25
–	–	8	6.00	200	150.00
0.50	.38	9	6.75	225	168.75
–	–	10	7.50	250	187.50
0.60	.45	11	8.25	275	206.25
–	–	12	9.00	300	225.00
0.70	.53	13	9.75	325	243.75
–	–	14	10.50	350	262.50
0.80	.60	15	11.25	375	281.25
–	–	16	12.00	400	300.00
0.90	.68	17	12.75	425	318.75
–	–	18	13.50	450	337.50
1.00	.75	19	14.25	475	356.25
–	–	20	15.00	500	375.00

CUSTOMS   Customs regulations are flexible in most respects, but visitors can expect at least a few probing questions at the border or the airport. Normal baggage and personal possessions should be no problem, but tobacco and alcoholic beverages face limitations. Only 50 cigars, 200 cigarettes, and 1 kilo (2.2 lbs.) of loose tobacco are allowed to individuals 16 years or over. In addition, an Imperial quart (just over a liter) of wine or liquor may be brought in, or a curiously generous case (24 cans) of beer, assuming the bearer is at or over the minimum drinking age in Québec, which is 18.

Pets with proper vaccination records may be admitted, but inquire in advance about necessary procedures at one of the Consulates General (see "Visitor Information" above, and "Pets" in "Fast Facts: Montréal" in Chapter 3). Talk to U.S. Customs about bringing pets back home.

There are strict regulations regarding the import of plants, food products, and firearms. Hunters with valid licenses can bring in some gear, but handguns and fully automatic firearms are prohibited. Fishing tackle poses no problems, as long as the proper nonresident license is obtained.

A car that is driven into Canada can stay for up to a year, but it must leave with the owner or a duty will be levied. The possession or use of a radar detector is prohibited, whether or not it is connected. Police officers can confiscate it and fine the owner $500 to $1,000.

REENTERING THE UNITED STATES   U.S. visitors who have been in Québec for fewer than 48 hours may bring back only $25 (U.S.) worth of Canadian goods duty free. Exceed that amount and duty must be paid on everything. That $25 limit may include only 50 cigarettes (2¹/₂ packs), 10 cigars, or 5 ounces of liquor.

Stays in Québec of more than two days have less strict limitations. Allowances expand to up to $400 (U.S.) duty-free Canadian goods per person, including up to 100 cigars (but none from Cuba), a carton of cigarettes (200), and 1 liter (1.06 U.S. qt.) of liquor, assuming the carrier is 21 or older. Note that the liquor regulation is that of U.S. Customs; state laws may demand an additional tax or specify a different quantity limit, and the U.S. officers enforce state laws as well as federal restrictions.

But considering the excellent discounts available on domestic and foreign bottles at border duty-free stores, even paying the duty on a couple of extra bottles represents a savings.

Individual states may collect duty on each and every bottle travelers carry when crossing the border by car. When traveling by air, they won't, because Customs inspection by U.S. government Customs agents takes place right there in Dorval (Montréal) and Québec City airports before U.S. passengers board their planes, not when they arrive at their destinations. There are two U.S. Customs inspections in Dorval—one right after check-in and one past the duty-free shops on the way to the departure gate for carry-on luggage.

For more detailed information concerning Customs regulations, write to: Canada Customs Office, 400 place d'Youville, 2nd floor, Montréal, PQ H2Y 2C2 (☎ 514/283-2949 or 514/283-2959).

MONEY
CASH/CURRENCY

Canada figures in dollars and cents, but with a favorable balance for Americans, since the Canadian dollar is worth around 75¢ in U.S. money, give or take a couple of points' daily variation. This means that American traveler's checks can gain you about 25% more spending power the moment they are changed for local currency (a return of approximately $500 Canadian for every $375 U.S.). And since prices are roughly on par with those in the States, the difference is real, not imaginary. The table below helps with calculations. All prices in this book, unless otherwise indicated, are in Canadian dollars.

Visitors can bring in or take out any amount of money they wish, but if you import or export sums of $5,000 (U.S.) or more, a report of the transaction must be filed with U.S. Customs.

Canadian coins are similar to American ones: 1¢, 5¢, 10¢, 25¢. Bills—$1, $2, $5, $10, $20, $50, $100—are all the same size but have different colors, depending on the denomination. The gold-colored $1 coin (called a "Loonie" by Canadians because there's a loon on one side) has all but replaced the $1 bill, but plenty of $2 bills are still in circulation.

What Things Cost in Montréal	U.S. $
Taxi from the airport to downtown	19.80
Bus from airport to downtown	7.40
Local telephone call	.21
Double at the Ritz-Carlton (very expensive)	151.10
Double at the Château Versailles (moderate)	98.00
Double at Les Passants du Sans Soucy Auberge (inexpensive)	78.70
Two-course lunch for one at La Marée (moderate)	12.50
Buffet lunch for one at Le Taj (inexpensive)	5.65
Three-course dinner for one at Toqué (expensive)	28.15
Three-course dinner for one at Stash's (moderate)	16.15
Three-course dinner for one at Sawatdee (inexpensive)	10.95
Bottle of beer	2.92
Coca-Cola	1.83
Cup of coffee	1.30
Roll of ASA 100 Kodacolor film, 36 exposures	5.75
Admission to the Museum of Fine Arts	7.50
Ticket for the Montréal Symphony Orchestra	19.80
Movie ticket	6.25

Note: Prices are listed here in U.S. dollars, minus tax. All other prices in the book are quoted in Canadian dollars.

Many establishments accept U.S. dollars, often posting a sign reading "U.S. Dollars," and beside it the percentage rate they offer. Usually, the rate is less than what the bank offers, but sometimes it is more favorable, as more and more establishments become eager to attract U.S. tourist dollars. As a rule, though, it's better to change money and traveler's checks at a bank.

CREDIT & CHARGE CARDS

Credit cards are accepted as widely in Québec as in the States. Visa and MasterCard dominate the market, followed by the American Express card, Diners Club, and its Canadian cousin, En Route. The Discover card falls well behind the others in usage. Charge slips are written up in Canadian dollars, and card companies convert the amount to U.S. dollars when they credit the transaction to your account.

AUTOMATED TELLER MACHINES

As ubiquitous in Québec as in the U.S., ATMs are found in most of the same places, such as outside or inside bank branches, but also increasingly at other locations, including the province's new casinos.

The principal networks are Cirrus and Plus for withdrawing funds from home checking accounts. A four-digit PIN (Personal Identifica-

What Things Cost in Québec City	U.S. $
Taxi from the airport to downtown	16.70
Bus from airport to downtown	8.35
Local telephone call	.21
Double at the Château Frontenac (expensive)	146.00
Double at the Château Bellevue (moderate)	74.00
Double at the Relais Charles-Alexandre (inexpensive)	52.10
Two-course lunch for one at Les Frères de la Côte (moderate)	7.82
Two-course lunch for one at Casse-Crêpe Breton (Inexpensive)	3.65
Three-course dinner for one at Laurie Raphaël (expensive)	23.00
Three-course dinner for one at Le Café du Monde (moderate)	15.65
Three-course dinner for one at Le Petit Coin Latin (inexpensive)	8.35
Bottle of beer	3.05
Coca-Cola	1.93
Cup of coffee	1.41
Roll of ASA 100 Kodacolor film, 36 exposures	6.75
Admission to the Museum of Civilization	4.50
Ticket for the Québec Symphony Orchestra	25.53
Movie ticket	6.25

Note: Prices are listed here in U.S. dollars, minus tax. All other prices in the book are quoted in Canadian dollars.

tion Number) is required, so people with fewer or more digits need to have another PIN assigned to their account(s) before leaving home. The exchange rate is usually more favorable than that offered by banks. This advantage can be wiped out, however, if your home bank charges high transaction fees, so check with your bank before departing. When using ATMs to obtain cash advances on credit cards, remember that interest is charged from the day of withdrawal.

2 When to Go

High season is late May through early September, when hotels are most likely to be full and charge their highest tariffs. Even then, though, weekends are cheaper, and package plans reduce the bite, so advance planning has its rewards. The Christmas-to-New Year's period is also busy, as are the days given to winter festivals in both Montréal and Québec City.

CLIMATE

Temperatures are usually a few degrees lower in Québec City than in Montréal. Spring, short but sweet, arrives around the middle of May. Summer (mid-June through mid-September) tends to be humid in Montréal, Québec City, and other communities along the St. Lawrence River, drier at the inland resorts of the Laurentians and Estrie. Intense but usually brief heat waves mark July and early August, but rarely remain oppressive in the evening. Autumn (September and October) is as short and changeable as spring, with warm days and cool or chilly nights. Canadian maples blaze with color for weeks. Winter brings dependable snows for skiing in the Laurentians, Estrie, and Charlevoix. After a sleigh ride or a ski run in Parc Mont-Royal, Montréal's Underground City is a climate-controlled blessing. Mid-February is the time for Québec City's robust Carnaval d'Hiver (Winter Carnival). Snow and slush are more-or-less constant presences from November to March.

Montréal's Average Monthly Temperatures (°F)

	Jan	Feb	Mar	Apr	May	June	July	Aug	Sept	Oct	Nov	Dec
High	21	25	34	52	65	74	78	77	70	56	43	26
Low	8	12	23	37	48	57	62	60	53	43	32	15

Québec City's Average Monthly Temperatures (°F)

	Jan	Feb	Mar	Apr	May	June	July	Aug	Sept	Oct	Nov	Dec
High	19	21	32	46	60	70	76	74	65	52	39	23
Low	5	8	19	32	43	53	57	56	48	37	28	12

HOLIDAYS

In Québec province, the important public holidays are: New Year's Day (January 1), Good Friday and Easter Monday (late March or April), Victoria Day (May 24 or nearest Monday), St-Jean-Baptiste Day, Québec's "national" day (June 24), Confederation (or Dominion) Day (July 1), Labor Day (first Monday in September), Canadian Thanksgiving Day (second Monday in October), Remembrance Day (November 11), Christmas Day (December 25).

MONTRÉAL & QUÉBEC CITY CALENDAR OF EVENTS

From June to September, only a serious misadventure in planning might allow visitors to miss a celebration of some sort in Montréal and Québec City. If something's not going on in one city, it's bound to be happening in the other, and it's easy to get from one to the other.

February

✪ **La Fete des Neiges (Snow Festival), Montréal.** Montréal's answer to Québec City's Carnaval d'Hiver (Winter Carnival).

Features outdoor events like harness racing, barrel jumping, racing beds on ice, canoe races, snowshoeing, skating, and cross-country skiing. The less athletically inclined can cheer from the sidelines, and then inspect the snow and ice sculptures. **Where:** Mostly on Île Notre-Dame, in the Port and Vieux-Montréal, and in Parc Maisonneuve. **When:** February 3–19. **How:** ☎ 514/872-6093 for details.

❁ **Carnaval D'Hiver (Winter Carnival), Québec City.** Usually, Québec is courtly and dignified, but all that is cast aside when the symbolic snowman called Bonhomme ("Good Fellow") appears to preside over these 10 days of merriment in early February every year. During the event, over a million revelers descend upon the city, eddying around the monumental ice palace and ice sculptures and attending a full schedule of concerts, dances, and parades. The mood is heightened by the availability of plastic trumpets and canes filled with a concoction called "Caribou," the principal ingredients of which are cheap whisky and sweet red wine. Perhaps its presence explains the eagerness with which certain Quebecers participate in the canoe race across the treacherous ice floes of the St. Lawrence. **Where:** In front of the Parliament Building, on grounds known during this time as place du Palais; just outside the walls to the Old City. **When:** February 2–12. **How:** Hotel reservations must be made far in advance. Scheduled events are free.

May/June

- **International Music Competition, Montréal.** Native and imported talent compete in an extended series of concerts and recitals during this annual event, held since 1969 at Place des Arts. ☎ 514/285-4380. May 21 to June 8.

❁ **La Tour de L'Île de Montréal.** Early in June some 45,000 cycling enthusiasts converge on Montréal to participate in a grueling day-long race before more than 120,000 spectators. The event, which began in 1984, attracts almost as many women as men. **Where:** Streets of Montréal. **When:** Usually first Sunday in June. **How:** ☎ 514/847-8356 for details.

- **International Festival of New Cinema and Video, Montréal.** Screenings of new and experimental films stimulate controversy and forums on the latest trends in film and video at halls and cinemas throughout the city. ☎ 514/843-4725. June 1–18.

- **Molson Grand Prix of Canada, Montréal.** Major international Formula I drivers burn rubber around the Gilles-Villeneuve racetrack on Île Notre-Dame for the running of the Grand Prix. ☎ 514/392-0000. Second weekend in June.

- **St-Jean Baptiste Day.** This holiday honors St. John the Baptist, the patron saint of French Canadians. It is marked by more festivities and far more enthusiasm throughout Québec province than national Dominion Day on July 1. It's their "national" holiday. June 24.

July

⭕ **International Jazz Festival, Montréal.** Montréal has a long tradition in jazz, and this enormously successful festival has been celebrating America's one true art form since 1979. Miles Davis, Chet Baker, and Dizzie Gillespie have been among the many headliners over the years, but it costs money to hear stars of their magnitude. Fortunately, hundreds of other concerts are free, often given on the streets and plazas of the city.

When: June 29–July 9. **Where:** Along rue Ste-Catherine and rue Jeanne-Mance. **How:** For information and tickets, ☎ 514/289-9472. Seats can be reserved through Ticketron.

⭕ **Festival d'Ete International (International Summer Festival), Québec City.** The largest cultural event in the French-speaking world, this festival has attracted artists from Africa, Asia, Europe, and throughout North America since it began in 1967. There are more than 250 events showcasing theater, music, and dance, with 600 performers from 20 different countries. One million people come to watch and listen. Jazz and folk combos perform for free in an open-air theater next to City Hall, visiting dance and folklore troupes put on shows, and concerts, theatrical productions, and related events fill the days and evenings.

When: July 6–16. **Where:** Throughout the city. **How:** ☎ 418/651-2882 for details.

• **Just for Laughs Festival, Montréal.** This is a celebration that almost equals the more famous jazz festival in magnitude. It even gave rise to the establishment of a humor museum. Comics perform in many venues, some for free, some not. Both Francophone and Anglophone comics from many countries participate. It's held along rue St-Denis and rue de Maisonneuve. ☎ 514/845-3155. Last two weeks of July.

• **Benson & Hedges International Fireworks Competition, Montréal.** The open-air theater in La Ronde amusement park on Île Ste-Hélène is the best place to view the pyrotechnics, although they can be enjoyed from almost any point overlooking the river. Tickets to the show also provide entrance to the amusement park. Kids, needless to say, love the whole explosive business. The 90-minute shows are staged by companies from several countries. Since parking is limited, it's best to use the metro. Saturdays in June, Sundays in July. ☎ 800/361-4595 for reserved seats.

August

⭕ **Les Medievales de Québec (Québec Medieval Festival), Québec City.** Hundreds of actors, artists, entertainers, and other participants from Europe, Canada, and the United States converge on Québec City in period dress to re-create daily scenes from five centuries ago, playing knights, troubadors, and ladies-in-waiting during this event, a giant costume party. Parades, jousting tournaments, recitals of ancient music, and the Grand Cavalcade (La Grande Chevauchée), featuring hundreds of costumed horsemen and women are just a few highlights. Fireworks are the one modern touch during this five-day festival. Come in medieval attire, if you wish. Held in Québec City only in odd-numbered years. (In even-numbered years, its sister event, the Festival des Remparts, takes place in Dinan, France.)

Where: In the streets and public grounds of Old Québec. **When:** August 5–13, 1995. **How:** ☎ 418/692-1993 for more information.

- **World Film Festival, Montréal.** An international film event since 1976. Some 500 screenings take place over 12 days, including 200 feature films from more than 50 countries, drawing the usual throngs of directors, stars, and wannabes. It isn't as gaudy as Cannes, but it's taken almost as seriously. Various movie theaters play host. ☎ 514/933-9699 for details. August 24–September 4.

September
- **Fall Foliage.** The maple trees blaze in color, and a walk in the parks and squares of Montréal and Québec City is a refreshing tonic. It's a perfect time for a drive in the Laurentians or Estrie (near Montréal) and Île d'Orléans or up into Charlevoix from Québec City. Mid- to late September.

October
- **International Festival of New Dance, Montréal.** This 12-day showcase invites troupes and choreographers from Canada, the United States, and Europe to various performance spaces. ☎ 514/287-1423. October 3–15.

December/January
- **Christmas/New Year's.** It's fun to celebrate these holidays à la française, especially in Québec City, with its streets banked with snow, and almost every ancient building sporting wreaths and decorated fir trees.

3 Tips for Special Travelers

FOR THOSE WITH DISABILITIES

When calling to make an airline reservation or talking with a travel agent, inquire where a wheelchair will be stowed on the plane or train, or if a seeing or hearing guide dog may accompany you. Find out about preordering special meals on the plane, or if there is anything else that might add to your comfort during the trip.

FOR SENIORS

When making an airline reservation, ask for the senior discount of 10% offered by many airlines on most fares and check to see if there is a special promotional fare that might be even more of a saving. Amtrak offers seniors 62 and older a 15% discount on the U.S. segment of some of its fares to Montréal, a trip that takes 10 to 12 hours. Remember to carry proof of age in order to obtain possible discounts at hotels, restaurants, and most museums and other attractions—driver's license, passport, Medicare card, and/or AARP membership card.

To meet other people and combine travel with learning, look into Elderhostel educational programs, which many seniors find worthwhile. Those qualified to participate must be 60 years of age or older, while their spouse, "significant other," relative, or friend must be 50 or older. For more information, contact Elderhostel, 75 Federal St., Boston, MA 02110 (☎ 617/426-7788).

FOR SINGLES

Two problems crop up most often for solo travelers: expenses and feelings of isolation, especially on Friday and Saturday nights when everyone else seems to be out in numbers divisible by two. Check the sections in this book on popular local bars (see Chapters 9 and 17) and consider them good possibilities for meeting the local folks and providing some lively conversation. Jazz and folk music spots, especially those that charge no cover—and most in Montréal and Québec City do not—are also fertile grounds for meeting and chatting with Quebecers.

The best kind of accommodation to choose in order to meet people is a bed and breakfast, and both Montréal and Québec City have wonderful ones. Guests come together over breakfast and sometimes end up going out to eat or explore together. Prices are also lower than hotels, many of which charge the same rate for a room whether it's occupied by one or two people. Another cost alternative is the YMCA or YWCA in Montréal, more desirable than many of their number in other cities and affording a relaxed way to encounter other travelers. So do walking tours, where an invigorating activity is closely shared with others for a couple of hours.

FOR GAYS & LESBIANS

In Montréal, gay and lesbian travelers may enjoy the Gay Village, primarily along rue Ste-Catherine est between rue St-Hubert and rue Papineau, where there are numerous meeting spots, shops, cafés, bars, and clubs. (See "Networks and Resources" in Chapter 3, and "The Gay & Lesbian Bars & Clubs" in Chapter 9.)

The gay community in Québec City is relatively small, centered in the Upper Town just outside the city walls. (See "Networks and Resources" in Chapter 11, and "The Bar & Café Scene" in Chapter 17.)

FOR FAMILIES

Montréal and Québec City are very family-oriented, with no lack for things to do, many of them outdoors, even in winter. History and the French language come alive for kids here, and many museums make special efforts to address their interests and enthusiasm.

FOR STUDENTS

Many of the tips that apply to single travelers apply to students (who may or may not be traveling solo). Always carry a university or similar ID card to obtain the many available discounts, especially at museums and other attractions. Both Montréal and Québec City have their designated Latin Quarters, centrally located university areas filled with students.

To save money on lodging, consider the YMCA or the YWCA in Montréal and the youth hostels in Québec City. For information about the 16 youth hostels in Québec province, contact Regroupment Tourisme Jeunesse, 4545 av. Pierre-de-Coubertin C.P. 1000, succursale, Montréal, Cananda H1V 3R2.

4   Getting There

Served by superhighways, transcontinental trains and buses, and the largest airport in the world (in acreage), Montréal and Québec City are easily accessible from any part of the United States.

BY PLANE
To Montréal

Montréal's two international airports, Dorval and Mirabel, are served by most of the world's major airlines. By far the greatest number of visitors fly into Dorval from other parts of North America on **Air Canada** (☎ 800/776-3000), **American Airlines** (☎ 800/433-7300), **Canadian Airlines International** (☎ 800/426-7000), **Continental** (☎ 800/525-0280), or **Delta** (☎ 800/241-4141). In the United States, Air Canada flies out of New York (Newark and LaGuardia), Miami, Tampa, Chicago, Los Angeles, and San Francisco.

Other carriers that serve Montréal include **United Airlines** (☎ 800/241-6522), **USAir** (☎ 800/428-4322), **Air France** (☎ 800/237-2747), and **British Airways** (☎ 800/247-9297). Regional airlines, such as Air Atlantic, American Eagle, and Inter-Canadian, also serve the city. Travelers arriving from Europe and other countries outside North America arrive at Mirabel.

To Québec City

Québec City is served from the U.S. by a number of major airlines, notably Air Canada, but most air traffic comes by way of Montréal or Toronto (see above). Direct flights are available from New York (Newark) on **Air Alliance,** a connector airline for Air Canada (☎ 800/776-3000), and from Boston on **Northwest Airlink/Precision** (☎ 800/225-2525). **Canadian Airlines International** flies into Québec City from international destinations outside the U.S. (☎ 800/426-7000).

AIRFARES

Given the volatile nature of the airline industry since deregulation, it's hard to predict what the fares will be tomorrow, let alone a year from now. Be on the lookout for special promotions and packages. Travelers who fly first or business class pay more for their seats, of course, but sometimes the upgrade from coach to business class costs very little and is worth the difference for those who need the extra legroom. Montréal and Québec City are close enough to northeastern U.S. cities, especially by air, to make a three-day weekend viable. But last-minute decisions to make the getaway mean it will be difficult to get a discounted fare.

Planning ahead is the best chance for obtaining the lowest fares, except when impromptu airfare wars make pricing go berserk, usually with brief windows of opportunity. Advance-purchase fares—those that must be purchased at least 14 days before date of departure—bring greater savings, but also involve certain restrictions. That might mean flying midweek rather than on weekends or staying through a Saturday. There are also 7-day advance-purchase fares, but they aren't as low as the 14-day versions.

BY TRAIN

For **VIA Rail** information from the United States, call 800/561-3949. If your calling area requires that you use a different number, it might be obtained through **Amtrak** (☎ 800/872-7245), or by dialing 800/555-1212 and asking for the VIA Rail number.

TO MONTRÉAL

Montréal is a major terminus on Canada's **VIA Rail** network, at 935 rue de la Gauchetière ouest (☎ 514/871-1331). The city is served by comfortable VIA Rail trains—some equipped with dining cars, sleeping cars, and cellular telephones—from other cities in Canada. There is scheduled service to Québec City via Trois-Rivières, and to Ottawa, Toronto, Winnipeg, and points west. **Amtrak** (☎ 800/872-7245) has one train a day to Montréal from Washington and New York that makes intermediate stops. While it is a no-frills affair, its scenic route passes along the eastern shore of the Hudson River and west of Lake Champlain. (The night train through Vermont has been discontinued.) The Adirondack takes about $10^1/_2$ hours, if all goes well, but delays aren't unusual. Passengers from Chicago can get to Montréal most directly by taking Amtrak to Toronto, then switching to VIA Rail.

The Queen Elizabeth hotel is located directly above the train station in Montréal, and less expensive lodging is only a short cab or metro ride away. Seniors 62 and older are eligible for a 15% discount on some Amtrak trains, on the U.S. segment of the trip. VIA Rail also has a senior discount. Don't forget to bring along proof of citizenship (a passport or birth certificate) for passing through Customs.

TO QUÉBEC CITY

Québec City's train station, the Gare du Palais, is in the Lower Town at 450 rue de la Gare-du-Palais (☎ 418/692-3940). Four commuter trains run between Montréal and Québec City daily from 7am to 6pm, and they have snack and beverage service. Travel time between the two cities is about 3 hours, and the trip costs $41 one-way for adults (half-price for children 2 to 11), or a discounted $25 if you buy the ticket 5 days in advance and don't travel on a Friday, Sunday, or holiday.

First-class passage isn't much more expensive, and the meal service and extra legroom are worth the cost to many travelers.

BY BUS
To Montréal

Montréal's main bus terminal is the Terminus Voyageur, 505 bd. de Maisonneuve est (☎ 514/842-2281). The Voyageur company operates buses between here and all parts of Québec, with frequent runs through the Eastern Townships to Sherbrooke, to the various villages in the Laurentians, and to Québec City. Morning, noon, early afternoon, and midnight buses cover the distance between Toronto and Montréal in about 7 hours. From Boston or New York there is daily bus service to Montréal on **Greyhound/Trailways** (☎ 800/231-2222). The trip from Boston takes about 8 hours; from New York City, with five departures daily, it takes 9 hours.

To Québec City

From New York or Boston take **Greyhound/Trailways** (☎ 800/231-2222) to Montréal and change for the bus to Québec City a 3-hour ride away. The bus traffic between Québec City and Montréal is intense, with the express buses of **Orléans Express** (☎ 514/395-4020 in Montréal, or 418/524-4692 in Québec City), running almost every hour on the hour from 7am to 1am. The bus line also links Québec City to the rest of Québec province, with connections to the rest of Canada. Ask about excursion tickets and discounts for seniors and children.

BY CAR

Highway distances and speed limits are given in kilometers (km) in Canada. The speed limit on the autoroutes (limited-access highways) is 100 kilometers per hour (62 m.p.h.), and seatbelt laws are strictly enforced. Passengers must buckle up in the backseat as well as in the driver's and passenger's seats up front.

Members of the American Automobile Association (AAA) should remember to take their membership cards. The 24-hour hotline for emergency service provided by the Canadian Automobile Association (CAA), which is affiliated with AAA, is 514/861-7575 in Montréal, 418/624-0708 in Québec City. Headquarters for CAA-Québec is 444 rue Bouvier, Québec City, PQ G2J 1E3.

For information on road conditions in and around Québec City from November through mid-April, there is a 24-hour hotline (☎ 418/643-6830). For the same information in Montréal, call 514/636-3026; outside Montréal, call 514/636-3248.

To Montréal

Interstate 87 runs due north from New York City to link up with Canada's Autoroute 15 at the border, and the entire 400-mile journey is on expressways. Likewise from Boston, I-93 north joins I-89 just south of Concord, N.H. At White River Junction there is a choice between continuing on I-89 to Lake Champlain, crossing the lake by

roads and bridges to join I-87 and Canada Autoroute 15 north or join-
ing I-91 at White River Junction to go due north toward Sherbrooke,
Québec. At the border, I-91 becomes Canada Route 55, and joins
Canada Route 10 through Estrie to Montréal. The Trans-Canada
Highway runs right through the city, connecting both ends of the
country. From Boston to Montréal is about 320 miles, from Toronto,
540 kilometers (350 miles), from Ottawa, 190 kilometers (120 miles).
Once in Montréal, Québec City is an easy 3-hour drive.

TO QUÉBEC CITY

Québec City is slightly over 500 miles from New York, and less than
400 miles from Boston. Coming from New York and points farther
south, pick up Interstate 91 at New Haven, and follow it right up to
the Canadian border. From Boston, take I-93 out of the city and link
up with I-91 at St. Johnsbury, Vt. After crossing the border, I-91
becomes Québec Autoroute 55, to Sherbrooke and Drummondville.
From Sherbrooke, there is a choice. To make the trip quickly, take
Autoroute 55 to Autoroute 20. But Rte. 116, which heads northeast
from Richmond, midway between Sherbrooke and Drummondville, is
more scenic if a bit slower.

On the approach to the city, follow signs for Pont (Bridge) Pierre-
Laporte. After crossing the bridge, turn right onto boulevard Wilfrid-
Laurier (Rte. 175), which later changes names and becomes the
Grande-Allée. Past the Old City walls it becomes rue St-Louis, which
leads straight to the Château Frontenac. For the most scenic entrance
into the city, take an immediate exit onto boulevard Champlain after
crossing the bridge and turn left at the entrance to Parc des
Champs-de-Bataille (Battlefields Park), up a steep hill to follow chemin
Grande-Allée to the Musée du Québec. Drive halfway around the circle
in front of the museum, and then take avenue Montcalm-Wolfe to the
Grande-Allée and turn right.

When driving to Québec City from Montréal (a car can be rented
in the train station), there are two choices: Autoroute 20, the favorite
of local commuters, or Autoroute 40.

PACKAGE TOURS

There are ample reasons for taking a package tour: to save money, to
have someone else make the arrangements and deal with glitches in a
foreign language, and to travel with built-in companions. There are
disadvantages, however, and they include: having to rise and eat and
sleep on someone else's schedule, abiding by the decisions of the group
and the tour guide, and traveling in a unilingual bubble that works
against interplay with members of the native population. In Québec,
the pros aren't as strong as they might be in, say, India or Egypt. While
French is the dominant language, there's almost always someone nearby
who speaks English. The money is easy to comprehend, since it uses
essentially the same denominations as in the U.S., and prices are lower
than at home. And the Québec tourism authorities are as helpful and
forthcoming as can be found anywhere in the world.

Having made the decision to check out package tours, here are some organizations that are regarded as reputable. Make sure to ask as many questions as necessary, and to make clear to the operator any special needs or requirements.

American Way Tours   (☎ 800/451-5250 or 212/683-3810) offers land packages in Québec that include lodging, a guided bus or boat tour in each city, and rail transportation between the two. Participants choose how long they stay in Montréal and/or Québec City.

Summit Ski Tours   (☎ 800/523-0710) offers ski packages to the Laurentians just north of Montréal.

Tauck Tours   (☎ 203/226-6911 or 800/468-2825) has a seven-day, six-night tour that includes Vermont, New Hampshire, Montréal, and Québec City. It's offered spring through mid-October, and is to be recommended for the opportunity to view the fall foliage in both countries.

Yankee Holidays   (☎ 800/225-2550) has package tours to Montréal or Québec City, as well as a combination tour of both cities. Participating hotels include the Queen Elizabeth and the Meridien in Montréal which are both superior. In Québec City, they work with the Château Frontenac and the contemporary Loews Le Concorde, among others.

3

Getting to Know Montréal

For a city of more than a million inhabitants, getting to know and getting around Montréal is remarkably easy. The two airports that serve it are nearby, one only 14 miles away, and, once in town, the Métro system is fast and efficient. Of course, walking is the best way to get to know this vigorous, multidimensional city, neighborhood by neighborhood.

1 Orientation

ARRIVING

BY PLANE   The **Aéroport de Dorval** (☎ 514/633-3105, or 800/465-1213 from Québec and eastern Ontario) is 14 miles (22km) southwest of downtown, and it handles all flights from North American cities (Canadian, American, and Mexican). The ride into town takes 30 minutes if the traffic is not badly tied up, and costs about $25, tip included, by taxi. Montréal's **Aéroport Mirabel** (☎ 514/476-3010, or 800/465-1213 from Québec and eastern Ontario), 34 miles (55km) northwest of the city, is the world's largest in terms of surface area. If you're flying in from Europe, Africa, South America (including the West Indies), or Asia, you'll land here. The ride into the city takes about 45 minutes in normal traffic, and costs about $60, tip included, if you go by taxi.

Both airports are served by **Autocar Connaisseur / Grayline** (☎ 514/934-1222), which will shuttle you from either airport to the other, or to major hotels in the center of the city. Buses from Dorval run every 20 to 30 minutes for $12 one way, $16 round-trip. From Mirabel, buses depart every hour for most of the day, every 30 minutes in the afternoon, for $14 one way, $20 round-trip. The fare between Mirabel and Dorval is $12.50 one way, $16.50 round-trip.

BY TRAIN   Montréal has one intercity rail terminus, **Central Station,** situated directly beneath the Queen Elizabeth Hotel at the corner of boulevard René-Lévesque and rue Mansfield (☎ 514/871-1331). Central Station is part of the Underground City, and

Impressions

Montréal is the only city in the world where the sun sets in the north.
　　　　　　　　　　　　　　　　　　　　　　　　　—L. Dudek (1971)

Impressions

You cannot fancy you are in America; everything about it conveys the idea of a substantial, handsomely built European town, with modern improvements of half English, half French architecture.

—Lt. Col. B. W. A. Sleigh,
Pine Forests and Hacmatack Clearings (1853)

is thus connected to the Métro (Bonaventure station), and to Windsor Station, the terminus for commuter and suburban trains.

BY BUS   The **Terminus Voyageur** (☎ 514/842-2281) has a bar, a cafeteria, and a travel agency selling tours, air tickets, and last-minute travel bargains. There's also a rental-car desk and a tourism information booth. The Terminus Voyageur is also the terminal for the airport buses to Mirabel and Dorval airports.

The Terminus Voyageur in Montréal is virtually on top of the Berri-UQAM Métro station, the junction of several important Métro lines and a starting point for a quick trip to any quarter of the city. ("UQAM" stands for Université de Québec à Montréal.) Alternatively, taxis usually wait outside the terminal building.

BY CAR   The Trans Canada Highway runs right through Montréal, connecting it with both ends of the country. Interstate 87 runs due north from New York City to link up with Canada's Autoroute 15 at the border, making the entire 377-mile (608 km) journey entirely on expressways. From Boston, I-93 north joins I-89 just south of Concord, N.H. At White River Junction there are two choices: Continue on I-89 to Lake Champlain, then follow various smaller roads to join I-87 and Canada Autoroute 15 north; or link up with I-91 at White River Junction to go due north toward Sherbrooke, Québec. At the border I-91 becomes Canada Autoroute 55, and joins Canada Autoroute 10 (the Estrie, or Eastern Townships, autoroute) to Montréal. The trip from Boston to Montréal is about 317 miles (512 km); from Toronto it's 339 miles (546 km); from Ottawa, 118 miles (190 km). Highway distances and speed limits are given in kilometers (km) and kilometers per hour (kmph) in Canada.

VISITOR INFORMATION

A great deal of carefully prepared information about Montréal, Québec City, and the score of touristic regions into which the province has carved itself is available to visitors. Sources are listed in Chapter 2, "Planning a Trip to Montréal & Québec City," as well as from offices in the cities themselves.

The main information center for visitors in Montréal is the large and efficiently organized **Infotouriste**, at 1001 rue du Square-Dorchester (☎ 514/873-2015, or 800/363-7777 from anywhere in Canada and the U.S.), between rues Peel and Metcalfe in the downtown hotel and business district. To get there, take the Métro to the Peel stop. The office is open daily: June to early September from 8:30am to 7:30pm, and early September to May from 9am to 6pm. Employed by the

Québec Ministry of Tourism, staff workers are knowledgeable—and bilingual—and the center is a useful information resource regarding dining, accommodations, and attractions throughout the province and in Montréal itself.

The city has its own **information bureau** convenient to Old Montréal and place Jacques-Cartier, at 174 rue Notre-Dame (corner of place Jacques-Cartier), near the monument to Lord Nelson (☎ **514/871-1595**). It's open Easter to mid-October, daily from 9am to 7pm; mid-October to Easter, Thursday through Sunday from 9am to 5pm.

CITY LAYOUT

For the duration of your visit, it is necessary to accept local directional conventions. The city borders the St. Lawrence River. As far as its citizens are concerned, that's south, looking toward the United States, although the river in fact runs more nearly north and south, not east and west. For that reason, it has been observed that Montréal is the only city in the world where the sun rises in the north. Don't fight it: Face the river. That's south. Turn around. That's north. When examining a map of the city, note that such prominent thoroughfares as Ste-Catherine and René-Lévesque are said to run "east" and "west," the dividing line being boulevard St-Laurent, which runs "north" and "south." To ease the confusion, the directions given below conform to local tradition, since they are the ones that will be given by natives.

MAIN ARTERIES & STREETS   In **downtown Montréal,** the principal streets running east-west include boulevard René-Lévesque, rue Ste-Catherine, boulevard de Maisonneuve, and rue Sherbrooke; the north-south arteries include rue Crescent, rue McGill, rue St-Denis, and boulevard St-Laurent, the line of demarcation between east and west Montréal (most of the downtown area of interest to tourists and businesspeople lies to the west). **Near Mont-Royal Park,** north of the downtown area, major streets are avenue du Mont-Royal and avenue Laurier. In **Old Montréal,** rue St-Jacques, rue Notre-Dame, and rue St-Paul are the major streets, along with rue de la Commune, which hugs the St. Lawrence River.

FINDING AN ADDRESS   Boulevard St-Laurent is the dividing point between east and west (*est* and *ouest*) in Montréal. There's no equivalent division for north and south—the numbers start at the river and climb from there, just as the topography does. For instance, when driving along boulevard St-Laurent and passing number 500, that's Old Montréal, near rue Notre-Dame; no. 1100 is near boulevard René-Lévesque; no. 1500 near boulevard de Maisonneuve; and no. 3400 near rue Sherbrooke. Even numbers are on the west side of north-south streets and the south side of east-west streets; odd numbers are on the east and north sides, respectively. For more help, check the handy "Address Locator" map in the free *Montréal Tourist Guide,* available everywhere.

In earlier days, Montréal was split ethnically between those who spoke English, living in the city's western regions, and those who spoke French, concentrated to the east. And things do sound more French as you walk east: Street names and Métro station names change from Peel and Atwater to St-Laurent and Beaudry. While boulevard St-Laurent is the east-west dividing line for the city's street-numbering system, the "spiritual split" comes farther east, at avenue de Bleury / avenue de Parc.

STREET MAPS   Good street plans are found inside the free tourist guide supplied by the Greater Montréal Convention & Tourism Bureau and distributed widely throughout the city. The bureau also provides a large, foldout city map for free.

NEIGHBORHOODS IN BRIEF

Downtown   This area contributes the most striking elements of the dramatic Montréal skyline, and contains the main railroad station, as well as most of the city's luxury and first-class hotels, principal museums, corporate headquarters, and largest department stores. Loosely bounded by rue Sherbrooke to the north, boulevard René-Lévesque to the south, boulevard St-Laurent to the east, and rue Drummond to the west, downtown Montréal incorporates the neighborhood formerly known as "The Golden Square Mile," an Anglophone district once character- ized by dozens of mansions erected by the wealthy Scottish and English merchants and industrialists who dominated the city's politics andsocial life well into this century. Many of those stately homes were torn down when skyscrapers began to rise here after World War II, but some remain, often converted to institutional use. At the northern edge of the downtown area is the handsome urban campus of prestigious McGill University, which retains its Anglophone identity.

The Underground City   During Montréal's long winters, life on the streets of downtown slows. The people escape down escalators and stairways into *la ville souterraine,* what amounts to a parallel subterra- nean universe. Down there, in a controlled climate that's forever spring, it's possible to arrive at the railroad station, check into a hotel, go out for lunch at any of hundreds of fast-food counters and full-service res- taurants, see a movie, attend a concert, conduct business, go shopping, and even take a swim—all without unfurling an umbrella or donning an overcoat. This "city" evolved when major building developments in the downtown area such as Place Ville-Marie, Place Bonaventure, Complexe Desjardins, Palais des Congrès, and Place des Arts put their below-street-level areas to profitable use, leasing space for shops and other purposes. Over time, in fits and starts and with no master plan in place, these spaces became connected with Métro stations and with each other. It became possible to ride long distances and walk the shorter ones, through mazes of corridors, tunnels, and plazas. Admit- tedly, the term "Underground City" is not entirely accurate, since some

Impressions

Concordia salus (Prosperity through Harmony)
—Motto for the city of Montréal, chosen by its first mayor, Jacques Viger, in 1833

parts, such as Place Bonaventure and Complexe Desjardins, define their own spaces, which may have nothing to do with "ground level." In Place Bonaventure, passengers may leave the Métro and then wander around on the same level only to find themselves, at one point, peering out a window several floors above the street. The city beneath the city has obvious advantages, including the elimination of traffic accidents and avoidance of the need to deal with winter slush or summer rain. But it covers a vast area, without the convenience of a logical street grid, and can be confusing at times. There are plenty of signs, but it's wise to make careful note of landmarks at key corners along your route in order to get back to your starting point. Expect to get lost anyway—but that's part of the fun.

Rue Crescent   One of Montréal's major dining and nightlife districts lies in the western shadow of the massed phalanxes of downtown skyscrapers. It holds hundreds of restaurants, bars, and clubs of all styles between Sherbrooke and René-Lévesque, centering on rue Crescent and spilling over onto neighboring streets. From east to west, the Anglophone origins of the quarter are evident in the surviving street names: Stanley, Drummond, de la Montagne (changed from "Mountain"), Crescent, Bishop, and MacKay. The wild party atmosphere that pervades after dark here never quite fades, and builds to crescendos as weekends approach, especially in warm weather when its largely twenty- and thirtysomething denizens spill out into sidewalk cafés and onto balconies in even greater numbers than during the winter months.

Vieux Montréal   The city was born here in 1642, down by the river at Pointe-à-Callière, and today, especially in summer, activity centers around place Jacques-Cartier, where café tables line narrow terraces and sun worshipers, flower sellers, itinerant artists, and strolling locals and tourists congregate. The area is larger than it might seem at first, bounded as it is on the north by rue St-Antoine, once the "Wall Street" of Montréal and still home to many banks, and on the south by the recently developed Old Port, a linear park bordering rue de la Commune that gives access to the river and provides welcome breathing room for cyclists, in-line skaters, and picnickers. To the east, Old Montréal is bordered by rue Berri, and to the west by rue McGill. Several small but intriguing museums are housed in historic buildings, and the architectural heritage of the district has been substantially preserved. Its restored 18th- and 19th-century structures have been adapted for use as shops, studios, cafés, bars, offices, and apartments.

St-Denis   Rue St-Denis, from rue Ste-Catherine est to avenue du Mont-Royal, running from downtown to the Plateau Mont-Royal section, is the thumping central artery of Montréal's Latin Quarter, thick with cafés, bistros, offbeat shops, and lively nightspots. It is to Montréal what boulevard St-Germain is to Paris, and indeed, once here, it isn't difficult to imagine yourself transported to the Left Bank. At the southern end of St-Denis, near the concrete campus of the Université du Québec à Montréal, the avenue is decidedly student-oriented, with alternative rock issuing from the inexpensive bars and clubs in which kids in jeans and black leather swap philosophical insights and telephone numbers. Farther north, above Sherbrooke, a raffish quality persists along the facing rows of three- and-four story rowhouses, but the average age of residents and visitors does lift past 30. Prices are higher too, and some of the city's better restaurants have located here. This is a district for taking the pulse of Francophone life, not for absorbing art and culture of the refined sort, for there are no museums or important galleries on St-Denis, nor is the architecture notable. But, then, that relieves visitors of the chore of obligatory sightseeing and allows them to take in the passing scene—just as the locals do—over bowls of *café au lait* at one of the numerous terraces that line the avenue.

Plateau Mont-Royal Due north of the downtown area, this may be the part of the city where Montréalers feel most at home—away from the chattering pace of downtown and the crowds of heavily touristed Vieux Montréal. Bounded by boulevard St-Joseph to the north, rue Sherbrooke to the south, avenue Papineau to the east, and rue St-Dominique to the west, it has a throbbing ethnicity that fluctuates in tone and direction with each new surge in immigration. Rue St-Denis (see above) runs the length of the district, but parallel boulevard St-Laurent has the more polyglot flavor. Known to all as "The Main," it was once the boulevard first encountered by foreigners tumbling off ships at the waterfront. They simply shouldered their belongings and walked north on St-Laurent, peeling off into adjoining streets when they heard familiar tongues, saw people who looked like them, or smelled the drifting aromas of food they once cooked in the old country. New arrivals still come here to start their lives again, and in the usual pattern, most work hard, save their money, and move to the suburbs. But some stay on. Without its people and their diverse interests, St-Laurent would be just another paper-strewn urban eyesore. But these ground-floor windows are filled with glistening golden chickens, collages of shoes and pastries and aluminum cookware, curtains of sausages, and even the daringly farfetched garments of those designers on the edge of Montréal's active fashion industry. Many warehouses and former tenements have been converted to house this panoply of shops, bars, and low-cost eateries, and their often-garish signs draw eyes from the still-dilapidated upper stories above. (See Chapter 7, "Montréal Strolls," for a detailed walking tour of this fascinating neighborhood.)

Prince Arthur & Duluth These two essentially pedestrian streets connect boulevard St-Laurent with St-Denis, eight blocks to the east. The livelier rue Prince-Arthur is lined with ethnic restaurants, primarily Greek and Portuguese, but with Asian establishments looking to take their place. Many allow customers to bring their own wine, readily available from nearby liquor stores. Mimes, jugglers, and street musicians try to wrest what spare change passersby can be persuaded into divesting. Four blocks north of rue Prince-Arthur, rue Duluth is fairly quiet in the blocks near St-Laurent, but more engaging near St-Denis. The mix of cuisines is much like that on Prince-Arthur. Tourists are evident in greater numbers on Prince-Arthur, many of them attracted by menus promising bargain lobster dinners for less than $10 at some times of the year.

Impressions

Montréal is French with a difference. Most of its citizens also speak English.

—"Montréal," Jules B. Billard, in *Exploring Canada from Sea to Sea* (National Geographic Society, 1967)

Parc du Mont-Royal   Not many cities have a mountain at their core. Okay, reality insists that it's a high hill, not a true mountain. Still, Montréal is named for it—the "Royal Mountain"—and it's a profound urban pleasure to drive, walk, or take a horse-drawn calèche to the top for a view of the city, the island, and the St. Lawrence River, especially at dusk. This park, which encompasses the mountain, was designed by the famous American landscape architect Frederick Law Olmsted, who was responsible for New York's Central Park, among many others. On its far slope are two cemeteries, one Anglophone, one Francophone, silent reminders of the linguistic and cultural division that persists in the city. With its skating ponds, hiking and running trails, and even a short ski run, the park is well used by Montréalers, who refer to it simply and lovingly as "the mountain."

Chinatown   Just north of Vieux-Montréal, south of boulevard René-Lévesque, and centered on the intersection of rue Clark and rue de la Gauchetière (pedestrianized at this point), Montréal's pocket Chinatown is mostly restaurants and a tiny park, with the occasional grocery, laundry, church, and small business. Knots of old men stand on streetcorners discussing the day's events. For the benefit of outsiders, most signs are in French or English as well as Chinese. Community spirit is strong, as it has had to be to resist the bulldozers of commercial proponents of redevelopment, and Chinatown's inhabitants remain faithful to their traditions despite the encroaching modernism all around them. In recent years, concerned investors from Hong Kong, wary of their uncertain future as part of mainland China, have poured money into the neighborhood, producing signs that its shrinkage has been halted, even reversed. The area is colorful and deserves a look, although the best Chinese restaurants are actually in other parts of the city.

The Gay Village   The city's gay and lesbian enclave runs east along rue Ste-Catherine from rue St-Hubert to rue Papineau. A small but vibrant district, it's filled with clothing stores, small eateries, a bar/club complex in a former post office building, and the Gay and Lesbian Community Centre, at 1355 rue Ste-Catherine est.

Ile Ste-Hélène   Ile Ste-Hélène (St. Helen's Island) in the St. Lawrence River was altered extensively to become the site of Expo '67, Montréal's very successful world's fair. In the four years before Expo opened, construction crews reshaped the island and doubled its surface area with landfill, then went on to create beside it an island that hadn't existed before, Ile Notre-Dame. Much of the earth needed to do this was dredged up from the bottom of the St. Lawrence River, and 15 million tons of rock from the excavation of the Métro and the

Décarie Expressway were carried in by truck. Bridges were built and 83 pavilions constructed. When Expo closed, the city government preserved the site and a few of the exhibition buildings. Parts were used for Olympic Games events in 1976, and today the island is home to Montréal's popular new casino and an amusement park, La Ronde.

2 Getting Around

BY PUBLIC TRANSPORTATION

BY MÉTRO For speed and economy, nothing beats Montréal's Métro system for getting around. Clean, relatively quiet trains whisk passengers through an ever-expanding network of underground tunnels, with 65 stations at present and more scheduled to open. **Single rides** cost $1.75 (90¢ for children); a strip of six tickets costs $7 ($3.25 for children). Depending on your actual use of the system, you can save money with the **one-day tourist pass** for $5, or the **three-day tourist pass** for $12. Buy tickets at the booth in any station, then slip one into the slot in the turnstile to enter the system. Take a transfer (*correspondence*) from the machine just inside the turnstiles of every station, which allows transfers from a train to a bus at any other Métro station for no additional fare. Remember to take the transfer ticket at the station where you first enter the system. (When starting a trip by bus and intending to continue on the Métro, ask the bus driver for a transfer.) Most connections from one Métro line to another can be made at the Berri-UQAM (Université de Québec à Montréal), Jean-Talon, and Snowdon stations. The Métro runs from about 5:30am to 12:30am Sunday through Thursday, until 1am on Friday and Saturday.

BY BUS Buses cost the same as Métro trains, and Métro tickets are good on buses, too. Exact change is required to pay bus fares in cash. Although they run throughout the city (and give riders the decided advantage of traveling above ground), buses don't run as frequently or as swiftly as the Métro.

BY TAXI

There are plenty of taxis run by several different companies. Cabs come in a variety of colors and styles, so their principal distinguishing feature is the plastic sign on the roof. At night, it's illuminated when the cab is available. Fares are not low. Most short rides from one point to another downtown cost about $5. Tip about 10% to 15%. Members of hotel and restaurant staffs can call cabs, many of which are dispatched by radio. They line up outside most large hotels or can be hailed on the street.

BY CAR

RENTALS Terms, cars, and prices are much like those in the United States. All the larger U.S. companies operate in Canada, or have affiliates (National is represented by Tilden, for instance). Basic rates are about the same from company to company. A charge is usually levied when returning a car in a city other than the one in which it was rented.

Montréal Métro

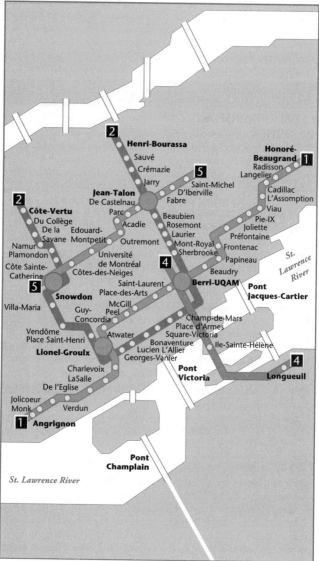

Henri-Bourassa ▣2
Sauvé
Crémazie
Jarry ▣5
Jean-Talon Saint-Michel
De Castelnau D'Iberville
Parc Fabre
Acadie Beaubien
Rosemont
Laurier
Outremont Mont-Royal
Sherbrooke

Côte-Vertu ▣2
Du Collège
De la Edouard-
Savane Montpetit
Namur
Plamondon
Côte Sainte-Catherine
▣5
Université
de Montréal
Côtes-des-Neiges
Villa-Maria **Snowdon**
Saint-Laurent
Place-des-Arts
McGill
Guy- Peel
Concordia
Vendôme
Place Saint-Henri Atwater
Lionel-Groulx
Charlevoix
LaSalle
De l'Eglise
Jolicoeur
Monk Verdun
▣1 **Angrignon**

Honoré-Beaugrand ▣1
Radisson
Langelier
Cadillac
L'Assomption
Viau
Pie-IX
Joliette
Préfontaine
Frontenac
Papineau
Beaudry
Berri-UQAM ▣4

St. Lawrence River

Pont Jacques-Cartier

Champ-de-Mars
Place d'Armes
Square-Victoria
Bonaventure
Lucien L'Allier
Georges-Vanier Ile-Sainte-Hélène
▣4 **Longueuil**
Pont Victoria
Pont Champlain

St. Lawrence River

Budget has a convenient car-rental location in Montréal, in Central Station, 895 rue de la Gauchetière ouest (☎ **514/937-9121** or 800/268-8900). Other car-rental companies include **Avis,** 1225 rue Metcalfe (☎ **514/866-7906** or 800/879-2847); **Hertz,** 1475 rue Aylmer (☎ **514/842-8537** or 800/263-0600); **Thrifty,** 1600 rue Berri, Suite 9 (☎ **514/845-5954** or 800/367-2277); and **Tilden,** 1200 rue Stanley (☎ **514/878-2771** or 800/387-4747).

GASOLINE Gasoline and diesel fuel are sold by the gallon or the liter at prices higher than those in the United States. If sales are by the gallon, it's the Imperial gallon that's used (1 Imperial gallon equals 1.2 U.S. gallons, or 4.546 liters). Gas in Québec is expensive; it costs about $25 to fill a tank with unleaded gasoline. To figure the approximate cost of Canadian gas to familiar U.S. standards, multiply the cost per liter in Canadian dollars by 4. Then convert the price to U.S. dollars.

PARKING It can be difficult on the heavily trafficked streets of downtown Montréal. There are plenty of parking meters, with varying hourly rates. (Look around before walking off without paying. Meters are set well back from the curb so they won't be buried by plowed snow in winter.) Most downtown shopping complexes have underground parking lots, as do the big downtown hotels. Some of the hotels don't charge extra to take cars in and out of their garages during the day, which can save money for those who plan to do a lot of sightseeing by car.

DRIVING RULES The limited-access expressways in Québec are called autoroutes, and distances and speed limits are given in kilometers (km) and kilometers per hour (kmph). Some highway signs are in French only, although Montréal's autoroutes and bridges often bear dual-language signs. Seatbelt use is required by law while driving or riding in a car in Québec. Turning right on a red light is prohibited in Montréal and throughout the province of Québec, except where specifically designated by an additional green arrow.

FAST FACTS: Montréal

American Express Offices of the American Express Travel Service are at 1141 bd. de Maisonneuve ouest (☎ **514/384-3640**), and in La Baie (The Bay), 585 rue Ste-Catherine ouest (☎ **514/281-4777**). For lost or stolen cards, call 800/268-9824.

Area Code Montréal's telephone area code is 514.

Babysitters Nearly all large hotels offer babysitting (*garderie des enfants*). In the smaller hotels and guesthouses, managers often know of sitters they believe to be reliable. Give as much notice as possible, and make certain about rates and extra charges, such as car fare, before making a commitment.

Bookstores Montréal has many bilingual bookstores. The W. H. Smith chain has a store in Central Station, beneath the Queen Elizabeth Hotel (☎ **514/861-5567**), with many others scattered throughout the city. **Coles** is centrally located downtown at 1171 rue Ste-Catherine ouest (☎ **514/849-8825**), and in many other locations. For travel-related books, guidebooks, maps, and travel accessories, try **Ulysses,** in the Latin Quarter at 4176 rue St-Denis, near rue Duluth (☎ **514/843-9447**); near the Delta Montréal Hotel at 560 av. du Président-Kennedy (☎ **514/843-7222**); and on the lower level of the Ogilvy department store, on rue Ste-Catherine at rue de la Montagne (☎ 514/842-7711, ext. 362). **L'Androgyne,** the gay, lesbian, and feminist bookstore at 3636 bd. St-Laurent (☎ 514/842-4765), has books in French and English.

Business Hours   Most **stores** are usually open 9am to 6pm Monday through Wednesday, 9am to 9pm on Thursday and Friday, and 9am to 5pm on Saturday. Many stores are now also open on Sunday from noon to 5pm. **Banks** are usually open Monday through Friday from 8 or 9am to 4pm.

Currency Exchange   There are currency-exchange offices near most locations where they're likely to be needed: at the airports, in the train station, in and near Infotouriste at Dorchester Square, and near Notre-Dame cathedral at 86 rue Notre-Dame. The Bank of America Canada, 1230 rue Peel, also offers foreign-exchange services, Monday through Friday from 8:30am to 5:30pm and on Saturday from 9am to 5pm.

Doctors and Dentists   The front desk at hotels can contact a doctor quickly. If it's not an emergency, call your country's consulate and ask for a recommendation (see "Embassies and Consulates," below). Consulates don't guarantee or certify local doctors, but they maintain lists of physicians with good reputations. Even if the consulate is closed, a duty officer should be available to help. For dental information, call the 24-hour hotline at 514/342-4444. In an emergency, dial 911.

Drugstores   Open 24 hours a day, 365 days a year, **Pharmaprix** has fairly convenient locations at 901 rue Ste-Catherine est, at rue St-André (☎ 514/842-4915), and 5122 côte-des-Neiges, at chemin Queen Mary (☎ 514/738-8464).

Electricity   Canada uses the same electricity (110–120 volts, 60 cycles) as the United States and Mexico, with the same flat-prong plugs and sockets.

Embassies and Consulates   All embassies are in Ottawa, the national capital. In Montréal, the American consulate general is at 1155 rue St-Alexandre (☎ 514/398-9695). The United Kingdom has a consulate general at 1155 rue University, Suite 901 (☎ 514/866-5863). Other English-speaking countries have their consulates in Ottawa.

Emergencies   Dial 911 for the police, firefighters, or an ambulance.

Holidays   See "When to Go" in Chapter 2.

Hospitals   Hotel staffs and consulates can offer advice and information. Hospitals with emergency rooms are **Hôpital Général de Montréal** (☎ 514/937-6011) and **Hôpital Royal Victoria** (☎ 514/842-1231). **Hôpital de Montréal pour Enfants** (☎ 514/934-4400) is a children's hospital with a poison center. Other prominent hospitals are **Hôtel-Dieu** (☎ 514/843-2611) and **Hôpital Notre-Dame** (☎ 514/876-6421).

Hotlines   For the **Sexual Assault Center** 24-hour crisis line, call 514/934-4604; for the **suicide action line,** call 514/723-4000; and for **Tel-Aide,** dial 514/935-1101.

Information   See "Visitor Information" in "Orientation," earlier in this chapter.

Liquor Laws   All hard liquor in Québec is sold through official government stores operated by the Québec Société des Alcools. Wine and beer can be bought in grocery stores and supermarkets. The legal drinking age in the province is 18.

Lost Property   For possessions lost in the Métro, call 514/ 280-4637. If something is left behind in a taxi, it will be difficult to recover unless you made a note of the name of the taxi company. In the event that that unlikely precaution was taken, call the company and tell them when and where the driver picked you up.

Luggage Storage and Lockers   Luggage can be checked at Central Station. Most hotels and guesthouses will store luggage for a day or two.

Mail   All mail posted in Canada must bear Canadian stamps. That might seem painfully obvious, but apparently large numbers of visitors use stamps from their home countries, especially the U.S. To receive mail in Montréal, have it addressed to you, c/o Poste Restante, Station "A," 1025 rue St-Jacques ouest, Montréal, PQ H3C 1G0, Canada. It can be claimed at the main post office (see below). Take along valid identification, preferably with a photo.

Money   See "Information, Entry Requirements & Money," in Chapter 2.

Newspapers and Magazines   Montréal's prime English-language newspaper is the *Montréal Gazette.* Most large newsstands and those in the larger hotels also carry the *Wall Street Journal,* the *New York Times, USA Today,* and the *International Herald Tribune.* So do the several branches of the Maison de la Presse Internationale, one of which is at 550 rue Ste-Catherine ouest, and the large bookstore, Champigny, at 4380 rue St-Denis. For information about current happenings in Montréal, pick up the Friday or Saturday edition of the *Gazette,* or the free monthly booklet called *Montréal Scope,* available in some shops and many hotel lobbies.

Pets   Dogs and cats can be taken into Québec, but the Canadian Customs authorities at the frontier will want to see a rabies vaccination certificate less than three years old signed by a licensed veterinarian. If a pet is less than three months old and obviously healthy, the certificate isn't likely to be required. Check with U.S. Customs about bringing your pet back into the States. Most hotels in Montréal do not accept pets, so inquire about their policy before booking a room.

Photographic Needs   Prices for film and other camera supplies are similar to those in the U.S., and many shops sell supplies. One specialist is Photo Service Ltée, 222 rue Notre-Dame ouest (☎ **514/ 849-2291**), in Old Montréal. They carry film, batteries, equipment, and accessories, and while they don't do repairs on premises, they can send cameras out for service.

Police   Dial 911 for the police. There are three types of officers in Québec: municipal police in Montréal, Québec City, and other towns; Sûreté de Québec officers, comparable to state police or highway patrol in the United States; and RCMP (Royal Canadian Mounted Police), who are similar to U.S. marshals or the FBI and handle cases involving infraction of federal laws. RCMP officers speak English and French. Other officers are not required to know English, though many do.

Post Office   The main post office is at 1250 rue University, near Ste-Catherine (☎ **514/395-4539**), open Monday through Friday from 8am to 6pm. A convenient post office in Old Montréal is at 155 rue St-Jacques (at rue St-François-Xavier). As of this writing, it costs 42¢ to send a first-class letter or postcard within Canada, and 48¢ to send a first-class letter or postcard from Canada to the United States. First-class airmail service to other countries costs 84¢ for the first 10 grams (about a third of an ounce). Rates are expected to go up.

Radio   For English-language FM radio, tune to CFQR (92.5), CBM (93.5), CJFM (95.9), or CHOM (97.7). A French station playing classical music is 100.7 FM. AM stations broadcasting in English are CFCF (600), CJAD (800), CBC (940), and CKGM (980). Some American AM and FM stations can be tuned in as well.

Restrooms   With so many shopping complexes throughout the city, convenient restrooms are usually available (the Québécois call them toilets). But when in dire need, duck into the nearest hotel or buy a cup of coffee in a handy café and use their facilities.

Safety   Montréal is a much safer city than its U.S. counterparts of similar size, but common sense insists that visitors stay alert to their surroundings. Tourists, after all, are prime targets of street criminals. In addition to the the usual precautions, using the hotel safe and carrying credit/charge cards and cash in belts or pouches worn under clothing are good ideas.

Taxes   Most goods and services in Canada are taxed 7% by the federal government. On top of that, the province of Québec adds an additional 6.5% tax on goods and services, including those provided by hotels. In Québec, the federal tax appears on the bill as the TPS (elsewhere in Canada, it's called the GST), and the provincial tax is known as the TVQ. Tourists may receive a rebate on both the federal and provincial tax on items they have purchased but not used in Québec, as well as on lodging. To take advantage of this, request the necessary forms at duty-free shops and hotels and submit them, with the original receipts, within a year of the purchase. Contact the

Canadian consulate or Québec tourism office for up-to-the-minute information about taxes and rebates.

Telephones   The telephone system, operated by Bell Canada, resembles the American system. All operators (dial "0"—zero—to get one) speak French and English, and respond in the appropriate language as soon as callers speak to them. Pay phones in Québec require 25¢ for a three-minute local call. Directory information calls (dial 411) are free of charge. Both local and long-distance calls usually cost more from hotels—sometimes a lot more, so check. Directories (*annuaires des téléphones*) come in white pages (residential) and yellow pages (commercial).

Television   Montréal has two English-language channels, 6 and 12, and cable-equipped TVs also receive some American stations with network affiliations, including CBS from Burlington, Vt. (Channel 3); NBC from Plattsburgh, N.Y. (Channel 5); and ABC from Burlington, Vt. (Channel 22).

Time   Montréal, Québec City, and the Laurentians are all in the eastern time zone. Daylight saving time is observed as in the States, moving clocks ahead an hour in the spring and back an hour in the fall.

Tipping   Practices are similar to those in the United States: 15% of restaurant bills, 10% to 15% for taxi drivers, $1 per bag for porters, $1 per night for the hotel room attendant. Hairdressers and barbers expect 10% to 15%. Hotel doormen should be tipped for calling a taxi or other services.

Transit Information   Dial "AUTOBUS" (☎ **514/288-6287**) for information about the Métro and city buses. For airport transportation, call Autocar Connaisseur / Grayline (☎ **514/934-1222**).

Useful Telephone Numbers   For Alcoholics Anonymous, call 514/376-9230; 24-hour pharmacy, 514/527-8827; the Gay and Lesbian Association of UQAM, 514/987-3039; Sexual Assault Center, 514/934-4504; lost or stolen Visa cards, 800/361-0152 (for American Express, see above); Canadian Customs, 514/283-2953; U.S. Customs, 514/636-3875.

Water   Unless specifically labeled nonpotable, the drinking water is as safe as in the States.

Weather   See "When to Go" in Chapter 2.

Impressions

While (Montréal) has a European flair which charms Americans, her carefree American attitude astonishes Europeans.
            —Jean-Claude Marsan, Preface to *Discover Montréal,*
                        by Joshua Wolfe and Cecile Grenier

3 Networks & Resources

FOR STUDENTS

This is a university town, with four large institutions enrolling tens of thousands of students. Anglophone visitors are assured of someone with whom to speak English on the McGill campus, while French-speaking or bilingual students from UQAM congregate in the cafés along rue St-Denis. A lot of students congregate in **Le St-Sulpice,** 1682 rue St-Denis (☎ **514/844-9458**), the **Shed Café,** 3515 bd. St-Laurent (☎ **514/842-0220**), and **Café Ciné-Lumière,** 5163 bd. St-Laurent (☎ **514/495-1796**). Activities of interest to students are noted in the free weeklies *Mirror* and *Hour,* both in English, and *Voir,* in French.

FOR GAY MEN & LESBIANS

There are several ways to plug into Montréal's gay and lesbian scene. Wander through the **Gay Village** along rue Ste-Catherine between rue St-Hubert and avenue Papineau, where you'll pass shops, bars, clubs, restaurants, and an upscale strip joint called Campus where Monday is ladies' night (to watch). The **Gay and Lesbian Community Centre** is at 1355 rue Ste-Catherine est (☎ **514/528-8424**). Montréal's gay neighborhood used to be along upper boulevard St-Laurent, and the gay, lesbian, and feminist bookstore **L'Androgyne,** established in 1973, is still there, at 3636 bd. St-Laurent (☎ **514/842-4765**). Books are in French and English, and the helpful staff is happy to answer travelers' questions.

FOR WOMEN

The **McGill Women's Union,** 3480 rue McTavish, Room 423, has drop-in hours from 10am to 4pm daily during the school year; at other times of year, call 514/398-6823 to see if they're open. The union has a large library, information about women's services, and a space in which to have coffee with some of the women students at McGill University.

Impressions

You can't throw a stone in Montréal without hitting stained glass.
                                        —Attributed to Mark Twain

4

Montréal Accommodations

Montréal hoteliers make everyone welcome, partly because there are
more hotel rooms here than can be filled with certainty throughout the
year. With that competition, and the robust value of the U.S. dollar
in relation to its Canadian counterpart, this is the place to splurge.
Accommodations range from aeries in one of the soaring glass skyscraper hotels to nests in hyper-luxurious hotels that would be at home
in Right Bank Paris to quiet rooms with iron bedsteads and garden fragrances in converted rowhouses in Vieux Montréal. Except in bed-and-
breakfasts, visitors can almost always count on special discounts and
package deals, especially on weekends, when the hotels' business clients
have packed their bags and gone home. B&Bs can offer a cozier setting at a lower price and give visitors the opportunity to get to know
a Montréaler or two. By the nature of the trade, bed-and-breakfast
owners are among the most outgoing and knowledgeable guides one
might ask.

A couple of bed-and-breakfasts are recommended below, but for
more information about other downtown B&Bs, contact **Relais
Montréal Hospitalité,** 3977 av. Laval, Montréal, PQ H2W 2H9
(☎ **514/287-9635;** fax 514/287-1007), or **Bed & Breakfast Downtown Network,** 3458 av. Laval (at rue Sherbrooke), Montréal, PQ
H2X 3C8 (☎ **514/289-9749** or 800/267-5180). These are referral
agencies for homeowners who have one or more rooms available for
guests. Accommodations and individual rules vary significantly, so
it's wise to ask all pertinent questions up front, such as if children are
welcome, if smoking is allowed, or if all guests share bathrooms.
Deposits are usually required, with the balance payable upon arrival.

Nearly all hotel staff members, from front-desk personnel to the
porters, are reassuringly bilingual. Rare exceptions are the occasional
immigrants in menial positions who speak neither French *nor* English.

The busiest times are in July and August, especially during the
several summer festivals, and during annual holidays (Canadian or
American). At those times, reserve well in advance, especially if special
rates or packages are desired. Most other times, expect to find plenty
of available rooms.

CATEGORIES For convenience, the recommendations below have
been categorized first by neighborhood, then by price. Expect to pay,
in Canadian dollars, $195 to $250 for two people per night in a hotel
designated "Very Expensive"; $150 to $195, "Expensive"; $100 to

$150, "Moderate"; and $60 to $100, "Inexpensive." A dollar sign beside an entry signifies an establishment that offers special value for money, and a star indicates that the hostelry is one of the author's particular favorites. All rooms have a private bath unless otherwise noted. In the top two categories, cable color TV and in-room movies are to be expected, as are restaurants, bars, meeting rooms, and parking garages. Business centers, health clubs, and concierges are less certain, so inquiries should be made if any these services are required.

TAXES   The provincial government imposes a 6.5% tax on accommodations (PST) in addition to the 7% federal goods and services tax (GST). Foreign visitors can get most of the hotel tax back, assuming they save their receipts and ask the hotel for the necessary duty-free form.

Note: Unless specifically noted, prices given here do *not* include taxes—federal or provincial.

1   Best Bets

- **Best Historic Hotel:** No contest. The Ritz-Carlton has been around since 1913, giving it a half-century lead on the nearest competition. The Ritz-Carlton Kempinski Montréal, 1228 rue Sherbrooke ouest (rue Drummond), Montréal, PQ H3G 1H6. ☎ **514/842-4212** or 800/426-3135. Fax 514/842-3383.
- **Best for Business Travelers:** A closer call, with several worthy candidates, but the La Reine Elisabeth / Queen Elizabeth gets the nod for its central location, Entrée Gold concierge floor, big health club, and excellent connections to the airports and railroad station. La Reine Elisabeth/Queen Elizabeth, 900 bd. René-Lévesque ouest (rue Mansfield) Montréal, PQ H3B 4A5. ☎ **514/861-3511** or 800/828-7447. Fax 514/954-2256.
- **Best for a Romantic Getaway:** With puffy duvets on the king-size beds, a Jacuzzi in every bathroom, champagne and caviar in the minibar, the Hotel Vogue gathers valentines by the armful. Hotel Vogue, 1425 rue de la Montagne (between bd. de Maisonneuve and rue Ste-Catherine), Montréal, PQ H3G 1G3. ☎ **514/285-5555** or 800/465-6654. Fax 514/849-8903.
- **Best Trendy Hotel:** Again, the Vogue, with an international crowd that eddies around the espresso bar in the lobby and through the there-to-be-seen Société Café. See "Best For a Romantic Getaway" for Hotel Vogue's address, phone and fax numbers.
- **Best Lobby for Pretending That You're Rich:** A tie—the woody, hushed Ritz-Carlton breathes Old Money, while the Vogue caters to the cell phone and Armani set. The Ritz-Carlton Kempinski Montréal, 1228 rue Sherbrooke ouest (rue Drummond), Montréal, PQ H3G 1H6. ☎ **514/842-4212** or 800/426-3135. Fax 514/842-3383. Hotel Vogue, 1425 rue de la Montagne (between bd. de Maisonneuve and rue Ste-Catherine),

Montréal, PQ H3G 1G3. ☎ **514/285-5555** or 800/465-6654.
Fax 514/849-8903.

- **Best for Families:** The Delta Montréal keeps the kids blissfully waterlogged with *two* pools, one inside, one out. They can also be placed under watchful eyes in the play center, giving their parents a break. Delta Montréal, 45D rue Sherbrooke ouest, Montréal, PQ H3A 2T4. ☎ **514/286-1986** or 800/877-1133. Fax 514/284-4306.

- **Best Moderately Priced Hotel:** True, there are no surprises, but the management keeps tinkering with the formula and the cheapest rooms dip into the budget category at the Holiday Inn Crowne Plaza Downtown, 420 rue Sherbrooke ouest (av. du Parc), Montréal, PQ H3A 1B4. ☎ **514/812-6111** or 800/ HOLIDAY. Fax 514/842-9381.

- **Best Budget Hotel:** Rates at L'Appartement start low and get even lower the longer you stay, and their studios and suites are as large or larger than the more expensive places in town. L'Appartement, 455 rue Sherbrooke ouest, Montréal, PQ H3A 1B7. ☎ **514/284-3634** or 800/363-3010. Fax 514/287-1431.

- **Best B&B:** Les Passants du Sans Soucy, the only bed-and-breakfast in Vieux-Montréal, is more upscale than its brethren, and near top restaurants and clubs in the old town. Les Passants du Sans Soucy, 171 rue St-Paul ouest, Montréal, PQ H2Y 1Z5. ☎ **514/842-2634**. Fax 514/842-2912.

- **Best Service:** It's tough to choose among the troops at the Hotel Vogue, the Ritz-Carlton, and the Inter-Continental—all display an almost equal amount of grace and care when it comes to tending their guests. The Hotel Vogue, ☎ **514/285-5555** or 800/465-6654; The Ritz-Carlton, ☎ **514/842-4212;** the Inter-Continental, ☎ **514/987-9900** or 800/361-3600.

- **Best Location:** Airport buses leave regularly from the front door of the La Reine Elisabeth/Queen Elizabeth, the main railroad station is just a couple of levels down in the hotel elevator, and most of the major corporate buildings are accessible through the corridors of the Underground City. See "Best for Business Travelers" above for this hotel's address, phone and fax numbers.

- **Best Health Club:** Le Westin Mont-Royal lays on aerobics classes with instructors, free weights *and* weight machines, and Exercycles, as well as saunas, a steam room, whirlpools, and massages to recover from the workout. Le Westin Mont-Royal, 1050 rue Sherbrooke ouest, Montréal, PQ H3A 2R6. ☎ **514/ 284-1110** or 800/228-3000. Fax 514/845-3025.

- **Best Hotel Pool:** Most of the big downtown hotels have heated pools, but at the Bonaventure Hilton, slip into the water indoors and stroke into the outdoors without leaving the water, even in January. Bonaventure Hilton International, 1 place Bonaventure (rue Mansfield), Montréal, PQ H5A 1E4. ☎ **514/878-2332** or 800/445-8667. Fax 514/878-0028.

An Important Note on Prices

Unless stated otherwise, **the prices cited in this guide are given in Canadian dollars,** which is good news for you because the Canadian dollar is worth 25% less than the American dollar, but buys nearly as much.

As we go to press, $1 Canadian is worth 75¢ U.S., which means that a $100-a-night hotel room costs only $75 U.S., and a $6 breakfast costs only $4.50 U.S.

For a conversion chart, see "Information, Entry Requirements & Money," in Chapter 2.

- **Best Views:** With 32 stories, Le Westin Mont-Royal has some of the loftiest rooms, with the most panoramic views, in town. See "Best Health Club" for this hotel's address, phone and fax numbers.

2 Downtown

VERY EXPENSIVE

Bonaventure Hilton International

1 place Bonaventure (at rue Mansfield), Montréal, PQ H5A 1E4. ☎ **514/878-2332,** or 800/268-9275 in Canada, 800/445-8667 in the U.S. Fax 514/878-0028. 375 rms, 18 suites. A/C MINIBAR TV TEL. $179–$234 double. AE, CB, DC, ER, MC, V. Weekend packages Apr–Oct. Children of any age stay free in parents' room. Valet parking $19.50; self-parking $12. Métro: Bonaventure.

From aloft, the top of the Place Bonaventure exhibition center looks as if it has a hole in it. That's the $2^{1}/_{2}$-acre rooftop garden, with strolling pheasants, paddling ducks, and a heated pool. All guest rooms have color TVs in the bedrooms and smaller black-and-white sets in the bathrooms, as well as views of city or garden. Furnishings hover somewhere between frumpy and gaudy. No-smoking rooms are available. The hotel's main entrance is at de la Gauchetière and Mansfield, and the lobby is on the 17th floor. It has underground access to Central Station.

Dining/Entertainment: Le Castillon is the hotel's well-regarded French restaurant. Another, La Bourgade, is less costly. Both have summer dining terraces.

Services: Room service (24-hour), babysitting.

Facilities: Year-round heated outdoor pool, fitness center with sauna.

✪ Hotel Vogue

1425 rue de la Montagne (between bd. de Maisonneuve and rue Ste-Catherine), Montréal, PQ H3G 1G3. ☎ **514/285-5555** or 800/465-6654. Fax 514/849-8903. 134 rms, 20 suites. A/C MINIBAR TV TEL. $195–$255 double; from $350 suite. Lower weekend rates. Children 15 and under stay free in parents' room. CB, DC, ER, MC, V. Valet parking $15. Métro: Peel.

The Vogue has been creating a stir since it opened in late 1990, a stunning conversion of an undistinguished office building. Not a few observers feel it has displaced the Ritz-Carlton at the apex of the local pantheon, an image achieved despite three changes in ownership in as many years (it's now part of the Loews chain). Confident gleams abound in fixtures and personnel, as if to proclaim, "We're good and getting better." Luxury breathes from the lobby to the guest rooms. Plump feather pillows and duvets dress the oversize beds, and the bedrooms are decked with fresh flowers, umbrella, cherrywood furniture, a fax, a safe, and a large bath with Mexican marble, separate shower, Jacuzzi, robes, hairdryer, telephone, scale, and TV. More proof? The minibars have been known to harbor caviar and foie gras. All of this suits the pronouncedly international clientele to a tee.

Dining/Entertainment: The Société Café serves three meals a day, with outside tables in summer. The lobby bar, L'Opéra, has piano music Thursday through Saturday.

Services: Concierge, room service (24 hours), dry cleaning, nightly turndown, babysitting available.

Facilities: In-room movies, small exercise room, coin-operated laundry, parking garage.

✪ Ritz-Carlton Kempinski Montréal

1228 rue Sherbrooke ouest (at rue Drummond), Montréal, PQ H3G 1H6. ☎ **514/ 842-4212,** or 800/363-0366 from Canada, 800/426-3135 in the U.S. Fax 514/ 842-3383. 185 rms, 45 suites. A/C MINIBAR TV TEL. $190–$220 double; from $350 suite. Children 13 and under stay free in parents' room. AE, CB, DC, ER, MC, V. Packages available. Parking $15 self or valet, with in/out privileges. Métro: Peel.

In 1912 the Ritz-Carlton opened its doors to the carriage trade, a clientele that has remained faithful (but who've traded in their carriages for Mercedes and Italian sportscars over the years). Limos purr in readiness near the porte-cochère. Soignée beauties and silver-haired tycoons glide past the gilt trim and crystal-and-brass sconces of the opulent Palm Court and gather out in the garden for the most gracious of high teas. Ducklings paddle about in the pond in the middle. Male patrons used to less formal modes of dress are apt to be annoyed when they are informed they must wear jackets in public rooms after 5pm, although the hotel's management seems to be easing up on that requirement. Robes and umbrellas are supplied for guests. The baths are equipped with hairdryers, makeup mirrors, and speakers carrying TV sound. The boutiques of Crescent and Sherbrooke streets and the big downtown department stores are only a few blocks away. Recent visits have revealed signs of slippage in service and maintenance, but not yet enough to damage its still-glowing reputation.

Dining/Entertainment: The Café de Paris is favored for its high tea, Sunday brunch, and weekday power breakfasts. Meals are served on the adjacent garden terrace in summer. There's piano music in the Ritz Bar and Le Grand Prix, with dancing nightly in the latter.

Services: Concierge, room service (24 hours), same-day dry cleaning and laundry, twice-daily maid service, babysitting, secretarial services, express checkout.

Montréal Downtown Accommodations

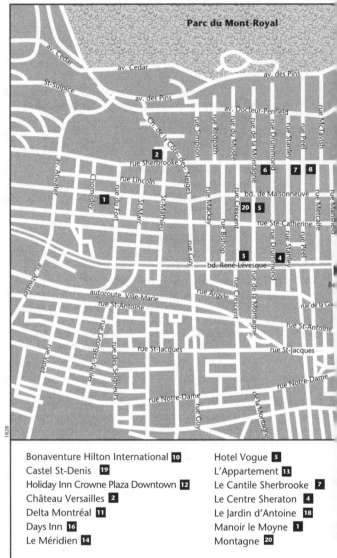

Bonaventure Hilton International **10**
Castel St-Denis **19**
Holiday Inn Crowne Plaza Downtown **12**
Château Versailles **2**
Delta Montréal **11**
Days Inn **16**
Le Méridien **14**

Hotel Vogue **5**
L'Appartement **13**
Le Cantile Sherbrooke **7**
Le Centre Sheraton **4**
Le Jardin d'Antoine **18**
Manoir le Moyne **1**
Montagne **20**

Facilities: In-room movies, modest fitness room, barbershop, newstand, gift shop.

✪ Le Westin Mont-Royal

1050 rue Sherbrooke ouest, Montréal, PQ H3A 2R6. ☎ **514/284-1110** or 800/228-3000. Fax 514/845-3025. 300 rms, 27 suites. A/C MINIBAR TV TEL. $205–$225 double; from $370 suite. Children 17 and under stay free with parents, or in an

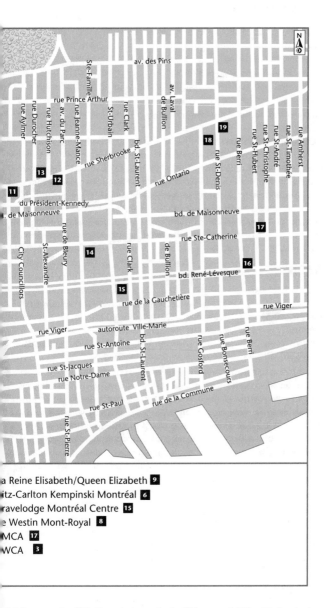

a Reine Elisabeth/Queen Elizabeth **9**

itz-Carlton Kempinski Montréal **6**

ravelodge Montréal Centre **15**

e Westin Mont-Royal **8**

MCA **17**

WCA **3**

djoining room for $75. Upgrade to a suite for $25, on availability. Weekend rates nd special packages. AE, CB, DC, ER, MC, V. Valet parking $19; self-parking $11. Métro: Peel.

This used to be Le Quatre Saisons, a member of the esteemed Four Seasons chain and a worthy competitor to the nearby Ritz-Carlton. A rather chilly lobby is softened by banks of plants and flowers. The guest rooms are large, with comfortable, if slightly dated, furnishings. Terrycloth robes are ready for guests' use, and security is enhanced by in-room safes. The bathrooms have hairdryers and retractable clotheslines. On-demand movies can be chosen from a library of over 60 titles. The impressive health club features a heated outdoor pool, open all year. It offers coffee and juice in the morning, aerobics classes, and workout gear or swimsuits upon request. There are 12 no-smoking floors.

Dining/Entertainment: Le Cercle is of mostly French inspiration, with an optional low-calorie menu. Zen, an upscale Chinese restaurant, offers lunch and dinner daily. Buffet breakfasts and lunches are served in the lobby bar, L'Apéro, which features piano music in the evenings.

Services: Concierge, room service (24 hours), nightly turndown, in-room massage, secretarial services.

Facilities: In-room movies, health club (with exercise classes, weight machines, whirlpool, sauna, and heated lap pool), car-rental desk, boutiques.

EXPENSIVE

Le Centre Sheraton

1201 bd. René-Lévesque ouest (between rue Drummond and rue Stanley), Montréal, PQ H3B 2L7. ☎ **514/878-2000** or 800/325-3535. Fax 514/878-3958. 826 rms, 40 suites. A/C TV TEL. $175–225 double; from $275 suite. Children 16 and under stay free in parents' room. Weekend rates. AE, CB, DC, DISC, ER, MC, V. Valet parking $10; self-parking $9 with in/out privileges. Métro: Bonaventure or Peel.

Le Centre Sheraton rises near Central Station, a few steps off Dorchester Square and within a short walk of the rue Crescent dining and nightlife district. A high glass wall transforms the lobby atrium into an immense greenhouse, big enough to shelter two royal palms and a luxuriance of tropical plants. This international chain can be impersonal, but the staff is efficient and the rooms are comfortable, if anonymous. Earnest people in suits make up most of the clientele. They gravitate to the executive Towers section, which bestows complimentary breakfast and a private lounge on its guests. Half the rooms have minibars; all have coffee makers. Some floors are reserved for nonsmokers.

Dining/Entertainment: The Boulevard restaurant serves three meals a day; the Musette, breakfast and lunch only. Jazz is performed Tuesday through Saturday evenings in the Impromptu Bar.

Services: Concierge (in Towers), room service (24 hours), dry cleaning, babysitting, secretarial services, express checkout, valet parking, airport transportation.

Facilities: In-room movies, indoor pool, fitness center (with whirlpool and sauna), barber, beauty salon, shopping arcade.

Le Méridien

4 Complexe Desjardins (C.P. 130), Montréal, PQ H5B 1E5. ☎ **514/285-1450** or 800/543-4300. Fax 514/285-1243. 572 rms, 28 suites. A/C MINIBAR TV TEL. $170–$190 double; from $285 suite. Children 17 and under stay free in parents' room. Packages available. AE, DC, DISC, ER, MC, V. Valet parking $15; self-parking $9. Métro: Place-des-Arts.

A unit of Air France's hotel chain, Le Méridien is an integral part of the striking Complexe Desjardins, across the street from place des Arts and the Montréal Museum of Contemporary Art. The guest rooms, decorated in restful tones, are comfortable enough, though the baths are on the skimpy side. Glass-enclosed elevators glide up to the bedrooms and down to the lower levels of the complex, which contain a shopping plaza and an indoor pool. Chinatown is a block away, and Vieux Montréal, the downtown district, and the ethnic neighborhoods along "The Main" are within easy walking distance. The hotel is usually the official headquarters of Montréal's popular jazz festival. No-smoking floors are available.

Dining/Entertainment: Café Fleuri provides all meals, while Le Club, with a French menu, serves only lunch and dinner. Le Bar overlooks Complexe Desjardins and has piano music nightly.

Services: Concierge, room service (24 hours), dry cleaning and laundry service, express checkout, valet parking.

Facilities: In-room movies, indoor pool, exercise room (with whirlpool and sauna), useful business center, shopping arcade.

La Reine Elisabeth/Queen Elizabeth

900 bd. René-Lévesque ouest (at rue Mansfield), Montréal, PQ H3B 4A5. ☎ **514/ 861-3511,** or 800/268-9411 in Canada, 800/828-7447 in the U.S. Fax 514/ 954-2256. 1,046 rms, 60 suites. A/C MINIBAR TV TEL. $166–$225 double (concierge-level rates approximately $50 more); from $310 suite. Various discounts, weekend, and excursion packages available. Children 18 and under stay free in parents' room. AE, CB, DC, DISC, ER, MC, V. Parking $12. Métro: Bonaventure.

Montréal's largest hotel has lent its august presence to the city since 1958. Its 21 floors sit atop VIA Rail's Central Station, with place Ville-Marie, place Bonaventure, and the Métro all accessible by underground arcades. This desirable location makes it a frequent choice of heads of state and touring celebrities, even though other hotels in town proffer higher standards of personalized pampering. These savvy guests close the gap by staying on the Entrée Gold floor, which has a lounge serving complimentary breakfasts and cocktail-hour canapés. The less exalted rooms are entirely satisfactory, with most of the expected comforts and gadgets, in price ranges to satisfy most budgets. Non-smoking floors are available.

Dining/Entertainment: The Beaver Club (see Chapter 5, "Montréal Dining," for a complete listing) has a dinner and dancing package on Saturday nights. Several other more casual bistro/bars serve meals in a variety of settings.

Services: Concierge, room service (24 hours), dry cleaning and laundry service, babysitting, valet parking.

Facilities: In-room movies, small health club with instructors, business center, beauty salon, shopping arcade, parking garage.

MODERATE

L'Appartement

455 rue Sherbrooke ouest, Montréal, PQ H3A 1B7. ☎ **514/284-3634** or 800/ 363-3010. Fax 514/287-1431. 125 apts. A/C TV TEL. $79–$119 apt for two. Weekly

rates 25% lower; monthly rates, 44% lower. AE, CB, DC, ER, MC, V. Parking $11 ($8 per day for stays of a week to 27 days). Métro: Place-des-Arts.

Accommodations range in size from small one-room studios with sitting areas to spacious three-room apartments, all with equipped kitchenette, full bath, and balcony. Guests have access to a glass-enclosed rooftop swimming pool, sauna, and washer and dryer. The cramped lobby is an afterthought. Housekeeping service is provided Monday through Friday. Rates for longer stays are negotiable.

Le Cantlie Sherbrooke

1110 rue Sherbrooke ouest (at rue Peel), Montréal, PQ H3A 1G9. ☎ **514/844-3951** or 800/567-1110. Fax 514/844-7808. 200 suites. A/C TV TEL. $145 suite for two. Children 11 and under stay free in parents' suite. Weekly and monthly rates available. AE, CB, DC, ER, MC, V. Parking $8 per day. Métro: Peel.

A neighbor to the Ritz-Carlton, this converted apartment house offers a prime location at lower-than-expected prices. The rooftop pool (open in summer only) offers a fine view of the city, and a fitness center was opened in 1993. There's a terrace café in warm months. Elegant, no, but the least expensive junior suites have ample room, and accommodations get bigger as the prices go up. Even casual requests usually bring immediate discounts. Voice mail and a business center enhance its appeal for executives on extended visits.

Château Versailles

1659 rue Sherbrooke ouest (at rue St-Mathieu), Montréal, PQ H3H 1E3. ☎ **514/ 933-3611,** or 800/361-7199 in Canada, 800/361-3664 in the U.S. Fax 514/ 933-7102. 70 rms. A/C TV TEL. $145 double. Children 16 and under stay free in parents' room. Special weekend rates Nov–May, and summer packages. AE, CB, DC, ER, MC, V. Valet parking $8.50. Métro: Guy. Bus: 24 (then half-a-block walk).

This has long been a local favorite, somewhat overpraised, considering rates that scrape the high edge of the moderate price scale. Although it began as a European-style pension in 1958, the owners have since expanded it into a total of four adjacent rowhouses. The guest rooms are spare but comfortable enough, some with minibars. A few antiques are spotted around the public rooms. Service remains more personal than in the big downtown hotels. Breakfast and afternoon tea are served in a small dining room with a fireplace and handmade quilts on the walls. Price and location keep it popular, so reserve well in advance. A modern annex, La Tour Versailles, is right across the street. The same prices prevail, amounting to greater value for rooms with some Shaker-style reproductions, minibars, and safes. There are two non-smoking floors and a French restaurant. Laptops and faxes are available on request. Go for the annex.

Delta Montréal

450 rue Sherbrooke ouest, Montréal, PQ H3A 2T4. ☎ **514/286-1986** or 800/ 877-1133. Fax 514/284-4306. 483 rms, 6 suites. A/C MINIBAR TV TEL. $115 double; from $250 suite. Weekend rates from $99 double. Children 17 and under stay free in parents' room; children 5 and under eat free. AE, ER, MC, V. Parking $12. Métro: Place-des-Arts.

A first impression of this unit of the Canadian chain is that it has been very well maintained. A second is that the target patron is the business traveler, given the expansively equipped business center and large health club. Then the supervised children's crafts and games center makes it clear that families are cosseted here, too. The bedrooms have angular dimensions, escaping the boxiness of too many contemporary hotels. Most have a small balcony; all have coffee machines. Room service is on call around the clock. A better-than-average health club has an aerobics instructor, whirlpool, sauna, massage, indoor lap pool, outdoor pool, and two squash courts. Enter the 23-story tower from Sherbrooke or avenue du Président-Kennedy (the sole entrance after 10:30pm). Courtesy airport transportation is on call.

Holiday Inn Crowne Plaza Downtown

420 rue Sherbrooke ouest (at av. du Parc), Montréal, PQ H3A 1B4. ☎ **514/ 842-6111** or 800/HOLIDAY. Fax 514/842-9381. 486 rms. A/C MINIBAR TV TEL. $104–$145 double. Two children 18 and under stay free in parents' room; children 11 and under eat free. Summer and family packages. AE, CB, DC, ER, MC, V. Parking $10. Métro: Place-des-Arts.

Not to be confused with the similarly named Holiday Inn Crowne Plaza Métro Centre, this upper-middle entry stands out among the clutch of hotels that cluster around the intersection of Sherbrooke and rue City Councillors. This is one of the city's best values in its class, especially for economizing families: Spouses and two children 18 and under stay free; kids 11 and under eat free too. The guest rooms all have city views and one king-size bed or two double beds. No-smoking and executive floors are available. Coin-operated washers and dryers are provided for guests' use. A large heated indoor pool is attended by a lifeguard. The adjoining fitness center has weights, Exercycles, whirlpool, and sauna.

Manoir Le Moyne

2100 bd. de Maisonneuve ouest (near rue Chomedey), Montréal, PQ H3H 1K6. ☎ **514/931-8861** or 800/361-7191. Fax 514/931-7726. 42 studios, 220 suites. A/C TV TEL. $80–$125 studio or suite for two. Weekend rates $59–$85 studio or suite for two, subject to availability. Two children 17 and under stay free in parents' unit. Weekly and monthly rates available. AE, DC, DISC, ER, MC, V. Parking $8. Métro: Atwater.

The unprepossessing Manoir Le Moyne is two blocks from the Forum concert and sports hall, and a cab ride west of the center of town. The accommodations, most with balconies, offer cable TV with in-room movies, coffee-making equipment, and refrigerators in fully equipped kitchenettes. Most units have queen-size beds. The studios are best for one person; the suites—which vary in dimension—are better for two people. The dining room has a summer terrace. A fair-sized fitness room has Exercycles and a weight machine, a large whirlpool, and men's and women's saunas. Families and businesspeople settling in for stays of several days are likely candidates, assuming the distance to downtown isn't a significant drawback. Obviously, it helps to have a car here, even though parking is limited.

✪ Montagne

1430 rue de la Montagne (north of rue Ste-Catherine), Montréal, PQ H3G 1Z5. ☎ **514/288-5656** or 800/361-6262. Fax 514/9658. 138 rms. A/C TV TEL. $125–$135 double. AE, CB, DC, ER, MC, V. Parking $10. Métro: Peel.

Two white lions stand sentinel at the front door, with a doorman in a pith helmet. Noah extends his influence inside, in a crowded lobby that incorporates a pair of 6-foot carved elephants, two gold-colored crocodiles, and a nude female figure with stained-glass butterfly wings sitting atop a splashing fountain. Clearly, you're not in Kansas. Up on the mezzanine is one of the city's more ambitious dining rooms, Le Lutetia (see Chapter 5, "Montréal Dining," for a complete listing). On the roof is a 20-story-high pool, with light meals and dancing under the stars. In back, a music lounge featuring jazz duos leads to a spangly disco which empties into a pubby bar with a terrace on rue Crescent. After all that, the relatively serene bedrooms seem downright bland. Stop in for a drink, anyway.

INEXPENSIVE

Castel St-Denis

2099 rue St-Denis, Montréal, PQ H2X 3K8. ☎ **514/842-9719.** Fax 514/843-8492. 18 rms, half with bath (shower). A/C TV. $45 double without bath, $55 double with bath. Additional person $10 extra. MC, V. Parking not available. Métro: Berri-UQAM or Sherbrooke.

Among the budget-priced tourist lodges in the Latin Quarter, the Castel St-Denis is one of the most desirable. It's a little south of rue Sherbrooke, among the cafés on the lower reaches of the street, and two long blocks from the Terminus Voyageur. Most of the rooms are fairly quiet, and all are tidy and simply decorated, if hardly chic. The friendly, bilingual owner is a good source for guidance about nearby restaurants and attractions.

Days Inn

1199 rue Berri, Montréal, PQ H2L 4C6. ☎ **514/845-9236** or 800/363-0363. Fax 514/849-9855. 148 rms, 6 junior suites. A/C TV TEL. In season, $82 single or double; $130 junior suite. Off-season, $75 single or double; $109 junior suite. Additional person $7 extra. AE, CB, DC, DISC, ER, MC, V. Parking $10 (outdoors). Métro: Berri-UQAM.

Formerly the Hotel Lord Berri, this new unit of the voracious U.S. economy chain is located between boulevard René-Lévesque and rue Ste-Catherine, not far from St-Denis and a five-minute walk from Old Montréal. Its Italian restaurant has a sidewalk terrace. The bedrooms have full baths and are equipped with color television sets connected for in-room movies. The room decor is as interesting as a bus schedule, but the Latin Quarter location and fair tariffs make up for it. Several floors are set aside for nonsmokers.

Le Jardin d'Antoine

2024 rue St-Denis, Montréal, PQ H2X 3K7. ☎ **514/843-4506** or 800-361-4506 between 8am and 6pm. Fax 514/281-1491. 18 rms, 2 suites. A/C TV TEL. $74–$120 double; $130–$140 suite. Rates include full breakfast. Rates about $10 less during the off-season (Oct–Apr). Additional person $10 extra. AE, MC, V. Parking $9. Métro: Berri-UQAM or Sherbrooke.

Near several good Latin Quarter restaurants, and more upscale than most of the other inns found along rue St-Denis, this bed-and-breakfast has no two rooms alike. That isn't necessarily a good thing, so ask

---

🙂 Family-Friendly Accommodations

L'Appartement *(see p.57)*   The glass-enclosed rooftop pool is the big attraction here, and the kitchenettes in the apartments are a gift to parents whose children get the fidgets in restaurants.

Delta Montréal *(see p. 58)*   The Activity Centre for supervised play and crafts-making is a big draw for small kids, along with the swimming pool and (for bigger kids) an electronic-games room.

Holiday Inn Crowne Plaza Downtown *(see p. 59)*   Two kids 17 and under stay free in their parents' room, kids 11 and under eat free, and everyone gets to enjoy the big swimming pool; plus, there are special packages for families.

Le Jardin d'Antoine *(see p. 60)*   Some rooms open onto the pleasant patio garden, where kids are welcome to play; all rooms have private baths, and breakfast is included in the price. The live-in owners have a child, too.

Manoir Le Moyne *(see p. 59)*   Kids have to flip a coin to see who gets the loft bed and who sleeps downstairs in these split-level accommodations. There's also cable TV and free in-room movies.

YMCA *(see p. 61)*   It has three family rooms, a cafeteria that serves three meals a day, and a big indoor pool that guests may use.

---

to see a room before accepting it. Most have brick walls, a brass or oak bed, and a cozily old-fashioned ambience. Some of the larger, more expensive rooms have whirlpools. Breakfast can be taken in the patio garden. Children are welcome, which is not always the case in bed-and-breakfasts.

Travelodge Montréal Centre

50 bd. René-Lévesque ouest (at rue Clark), Montréal, PQ H2Z 1A2. ☎ **514/ 874-9090,** or 800/363-6535 in Canada, 800/578-7878 in the U.S. Fax 514/ 874-0907. 242 rms. A/C TV TEL. $79 double. Additional person $7 extra; children 11 and under stay free in their parents' room. AE, CB, DC, DISC, ER, MC, V. Parking $10. Métro: St-Laurent or Place d'Armes.

An anonymous mid-rise slab next to the Complexe Desjardins and midway between east and west Montréal, the former Hotel Arcade's low rates and convenient location are its primary virtues. Its guest rooms are small but bright, with single or twin beds (some rooms have up to four beds), cable TV with remote, and coffee machines. There's a lobby bar, and the dining room one flight up serves breakfast and dinner daily, but not lunch. There are two no-smoking floors.

YMCA

1450 rue Stanley (between bd. de Maisonneuve and rue Ste-Catherine), Montréal, PQ H3A 2W6. ☎ **514/849-8393.** Fax 514/849-8017. 331 rms. $54 double without bath, $59 double with bath. Lower rates for students and seniors. AE, MC, V. Parking not available. Métro: Peel.

This cavernous "Y" has rooms—and over 420 beds—in an assortment of configurations, most with telephone and color TV. Men, women, and families can be accommodated. An inexpensive cafeteria is available for all meals except weekend dinners. Guests may use the training room, indoor pool, saunas, squash courts, and jogging track for free. Reserve ahead. There's no curfew. The restaurants and nighttime distractions of the rue Crescent district are right around the corner.

YWCA

1355 bd. René-Lévesque ouest (at rue Crescent), Montréal, PQ H3G 1T3. ☎ **514/ 866-9941** ext. 505. Fax 514/861-1603. 150 rms, 3 with semiprivate bath. $50 double without bath, $54 double with semiprivate bath. Weekly rates available. MC, V. Métro: Lucien-l'Allier or Peel.

The YWCA provides adequate lodging for women only, plus their children (boys to about age eight and girls of all ages). Guests may use the weight-training room, pool, sauna, and fitness classes at no additional charge. Reservations are accepted, but be aware that many of this Y's rooms are rented to students during the school year. There's no curfew. The popular restaurants along Crescent Street are within walking distance. Parking is available in a lot across the street.

3 Vieux-Montréal

EXPENSIVE

✪ Inter-Continental Montréal

360 rue St-Antoine ouest (at rue de Bleury), Montréal, PQ H2Y 3X4. ☎ **514/ 987-9900** or 800/361-3600. Fax 514/987-9904. 335 rms, 22 suites. A/C MINIBAR TV TEL. $180–$195 double; from $350 suite. Packages available. AE, CB, DC, ER, MC, V. Valet parking $16. Métro: Square Victoria.

A striking new addition to the downtown hotel scene, the Inter-Continental became an instant candidate for inclusion among the top five hotels in town when it opened in mid-1991. It's equal to the Westin Mont-Royal on virtually all counts *and* less expensive. A commingling of old and new, its new tower houses the sleek reception area and guest rooms, while the restored annex, the Nordheimer building (1888), contains some of the hotel's restaurants and bars. (Take a look at the early 19th-century vaults down below.) The guest rooms are quiet and well lit, with photographs and lithographs by local artists on the walls. The turret suites are fun, with their round bedrooms and wraparound windows. All rooms have two or three telephones and coffee machines. Robes are supplied. Four floors are reserved for nonsmokers and there are executive floors with a lounge. The Inter-Continental is only a few minutes' walk from Notre-Dame Cathedral and the restaurants and nightspots of Vieux-Montréal.

Dining/Entertainment: Les Continents serves all three meals and Sunday brunch. Le Cristallin, the lobby-level piano bar, has music nightly. In the Nordheimer building is congenial Chez Plume, popular for lunch and after-work get-togethers.

Vieux-Montréal Accommodations & Attractions

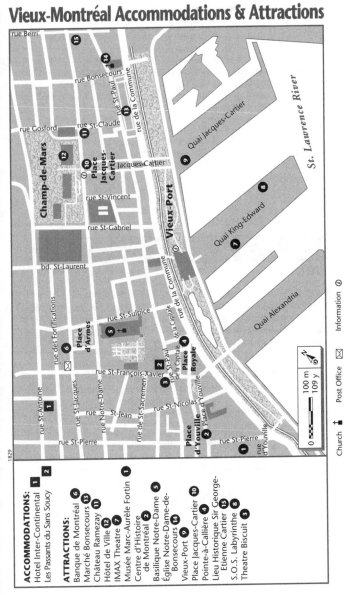

ACCOMMODATIONS:

1. Hotel Inter-Continental
2. Les Passants du Sans Soucy

ATTRACTIONS:

6. Banque de Montréal
13. Marché Bonsecours
11. Château Ramezay
12. Hôtel de Ville
7. IMAX Theatre
1. Musée Marc-Aurèle Fortin
2. Centre d'Histoire de Montréal
5. Basilique Notre-Dame
14. Église Notre-Dame-de-Bonsecours
9. Vieux-Port
10. Place Jacques-Cartier
4. Pointe-à-Callière
15. Lieu Historique Sir George-Etienne Cartier
8. S.O.S. Labyrinthe
3. Theatre Biscuit

Church + ■ Post Office ⊠ Information ⊘

Services: Concierge, room service (24 hours), same-day laundry/valet (Mon–Fri), complimentary newspaper, nightly turndown, express checkout, valet parking.

Facilities: In-room movies, health club (with a small, enclosed rooftop pool, sauna and steamrooms, massage, and weight room), business center.

INEXPENSIVE

Les Passants du Sans Soucy

171 rue St-Paul ouest, Montréal, PQ H2Y 1Z5. ☎ **514/842-2634.** Fax 514/842-2912. 8 rms, 1 suite. A/C TV TEL. $85–$105 double; $150 suite. Rates include full breakfast. Additional person $10 extra. AE, ER, MC, V. Parking $7.50 Mon-Fri, free Sat–Sun. Métro: Place d'Armes.

The only bed-and-breakfast in Old Montréal is this 1723 house craftily converted by the bilingual owners, Daniel Soucy and Michael Banks. Exposed brick and beams and a marble floor form the vestibule, beyond which are a sitting area and a breakfast nook with a skylight. Nine guest rooms are upstairs, each with stucco-and-rock walls, fresh flowers, lace curtains, and wrought-iron or brass beds. The inn is eight blocks from place Jacques-Cartier. Substantial breakfasts include chocolate croissants and café au lait.

4 Plateau Mont-Royal

MODERATE

✪ Auberge de la Fontaine

1301 rue Rachel est (at rue Chambord), Montréal, PQ H2J 2K1. ☎ **514/597-0166** or 800/597-0597. Fax 514/597-0496. 18 rms, 3 suites. A/C TV TEL. $105–$140 double; $175 suite. Rates include buffet breakfast. Additional person $10 extra; children 11 and under stay free in parents' room. AE, ER, MC, V. Free parking in back of the inn or on the street. Métro: Mont-Royal or Sherbrooke.

For those who like to stay a little distance away from frenetic downtown districts, this urban inn at the northern edge of Lafontaine Park may be just the ticket. The park is a bit far from the action, except in summer, when free concerts are performed there and its tennis courts and jogging and cycling paths get vigorous use. The inn has clean, sprightly rooms and bathrooms equipped with hairdryers. The suites have whirlpools, while many of the other rooms have terraces or balconies. Those in the new section are roomier; units in back are quieter. Guests may use the terrace on the third floor, as well as a small kitchen that's kept stocked with complimentary cookies, tea, and juice.

5

Montréal Dining

Montréal has an estimated 5,000 restaurants. Until only a few short years ago, they were overwhelmingly French, in the several variations and subcategories that culinary tent can contain. There were a few temples de cuisine that delivered, or pretended to, haute standards of gastronomy, followed by scores of accomplished bistros employing humbler ingredients and less grand settings, and other places that trafficked in the hearty fare of the days of the colonial era, which used the ingredients available in New France—game, maple sugar, and root vegetables. Everything else was ethnic. Yes, there were establishments that presented the cooking of Asia and the Mediterranean, but they didn't enjoy the same favor they did in other cities of North America. Québec was French, and that was that.

When recurring waves of food crazes washed over Los Angeles, Chicago, Toronto, and New York in the 1980s, introducing their citizens to Cajun, Tex-Mex, southwestern, and the fusion cuisines variously known as Franco-Asian, Pacific Rim, and Cal-Ital, the diners of Montréal were resolute. They stuck to their Frenchphilic traditions. Now that's changing, for a number of reasons. The recession of the early 1990s, from which Canada was slow to recover, put many restaurateurs out of business and forced others to reexamine and streamline their operations. Immigration continued to grow, and the introduction of still more foreign cooking styles stayed apace. Montréalers, secure in their status as epicures, began sampling the exotic edibles emerging in new storefront eateries all around them—Thai, Moroccan, Vietnamese, Portuguese, Turkish, Mexican, Indian, Créole, Szechuan, and Japanese. Innovation and intermingling of styles, ingredients, and techniques was inevitable. The city, long among the elite gastronomic centers, is now as cosmopolitan in its tastes and offerings as any on the Continent.

Picking through this forest of ever-tempting choices can be both gratifying and bewildering. The establishments suggested below point you in several fruitful directions. While they represent the barest hint of the cornucopia that awaits visitors, they include some of the most popular and honored restaurants in town, and getting to any of them involves passing many other worthy possibilities, for numbers of good restaurants often cluster in concentrated neighborhoods or along particular streets, such as rue Crescent, St-Denis, or St-Laurent. Nearly all of them have menus posted outside, prompting the local pastime of stopping every few yards for a little mouth-watering reading and comparison shopping before deciding on a place for dinner. Additional resources are the useful annual guides produced by the Greater Montréal Convention and Tourism Bureau and the Association des restaurateurs du Québec.

It's a good idea, and an expected courtesy, to make a reservation to dine at one of the city's top restaurants. Unlike larger American and European cities, however, a few hours or a day in advance is usually sufficient. A hotel concierge can make the reservation, but nearly all reservation clerks will switch immediately into English when they sense that a caller doesn't speak French. As everywhere, it's bad form to arrive late or not at all, so thoughtful patrons call and cancel if they can't make it. Dress codes are all but nonexistent, except in a handful of luxury restaurants, but adults who show up in the equivalent of T-shirts and jeans are likely to feel uncomfortably out of place at the better establishments. Montrealers are a fashionable lot, and manage to look smart even in casual clothes.

Few people want to dine in five-fork restaurants all the time, and they miss a great deal if they do. This city's moderately priced bistros, cafés, and ethnic eateries offer outstanding food, congenial surroundings, and amiable service at an agreeable cost. And, speaking of value for money, the city's *table d'hôte* (fixed-price) meals are eyeopeners. Entire two- to four-course meals, often with a beverage, can be had for little more than an à la carte main course alone. Even the best restaurants offer them, so table d'hôte represents a considerable saving and the chance to sample some excellent restaurants at a reasonable price. Making lower-priced lunch the main meal of the day keeps costs down too, and is the most economical way to sample the top establishments. The delectable bottom line of dining in Montréal is that a meal can be had here that is the equal in every dimension to the best offered in Los Angeles, Chicago, or New York—for one-third the cost.

When "cuisine" is the last thing on your mind and what is required is a quick meal that will do minimal damage to a credit- or charge-card balance, Montréal doesn't disappoint, either. There are a multitude of places that serve sandwiches and fries for only a few dollars and a number of restaurants, mostly ethnic eateries, that serve two-course lunch specials for under $8. Look, in particular, to Thai, Chinese, and Indian restaurants for all-you-can-eat lunch buffets at that price.

CATEGORIES   The restaurants recommended below have been categorized by neighborhood and then by price. The category is determined by the price range—in Canadian dollars—of the main courses served at dinner: "Very Expensive," $25 to $35 per person; "Expensive," $20 to $25; "Moderate," $12 to $20; and "Inexpensive," $12 and under. A dollar sign beside a listing denotes special value for money, and a star identifies one of my particular favorites. Prices *do not* include the 7% federal tax and 8% provincial tax that are added to the restaurant bill. (Food purchased in a market or grocery store is not taxed.)

PARKING   Since parking space is at a premium in most restaurant districts in Montréal, take the Métro or a taxi to the restaurant (most are within a block or two of a Métro station), or ask if valet parking is available when making a reservation.

1 Best Bets

- **Best Spot for a Romantic Dinner:** Tucked into an 18th-century stone house in Old Montréal is La Marée, whose tables are bathed in candlelight and set with elegant crystal and silver. Its food is excellent without being distracting, and the staff is attentive yet unobtrusive. La Marée, 404 place Jaques-Cartier (near rue Notre-Dame). ☎ **514/861-8126.**
- **Best Spot for a Business Lunch:** The classic power place since 1958 has been the Beaver Club in the La Reine Elisabeth Hôtel, but as its men's-club air might be unpalatable to some women business travelers who have to entertain while on the road, the elegantly neutral Café de Paris at the Ritz-Carlton won't disappoint. The Beaver Club in La Reine Elisabeth, 900 bd. René-Lévesque ouest, ☎ **514/861-3511.** Café de Paris at the Ritz-Carlton, 1228 rue Sherbrooke ouest (rue Drummond), ☎ **514/842-4212.**
- **Best Spot for a Celebration:** Not a whiff of stuffy pretension gets in the way of the always-festive gatherings at Claude Postel, and the ever-gracious Claude himself is usually on hand to ensure that your celebration is memorable. Claude Postel, 443 rue St-Vincent (near rue Notre-Dame). ☎ **514/875-5067.**
- **Best Decor:** Exposed stone walls here, wallpaper with delicate traceries there, gilt- and carved framed paintings of game, fireplaces ablaze much of the year, velvet drapes at the windows— La Marée pleases the eye at every turn. La Marée, 404 place Jaques-Cartier (near rue Notre-Dame). ☎ **514/861-8126.**
- **Best View:** Assuming no objections to rooms that move while its occupants are eating, the room with *the* vista is the Tour de Ville in the Radisson Hôtel des Gouverneurs. Le Tour de Ville in Radisson Hôtel des Gouverneurs, 777 rue Université. ☎ **514/879-1370.**
- **Best Wine List:** Les Halles has a cellar of nearly 300 bottles, carefully arranged not simply by such broad regional categories as bourdeaux and burgundies, but by district appellation. Les Halles, 1450 rue Crescent (between rue Ste-Catherine and bd. de Maisonneuve). ☎ **514/844-2328.**
- **Best Value:** At lunch, the all-you-can-eat Indian buffet at Le Taj is a wonder. At dinner, the *expensive* four-course table d'hôte at Le Boulingueur comes in under $15. Le Taj, 2077 rue Stanley (near rue Sherbrooke). ☎ **514/845-9015.**
- **Best for Kids:** A former train station full of railroad memorabilia, including gumball machines and old-time signs, Il Etait Une

Fois . . . has enough variations on the burger theme to satisfy a tableful of picky 10-year-olds. There's a hot dog called Big Foot, too. Il Etait Une Fois . . . , 600 rue d'Youville (av. McGill College). ☎ **514/842-6783.**

- **Best French Cuisine:** Les Halles has clung to the crest of the *haute* pinnacle for over a quarter century by judicious evolution in its cookery, not wrenching overhauls. See "Best Wine List" above for Les Halles' address and phone number.

- **Best Italian Cuisine:** Funky-chic Buona Notte may look as if it's more concerned with being a place to be seen than with what it sends out of the kitchen, but the pastas, focaccias, and risottos are the big events, not the occasional celebrity diners. Buona Notte, 3518 bd. St-Laurent (near rue Sherbrooke). ☎ **514/848-0644.**

- **Best Mexican Cuisine:** There's a party every night at Casa de Matéo, starting with the birdbath margaritas and dancing on through fried cactus, ceviche, and fish Veracruz. The infectious enthusiasm of the staff is often heightened by live mariachi music. Casa de Matéo, 440 rue St-François-Xavier (near rue St-Paul). ☎ **514/844-7448.**

- **Best Thai Cuisine:** Standard-bearer Sawatdee purveys revelatory examples of a most complex Asian cooking style at good value in a setting of museum-quality Thai statuary and artworks. Sawatdee, 3453 rue Notre-Dame ouest (av. Atwater) ☎ **514/938-8188.**

- **Best Seafood:** Some say the best French food is Belgian, and everyone knows how good the French are with fish. Following that logic, get over to Witloof for waterzooi and fat steamed mussels with heaps of super frites. Witloof, 3619 rue St-Denis (rue Sherbrooke). ☎ **514/281-0100.**

- **Best Burgers & Beer:** The meal of choice at the mingle bars along rue Crescent comes closest to the ideal at Sir Winston Churchill Pub. Sir Winston Churchill Pub, 1459 rue Crescent (between bd. de Maisonneuve and rue St-Catherine). ☎ **514/288-3814.**

- **Best Pizza:** Names are destiny, as with Pizzédélic, where they do anything from same-old, same-old tomato and cheese to forward-edge designer concoctions with unlikely toppings, like snails. Pizzédélic, 3509 bd. St-Laurent (near rue Sherbrooke). ☎ **514/282-6784.**

- **Best Desserts:** With pâtisseries on every other corner, indulging in creamy, gooey, blissfully caloric sweets isn't a chore. But along boulevard St-Laurent, make the effort to seek out Kilo. Kilo, 5206 bd. St-Laurent (between rue Maguire and rue Fairmount). ☎ **514/277-5039.**

- **Best Late-Night Dining:** The Latin Quarter's hippest bistro, L'Express doesn't need a sign out front, since it stays filled nightly until 3am (Sunday only until 1am). Simple but toothsome recipes with the freshest ingredients keep the nightbirds coming. L'Express, 3927 rue St-Denis (rue Roy). ☎ **514/845-5333.**

- **Best Outdoor Dining:** Claude Postel has a new dining terrace. While his cold-weather game dishes are memorable, his minions also have a light touch with summery seafood dishes. See "Best Spot for a Celebration" above for Claude Postel's address and phone number.

- **Best People-Watching:** Any of a dozen cafés along St-Denis will fill this bill, especially on weekends, when the Plateau Mont-Royal boulevard comes alive. But Fonduementale might be the most fun. Fonduementale, 4325 rue St-Denis (av. Marie-Anne). ☎ **514/499-1446.**

- **Best Afternoon Tea:** Gentility and correctness prevail at the Café de Paris in the Ritz-Carlton, where high tea is sublimely reassuring at any time of year, but best in spring and summer, when they move outdoors next to the duck pond. Café de Paris in the Ritz Carlton, 1228 rue Sherbrooke ouest (rue Drummond). ☎ **514/ 842-4212.**

- **Best Brunch:** Crêpes with multitudes of fillings make for Frenchified brunches at Le Jardin Nelson, in the garden, inside, or on the terrace facing place Jacques-Cartier. Le Jardin Nelson, 407 place Jaques-Cartier (rue de la Commune). ☎ **514/ 861-5731.**

- **Best for Before-Theater Dinner:** Polish café Stash is only a block down the hill from the English-language Centaur Theater, and they're open continuously from 11am to late evening. Stash's, 200 rue St-Paul ouest (rue St-François-Xavier). ☎ **514/ 845-6611.**

- **Best Smoked Meat:** It'll only throw another log on a local controversy that's blazed for at least a century, but Schwartz's on the Main serves up the definitive version of Montréal's untransplantable deli treat. Chez Schwartz Charcuterie Hébraique de Montréal, 3895 bd. St-Laurent (north of rue Prince-Arthur). ☎ **514/842-4813.**

- **Best Fast Food:** Where else but Chez Better, where sausages and schnitzels dominate the card, washed down with any of dozens of foreign beers. Six branches and growing. Chez Better, 160 rue Notre-Dame (near place Jaques-Cartier). ☎ **514/ 861-2617.**

- **Best Restaurant, Period:** Fresh-faced, ever-questing Normand Laprise and partner Christine Lamarche keep Toqué! in a league of its own. Toqué!, 3842 rue St-Denis (rue Roy). ☎ **514/ 499-2084.**

2 Restaurants by Cuisine

ALGERIAN

Au Coin Berbère
(Plateau Montréal, M)

BELGIAN

Witloof (Plateau
Montréal, E)

BISTRO FRENCH
Le Bourlingueur
(Vieux-Montréal, M)

CANTONESE/MANDARIN
La Maison Kam Fung
(Downtown, M)

CONTEMPORARY FRENCH
La Marée
(Vieux-Montréal, VE)
Le Lutétia (Downtown, E)
Toqué! (Plateau Mont-Royal, E)

CONTEMPORARY ITALIAN
Buona Notte
(Plateau Montréal, M)
La Sila (Downtown, M)

DELI
Chez Schwartz Charcuterie
Hébraique de Montréal
(Plateau Montréal, IE)

FRENCH
The Beaver Club
(Downtown, VE)
Café Ciné-Lumière
(Plateau Montréal, IE)
Claude Postel
(Vieux-Montréal, VE)
L'Express (Plateau Montréal, M)
Le Jardin Nelson
(Vieux-Montréal, IE)
Les Halles (Downtown, VE)

GERMAN
Chez Better
(Vieux-Montréal, IE)

INTERNATIONAL
Fonduementale (Plateau
Montréal, M)

Le Tour de Ville (Downtown, E)
Sir Winston Churchill Pub
(Downtown, IE)

JAPANESE
Katsura (Downtown, M)

LIGHT FARE
Galaxie Diner (Plateau
Montréal, IE)
Il Etait Une Fois. . .
(Vieux-Montréal, IE)
La Tulipe Noire
(Downtown, M)
Le Jardin Nelson
(Vieux-Montréal, IE)
Le 9e (Downtown, IE)
Les Pres (Downtown, IE)
Santropole (Plateau
Montréal, IE)
Wilensky's (Plateau
Montréal, IE)

MEXICAN
Casa de Matéo (Vieux-
Montréal, M)

NORTHERN INDIAN
Le Taj (Downtown, M)

PIZZA
Pizzédélic (Plateau
Montréal, IE)

POLISH
Stash's (Vieux-Montréal, IE)

THAI
Sawatdee (Downtown, M)

VEGETARIAN
Le Commensal
(Downtown, IE)

3 Downtown

VERY EXPENSIVE

✪ The Beaver Club

In La Reine Elisabeth, 900 bd. René-Lévesque ouest. ☎ **514/861-3511.** Reservations recommended. Main courses $16–$21 at lunch, $30–$35 at dinner; table d'hôte $16–$23 at lunch, $30–$35 at dinner. AE, CB, DC, ER, MC, V. Daily noon–3pm and 6–11pm. Métro: Bonaventure. FRENCH.

Dine here under the glassy gazes of a polar bear, musk ox, and bison, for the restaurant takes its name from an organization of socially prominent explorers and trappers established in 1785. Stained glass and carved wood panels depict the group's early adventures in the wilderness and undergird the clubby tone of the main dining room of the Hôtel La Reine Elisabeth, a magnet for the city's power brokers for decades. It's hardly exclusive, though, not with 225 seats to fill. Lunch is the time for the gentlest prices and to watch the pinstriped CEOs and VPs schmoozing and dealing at the back. The menu changes twice a year, but if only one meal is to be taken here, lean to the emblematic roast beef. This is no place for food frippery. Still, the determined dieter is grateful to learn that nutritional information is provided for each lunch dish. On Saturday a trio begins playing at 7:30pm for dancing.

Les Halles

1450 rue Crescent (between rue Ste-Catherine and bd. de Maisonneuve). ☎ **514/ 844-2328.** Reservations recommended. Main courses $9.75–$14.50 at lunch, $25–$31 at dinner; table d'hôte $21.50 at lunch, $29.50 at dinner. AE, DC, ER, MC, V. Mon 6–11pm, Tues–Fri 11:45am–2:30pm and 6–11pm, Sat 6–11pm. Métro: Guy-Concordia or Peel. FRENCH.

Opened in 1971, Les Halles continues to thrive as one of the most accomplished French restaurants in town. It's more expensive than it should be, however, so the meal to try it out is lunch. That's no loss for the romantics among us. Despite the prices, this isn't an "event" establishment, draped with brocades and glinting with Baccarat. The tables are close, service is correct but chummy, and mock storefronts intended to recall the old Paris market of the same name take up the walls—all of which promotes the idea of bistro, not *temple de cuisine*. Those mild caveats aside, beef, lamb, and game dishes are the stars, seafood the featured players, suitably light-spirited. The central ingredients are rarely exotic, but the kitchen dresses them in unexpected ways. Frogs' legs, for example, are splashed with Pernod during cooking for a distinctive finish, chunks of lobster are tossed with scallops and grapefruit sections, and these are pale descriptions of the resulting compositions. Main courses and desserts are in sufficiently hefty portions to obviate the need for appetizers.

An Important Note on Prices

Unless stated otherwise, **the prices cited in this guide are given in Canadian dollars,** which is good news for visitors because the Canadian dollar is worth about 25% less than the American dollar, but buys just about as much.

As we go to press, $1 Canadian is worth 75¢ U.S., which means that an $80 dinner for two will cost only $60 U.S., and a $5 breakfast will cost only about $3.75 U.S.

For a conversion chart, see "Information, Entry Requirements & Money," in Chapter 2.

EXPENSIVE

Le Lutétia

In the Hôtel de la Montagne, 1430 rue de la Montagne. ☎ **514/288-5656.**
Reservations recommended. Main courses $12–$18. AE, DC, ER, MC, V. Mon 7–
11am, Tues–Fri 7–11am and noon–3pm, Sat 7–11am and 6–11pm, Sun 7–11am,
noon–3pm, and 6–11pm. Métro: Peel. CONTEMPORARY FRENCH.

Underrated and undermentioned, this is as amusing and provocative
a restaurant as the hotel in which it's situated. On the mezzanine floor,
ranged around a rectangular opening to the floor below with oversize
teardrop chandeliers, it incorporates snippets of every decorative style
of the late 19th century, including—but not confined to—baroque,
Victorian, neo-Italian, and French Second Empire. On the pink-clad
table await bowls of pickled beans, piquant mushrooms, and black
olives. All subsequent courses arrive on trolleys under silver bells,
removed with due ceremony. The contents of the plates beneath can
be uneven in execution, especially fish, which is apt to be slightly
overcooked, and beef, a specialty, cooked precisely to order. With a
caution to choose the simpler dishes and a little luck, the end result can
be a memorably romantic meal for two. Dress can be casual, although
the serving staff is in tuxedos. Note the odd hours, dictated in part by
its function as a hotel dining room.

Le Tour de Ville

On the 30th floor of the Radisson Hôtel des Gouverneurs, 777 rue Université.
☎ **514/879-1370.** Reservations required. Buffet $33. AE, CB, DC, DISC, ER,
MC, V. Daily 6–11pm. Métro: Square Victoria. INTERNATIONAL.

Memorable, breathtaking. The view, that is, from this, Montréal's only
revolving restaurant. The food, on the other hand, while varied enough
and not numbingly expensive, does little to dispel the notion that
elevated venues rarely inspire high culinary achievement. Served at a
buffet, the food is themed as "from the four corners of the world," they
insist. Make that two corners, since the usual sources are Switzerland,
France, Italy, and California. The best time to go is when the sun is
setting and the city lights are beginning to wink on. One flight down
is a bar with the same wonderful vistas, along with a dance floor, and
a band three nights a week (Thursday through Saturday from 9pm to
1am, 2am on Saturday). There's no cover, but drinks are steep, from
$5.50 to $9. The bar opens at 6pm.

MODERATE

Katsura

2170 rue de la Montagne (between bd. de Maisonneuve and rue Sherbrooke).
☎ **514/849-1172.** Reservations recommended. Main courses $13–$25; table
d'hôte $8–$19 at lunch, $27–$43 at dinner. AE, DC, ER, MC, V. Mon–Thurs 11:30am–
2:30pm and 5:30–10:30pm, Fri–Sat 11:30am–2:30pm and 5:30–11:30pm, Sun
5:30–9:30pm. Métro: Peel or Guy-Concordia. JAPANESE.

A tuxedoed maître d' welcomes patrons at the door and conducts them
into a conventional Western dining room with plush chairs, or to
tatami mats at low Japanese tables in rooms enclosed by opaque paper
screens. Waitresses in kimonos move quickly but almost silently

under the soothing tinkle of music on the stereo. The house special is a nine-course extravaganza—from baked clams and sashimi through shrimp tempura, salad, egg-flower soup, and sirloin teriyaki to ice cream with segments of mandarin oranges. Katsura has been around long enough to be accorded credit for introducing sushi to Montréal—it's no longer a novelty, but it's still done to near-perfection here. There's a sushi bar in the back, which is also a refuge for those who arrive without a reservation when the place is full. A caution applies back there, for too-enthusiastic ordering of products of the sushi chef's flashing knives can send the final cost skyrocketing beyond reason.

⑤ La Maison Kam Fung

1008 rue Clark (near rue de la Gauchetière est). ☎ **514/878-2888.** Main courses $6.95–$11.95. AE, DC, ER, MC, V. Daily 10am–2pm and 5–10:30pm. Métro: Place d'Armes. CANTONESE/MANDARIN.

Kam Fung mysteriously closed its old Chinatown location around the corner in 1992, then as abruptly reopened here two years later. New owners and new chefs now conduct business in an even-larger room. Weekends are the event days, when Chinese dispersed throughout the suburbs return for needed ingestions of comfort food. While regular meals are served in the evening, midday is reserved for dim sum. Here's the drill: Go to the second floor, obtain a ticket from the young woman at the podium, and wait. Once summoned to a table, be alert to the carts being trundled out of the kitchen. They're stacked with covered baskets and pails, the contents of each displayed for your consideration. Most of these are dumplings of one kind or another, balls of curried shrimp or glistening envelopes of pork nubbins or scallops, supplemented by such items as fish purée slathered on wedges of sweet pepper and, for the venturesome, steamed chicken feet and squid. Simply order until you're sated, being selective enough not to gather up the first five items that appear. Much more is on the way. For dessert, there are trolleys with slices of fruit. And a hint: Dumplings with sesame seeds are almost always sweet.

✪ Sawatdee

3453 rue Notre-Dame ouest (at av. Atwater). ☎ **514/938-8188.** Main courses $7.95–$19.95. AE, MC. Tues–Fri noon–2:30pm and 5–10pm, Sat–Sun 5–11pm. Métro: Lionel-Groulx. THAI.

While it may be a stretch to describe this as "one of the hundred best restaurants in Canada," as it has been proclaimed, Sawatdee is certainly a welcome addition. It's well west of downtown, in a seedy neighborhood of second-rate clothing stores and fast-food outlets. Think of it for lunch after a morning of browsing along rue Notre-Dame east of Atwater, which has at least 30 antiques shops in just a few blocks. That meal can be an all-you-can-eat buffet at under $8 per person. Cheap and filling, but not wonderful. For something memorable, show up for dinner, and make it clear that you want genuine Thai seasonings, not the wan versions usually served to non-Asians. Sharing dishes is the way to go, since many of them will be unfamiliar to most diners. Thai cooking borrows from its neighbors, India and China, and applies their seasonings and techniques to native ingredients. Curries, coconut milk, and lemon grass appear frequently in concert with chicken, shrimp, and pork. Take time to examine the abundance of museum-quality statuary and tapestries.

La Sila

2040 rue St-Denis (north of rue Ontario). ☎ **514/844-5083.** Reservations recommended. Main courses $8–$15; table d'hôte $9–$12 at lunch, $27–$30 at dinner. AE, DC, ER, MC, V. Mon–Fri 11:30am–2:30pm and 5:30–11pm, Sat 5:30–11pm. Métro: Sherbrooke. CONTEMPORARY ITALIAN.

Apart from a determination to deemphasize the heavier cream sauces of the past, La Sila remains something of a traditionalist on a dining scene that only recently has succumbed to the continent-wide enthusiasm for flashy Cal-Ital-Asian preparations. The reasons to go are the pastas, made in-house, and the trademark milk-fed veal that practically parts at a loving look. Service is by careerists, not models and actors between shoots and auditions, a difference gratifying to behold. (These things were true before the founding owner retired and so far apply to practices under the current regime.) Redecoration has brightened the interior and added a bar, and the terrace still invites diners in the warm months. Little on the menu is likely to disappoint, but the chef's special fettuccine and the veal scaloppine La Sila are all but certain to please. There's free parking in back.

✪ Le Taj

2077 rue Stanley (near rue Sherbrooke). ☎ **514/845-9015.** Main courses $9–$17; luncheon buffet $7.50. AE, DC, ER, MC, V. Sun–Fri 11:30am–2:30 and 5–10:30pm, Sat 5–10:30pm. Métro: Peel. NORTHERN INDIAN.

A large relief temple sculpture occupies pride of place in this dramatic setting of cream and apricot, completely overhauled in recent years. Back in the corner, a chef works diligently over an open tandoor oven. His specialty is the mughlai repertoire of northern India. Seasonings on the scores of dishes he sends forth are more tangy than incendiary (but watch out for the coriander sauce). Spicy or mild, all are perfumed with turmeric, saffron, ginger, cumin, mango powder, and garam-masala.

For a rare treat, the marinated lamb chops roasted in the tandoor and arriving at table still sizzling and nested on braised vegetables are a surprise. Vegetarians have a choice of eight dishes, the chickpea-based channa masala among the most complex. The main courses are huge, making appetizers irrelevant. They arrive in a boggling array of bowls, saucers, cups and dishes, including naan (the flat bread) and basmati rice. Evenings are quiet, lunchtimes busy, because of the cheap buffet, but not hectic.

La Tulipe Noire

2100 rue Stanley (near rue Sherbrooke). ☎ **514/285-1225.** Salads and sandwiches $6–$14. MC, V. Daily 8am–midnight. Métro: Peel. LIGHT FARE.

This is a place to know for its perky reliability and extended hours, as when breakfast at a nearby hotel turns out to cost $20 or for a pause in a club crawl in the rue Crescent district. Basically a combination coffee shop and pastry shop, it's best for snacks or late-evening dessert rather than dinners, although full meals are available. At lunchtime or as night wears on, crowds stack up at the door and it can get a little frantic. You'll find it in the back of the Maison Alcan building on rue Sherbrooke. They only close two or three days a year.

INEXPENSIVE

ⓢ Le Commensal

1204 av. McGill College (at rue Ste-Catherine). ☎ **514/871-1480.** Reservations not accepted. Dishes priced by weight, $1.40 per 100 grams (about 3¹/₂ oz.). AE, MC, V. Daily 11am–11:30pm. Métro: McGill. VEGETARIAN.

Le Commensal serves strictly vegetarian fare with not a hint of animal flesh in any of the many platters that fill its buffet table. Most of the dishes are so artfully conceived, with close attention to aroma, color, and texture, that even avowed meateaters are unlikely to feel deprived. The only likely complaint is that those dishes that are supposed to be hot are too often lukewarm. Patrons circle the table helping themselves, then pay the cashier by weight. The second-floor location affords a view, which compensates for the utilitarian decor.

Le Commensal has eight other locations, at recent count, one of the most convenient being the one at 2115 rue St-Denis, at rue Sherbrooke (☎ **514/845-2627**).

Le 9e

In the Eaton department store, 677 rue Ste-Catherine. ☎ **514/284-8421.** Table d'hôte $7.75–$9.50. AE, MC, V. Mon–Wed and Sat 11:30am–3pm, Thurs–Fri 11:30am–3pm and 4:30–7pm. Métro: McGill. LIGHT FARE.

"Le Neuvième," on the ninth floor of the old-line department store, is a replica of an art deco dining room aboard the ocean liner *Ile de France*, complete with murals, marble columns, and giant alabaster vases. Menu items include soups, sandwiches, and salads; and daily specials—lamb, fish, and pasta, usually—come with soup, dessert, and coffee. They couldn't be much more ordinary in concept and execution, but sustenance here is more visual than gustatory. Le 9e opened in 1931, and some of the waiters and waitresses, in their starched black-and-white uniforms, look as if they might have been around at the inauguration. Expect noise and children.

Les Pres

902 rue Ste-Catherine (between av. McGill College and rue Mansfield). ☎ **514/876-1096.** Main courses $5.50–$13; table d'hôte $6–$10 at lunch, $10–$15 at dinner. AE, ER, MC, V. Mon–Thurs 11am–11:30pm, Fri–Sat 11am–midnight, Sun noon–11pm. Métro: McGill. LIGHT FARE.

Admittedly, gastronomic societies will always give this coffee shop a miss. It's mentioned here because it's at the heart of the downtown shopping district, steps away from La Baie and Henry Birks, and it provides filling meals without emptying wallets. A typical lunch special, at $9.95, included broccoli-cream soup, a plate of mildly spicy "Cajun" chicken, mixed vegetables, rice or fries, salad, and coffee or tea. They have beer on tap.

Sir Winston Churchill Pub

1459 rue Crescent (between bd. de Maisonneuve and rue Ste-Catherine). ☎ **514/ 288-3814.** Most items under $12. AE, DC, ER, MC, V. Daily 11:30am–3pm and 5pm–3am. Métro: Guy-Concordia or Peel. INTERNATIONAL.

Sidewalk tables here are enclosed by glass in winter, open to the sun in summer—just the place to pass an hour of people-watching, burger-munching, and beer-quaffing. To be reasonably certain of snagging a table, arrive before noon or after 2pm. Variations on the soup-and-sandwich theme are provided by the lunch buffet and Sunday brunch.

4 Vieux-Montréal

VERY EXPENSIVE

✪ La Marée

404 place Jacques-Cartier (near rue Notre-Dame). ☎ **514/861-8126.** Reservations required. Main courses $15–$17 at lunch, $24–$30 at dinner; table d'hôte lunch $14–$17. AE, CB, DC, ER, MC, V. Mon–Fri noon–3pm and 5:30–11:30pm, Sat–Sun 5:30–11:30pm. Métro: Champ-de-Mars. CONTEMPORARY FRENCH.

Look for the historic 1807 del Vecchio house on the west side of the plaza, a site occupied by previous structures since 1655. Fine dining is generally not to be expected at the epicenter of a city's most heavily trampled tourist district. This restaurant demolishes that negative expectation. Begin with the setting: stone walls, fireplaces, paintings of fish and game, delicately figured wallpaper, furnishings recalling the eras of Louis XIII and the Sun King. Candlelight enhances the mood for romantic couples in the evening, while power lunches prevail at midday. (A lunchtime express menu costs only $9.50 to $12.) Known especially for its refined and precise treatment of seafood, the kitchen is lauded—correctly—for such fabrications as trout stuffed with salmon and lobster mousse and lobster with tomato and fresh basil with a white-wine sauce. In cooler weather, chateaubriand tops the list. Service is disciplined and unobtrusive. There's no dress code, but you'll want to look at least stylish casual.

EXPENSIVE

✪ Claude Postel

443 rue St-Vincent (near rue Notre-Dame). ☎ **514/875-5067.** Reservations recommended. Main courses $17–$30; table d'hôte lunch $20. AE, CB, DC, ER, MC, V. Mon–Fri 11:30am–2:30pm and 5:30–11pm, Sat–Sun 5:30–11pm. Métro: Place d'Armes or Champ-de-Mars. FRENCH.

One of the most upbeat places in Vieux-Montréal is named for its chef-owner, who once shook the skillets at Bonaparte, a few blocks away. He has surpassed his former employer on every count, and continues to widen the gap, as with recent renovations that added a summer dining terrace with 50 seats. The building, which dates from 1862, has been a morgue and a hotel that once had Sarah Bernhardt as a guest. The animated Postel almost dances through his dining room, greeting regulars and newcomers with equal warmth, suggesting off-menu items and possible wines. While his customers are largely businesspeople and government employees, he frequently attracts visiting celebs, including Madonna and Donald Sutherland. They come for such creations as sweetbreads braised in wine and cream with fistsful of morels and slivers of air-cured ham, a triumph even for those who ordinarily shun organ meats. Caribou, venison, scallops, and salmon appear on the menu in equally creative guises. There is valet parking from 6pm.

Postel has a take-out shop nearby, at 75 rue Notre-Dame, with most of the makings of a satisfying picnic, including baguettes, cheeses, sandwiches, and quiches.

MODERATE

⑤ Le Bourlingueur

363 rue St-François-Xavier (near rue St-Paul). ☎ **514/845-3646.** Reservations recommended. Table d'hôte lunch or dinner $9–$14. AE, ER, MC, V. Mon 11:30am–3pm, Tues–Fri 11:30am–9pm, Sat 5:30–9pm. Métro: Place d'Armes. BISTRO FRENCH.

While it doesn't look especially promising upon first approach, this registers as a real find in Vieux Montréal. For the almost unbelievably low prices indicated above, they offer 8 to 10 four-course meals daily. The chalkboard menu changes with market availability, making it possible to dine here twice a day for a week without repeating anything except the indifferent salad. The specialty of the house is seafood— watch for the cold lobster with herb mayonnaise and for the turbot (the sturdy Canadian kind) with mustard sauce. Well short of chic, it doesn't make the most of the its stone walls and old beams, and chooses to put paper placemats on the pink tablecloths. No matter, especially with such low prices and relative quality. Le Bourlingueur attracts a mixed crowd of the widest possible range in age, sex, occupation, and proclivity. They arrive in greatest numbers at lunchtime.

✪ Casa de Matéo

440 rue St-François-Xavier (near rue St-Paul). ☎ **514/844-7448.** Reservations not required. Main courses $14–$18; daily lunch specials $8–$10. AE, MC, V. Mon–Fri 11am–11pm, Sat–Sun 2–11pm. Métro: Place d'Armes. MEXICAN.

Step into what feels like a party about to kick into high gear every night. You'll receive a downright gleeful greeting from the host and, on Friday and Saturday, mariachis come to carry the fiesta to a higher register. Birdbath-size margaritas arrive with chips and salsa at the center horseshoe bar, which is encased with rough terra-cotta tiles. Lending authenticity is a shy but cheerful staff from Mexico, Guatemala, Ecuador, and other Latin American countries, most of them delighted to be addressed in even a few words of Spanish. With these generous servings, appetizers can be skipped in deference to cost and calories. But that would mean missing the *plato Mexicano*, a sampler of all the starters. Since that's a meal in itself, judicious sorts can stop there. But *that* would mean missing the pescado Veracruzano, the whole red snapper quickly marinated and fried and served with a nest of crisp vegetables. The usual burritos and enchiladas are entirely missable, a sop to timid appetites.

🅼 Family-Friendly Restaurants

Le Faubourg Ste-Catherine *(see p. 86)*   This market and fast-food complex blends tempting foods from many countries and is a great place to buy picnic fare. Kids reluctant to try exotic foods can find all the burgers, sandwiches, fruits, and ice cream they want.

Il Etait Une Fois . . . *(see p. 79)*   Kids think this restaurant, in an old train station, is a big playhouse. Besides the decorative memorabilia, there are ice-cream sundaes, burgers, and a hot dog called Big Foot. Just the place to celebrate a birthday.

Le 9e *(see p. 75)*   What looks like a ship's dining room is found on the ninth (9e) floor of Eaton's department store. Kids can pretend they're on a fantasy voyage, and since "Le Neuvième" is a noisy place, they can be as enthusiastic as they like.

McDonalds's   For something familiar, but with a twist, this McDonald's, only a block from Notre-Dame Basilica at 1 rue Notre-Dame where it meets bvd. St-Laurent, deserves a mention. It's located in a house that was once the home of Antoine Lamet de la Mothe Cadillac, the founder of Detroit and a governor of Louisiana. It offers the usual menu, along with pizzas and the Québec favorite, poutine (french fries covered with a cheese sauce).

INEXPENSIVE

🅢 Chez Better

160 rue Notre-Dame (near place Jacques-Cartier). ☎ **514/861-2617.** Main courses $6.25–$8.50. AE, MV, V. Daily 11am–11pm. Métro: Champ-de-Mars. GERMAN.

They aren't making a half-hearted boast. This and the other five outposts of this growing local chain are named for the founder, a Canadian born in Germany. Presumably he grew homesick for the viands of his native land and opened his first restaurant to assuage that hunger. Think knackwurst, sauerkraut, fries, and beer, with variations, and that gives the general outline of the menu. Forget grease and oozing globules of fat, for these are remarkably lighthearted sausages, brightly seasoned with herbs, curry, hot pepper, even truffle shavings. A trivet of three mustards sits on each table. While sausage plates are the stars, there are also mixed grills, chicken schnitzels, grilled smoked pork chops, and salads. In this 1811 building in Vieux Montréal, the ground floor is for nonsmokers, while upstairs is for puffers. Service can be disjointed, but rarely to the point of irritation.

Two other branches tourists are likely to encounter are at 4382 bd. St-Laurent (☎ **514/845-4554**) and 1430 rue Stanley (☎ **514/848-9859**).

Le Jardin Nelson

407 place Jacques-Cartier (at rue de la Commune). ☎ **514/861-5731.** Reservations not accepted. Main courses $5.75–$9.50. MC, V. May–Labor Day, daily 11:30am–3am; Labor Day–Nov, daily 11:30am–midnight (later on weekends); Dec–Apr, more limited hours (call ahead). Métro: Place d'Armes. FRENCH/LIGHT FARE.

Near the foot of the hill, a passage leads into the paved garden court in back of a handsome stone building dating from 1812. The kitchen specializes in crêpes, their fillings determining their destinies as main courses or desserts. Mild invention keeps the results intriguing, as with the melange of semicrispy veggies rolled in a thin buckwheat pancake laced with threads of spinach. Soups, omelets, salads, and sandwiches are also available. A crab-apple tree shades the garden, a horticultural counterpoint to midday concerts by jazz combos (Friday through Sunday) and classical chamber groups (Monday through Thursday).

Stash's

200 rue St-Paul ouest (at rue St-François-Xavier). ☎ 514/845-6611. Reservations recommended. Main courses $9–$13; table d'hôte $18.75–$24.50. AE, MC, V. Mon–Fri 11am–10:30pm, Sat–Sun noon–10:30pm. Métro: Place d'Armes. POLISH.

Even after moving from its former spot beside Notre-Dame cathedral, this *restauracja polska* continues to draw enthusiastic throngs for its munificent offerings and low prices. The new setting features brick and stone walls, exposed beams, colorful hanging lamps, blond-wood furniture, and shelves of secondhand books and newspapers to peruse. An old convent was the source of the several refectory tables and pews. A roast wild boar is a new addition to an already-ample card of pirogies (a kind of Polish ravioli stuffed with meat or cheese), potato pancakes, borscht with sour cream, roast duck, and beef Stroganoff. The place is named after the original owner, now in Europe. A jolly tenor persists, with animated patrons and such menu admonitions as "anything tastes better with wodka, even wodka. Read, eat, and enjoy."

Il Etait Une Fois . . .

600 rue d'Youville (at av. McGill College). ☎ 514/842-6783. Most items under $10. MC, V. Daily 11am–9pm. Métro: Victoria. LIGHT FARE.

At the western edge of Vieux Montréal is this 1909 former brick train station, now converted to a popular casual eating place. The name means "Once Upon a Time . . .," referring to the railroad memorabilia that constitutes the decor—a pot-belly stove, gumball machines, vintage signs. Kids may not grasp the nostalgia, but they go for the dozen different burgers, which include a veggie version. All come with a variety of trimmings, as does the "Big Foot" hot dog. They don't disdain the malteds, sundaes, apple pie à la mode, or strawberry-rhubarb pie either, while their grownup companions can have beer or wine. Fish and chips, lobster rolls, and salads are also on the unambitious menu. It's a short two-block walk west from the Centre d'Histoire de Montréal.

5 Plateau Mont-Royal

EXPENSIVE

✪ Toqué!

3842 rue St-Denis (at rue Roy). ☎ 514/499-2084. Reservations recommended. Main courses $22–$26. AE, MC, V. Daily 6–11pm. Métro: Sherbrooke. CONTEMPORARY FRENCH.

This restaurant is the sort of adornment that can singlehandedly raise the gastronomic standards of an entire city. Since Montréal already ranked quite high in that regard, a meal here is virtually obligatory for anyone who admires superb food dazzlingly presented, especially since the former champ, Les Mignardies, has closed its doors. Normand Laprise, previously associated with a well-regarded venture called Citrus, has teamed up with Christine Lamarche to create a place as postmodernist in its cuisine as in its decor, which is largely bright colors and minimalist fixtures, with a wall down the middle to separate smokers from non. "Postnouvelle" might also apply, for while the presentations are dazzlers, the portions are quite sufficient and the singular combinations of ingredients are intensely flavorful. Alice Waters and Wolfgang Puck-ish comparisions might be made, for this food bears resemblances to those Californians' inclination to apply French and Asian techniques to top-of-the-bin ingredients. (This is Montréal, though, and on those rare occasions when the kitchen stumbles, it tends to be with items like updated spring rolls.) Experimentation is kept on a tether by the chefs' professionalism, and missteps are few. The menu is never set in stone. If fiddleheads are good at market in the morning, they might well replace the listed asparagus that night. Consider just one recent dish: a timbale of creamy risotto touched with Parmesan hides under a cascade of thread-thin strips of deep-fried sweet potato, all to nestle against lightly grilled leaves of palest veal. Duck and foie gras are memorable, while salmon is often the desirable fish dish. An exciting cheese selection can precede dessert. Success has forced a move downstairs of the open kitchen that used to be in front—they need the space for tables. The restaurant fills up later than most local restaurants, with prosperous-looking suits and women with glints of gold at throat and wrist. Allow two hours and call at least a day ahead for reservations.

Witloof

3619 rue St-Denis (at rue Sherbrooke). ☎ **514/281-0100.** Reservations recommended. Main courses $13.50–$18.50; table d'hôte $13–$22. AE, DC, ER, MC, V. Mon–Wed 11:30am–11pm, Thurs–Fri 11:30am–midnight, Sat 5pm–midnight, Sun 5–11pm. Métro: Sherbrooke. BELGIAN.

Its name is Flemish for "endive," and when Witloof sticks to the Belgian dishes in which it specializes, it's one of the most gratifying restaurants in town. It contrives to be both a casual and an elegant place, with snowy linen tablecloths covered with butcher paper. Steaming casseroles of mussels with tents of frites on the side are deservedly most popular, but the classic Belgian stew, waterzooi, is a close second. Pastas are no better than adequate. Because it's always busy, the kitchen can fall behind on orders, but the convivial atmosphere dissuades grousing. Several Belgian beers, including Blanche de Bruges, are available and go well with most of this food. The restaurant has a large selection of desserts, from crème caramel to praline crêpes.

MODERATE

Au Coin Berbère

73 rue Duluth est (between bd. St-Laurent and av. Coloniale). ☎ **514/844-7405.** Main courses $9–$17. MC, V. Tues–Wed 5–11pm. Thurs–Sun 5pm–midnight. Métro: Mont-Royal or Sherbrooke. ALGERIAN.

A change of pace from prevailing French and Italian menus, this earnest little retreat specializes in couscous, with 10 variations on the theme. It may be particularly appealing for vegetarians hungry for something other than salads or vegetable plates. Couscous is both the name of the famous North African dish, which involves a great number of various toppings, and the name of the grainy pasta that's the one essential ingredient. White tablecloths and somber, unobtrusive service add a touch of class, a needed quality along rue Duluth. Although similar to Prince Arthur in architectural character, this passageway between St-Laurent and St-Denis continues to look wind-blown and shabby, with much less pedestrian traffic. Still, Au Coin Berbère is pleasantly intimate and fully licensed, not routinely the case with ethnic eateries in this area.

Buona Notte

3518 bd. St-Laurent (near rue Sherbrooke). ☎ **514/848-0644.** Reservations recommended. Main courses $6.95–$9.50; table d'hôte $16.95–$25.95. AE, DC, MC, V. Mon–Fri 11:30am–midnight, Sat 5pm–midnight, Sun 10am–3pm and 5pm–midnight. Métro: St-Laurent. CONTEMPORARY ITALIAN.

It could as easily be in New York's Soho, with its high ceiling masked by fans, wrapped pipes, and heating ducts. A principal component of the decor are plates painted by celebrity diners—Michael Bolton, Danny DeVito, and the Gypsy Kings, among them. They're boxed (the plates, that is) and arrayed along one wall. This is the kind of place that attracts that sort of patron. Funk and hip-hop thump over the stereo, people in black or spangles-of-the-moment cruise the tables, and the service staff looks ready to leap at the next casting call. Yet while food inevitably takes second place to preening, it's surprisingly worthwhile. Pastas rule, tumbled with crunchy vegetables or with silky walnut sauce or any of 10 or more combinations. The kitchen exhibits less reliance on flesh than the norm. There are several more complete meals, with chicken or beef prevailing, but also an imaginative risotto with two cheeses and two sauces. The rims of the plates are usually dusted with minced parsley and paprika, a presentational device that tends to look messy rather than decorative. The breads are gratifyingly dense and chewy.

۞ L'Express

3927 rue St-Denis (at rue Roy). ☎ **514/845-5333.** Reservations recommended. Main courses $10–$16. AE, CB, DC, ER, MC, V. Mon–Fri 8am–3am, Sat 10am–3am, Sun 10am–2am. Métro: Sherbrooke. FRENCH.

No obvious sign announces the presence of this restaurant, only its name discreetly spelled out in white tiles embedded in the sidewalk.

Apart from that bit of implicit snobbery, there's no need to call attention to itself, since *tout* Montréal knows exactly where it is. Blazing onto the scene as the newest, hottest bistro a few years back, L'Express has now settled into coveted status as an established place-to-be-seen. Best of all, for its owners, at least, that elevation was seemingly effortless. The constant presence of vaguely familiar faces—media types, politicians, actors, artists, and platoons of stylish, very pretty people—sustains a cachet that shows no signs of wearing thin. They lean toward each other over black café tables and chairs, snatching glimpses of themselves in the many mirrors. With all this place has going for it, the food could be less than mediocre without much harm. Instead, it's fairly priced, prepared with a sensitivity to lightness in saucing, and in substantial portions. Seasonal adjustments veer from vinegary octopus and lentil salad in summer to full-flavored duck breast with chewy chanterelles in a sauce with the scent of deep woods. Or simply stop by for a croque monsieur or a bagel with smoked salmon and cream cheese. While reservations are usually necessary for tables, single diners can often find a seat at the bar, where meals are also served.

Fonduementale

4325 rue St-Denis (at av. Marie-Anne). ☎ **514/499-1446.** Main courses $11.75–$18; table d'hôte $17.50–$25. AE, CB, DC, ER, MC, V. Mon–Sat 5:30–11pm. Métro: Mont-Royal. INTERNATIONAL.

Fondue sets have been gathering dust in attics all over North America for 30 years, when the fad reached its last apogee. That may explain why the bulk of this clientele was either born since then or has been seized by a fit of nostalgia. More kinds of fondue than they might have thought existed comprise the bulk of the menu. Among the most frequently ordered are the strictly beef variety, at $20 per person, and the Chinese variation, with beef, chicken, and shrimp. Joined with fondue appetizers and followed by chocolate fondue, overdosing is an ever-present danger. Those diners who prefer that their meals be prepared in the kitchen have access to an extensive card of game, including cuts of elk, caribou, bison, deer, boar, rabbit, and pheasant, most of which comes from farms in Québec and Ontario. Sample three different kinds of game for $18. The restaurant is in a turn-of-the-century house on one of the busiest stretches of rue St-Denis. In summer, there is terrace dining in front for observing the passing parade, or in back, for those who prefer the shelter of a shade tree.

INEXPENSIVE

Café Ciné-Lumière

5163 bd. St-Laurent (north of av. Laurier). ☎ **514/495-1796.** Main courses $7–$10; table d'hôte $6–$13 at lunch, $7–$14 at dinner. AE, MC, V. Sun–Wed 10am–11pm, Thurs 10am–midnight, Fri 10am–1am, Sat 10am–2am. Métro: Laurier. FRENCH.

Classic film enthusiasts delight in this dowdy little room of uncertain origin, for standards from the golden age of film are shown every night from 7pm until closing. Conversation is optional, since headsets are provided free of charge for each customer. The soundtrack is in the original language, usually French, but often English. Considering the low prices, the quality of the largely bistro-style food is quite good, if uneven. As in so many Montréal restaurants, mussels are featured in several versions here, all accompanied by frites. Among the items that aren't seen on every other menu in town are the boned chicken legs stuffed with ground bison and wild boar, sliced and served with a creamy peppercorn sauce. Daily specials are listed on a chalkboard. What passes for decor (hardly critical in a place where the central attraction is flickering images on a wall) is composed primarily of still photos of James Dean, Elizabeth Taylor, and their compatriots.

✪ Chez Schwartz Charcuterie Hébraïque de Montréal

3895 bd. St-Laurent (north of rue Prince-Arthur). ☎ **514/842-4813.** Most items $4–$12. No credit cards. Sun–Thurs 9am–1am, Fri 9am–2am, Sat 9am–3am. Métro: St-Laurent. DELI.

A woman in the line of people waiting for a seat inside is heard to claim that she never wants to eat anything that used to be alive. Is *she* in the wrong place! This, after all, is what used to be called Schwartz's Montréal Hebrew Delicatessen before the imposition of French-first language laws. To many ardent fans, including this writer, this is the only place on the continent to indulge in the guilty treat of smoked meat. It's a long, narrow space with a lunch counter and a collection of simple tables and chairs crammed together almost hip to hip. Any empty seat is up for grabs. Few mind the inconvenience or proximity to strangers, for they're soon delivered plates described either as small (meaning large) or large (humongous) heaped with slices of the trademark delicacy, along with piles of rye bread. Most people also order sides of french fries and one or two mammoth garlicky pickles. There are a handful of alternative edibles—broiled rib steak or beef liver—but go not for tofu and leafy green vegetables. Schwartz's has no liquor license.

Ⓢ Galaxie Diner

4801 rue St-Denis (at rue Gilford). ☎ **514/499-9711.** Most items $3.50–$7.50. MC, V. Sun–Wed 7am–midnight, Thurs–Sat 7am–1am. Métro: Mont-Royal; turn left at the Métro, right at St-Denis, and walk four blocks. LIGHT FARE.

This started out in 1952 as Uncle Will's Diner on Route 23 near Newark, N.J. The French Canadian owner found it on a scrap heap near Boston, rebuilt it, moved it here, and added a terrace. Neon proclaims its presence. On the jukebox are Dion and the Belmonts, the Big Bopper, Aretha, and the Mamas and Papas, and found on the big menu are Rice Krispies, hamburgers, hot dogs, root beer, and cherry Cokes. But you can also get such Québécois faves as oeufs au choix, poutine, and sugar pie and the waitresses are an improvement on their gum-snapping Stateside compatriots.

Ⓢ Pizzédélic

3509 bd. St-Laurent (near rue Sherbrooke). ☎ **514/282-6784.** Most items $3.50–$6.25. MC, V. Tues 11:30am–2am, Wed–Thurs and Sun 11:30am–1am, Fri–Sat 11:30am–3am. Métro: St-Laurent. PIZZA.

Pizza here sweeps from as traditional as to as imaginative as anyone might imagine, with toppings from feta cheese to escargots to artichokes to pesto. All arrive on thin, not-quite-crispy crusts.

Another conveniently located Pizzédélic is downtown at 1329 rue Ste-Catherine (☎ **514/526-6011**).

Santropole

3990 rue St-Urbain (at rue Duluth). ☎ **514/842-3110**. Most items $3–$8. No credit cards. Mon–Thurs 11:30am– midnight, Fri 11:30am–2am, Sat noon–2am, Sun noon–midnight. Closed Mon Oct–Apr. Métro: Mont-Royal; then walk through Jeanne Mance Park. LIGHT FARE.

Santropole has 20-year reputation for abundant salads and hefty sandwiches. Even the allegedly "small" salads are large, so order accordingly. The menu, in French and English, features 24 sandwiches, hot vegetarian pies, 18 different kinds of milkshakes (almond, mint, maple, and peach-apricot are among the choices), and a variety of herbal teas. Occupying a three-story red-brick house, there are several dining nooks, along with a flower-filled courtyard in summer. One percent of the bill is sent to organizations that ease hunger in Québec and Third World countries. Take-out is available.

Wilensky's

5567 rue Clark (at rue Fairmount). ☎ **514/271-0247**. Most items $1.50–$2.35. No credit cards. Mon–Fri 9am–4pm. Métro: Laurier; then walk about 12 blocks. Bus: 55 to St-Laurent and Fairmount; then walk a block. LIGHT FARE.

Wilensky's has been a Montréal tradition since 1932, known for its grilled-meat sandwiches, low prices, curt service, and utter lack of decor. Expect to find nine stools at a counter, some boxes, heavily worn surfaces. Some scenes from the film *The Apprenticeship of Duddy Kravitz* were shot here, for this is Mordecai Richler territory, and the ambience is Early Immigrant. The food selections are limited to a few sandwiches—not much more than bologna, salami, and mustard thrown on a bun and squashed on a grill—and hot dog sandwiches, also squashed. They're washed down with root beer or a drink jerked from their rank of syrups, like the old-time soda fountain it is. Cherry-pineapple is a possibility. I'm talking tradition, not cuisine. Pay when served.

6 Early-Morning & Late-Night Bites

BREAKFAST/BRUNCH

Le Café Cherrier

3635 rue St-Denis (at rue Cherrier). ☎ **514/843-4308**. Main courses $5.50–$12.50; brunch $5–$11. AE, MC, V. Mon–Fri 8am–11pm, Sat–Sun 9am–11pm (to 3am in summer); brunch Sat–Sun 8:30am–3pm. Métro: Sherbrooke. FRENCH.

Breakfast or brunch consists of fresh-squeezed juice with eggs any style, including Benedict. None of of the standard breakfast fare sets new standards, admittedly, but they also offer cheeses, pastas, sandwiches, and fish and beef dishes. The portions are ample. An easygoing atmosphere prevails, and it's said to be popular with local journalists.

PATISSERIES

The word means "pastry shops," and Montréal has some delightful ones. Most of them also serve light items—quiches, salads, sandwiches—

but many patrons settle for a sweet or a croissant and coffee. These are great spots for breakfast or a break while sightseeing.

La Brioche Lyonnaise

1593 rue St-Denis (near bd. de Maisonneuve). ☎ **514/842-7017.** Most items $3–$8. MC. Mon–Sat 8:30am–midnight, Sun 10am–midnight. Métro: Berri-UQAM. LIGHT FARE/PASTRIES.

After a Latin Quarter dinner, a show at the St-Denis Theatre across the street, or just for a break in sightseeing, this is a welcome stop. Check out what's available in the display case—from chocolate-filled triangles to Marie Claires to mega-meringues—then find a table in one of the several seating areas. Eventually, someone comes to take orders. As in most pâtisseries, there's no pressure to move on.

Kilo

5206 bd. St-Laurent (between rue Maguire and rue Fairmount). ☎ **514/277-5039.** Most items $2.25–$6.25. MC, V. Mon 5pm–midnight, Tues–Thurs 10:30am–midnight, Fri 10:30am–3am, Sat 1pm–3am, Sun 1pm–midnight. Métro: Laurier. LIGHT FARE/DESSERTS.

When dining in the area, skip the last course and make a beeline to Kilo. The mousses and pies sold here are arrayed as enticingly as jewels in a display case. Desserts, in fact, are the order of the day—or night—at Kilo. Light lunches are served, and some refreshing juices, but it's the desserts, sweet and creamy or tartly piquant, that draw the crowds. Strong coffee laced with cognac, amaretto, or Grand Marnier is often chosen to complement. Kilo, metric for 2.2 pounds, may be closer to a promise than a tease, a challenge to the most determined dieters.

LATE-NIGHT/24-HOUR EATERIES

The Bagel Factory

74 rue Fairmount ouest. ☎ **514/272-0667.** Most items $3–$9. No credit cards. Daily 24 hours. Métro: Laurier. BAGELS.

Québec bagels are a must-try treat when in Montréal. Natives insist that they're superior to the more famous New York version, and they have a case. Thinner and lighter, these bagels have an agreeably chewy texture that doesn't remind eaters of teething rings. This tiny place is as good a place as any to sample them. It offers a good variety, including an extra-large one called Bozo, available for take-out only. Potato latkes, cheese blintzes, and bagel spreads are also sold.

Bens Delicatessen

990 bd. de Maisonneuve (at rue Metcalfe). ☎ **514/844-1000.** Most items under $12. MC, V. Sun–Thurs 7am–4am, Fri–Sat 7am–5am. Métro: Peel. DELI.

This deli-restaurant was founded by Ben and Fanny Kravitz in 1908 and is still in the family. Subsequent owners persist in the claim that this is where Montréal's famous smoked meat originated. Besides the inevitable variations on that much-loved ingredient, the menu meanders through cheese blintzes, potato latkes, chicken potpie, corned beef and cabbage, and much more. They are licensed to sell wine, beer, and liquor.

Its major competitor, **Dunn's,** open 24 hours, is nearby at 892 rue Ste-Catherine ouest.

Lux

5220 bd. St-Laurent. ☎ **514/271-9277.** Most items $3.25–$8.95. AE, MC, V. Daily 24 hours. Métro: Laurier. LIGHT FARE.

Buy jawbreakers, pick up a copy of *Vanity Fair* or the *New York Times,* shop for T-shirts, and have a Bloody Mary or a hot dog in the same space—all at three in the morning. The place is a combination café, shop, newsstand, and bar—in effect, a 24-hour mall for Montréal night owls. The interior of the converted textile mill looks like a cross between a Left Bank club and an industrial loft, with a circular main room and two stainless-steel staircases spiraling up to a glass-domed second floor. The centerpiece is the café, surrounded by racks holding more than 1,000 magazines. Popular items in the café-bar are the homemade desserts, particularly the cheesecake with fresh raspberry sauce; the eggs Benelux, served 24 hours a day; and local beers, including Maudite and Blanche de Chambly.

7 Picnic Fare & Where to Eat It

When planning a picnic or a meal back in your hotel room, consider a stop at **La Vieille Europe,** at 3855 bd. St-Laurent, near St-Cuthbert (☎ 514/842-5773), a storehouse of culinary sights and smells. Choose from wheels of pungent cheeses, garlands of sausages, pâtés, cashews, honey, fresh peanut butter, or dried fruits. Coffee beans are roasted in the back, adding to the admixture of maddening aromas. A large grocery store, **Warshaw,** is next door, should more supplies be required. A stroll to the north along St-Laurent reveals other possibilities for mobile edibles. From there, it isn't far by taxi to Parc du Mont-Royal, a wonderful place to enjoy the bounty of a shopping excursion.

In Old Montréal, pick up supplies at the **dépanneur** (convenience store) at 8 rue St-Paul, at rue St-Jean-Baptiste, which keeps late hours, and then take them to place Jacques-Cartier or the Vieux-Port, both only steps away. Dépanneurs also sell wine, but there's a bigger selection at the **Maison des Vins,** 505 av. du Président-Kennedy, at Aylmer, near the Delta hotel, and a shop selling cheeses and crackers is conveniently located right across the hall or at **Faubourg Ste-Catherine,** on rue Ste-Catherine ouest between Guy and St-Mathieu, which also sells fresh fruits and vegetables.

6

What to See & Do in Montréal

A superb métro system, a fairly logical street grid, wide boulevards, and the vehicle-free Underground City all aid in the swift, uncomplicated movement of people from one place to another in Montréal. The difficulty for tourists, as in every great city, lies in making choices that fit their interests and the time available. After all, the possibilities include hiking up imposing Mont-Royal in the middle of the city, biking along the redeveloped waterfront or beside the Lachine Canal, visiting museums or historic homes, or attending a hockey or baseball game. And with riverboat rides, the fascinating new Biodôme, a sprawling amusement park, and the unique Cirque du Soleil, few cities assure kids of as good a time as this one.

A number of the following attractions opened or expanded in 1992. That's no coincidence. They were planned to coincide with that year's celebration of Montréal's 350th birthday. Efforts to enhance cultural opportunities have continued since then, as with the new (it opened in 1995) Biosphère on Ile Sainte-Hélène. To help boost public awareness of Montréal's museum collections, a Montréal Museums Day has been inaugurated. Usually scheduled for the last Sunday in May, on this day 21 museums are open to all for free, and shuttle buses carry visitors to most of them, also free of charge. Of greater utility is the **Montréal Museums Pass,** available year round. It allows entry to 17 of the city's museums and costs $12 per adult for one day, or $25 for three days. For families, the price is $24 for one day, $50 for three days. For information, call 514/861-9609.

1 Suggested Itineraries

If You Have 1 Day

Explore the oldest part of town, called Vieux-Montréal (Old Montréal), with many restored buildings dating from the 1700s. Don't miss the unusual interior of the stunning Notre-Dame Basilica. The Pointe-à-Callière, Montréal's Museum of Archeology and History, opened in 1992 and provides a clever and engaging orientation to the city, holding kids and adults alike enthralled.

Then, for contrast, stroll through the downtown sections of the modern city, including its tiny but vibrant Chinatown, and visit the new pavilion of the Museum of Fine Arts, which has a big bookstore and gift shop. Enjoy a table d'hôte lunch or dinner in one of the city's fine downtown restaurants.

If You Have 2 Days

Spend your first day as outlined above.

On the second day, take the Métro to the architecturally daring Olympic Complex with its inclined tower and observation deck. Across the street is the Botanical Garden, its carefully cultivated acres providing hours of peaceful meditation. While there, see the new Chinese Garden and take the informative open-air train tour. In summer, make a day of it on Ile Ste-Hélène by visiting the Old Fort, with its museum and changing-of-the-guard ceremony, and the new Biosphère. Afterward, go to La Ronde Amusement Park, where fireworks displays are mounted many evenings. Or head that night to Vieux-Montréal and take in a performance at the English-language Centaur Theatre, listen to jazz or folk in one of the clubs along rue St-Paul, or (in the spring) thrill to the magic of the acclaimed Cirque du Soleil.

If You Have 3 Days

Spend your first two days as suggested above.

In the morning of Day 3, take an exhilarating jet-boat ride through the Lachine Rapids, or a calmer harbor cruise aboard the sleek Bâteau-Mouche. Get to know the Montréal of the Montréalers by wandering along boulevard St-Laurent, the axis of the city's ethnic neighborhoods, to rue Prince-Arthur and rue Duluth, then through carré St-Louis (St. Louis Square) to the Latin Quarter, the center of activity for the Francophone population. In the evening, listen to music or dine in one of the fine restaurants in the quarter.

If You Have 5 Days or More

Spend Days 1 to 3 as recommended above.

On the fourth day, fit and athletic visitors might choose to climb up Mont-Royal from rue Peel and admire the view of the city and river from the lookout, then stroll or take a picnic in the surrounding park. (If the prospect of that hike is daunting, take the Métro to the Guy station, then bus no. 165.) In the afternoon take in a specialized museum, such as the Canadian Centre for Architecture or the McCord Museum of Canadian History.

On Day 5, visit St. Joseph's Oratory, one of the city's prominent shrines, which gives a glimpse of the spiritual life of devout Montréalers. If the weather's good, rent a bike and follow the Lachine Canal for 7 miles (11km) to Lake St-Louis. If the weather turns dicey, descend to the climate-controlled world of Montréal's Underground City, a labyrinth of passages, subway tunnels, shops, and cinemas, that can be enjoyed without once stepping outdoors.

2 The Top Attractions
DOWNTOWN

Musée Juste Pour Rire (Just for Laughs Museum)

2111 bd. St-Laurent (north of rue Sherbrooke). ☎ **514/845-2322.** Admission $10 adults; $5 seniors, students, and children 5–12; free for children 4 and under; $20 family ticket. Tues–Sun 1–10pm (last visit 8pm). Closed two months in winter when the new exhibition is being installed. Métro: St-Laurent. Bus: 55.

This engagingly off-center museum opened in Montréal on April Fool's Day 1993. Gilbert Rozon, who created the "Just for Laughs" comedy festival, was responsible. It may seem a quixotic endeavor, given the differences in tastes between the French and English (witness Jerry Lewis). But it must be remembered that Francophone Quebecers share a North American culture and sensibility, and therefore a similar sense of humor. Mammoth shows with lavish exhibits are mounted for six to eight months at a time. They have included clips of world-famous clowns, cartoons, TV sitcoms, and comic shorts. Puns, one-liners, and double entendres abound, not a few of them risqué, others as black as humor gets. Preteens are likely to be simply baffled. Videos and historic film clips hold museumgoers, many of them students, enthralled for hours. The museum closes for two months while another multi-faceted exhibition filling three floors is put together, so call ahead to make sure it's open. It also houses a 250-seat cabaret-theater, a humor hall of fame, a shop, and a café.

Musée McCord (McCord Museum of Canadian History)

690 rue Sherbrooke ouest (at Victoria). ☎ **514/398-7100.** Admission $5 adults, $3 seniors, $2 students, free for children 11 and under; $8 family ticket. Tues–Sun 10am–5pm. Métro: McGill.

This museum, associated with McGill University, showcases the eclectic—and not infrequently eccentric—collections of scores of 19th- and 20th-century benefactors. The museum was founded by David Ross McCord (1844–1930), a lawyer whose family immigrated to Québec from Northern Ireland in 1760. Objects from its holdings of 80,000 artifacts are rotated in and out of storage, so it isn't possible to be specific about what will be on exhibit at any given time. In general, expect to view furniture, costumes, china, silver, paintings, photographs, and folk art that reveal rural and urban life as it was lived by English-speaking European immigrants of the past three centuries. A new atrium connects the original 1905 building and a wing added during extensive renovations in 1992. Beyond it are galleries given over to temporary exhibits. The First Nations room displays portions of the museum's extensive collection of ethnology and archeology, including clothing, jewelry, and meticulous beadwork. The exhibits are intelligently mounted, with texts in English and French, although the upstairs rooms are of narrower interest. A permanent gallery is devoted to the Notman Photographic Archives, a collection of 700,000 photographs chronicling life in Canada, and Montréal in particular, in

Montréal Downtown Attractions

Parc du Mont-Royal ③

av. Cedar
av. Cedar
St-Sulpice
av. des Pins
av. des Pins
av. Docteur-Penfield
Ch. de la Côte-des-Neiges
rue Simpson
rue Redpath
rue du Musée
rue de la Montagne
rue Drummond
rue Stanley
rue Peel
rue McTavish
rue Sherbrooke ②
rue Lincoln
av. Atwater
Chomedey
rue du Fort
St-Marc
St-Mathieu
rue Mackay
rue Crescent
rue Bishop
rue Guy
bd. de Maisonneuve
rue Ste-Catherine
rue Drummond
rue Stanley
rue Peel
rue Mansfield
rue Metcalfe
⑤
bd. René-Lévesque
①
autoroute Ville-Marie
rue St-Antoine
rue Argyle
rue Crescent
rue de la Montagne
⑦
Bel
rue de la Gauc
rue St-Antoine
rue Vinet
rue Georges-Vanier
rue des Seigneurs
rue St-Jacques
rue St-Jacques
⑧
rue Notre-Dame
rue Notre-Dame
de la Montagne
rue Guy

1830

Centre Canadien
   d'Architecture ①
Cathédral Christ Church ⑥
Planétarium de Montréal ⑧
Musée Juste Pour Rire ⑩

Cathédrale-Basilique
   Marie-Reine-du-Monde ⑦
Musée McCord
   d'Histoire Canadienne ⑤
Musée d'Art Contemporain
   de Montréal ⑨

the 19th and early 20th centuries. A library is on the third floor, and the museum has a gift shop and tearoom.

✪ Musée des Beaux-Arts (Museum of Fine Arts)

1379–1380 rue Sherbrooke ouest (at rue Crescent). ☎ **514/285-1600** or 514/ 285-2000. Admission permanent collection only, $4.75 adults, $3 students and children 12 and over, $1 seniors 65 and older and children 3–12; $9.50 family ticket. Special temporary exhibitions plus the permanent collection, $9.50 adults,

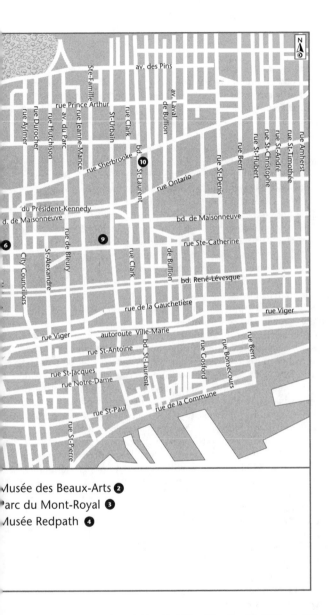

Musée des Beaux-Arts ❷

Parc du Mont-Royal ❸

Musée Redpath ❹

$4.75 students and seniors 65 and older, $2 children 12 and under; $19 family ticket.
Wed 5:30–9pm 50% or more off regular admission. Tues and Thurs–Sun 11am–6pm,
Wed 11am–9pm. Métro: Peel or Guy-Concordia.

Montréal's most prominent museum was opened in 1912, in Canada's
first building designed specifically for the arts. The original neoclassical pavilion is on the north side of rue Sherbrooke. Years ago it was
recognized that the collection had outstripped the building, forcing

curators to make painful decisions about what few items could be placed on view at any one time. The result was exhibits that often seemed sketchy, incomplete. That problem was solved with the completion of a stunning new annex, the Jean-Noël Desmarais Pavilion, directly across the street. Opened in late 1991, it was designed by Montréal architect Moshe Safdie, who first gained international notice with his Habitat housing complex at the 1967 Expo. Five stories high, it's sheathed in white marble, with an entrance that is 40 feet high opening into an atrium that shoots all the way to the roof. The adjacent 1905 apartment building kept its facade, but was stripped to the walls to accommodate offices and the large museum store. Along with two below-street-level floors and the underground galleries that connect the new building with the old, exhibition space was tripled. The result is not unlike what a thoughtful couple with taste would end up with if they emptied every closet in an old house, took a hard look at what should occupy the bare walls, and disposed of all the rest.

For the best look at the results, enter the new annex, take the elevator to the top, and work your way down. It's largely devoted to international contemporary art and Canadian art after 1960, and to European paintings, sculpture, and decorative arts from the Middle Ages to the 19th century. On the upper floors, for example, are many of the gems of the collection—paintings by El Greco, Reynolds, Renoir, Monet, Picasso, and Cézanne, and sculptures by Rodin and Lipshitz, among others. On the subterranean levels are works by 20th-century modernists, including abstract expressionists of the post–World War II New York School. But the museum casts a wider net, as with the 18th- and 19th-century English crystal and porcelains and Italian ceramics just steps away from furniture designs by Charles Eames. In 1995 a great deal of space and public-relations dollars were devoted to a six-month exhibition of a century of automobile design.

From the lowest level of the new pavilion, follow the under-street corridor past primitive artworks from Oceania and Africa, then up the elevator into the old building, with its displays of pre-Columbian ceramics, Inuit carvings, and Amerindian crafts. The rest of that building is used primarily for temporary exhibits. Across the street, the street-level store has an impressive selection of books, games, and folk art, and there's a café. If you have time for only a short visit, make it to the fourth floor. For an extra bonus, be sure to walk to the sculpture court on that level for a splendid panoramic view of the city.

Parc du Mont-Royal

☎ **514/844-4928** for general information or 514/872-6559 for special events. Admission free. Daily 6am–midnight. Métro: Mont-Royal. Bus: 11; hop off at Lac des Castors. From downtown, go north on rue Peel to connect with a stairway and a switchback bridle path, called Le Serpent, that leads to the Chalet Lookout and beyond.

Montréal is named for the 761-foot (232m) hill that rises at its heart. Joggers, cyclists, dogwalkers, lovers, and anyone else in search of pleasurable exercise or a little pastoral serenity won't want to miss it. On Sunday, hundreds of folks congregate around the statue of

George-Etienne Cartier to listen and sometimes dance to improvised music, and Lac des Castors (Beaver Lake) is surrounded by sunbathers and picnickers in summer (no swimming is allowed). In wintertime, cross-country skiers follow the miles of paths and snowshoers tramp and crunch along other trails laid out especially for them. In the cold months, the lake fills with whirling ice skaters of various levels of aptitude. The large, refurbished Chalet Lookout near the crest of the hill provides both a sweeping view of the city and an opportunity for a snack. The five mountains seen rising from the St. Lawrence plains, along with Mont-Royal itself, make up the Monteriegiennes chain. Up the hill behind the chalet is the spot where, tradition has it, de Maisonneuve erected his wooden cross in 1642 (in 1535, Jacques Cartier gave the mountain its name, which in ancient French was spelled Mont-Réal—"Royal Mountain"). Today the cross is a 100-foot-high steel structure rigged for illumination at night and visible from all over the city. Park security is provided by mounted police. There are three cemeteries on the northern slope of the mountain—Catholic, Protestant, and Jewish.

VIEUX-MONTRÉAL

✪ Basilique Notre-Dame

116 rue Notre-Dame ouest (at place d'Armes). ☎ **514/842-2925.** Basilica, free; museum, $1 adults, 50¢ students. Basilica, June 25–Labor Day, daily 7am–8pm; Labor Day–June 24, daily 7am–6pm. Tours given mid-May to June 24 and Labor Day to mid-Oct, Mon–Fri 9am–4pm; June 25–Labor Day, Mon–Fri 9am–4:30pm. Museum, Sat–Sun 9:30am–4pm. Métro: Place d'Armes.

Big enough to hold 4,000 worshipers, and breathtaking in the richness of its interior furnishings, this magnificent structure was designed in 1829 by an Irish-American Protestant architect, James O'Donnell. He was said to have been so inspired by his work that he converted to Catholicism after it was done. He had good reason. None of the hundreds of churches on the island of Montréal approaches this interior in its wealth of exquisite detail, most of it carved from rare woods delicately gilded and painted. O'Donnell, one of the proponents the gothic revival style in the middle decades of the 19th century, is one of only a few people honored by burial in the crypt. The main altar was carved from linden wood, the work of Victor Bourgeau. Behind it is the Chapel of the Sacred Heart, much of it destroyed by a deranged arsonist in 1978 but rebuilt and rededicated in 1982. It's such a popular place for weddings that couples have to book it a year and a half in advance. The chapel altar was cast in bronze by Charles Daudelin of Montréal, with 32 panels representing birth, life, and death. Next to the chapel is a small **museum** (☎ 514/842-2925) dealing with the history of the church and of Roman Catholicism in Québec. Of fleeting interest are the near-surrealist paintings of Father Guindon (1864–1923) but the basilica's organ is one of the largest in the world, with five keyboards and 5,772 pipes. Because of its remarkable acoustics, the church is often used for jazz and classical performances, including one celebrated Christmas performance by Luciano Pavarotti. The basilica's oversize bell, nicknamed Le Gros Bourdon, weighs over 12 tons and has a low, resonant rumble that vibrates right up through the feet. It is tolled only on special occasions.

Vieux-Port (Old Port)

333 rue de la Commune ouest (at rue McGill). ☎ **514/496-7678.** Admission port and interpretation center, free; tram rides, $2 adults, $1 children 3–12; charges vary for other attractions. Interpretation Centre, mid-May to early Sept, daily 10am–9pm; hours for specific attractions vary. Métro: Champ-de-Mars, Place d'Armes, or Square-Victoria.

Since 1992 Montréal's once-dreary commercial wharf area has metamorphosed into an appealing 1.2-mile-long (2km), 133-acre promenade and park with public spaces, exhibition halls, family activities, bike paths, a tall ship called the *Pelican* to explore, and a big, browsable flea market. Cyclists, in-line skaters, joggers, strollers, lovers, and sunbathers all make use of the park in good weather or to attend scheduled outdoor events or take a boat ride. To get an idea of all there is to see and do here, hop aboard the small Balade tram that travels throughout the port. During even-numbered years in spring, the acclaimed Cirque du Soleil sets up at the port under its bright yellow-and-blue big top. There's also a large-scale, wraparound IMAX theater. At the far eastern end of the port is a clock tower built in 1922, with 192 steps leading past the exposed clockworks to observation decks at three different levels (admission free). Most cruises, entertainments, and special events take place from mid-May to October. Information booths with bilingual attendants assist visitors during that period. The Old Port stretches along the waterfront from rue McGill to rue Berri. Quadricycles, bicycles, and in-line skates are available for rent.

Place Jacques-Cartier

Between rue Notre-Dame and rue de la Commune. Métro: Place d'Armes.

Across the street from City Hall is the focus of summer activity in Vieux-Montréal and the most enchanting of the old city's squares. Its cobblestone streets slope down toward the port past ancient stone buildings that survive from the 1700s, while its outdoor cafés, street musicians, flower sellers, and horse-drawn carriages recall the Montréal of a century ago. Montréalers insist that they never go to a place so frequented by tourists, which begs the question of why so many of them congregate here. On warm days especially, they take the sun and sip sangría on the bordering terraces, while enjoying the flowing pageant of activities in the square.

✪ Pointe-à-Callière (Montréal Museum of Archeology and History)

350 place Royale. ☎ **514/872-9150.** Admission $7 adults, $5 seniors, $4 students, $2 children 6–12; $14 family ticket. To view temporary exhibits only, 50% off. July–Aug, Tues–Sun 10am–8pm; Sept–June, Tues and Thurs–Sun 10am–5pm, Wed 10am–8pm. Métro: Place d'Armes.

A first visit to Montréal might best begin here. Built on the very site where the original colony was established in 1642 (Pointe-à-Callière), the modern Museum of Archeology and History engages visitors in rare and beguiling ways. Go first to the 16-minute multimedia show in an auditorium that actually stands above exposed ruins of the earlier city that once stood here. Images pop up, drop down, and slide out on rolling screens accompanied by music and a playful bilingual narration that keeps the history slick and utterly painless, with enough quick cuts and changes to keep even the youngest viewers from fidgeting.

Pointe-à-Callière was the point where the St-Pierre River merged with the St. Lawrence. Evidences of the many layers of occupation at this spot—from Amerindians to French trappers to Scottish merchants—were unearthed during archeological digs that persisted here for more than a decade. They are on view in display cases set among ancient building foundations and burial grounds down below street level. The bottom shelves are for items dating to before 1600, and there are other shelves for consecutive centuries. Walks wind through the remains of the ghost city, across a section of the canalized St-Pierre, and up through the basements of the 1838 Custom House. Along the way are interactive games meant to illuminate fragments of the site's dense history and holographic devices that allow "conversations" with an Indian sachem and a French colonial woman.

The complex incorporates the dynamic new building first entered, which echoes the triangular Royal Insurance building (1861) that stood there for many years. Its tower contains L'Arrivage café and provides a fine view of Old Montréal and the Old Port. At the end of the self-guided subterranean tour, in the Custom House, are more exhibits and a well-stocked gift shop. Allow at least an hour for a visit.

ELSEWHERE IN THE CITY

✪ Biodôme de Montréal

4777 av. Pierre-de-Coubertin (next to the Olympic Stadium). ☎ **514/868-3000.** Admission $8.50 adults, $6 seniors and students, $4.25 children 6–17. Daily 9am–6pm (to 8pm in summer). Métro: Viau.

Near Montréal's Botanical Garden and next to the Olympic Stadium is the engrossing Biodôme, possibly the only environmental museum of its kind. Originally built as the velodrome for the 1976 Olympics, it has been refitted to house replications of four distinct ecosystems, complete with appropriate temperatures, flora, fauna, and changing seasons. Visitors stroll at leisure through a steamy Amazonian rain forest with fish swimming in its pools and monkeys and parrots in the leafy canopy. A corridor lined with tanks of tropical fish leads into a refreshing Laurentian forest, with stands of live birch and maple rising above streams with playful otters, ducks, and trout. The next encapsulated microworld is devoted to the marine life of the St. Lawrence River, with tidal pools and marshlands, and last is the chilly Antarctic, with squads of waddling puffins and penguins besporting themselves. With 4,000 creatures and 5,000 trees and plants, the Biodôme incorporates exhibits gathered from the old aquarium and the modest zoos at the Angrignon and LaFontaine parks. It also has a games room for kids called Naturalia, a shop, and a café.

✪ Jardin Botanique (Botanical Garden)

4101 rue Sherbrooke est (opposite Olympic Stadium). ☎ **514/872-1400.** Admission outside gardens, greenhouses, and insectarium, May–Nov $7 adults, $5 seniors over 65 and students, $3.50 children 6–17; Dec–Apr $5 adults, $3.50 seniors and students, $2.50 children. Botanical Garden, Insectarium, and Biodôme (good for two consecutive days), $12.50 adults, $9.50 seniors, $6.25 children. Daily 9am–6pm (to 8pm in summer). Métro: Pié-IX; then walk up the hill to the gardens, or from mid-May to mid-Sept take the shuttle bus from Olympic Park.

Across the street from the Olympic sports complex, the Botanical Garden spreads across 180 acres. Begun in 1931, it has grown to include 26,000 different types of plants in 31 specialized gardens, ensuring something beautiful and fragrant for visitors year round. Ten large conservatory greenhouses shelter tropical and desert plants and bonsai from the Canadian winter. One greenhouse, called the Wizard of Oz, is especially fun for kids. Roses bloom here from mid-June to the first frost, May is the month for lilacs, and June for the flowering hawthorn trees.

Inaugurated in summer 1991, the 6-acre Chinese Garden, a joint project of Montréal and Shanghai, is the largest of its kind ever built outside Asia, with pavilions, inner courtyards, ponds, and myriad plants indigenous to China. The serene Japanese Garden fills 15 acres and contains a cultural pavilion with an art gallery, a tearoom where the ancient tea ceremony is observed, and a Zen garden. The striking green stone that dominates its manicured landscape, peridotite, comes from Quebec's Estrie region.

The grounds are also home to the relatively new Insectarium, which displays some of the world's most beautiful insects, not to mention some of its more sinister ones (see "Especially for Kids," later in this chapter). Birders should bring along binoculars on summer visits to spot some of the more than 130 species of birds that spend at least part of the year in the Botanical Garden. In summer, an outdoor aviary is filled with Québec's most beautiful butterflies.

Year round, a free shuttle bus links the Botanical Garden and nearby Olympic Park; a small train runs regularly through the gardens and is worth the small fee charged to ride it.

Stade Olympique (Olympic Stadium)

4141 av. Pierre-de-Coubertin (at bd. Pié-IX). ☎ **514/252-8687.** Round-trip cable-car ride, $7 adults, $5 students and children. Guided tours, recorded train tours, and a multimedia presentation available; public swim periods scheduled daily, with low admission charges. Cable car, mid-June to early Sept, Mon noon–9pm, Tues–Thurs 10am–9pm, Fri–Sat 10am–11pm; early Sept to mid-Jan and mid-Feb to mid-June, Tues–Sun noon–6pm. Closed mid-Jan to mid-Feb. Métro: Pié-IX or Viau (choose the Viau station for the guided tour).

Centerpiece of the 1976 Olympic Games, Montréal's controversial stadium and its associated facilities provide considerable opportunities for both active and passive diversion. It incorporates a natatorium with six different pools, including one of competition dimensions with an adjustable bottom and a 50-foot-deep version for scuba-diving. The stadium seats 60,000 to 80,000 spectators, who come here to see the Expos, rock concerts, and trade shows. It has a 65-ton retractable Kevlar roof winched into place by 125 tons of steel cables, which are attached to a 626-foot inclined tower that looms over the arena like a egret looking for a fish in a bowl. When everything functions as intended, it takes about 45 minutes to raise or lower the roof. In reality, the roof malfunctions frequently and high winds have torn large rips in the fabric. That's only one reason that what was first known as "The Big O" was scorned as "The Big Owe" after cost overruns led to heavy increases in taxes. The tower, which leans at a 45° angle, also does duty as an observation deck, with a funicular that whisks 90 passengers to the top in 95 seconds. On a clear day, the deck bestows a 35-mile view over Montréal and into the neighboring Laurentians. A free shuttle bus links the Olympic Park and the Botanical Garden.

3 More Attractions

DOWNTOWN

Cathédral Christ Church
1444 Union Ave. (at rue Ste-Catherine and rue Université). ☎ **514/843-6577.** Admission free; donations accepted. Daily 8am–6pm; services Sun at 8am, 10am, and 4pm. Métro: McGill.

This Anglican cathedral stands in glorious gothic contrast to the city's glassy downtown skyscrapers, reflected in the postmodernist Maison des Coopérants office tower. Sometimes called the "floating cathedral" because of the many tiers of malls and corridors of the Underground City beneath it, the building was erected in 1859. The original steeple, too heavy for the structure, was replaced by a lighter aluminum version in 1940. The cathedral hosts concerts throughout the year, notably from June to August on Wednesday at 12:30pm.

Cathédrale-Basilique Marie-Reine-du-Monde (Mary Queen of the World Cathedral)
Bd. René-Lévesque (at rue Mansfield). ☎ **514/866-1661.** Admission free; donations accepted. Summer daily 7am–7:30pm; fall–spring Sat 8am–8:30pm, Sun 9:30am–7:30pm. Métro: Bonaventure.

No one who has seen both will confuse this with St. Peter's Basilica in Rome, but a scaled-down homage was the intention of its guiding force, Bishop Ignace Bourget, in the middle of the last century. He was moved to act after the first Catholic cathedral burned to the ground in 1852. Construction lasted from 1875 to 1894, delayed by his desire to place it not in Francophone east Montréal but in the heart of the Protestant Anglophone west. The resulting structure covers less than a quarter of the area of its Roman inspiration, and there are no curving arcades to embrace a sweeping plaza in front. The stairs to the entrance are only a few yards away from the boulevard. Most impressive is the 252-foot-high dome, about half the height of the original. A local touch is provided by the statues standing on the roofline, representing local patron saints. The interior is less rewarding visually than the outside. A planned restoration is expected to cost at least $7.5 million.

Musée d'Art Contemporain de Montréal (Museum of Contemporary Art)
185 rue Ste-Catherine ouest. ☎ **514/847-6212.** Admission $6 adults, $4 seniors, $3 students, free for children 11 and under; $12 family ticket; free to all Wed 6–9pm. Tues and Thurs–Sun 11am–6pm, Wed 11am–9pm. Métro: Place-des-Arts.

The only museum in Canada devoted exclusively to contemporary art moved into this new facility at place des Arts in 1992 after years in an isolated riverfront building. "Contemporary" is defined here as art produced since 1939, showcasing the work of Québec and other Canadian artists, but supplemented by a collection of 3,400 works by such notables as Jean Dubuffet, Max Ernst, Jean Arp, Ansel Adams, Larry Poons, Antoni Tàpies, Max Ernst, Robert Mapplethorpe, and Montréal photographer Michel Campeau. A few larger pieces are seen on the ground floor, but most are one flight up, with space for temporary exhibitions to the right and selections from the permanent collection on the left.

As is to be expected, many of the most recent works will be seen as baffling, enigmatic, or simply fraudulent, for the Canadian artists shown are no less provocative or venturesome than their counterparts in New York, London, or Paris. In these unsettled times for the visual arts, no single style prevails, so expect to see minimalist installations small and large, video displays, evocations of pop, op, and abstract expression, and accumulations of objects simply piled on the floor. That the works often arouse strong opinions signifies a museum that's doing something right. A shop and restaurant are on the premises. When you're standing in front of the place des Arts complex, the museum is to the left.

Redpath Musée

859 rue Sherbrooke ouest (at rue McGill). ☎ **514/398-4086.** Admission free. July–Aug Mon–Thurs 9am–5pm, Sun 1–5pm (closed holiday weekends); Sept–June, Mon–Fri 9am–5pm. Métro: McGill.

The Redpath Museum is part of McGill University, in a building dating from 1882. The main draw here is the Egyptian antiquities, the second-largest collection in Canada, but also on view are fossils and geological fragments. If the unusual name seems glancingly familiar, think of the wrappings on sugar cubes in many restaurants. John Redpath was a 19th-century industrialist who built Canada's first sugar refinery and later distributed much of his fortune in philanthropy.

VIEUX-MONTRÉAL

Château Ramezay

280 rue Notre-Dame (east of place Jacques-Cartier). ☎ **514/861-3708.** Admission $5 adults, $3 seniors and students, free for children 5 and under; $10 family ticket. May–Sept, daily 10am–6pm; Oct–Apr, Tues–Sun 10am–4:30pm. Métro: Champ-de-Mars.

Built by Gov. Claude de Ramezay in 1705, the château was the home of the city's royal French governors for four decades, before being taken over and used for the same purpose by the British conquerors. In 1775 an army of American revolutionaries invaded and held Montréal, using the château as their headquarters. Benjamin Franklin, sent to persuade Quebecers to rise with the colonists against British rule, stayed in the château and no doubt enjoyed his visit even though he failed to persuade the city's people to join his cause. After the short American interlude, the house was used as a courthouse, government office building, teachers' college, and headquarters for Laval University before being converted into a museum in 1895. Old coins, furnishings, tools, and other memorabilia related to the economic and social activities of the 18th century and first half of the 19th century fill the main floor. In the cellar are seen the original vaults of the house. Across rue Notre-Dame is the City Hall.

Hôtel de Ville (City Hall)

275 rue Notre-Dame (at rue Gosford). ☎ **514/872-3355.** Admission free. Daily 8:30am–4:30pm; 15-minute guided tours given Mon–Fri May–Oct. Métro: Champ-de-Mars.

This is a relatively recent building by Old Montréal standards, finished in 1878. The French Second Empire design makes it look as though it had been imported from Paris, stone by stone. Balconies, turrets, and mansard roofs detail the exterior, seen to particular advantage when illuminated at night. It was from the balcony above the awning that Charles de Gaulle proclaimed, "Vive le Québec Libre!" in 1967. Presumably he did not reflect that there were several active separatist movements in his own country at the time, nor consider how he might've felt if a Canadian prime minister arrived in France and shouted "Long live Free Breton!" from the banks of the Seine.

Inside, the bust to the left is of Jacques Viger, Montréal's first mayor, while the one to the right is of Peter McGill, the city's first Anglophone mayor. The Hall of Honour is made of green marble from Campagna, Italy, with art deco lamps from Paris and a bronze-and-glass chandelier, also from France, that weighs a metric ton. In the display cabinet to the left by the elevator are gifts from mayors of other cities from around the world. Council Chamber meetings, on the first floor, are open to the public. The chamber has a hand-carved ceiling and five stained-glass windows representing religion, the port, industry and commerce, finance, and transportation. The mayor's office is on the fourth floor.

Eglise Notre-Dame-de-Bonsecours (Notre Dame de Bon Secours Chapel)

400 rue St-Paul (at the foot of rue Bonsecours). ☎ **514/845-9991.** Chapel, free; museum, $2 adults, 50¢ children. May–Oct, chapel, daily 9am–5pm; museum, Tues–Sun 9am–4:30pm. Nov–Apr, chapel, daily 10am–3pm; museum, Tues–Sun 10:30am–2:30pm. Métro: Champ-de-Mars.

Just to the east of Marché Bonsecours is the Sailors' Church, so called because of the wooden ship models hanging inside, given as votive offerings by sailors. The first church building, the project of an energetic teacher named Marguerite Bourgeoys, was built in 1678. She arrived with de Maisonneuve to undertake the education of the children of Montréal in the latter half of the 17th century. Later on, she and several sister teachers founded a nuns' order called the Congregation of Notre-Dame, Canada's first. The present church, which dates from 1771–73, has a small museum downstairs with 58 stage sets dedicated to her life and work. A carving of the Madonna has been displayed in both churches (because of a theft, the carving now on view is a replica—the original is locked up). The pioneering Bourgeoys was recognized as a saint in 1982. There's an excellent view of the harbor and the old quarter from the church's tower.

Marché Bonsecours (Bonsecours Market)

350 rue St-Paul (at the foot of rue St-Claude). ☎ **514/872-4560.** Métro: Champ-de-Mars.

This imposing neoclassic building with a long facade and a colonnaded portico and a handsome silvery dome was built in the mid-1800s and first used as Montréal's City Hall, then for many years after 1878 as the central market. Restored in 1964, it housed city government offices, and in 1992 became the information and exhibition center for the celebration of the city's 350th birthday. It continues to be used as an exhibition space. The architecture alone makes a visit worthwhile.

Lieu Historique Sir George-Etienne Cartier

458 rue Notre-Dame (at rue Berri). ☎ **514/283-2282.** Admission free (this may change, however). May to early Sept, daily 10am–6pm; Feb–Apr and mid-Sept to Dec, Wed–Sun 10am–noon and 1–5pm. Closed Jan. Métro: Champ-de-Mars.

Operated by Parks Canada, this national historic site is actually two houses. One has been reconstructed to its appearance in the 1860s as the Victorian residence of Sir George-Etienne Cartier (1814–73), one of the fathers of Canada's 1867 Confederation. The adjacent house is devoted to Cartier's career and work. During the summer, the site has costumed guides and hosts concerts and other activities.

PLATEAU MONT-ROYAL

Musée des Hospitalières de l'Hôtel-Dieu

201 av. des Pins ouest. ☎ **514/849-2919.** Admission $5 adults, $3 seniors and students 12 and over, free for children 11 and under. Mid-June to mid-Oct, Tues–Fri 10am–5pm, Sat–Sun 1–5pm; mid-Oct to mid-June Wed–Sun 1–5pm. Métro: Sherbrooke. Bus: 144.

Opened in 1992 to coincide with the city's 350th birthday, this unusual museum, in the former chaplain's residence of Hôtel-Dieu Hospital, traces the history of Montréal from 1659 to the present, focusing on the evolution of health care during the three centuries of the history of the hospital, including an exhibit of medical instruments. It bows to the missionary nurse Jeanne Mance, the founder of the first hospital in Montréal, who arrived in 1642, the only woman among the first settlers who left France with Sieur de Maisonneuve. The museum's three floors are filled with memorabilia, including paintings, books, reliquaries, furnishings, and a reconstruction of a nun's cell. Its architectural highpoint is a marvelous "floating" oak staircase brought to the New World in 1634 from the Maison-Dieu hospital in La Flèche, France. The original Hôtel-Dieu was built in 1645 near the site of the present Notre-Dame Basilica, in Old Montréal. This building was erected in 1861.

Parc Lafontaine

Rue Sherbrooke and av. Parc-Lafontaine. ☎ **514/872-2644.** Admission free; small fee for use of tennis courts. Park, daily 24 hours; tennis courts, summer only, daily 9am–10pm. Métro: Sherbrooke.

This European-style park near downtown is one of the city's oldest. In testament to the dual identities of the populace, half the park is landscaped in formal French manner, the other half in more casual English style. Among its several bodies of water is a lake that's used for paddle-boating in summer and ice skating in winter. Snowshoeing and cross-country trails curl through the trees. The amphitheater is the setting for outdoor theater and movies in summer. Joggers, bikers, picnickers, and tennis buffs (there are 14 outdoor courts) share the space. Look for the bust of Félix Leclerc, the renowned French-Canadian poet and songwriter, near the esplanade.

Oratoire St-Joseph (St. Joseph's Oratory)

3800 chemin Queen-Mary (on the north slope of Mont-Royal). ☎ **514/733-8211.** Admission free, but donations are requested at the museum. Oratory, daily 7am–8pm; museum, daily 10am–5pm. The 56-bell carillon plays Wed–Fri noon–3pm, Sat–Sun noon–2:30pm. Métro: Côtes-des-Neiges.

This huge basilica, with its monster copper dome, was built by Québec's Catholics to honor St. Joseph, patron saint of Canada. Dominating the north slope of Mont-Royal, its imposing dimensions are seen by some as inspiring, by others as forbidding. It came into being through the efforts of Brother André, a lay brother in the Holy Cross order who enjoyed a reputation as a healer. By the time he had built a small wooden chapel in 1904 near the site of the basilica, he was said to have effected hundreds of cures. Those celebrated powers attracted supplicants from great distances, and Brother André performed his work until his death in 1937. His dream of building this shrine to his patron saint became a reality only years after his death, in 1967. He is buried in the basilica, and was beatified by the pope in 1982, a status one step below sainthood.

The basilica is largely Italian Renaissance in style, its dome recalling the shape of the Duomo in Florence, but of much greater size and less grace. Inside is a museum where a central exhibit is the heart of Brother André. Outside, a Way of the Cross lined with sculptures was the setting of scenes for the film *Jesus of Montréal.* Brother André's wooden chapel, with his tiny bedroom, are on the grounds and open to the public. Pilgrims, some ill, come to seek intercession from St. Joseph and Brother André, and often climb the middle set of steps on their knees. At 862 feet (263m), the shrine is the highest point in Montréal. A cafeteria and snack bar are on the premises. Guided tours are offered at 10am and 2pm daily in summer and on weekends in September and October (donation only).

ELSEWHERE IN THE CITY

La Biosphère

160 chemin Tour-de-l'Isle (on Ile Ste-Hélène). ☎ **514/283-5000.** Admission $6.50 adults, $5 seniors and students, $4 children 7–17; $16 family ticket. June–Sept, daily 10am–8pm; Oct–May, Tues–Sun 9am–6pm. Métro: Ile Ste-Hélène; then the shuttle bus.

Not to be confused with the Biodôme at Olympic Park, this new project is located in the geodesic dome designed by Buckminster Fuller to serve as the American Pavilion for Expo '67. A fire destroyed the acrylic skin of the sphere in 1976, and it served no purpose other than as a harbor landmark until 1995. The motivation behind the Biosphère is unabashedly environmental, with four exhibition areas, a water theater, and an amphitheater all devoted to promoting awareness of the St. Lawrence–Great Lakes ecosystem. Multimedia shows and hands-on displays invite the active participation of visitors. In the highest point of the so-called Visions Hall is an observation level with an unobstructed view of the river. Connections Hall offers a "Call to Action" presentation employing six giant screens and three stages. There's a preaching-to-the-choir quality to all this that slips over the edge of the edutainment border into zealous philosophizing. But the various displays and exhibits are put together thoughtfully and will divert and enlighten most visitors, at least for a while.

Musée des Arts Decoratifs de Montréal (Decorative Arts Museum)

2929 rue Jeanne-d'Arc (enter on bd. Pié-IX). ☎ **514/259-2575.** Admission $3 adults, $2 seniors, $1.50 students 13–25, free for children 12 and under. Fri–Sun 11am–5pm. Métro: Pié-IX.

In 1915 Oscar and Marius Dufresne began construction of a 44-room Beaux Arts mansion in a then-distant precinct of Montréal. The two brothers, one an industrialist and the other an engineer, divided the house down the middle and proceeded to fill it with silverware, porcelain, paintings, sculpture, furniture, and textiles of the period. Besides the lavish use of Italian marble and African mahogany, and the Dufresnes' original furnishings, the museum displays religious sculptures from the 1700s and 1800s, a collection devoted to the Hébert family of artists from Québec, and an assembly of avant-garde furnishings of the 1930s to the 1950s by such designers as Frank Lloyd Wright and Marcel Breuer. The contrasts between the various components of the collections are somewhat jarring, and the museum doesn't justify the longish trip from downtown on its own. However, it can easily be combined with visits to nearby Olympic Park, the Biodôme, and the Botanical Garden.

St-Lambert Lock, St. Lawrence Seaway

Rte.132 under east end of Victoria Bridge. ☎ **514/672-4110.** Admission free. Daily, mid-Apr to mid-Nov. Drive or take a taxi across Victoria Bridge to the exit marked ECLUSES; park in the "Observatory" lot, and walk from there to the observation deck overlooking St-Lambert Lock.

The St. Lawrence Seaway was inaugurated by Elizabeth II and President Eisenhower in 1959, after a century of planning and a remarkably short five years of construction. The system of canals and 15 locks meant that oceangoing vessels could sail all the way to Lake Superior in the North American heartland, 2,300 miles (3,700 km) from the Atlantic. To learn more about the seaway, visit the observation deck and exhibition space overlooking St-Lambert Lock. In the mammoth lock, 860 feet long by 80 feet wide, ships are raised about 15 feet, and then the upriver gates are opened for them to continue the journey to the center of the continent. The specially constructed ships, called "lakers," are narrow, to fit the locks, but often more than 700 feet long. A TV monitor in the tower runs a short video about the history and operation of the seaway. Obviously, the ideal time to be here is when a ship enters the lock, but there's no way to predict that circumstance. January to March, ice on the river prevents ships from sailing.

4 Especially for Kids

IMAX Theatre

Old Port, Quai King Edward (at the end of bd. St-Laurent). ☎ **514/349-4629** for shows and times. Admission $11.75 adults, $9.75 seniors and students, $7.50 children 4–11. Call for current schedule of shows in English. Métro: Place d'Armes.

The images and special effects are larger-than-life, sometimes in 3-D, and always visually dazzling, thrown on a seven-story screen. Arrive for shows at least 10 minutes early, earlier on weekends and evenings.

Insectarium

In the Botanical Garden, 4101 rue Sherbrooke (at bd. Pié-IX). ☎ **514/872-1400.** May–Oct $7 adults, $5 seniors over 65, $3.50 children 6–17; Nov–Apr $5 adults, $3.50 seniors, $2.50 children. Summer, daily 9am–8pm; the rest of the year, daily 9am–6pm. Métro: Pié-IX; then walk up the hill to the gardens or (in summer) take the shuttle bus from Olympic Park.

A recent addition to the Botanical Garden, this two-level structure near the rue Sherbrooke gate exhibits the collections of two avid entomologists, Georges Brossad (whose brainchild this place is) and Father Firmia Liberté. Over 3,000 mounted butterflies, scarabs, maggots, locusts, beetles, tarantulas, and giraffe weevils are displayed, and live exhibits feature scorpions, tarantulas, crickets, cockroaches, and praying mantises. Needless to say, kids are delighted by the creepy critters. Their guardians are apt to be less enthusiastic.

La Ronde Amusement Park

Parc des Iles, Ile Ste-Hélène. ☎ **514/872-6222** or 800/361-8020. Admission unlimited all-day pass, $18.85 for those 12 and older, $9.45 for children 11 and under; $42 family pass. Reserved seating for fireworks, from $21.50 including all rides. Grounds only, $9.85. (Taxes not included.) Mid-May to late June, Sun–Fri 10am–10pm, Sat 11am–1am; late June to early Sept, Sun–Thurs 11am–midnight, Fri–Sat 11am–1am. Parking $6.15. Métro: Papineau (and then bus no. 169) or Ile Ste-Hélène (and then bus no. 167).

Montréal's ambitious amusement park fills the northern reaches of the Ile Ste-Hélène with over 30 rides, family entertainment, an international circus, a medieval village, roller coasters, and places to eat and drink. Thrillseekers will love the Cobra, a stand-up roller coaster that incorporates a 360° loop and reaches speeds in excess of 60 m.p.h. A big attraction every year is the Benson & Hedges International Fireworks Competition, held on Saturday in June and Sunday in July. The pyromusical displays are launched at 10pm and last at least 30 minutes. (Some Montréalers choose to watch them from the Jacques Cartier Bridge, which is closed to traffic then; they take along a portable radio to listen to the accompanying music.)

Planetarium de Montréal

1000 rue St-Jacques (at rue Peel). ☎ **514/872-4530.** Admission $5.50 adults; $3.25 seniors, students, and children 6–17. Jan 9 to mid-June and Labor Day to Dec 23,

Tues–Sun and hols 2:30–7:30pm; Jan 2–9, mid-June to Labor Day, and Dec 24 daily 2:30–7:30pm. Métro: Bonaventure (Windsor Station exit).

A window on the night sky with its mythical monsters and magical heroes, Montréal's planetarium is right downtown, only two blocks south of Windsor Station. Changing shows under the 65.6-foot (20m) dome dazzle kids while informing them at the same time. Shows change with the seasons, exploring time and space travel and collisions of celestial bodies. The special Christmas show, "Star of the Magi," is the attraction throughout December and early January, based on recent investigations of historians and astronomers into the mysterious light that guided the Magi. Shows in English alternate with those in French.

S.O.S. Labyrinthe

Old Port, Quay King Edward (at the end of bd. St-Laurent). ☎ **514/982-9660** or 800/361-8020. Admission $8.75 adults, $7.50 students; $18 family ticket. May–Oct 9, daily 10am–10pm. Métro: Champ-de-Mars.

True to its name, it offers over a mile (2km) of indoor twisting paths, obstacles, and challenges, including a tunnel and a secret passage, all connected by a maze of corridors. Fogs and spouting water complicate the journey. The course changes weekly and incorporates a treasure hunt. Kids, up to teenagers, love it. Most adults can bear it, if without much enthusiasm. Guides on in-line skates are on duty for those who can't find their way out.

Theatre Biscuit

221 rue St-Paul ouest (near rue St-François-Xavier). ☎ **514/845-7306.** Admission $12.50 adults, $9.50 children. Sat–Sun only, performances at 3pm (pick up tickets at 2:30pm). Métro: Place d'Armes.

Montréal's only permanent puppet theater has shows on weekends, and reservations are required. Visitors may explore its small puppet museum. This is good family fun, and understanding French is not essential.

5 Special-Interest Sightseeing

Centre Canadien d'Architecture

1920 rue Baile (at bd. René-Lévesque). ☎ **514/939-7026.** Admission $5 adults, $3 students and seniors, free for children 11 and under. June–Sept, Tues–Wed and Fri–Sat 11am–6pm, Thurs 11am–8pm; Oct–May, Wed and Fri 11am–6pm, Thurs 11am–8pm, Sat–Sun 11am–5pm. Guided tours available on request. Métro: Atwater, Guy-Concordia, or Georges-Vanier.

The understated but handsome CCA building fills a city block, joining a thoughtfully contemporary structure with an existing older building, the 1875 Shaughnessy House. Founded in 1979 by architect Phyllis Lambert, the CCA doubles as a study center and a museum with changing exhibits devoted to the art of architecture and its history. Materials on view include architects' sketchbooks, elevation drawings, and photography. The collection is international in scope and encompasses architecture, urban planning, and landscape design. Texts are in both French and English. Opened only in 1989, the museum has received rave notices from scholars, critics, and serious architecture buffs. That said, it's only fair to note that the average visitor is likely to find it as enthralling as a train timetable. The bookstore has a special section on Canadian architecture with emphasis on Montréal and Québec City. The sculpture garden across the Ville-Marie autoroute is part of the CCA, designed by artist/architect Melvin Charney.

Centre d'Histoire de Montréal

335 place d'Youville (at rue St-Pierre). ☎ **514/872-3207.** Admission $4.50 adults; $3 seniors, students, and children 6–17. Late Jan to early May and early Sept to mid-Dec, Tues–Sun 10am–5pm; early May to mid-June, daily 9am–5pm; late June to early Sept, daily 10am–6pm. Closed mid-Dec to late Dec. Métro: Square-Victoria.

Built in 1903 as Montréal's Central Fire Station, the red-brick and sandstone building is now the Montréal History Center, which traces the history of the city from its first occupants, the Amerindians, to the European settlers who arrived in 1642, to the present day. Throughout its 14 rooms, carefully conceived presentations chart the contributions of the city's founders and subsequent generations. The development of the railroad, Métro, and related infrastructures are recalled, as is that of domestic and public architecture in imaginative exhibits, videos, and slide shows. On the second floor, reached by a spiral staircase, are memorabilia from the early 20th century. Labels are in French, so ask at the front desk for a visitor's guide in English.

Musée de la Banque de Montréal (Bank of Montréal Museum)

119 and 129 rue St-Jacques (at place d'Armes). ☎ **514/877-6892.** Admission free. Museum, Mon–Fri 10am–4pm; bank, Mon–Fri 8am–5pm. Métro: Place d'Armes.

Facing place d'Armes is Montréal's oldest bank building, with a classic facade, a graceful dome, a carved pediment, and six Corinthian columns, mostly unchanged since its completion in 1847 (the pediment was carved in 1867). The interior was renovated in 1901–05 by the famed U.S. firm McKim, Mead, and White with Ionic and Corinthian columns of Vermont granite, walls and piers of pink marble from Tennessee, and a counter of Levanto marble. The bank contains a small museum with a replica of its first office (and its first bank teller, Henry Stone from Boston), gold nuggets from the Yukon, a $3 bill (one of only two known), and a collection of 100-year-old mechanical banks. A bilingual guide is available to answer questions.

Musée Marc-Aurèle Fortin

118 rue St-Pierre (at rue d'Youville). ☎ **514/845-6108.** Admission $3 adults, $1 students and seniors, free for children 11 and under. Tues–Sun 11am–5pm. Métro: Place d'Armes.

This is Montréal's only museum dedicated to the work of a single French-Canadian artist. Landscape watercolorist Marc-Aurèle Fortin (1888–1970) interpreted the beauty of the Québec countryside, such as the Laurentians and Charlevoix. His work is on the ground floor, while temporary exhibits, mounted downstairs, usually feature the work of other Québec painters.

Musée David M. Stewart

Vieux Fort, Ile Ste-Hélène. ☎ **514/861-6701.** Admission $5 adults, $3 seniors and students, free for children 6 and under; $10 family ticket. Summer, Wed–Mon

10am–6pm; the rest of the year, Wed–Mon 10am–5pm. Métro: Ile Ste-Hélène; then a 15-minute walk.

After the War of 1812, the British prepared for a possible future American invasion by building this moated arsenal. The duke of Wellington ordered its construction as another link in the chain of fortifications along the St. Lawrence. Completed in 1824, it was never involved in armed conflict. The British garrison left in 1870 after Confederation of the former Canadian colonies. Today the low stone barracks and blockhouses contain the museum, which display maps and navigational and scientific instruments that helped Europeans explore the New World, as well as military and naval artifacts, uniforms, and related paraphernalia from the time of Jacques Cartier (1535) through the end of the colonial period. From late June through late August, the fort comes to life with reenactments of military parades by La Compagnie Franche de la Marine and the 78th Fraser Highlanders, at 11am, 2:30pm, and 5pm. The presence of the French unit is an unhistorical sop to Francophone sensibilities, since New France had become English Canada almost 65 years before the fort was erected.

6 Organized Tours

A generalized guided tour is often the most desirable way to begin explorations of a new city. Even a mediocre tour with a guide who imagines himself a great wit can provide a timesaving sense of the topography of the city, its history, and which attractions are most likely to reward a return visit in depth.

For a complete listing of tours and tour operators, check under "Guided Tours" in the annually revised *Montréal Tourist Guide,* or at **Infotouriste** (☎ **514/873-2015** or 800/363-7777). Most of the land tours leave from Infotouriste, downtown at Dorchester Square. Boat tours depart from the Old Port in Old Montréal. Parking is free at the dock, or take the Métro to the Champ-de-Mars station and walk six blocks.

BOAT TOURS Numerous opportunities for experiencing Montréal and environs by water are laid out under "Cruises" in the *Montréal Tourist Guide.* Among the better are:

Le Bateau-Mouche (☎ **514/849-9952**), an air-conditioned, glass-enclosed vessel reminiscent of those in Paris. It plies the St. Lawrence River from May to October. Cruises depart for 90-minute excursions at 10am, noon, 2pm, and 4pm, and for a three-hour dinner cruise at 7pm. The shallow-draft boat takes up to 158 passengers on a route inaccessible by traditional vessels. It passes under seven bridges and provides sweeping views of the city, Mont-Royal, the St. Lawrence, and its islands. Snacks are available on board. Families get a discount on the first trip of the day, at 10am. Le Bateau-Mouche departs from the Jacques Cartier Pier, opposite place Jacques-Cartier.

Croisières du Port de Montréal (Montréal Harbor Cruises) (☎ 514/842-3871) also travels the harbor and the St. Lawrence. The boats depart up to five times a day from May to mid-October from the Clock Tower Pier at the foot of rue Berri in Vieux Montréal, for tours, dinner and dancing, or extended sightseeing for one to nine hours.

The *Croisières Nouvelle-Orléans* (☎ **514/842-7655**), a fairly accurate imitation of a Mississippi paddle wheeler, plies the St. Lawrence regularly, departing from the Jacques Cartier Pier at the Old Port.

For an exciting—and wet—experience, consider a ride on a **Saute-moutons** (wave-jumper) powerboat on the roiling Lachine Rapids of the St. Lawrence River. The streamlined boat makes the 90-minute trip May to September, daily every two hours from 10am to 6pm. It takes half an hour to get to and from the rapids, which leaves 30 minutes for storming up the river. Arrive 45 minutes early to obtain and don rain gear and life jacket. Wearing a sweater and bringing a change of clothes are good ideas, as you almost certainly will get splashed or even soaked through. Cruises depart from the Clock Tower Pier. For information, call 514/284-9607.

BUS TOURS   Now for something a little different. **Amphitour Kamada** tours Vieux Montréal much like any other bus—until it waddles into the waters of the harbor for a dramatic finish. Inventor/driver Jacques Tourigny originally designed the vehicle, essentially a bus with a hull, for his family to tour the Amazon. Since launching the "amphi-bus" in 1985, he's never had an accident. The one-hour excursion is offered May to October, daily from 10am to 11pm. The point of debarkation is place Jacques-Cartier; book through Amphi Tour Ltée (☎ **514/849-5181**).

For a more traditional way to see the city, there's the **Murray Hill Trolley Bus** (☎ **514/841-4733**). A particular benefit of these tours is that in summer passengers can get on and off the bus as often as they wish and explore on their own, boarding the next bus to come along. The narrated tour is bilingual. Tours depart year round from Infotouriste, at Dorchester Square, and there's free shuttle service from major hotels.

Commercial guided tours in air-conditioned buses are offered daily year round by **Gray Line** (☎ **514/934-1222**). The basic city tour takes three hours; the deluxe, five hours, which includes an hour-long stop at the Botanical Garden. Other tours take you to the Ile Ste-Hélène, the St. Lawrence Seaway, the Laurentians, and Québec City. Tours depart from Dorchester Square.

Montréal's romantic **calèches** (☎ **514/653-0751**) are horse-drawn open carriages whose drivers serve as guides. In winter they hitch their steeds to old-fashioned sleighs for a ride around the top of Mont-Royal, the horses puffing steam, the passengers bundled in lap rugs. Prices run about $40 for an hour's tour in the carriage or sleigh, which can seat four comfortably, five if one sits with the driver. In addition to Mont-Royal, calèches depart from Dorchester Square and in Vieux Montréal at place Jacques-Cartier and rue de la Commune, rue Notre-Dame opposite rue St-Vincent, and place d'Armes opposite Notre-Dame Basilica.

Drivers for **Taxi Lasalle** (☎ 514/277-2552) provide a similar service. They are based at Dorchester Square and will take up to four people on tours of the city for about $25 per hour.

WALKING TOURS Walking tours of Vieux Montréal, the Underground City, or any other section that piques interest are available through **Guidatour** (☎ 514/844-4021) or **Visites de Montréal** (☎ 514/933-6674).

Free guided tours of the campus of **McGill University** are available, but it is necessary to call 514/398-6555 at least 24 hours in advance.

7 Spectator Sports

Montrealers are as devoted to their demi-religion, ice hockey, as other Canadians, but they still manage to have plenty of enthusiasm left over for baseball or soccer. Some boosters have even floated the idea of bidding for a future NFL Super Bowl, if they can ever get the roof of the Olympic Stadium to work properly. In the meantime, there are several regularly ongoing sporting events, such as the **Molson Grand Prix** in June, **The Player's Ltd. International men's tennis championship** in late July, and the **Montréal Marathon** in September.

BASEBALL

The **Montréal Expos,** Montréal's baseball team, is a member of the National League. They play at Olympic Stadium from April to September, with games usually at 1:35 or 7:35pm. Ticket reservations can be made by telephone, with a credit or charge card. Olympic Stadium, 4549 av. Pierre-de-Coubertin. ☎ 514/846-3976 for information. Admission from $15.25 adults, $9 seniors, $5.50 students, $4 children. Métro: Pié-IX.

HARNESS-RACING

Blue Bonnets Racetrack, is the dedicated facility for international harness-racing events, including the Prix d'Eté, the Prix de l'Avenir, the Blue Bonnets Challenge, and the Breeders Cup. Restaurants, bars, a snack bar, and pari-mutuel betting can make for a satisfying evening or Sunday-afternoon outing. There are no races on Tuesday or Thursday. 7440 bd. Décarie (at rue Jean-Talon). ☎ 514/739-2741. Admission $5 clubhouse, $3.75 stands, free for children 15 and under. Mon, Wed, and Fri–Sat at 7:30pm; Sun at 1:30pm. Métro: Namur; then take the shuttle bus.

HOCKEY

The **Montréal Canadiens,** stars of the National Hockey League, have won 24 Stanley Cup championships since 1929. They perform at the Forum from October into mid-June. Montréal Forum, 2313 rue Ste-Catherine ouest (between rue Lambert-Closse and av. Atwater). ☎ 514/932-2582. Admission $23.50 seats, $10 standing room. Métro: Atwater.

ROLLER HOCKEY

Road Runners Roller Hockey is hockey with a twist—played entirely on in-line skates. The Road Runners have created a stir in Montréal since they started to play in 1994, and their talented female goalie, Manon Rheaume, is a particular favorite. Games are in summer only. Montréal Forum, 2313 rue Ste-Catherine ouest (between rue Lambert-Closse and av. Atwater). ☎ **514/932-2582.** Admission $5, $11.50, or $27.50. Summer only, 7:30pm. Métro: Atwater.

8 Outdoor Activities

BICYCLING Montréal enjoys a network of 149 miles (240km) of cycling paths. Popular routes include the 6.8-mile (11km) path along the **Lachine Canal** that leads to Lake St-Louis; the 10-mile (16km) path west from the **St-Lambert Lock** (see above) to the city of Côte Ste-Catherine; and **Angrignon Park** with its 4-mile cycling path and inviting picnic areas (take the Métro, which accepts bikes in the last two doors of the last car, to the Angrignon station). Bikes can be rented at the Old Port (at boulevard St-Laurent) for $6 an hour or $20 a day. Bikes, along with the popular four-wheel "Q Cycles," may also be rented at the place Jacques-Cartier entrance to the Old Port. The Q Cycles, for use in the Old Port only, cost $4.25 per half hour for adults and $3.50 per half hour for children.

CROSS-COUNTRY SKIING Parc Mont-Royal has a 1.3-mile (2.1km) cross-country course called the *parcours de la croix*. The Botanical Garden has an ecology trail used by cross-country skiers. The problem for either is that skiers have to supply their own equipment. Just an hour from the city, in the Laurentians, is one of the finest centers for cross-country skiing in North America, the Far Hills Inn and Ski Centre, where equipment can be rented.

HIKING The most popular—and obvious—hike is up to the top of **Mont-Royal.** Start downtown on rue Peel, which leads north to a stairway, which in turn leads to a half-mile (800m) path of switchbacks called Le Serpent. Or opt for the 200 steps that lead up to the Chalet Lookout, with the reward of a panoramic view of the city. Figure about 1¼ miles one way.

IN-LINE SKATING In-line skates (or Rollerblades) and all the relevant protective gear can be rented from **Velo Adventure** on Quai King Edward in the Old Port (☎ 514/847-0666). The cost is $8.50 (weekdays) or $9 (weekends) for the first hour and $4 for each additional hour. A deposit is required. Lessons on skates are available for $25 for two hours.

JOGGING There are many possibilities. One is to follow rue Peel north to Le Serpent switchback path on **Mont-Royal,** continuing uphill on it for half a mile (800m) until it peters out. Turn right and continue 1 mile (1.6km) to the monument of George-Etienne Cartier, one of Canada's fathers of Confederation. From here, either take a bus back downtown or run back down the same route or along avenue du Parc and avenue des Pins (turn right when you get to it). It's also fun to jog along the **Lachine Canal.**

SWIMMING Unfortunately, most of the water around Montréal is too polluted for swimming, with one notable exception: the artificial

---

❓ Did You Know?

* Montréal has a museum devoted to humor and an annual Just for Laughs festival.
* Montréal is Canada's second-largest city, after Toronto.
* The Montréal Botanical Garden is frequently compared to London's Kew Gardens.
* The Musée des Beaux-Arts, founded in 1860, is the oldest museum in Canada.
* The largest Chinese garden outside Asia is in Montréal.
* When Montréal's Victoria Bridge opened in 1860, it was regarded as the Eighth Wonder of the World.
* Mont-Royal Park was designed by Frederick Law Olmsted, an American, who also designed New York's Central Park.
* St. Joseph's Oratory is the largest pilgrimage center in the world dedicated to the saint.
* The Canadian Centre for Architecture has the largest collection of documents on architecture in the world.
* The city's tallest building, 51-story 1000 rue de la Gauchetière, has a year-round ice-skating rink inside.

Plage de l'Ile Notre-Dame (☎ **514/872-6093**) is the former Regatta Lake from Expo '67. The water is drawn from the Lachine Rapids and treated by a mostly natural filtration system of sand, aquatic plants, and ultraviolet light (and a bit of chlorine) to make it safe for swimming. Admission is $7 for adults, seniors, and students; $2.50 for children 6 to 17. To get there, take the Métro to the Ile Ste-Hélène station.

Those who prefer a pool but are staying in a hotel that doesn't have one, take the Métro to the Viau station and **Olympic Park,** 4141 av. Pierre-de-Coubertin (☎ **514/252-4622**), which has six pools, open Monday through Friday from about 9:30am to 9pm and on Saturday and Sunday from 1 to 4pm. Call ahead to confirm swim schedules, which are affected by competitions and holidays.

The **City of Montréal Department of Sports and Leisure** (☎ **514/872-6211**) can provide information about other city pools, indoor or outdoor. Admission to the pools varies from free to about $4 ($2 for children).

7

Montréal Strolls

Cities best reveal themselves to the traveler on foot, and Montréal is one of the most amenable to walkers in North America. Its layout is fairly straightforward, easy to get around, and there's much to see in the more concentrated districts—the old town, center city, around rue Crescent, the Latin Quarter, and on "the mountain."

WALKING TOUR 1
VIEUX-MONTRÉAL

Start: Eglise Notre-Dame-de-Bonsecours.
Finish: Vieux-Port.
Time: Two to three hours.
Best Times: Almost any day the weather is decent. Old Montréal is lively and relatively safe day or night. Note, however, that most of the museums in the area are closed on Monday. On weekends and holidays, Montréalers turn out in full force, enjoying the plazas, the 18th- and 19th-century architecture, and the ambience of the most picturesque part of their city.
Worst Times: Evenings, when attractions are closed and rue St-Paul can get a little rowdy with bar-hoppers.

Take the Métro to the Champ-de-Mars station and follow the signs to Vieux-Montréal (Old Montréal), proceeding up the hill to rue Notre-Dame. Turn left, then right on rue Bonsecours, descending one block to rue St-Paul, the oldest thoroughfare in Montréal (1672). There stands the small:

1. **Eglise Notre-Dame-de-Bonsecours** (1673), or Sailors' Church. The church was founded in 1657 by Marguerite Bourgeoys, a nun and teacher who was made a saint in 1982. A small museum downstairs tells the story of her life and work in 58 small scenes. Sailors have historically made pilgrimages to the church to give thanks for being saved at sea. Climb up to the tower for a memorable view of the harbor and the Old Town.

Right across rue St-Paul from the church, at no. 401, is a house that offers a look at what life was like in Montréal in the late 18th century. The:

2. **Maison Calvet (Calvet House)** was built in 1725 and restored from 1964 to 1966. It's now a bakery and café, with an antique fireplace taking pride of place. While it appears to be a modest dwelling, in the early days such a house would have been inhabited by a fairly well-to-do family. Pierre du Calvet, believed to be the house's original owner, was a French Huguenot who supported the American Revolution. Calvet met with Benjamin Franklin in Montréal in 1775, and was imprisoned from 1780 to 1783 for supplying money to the Americans. The house, with its characteristic sloped roof meant to discourage snow buildup, is constructed of Montréal graystone.

Just beyond the Sailor's Church, heading west down rue St-Paul, is an imposing building with a colonnaded facade and silvery dome, the graystone:

3. **Marché Bonsecours (Bonsecours Market)**. Built between 1845 and 1850, it was briefly used as the Parliament of United Canada, the City Hall, the central market, and later the home of the municipality's housing and planning offices. The building was restored in 1992 to serve as a center for temporary exhibitions and musical performances during the city's 350th-birthday celebration. It's expected to continue to be used for exhibitions, celebrations, and the like.

When the Bonsecours Market was first built, the dome could be seen from everywhere in the city. The Doric columns of the portico were cast in England, and the prominent dome has long served as a landmark for seafarers coming into the harbor.

Continue down rue St-Paul. At no. 281 is the former:

4. **Hotel Rasco,** built in 1836 for Francisco Rasco, an Italian who came to Canada to manage a hotel for the Molson family. Soon after, he became successful with his own hotel. The 150-room Rasco was the Ritz of its day in Montréal, hosting, among other honored guests, Charles Dickens and his wife in 1842 when the author was directing some of his plays at the theater across the street. The hotel lives on in legend if not in fact, devoid of much of its original architectural detail. Rasco left in 1844, and the hotel slipped into decline. Between 1960 and 1981 it stood empty, but the city took it over and restored it in 1982. Now, however, its future again looks uncertain.

Continue along rue St-Paul one more block to arrive at the focus of activity in Old Montréal, a magnet for both citizens and tourists year-round.

5. **Place Jacques-Cartier** opened as a marketplace in 1804. Easily the most appealing of the Old City's squares, its cobbled streets, gentle downhill slope, ancient buildings, and horse-drawn carriages set the mood, while outdoor cafés, street entertainers, itinerant artists, and flower vendors invite lingering. Horse-drawn calèches depart from the southern end of the square for tours of Old Montréal.

Walking Tour—Vieux-Montréal

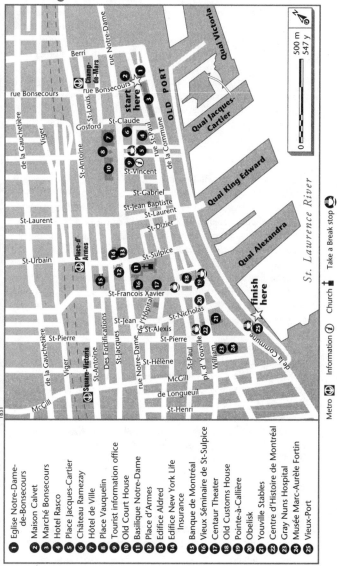

1. Eglise Notre-Dame-de-Bonsecours
2. Maison Calvet
3. Marché Bonsecours
4. Hotel Rasco
5. Place Jacques-Cartier
6. Château Ramezay
7. Hôtel de Ville
8. Place Vauquelin
9. Tourist information office
10. Old Court House
11. Basilique Notre-Dame
12. Place d'Armes
13. Edifice Aldred
14. Edifice New York Life Insurance
15. Banque de Montréal
16. Vieux Séminaire de St-Sulpice
17. Centaur Theater
18. Old Customs House
19. Pointe-à-Callière
20. Obelisk
21. Youville Stables
22. Centre d'Histoire de Montréal
23. Gray Nuns Hospital
24. Musée Marc-Aurèle Fortin
25. Vieux-Port

Metro Ⓜ   Information ⓘ   Church ✝   Take a Break stop ☕

☕ **TAKE A BREAK**   Some of the old buildings in and around place Jacques-Cartier harbor restaurants and cafés. For a drink or a light meal, try to find a seat in **Le Jardin Nelson** (no. 407), on the east side of the square near the bottom of the hill. Sit in the courtyard in back when the weather is good—there might be live music playing—or on the terrace overlooking the activity of the square.

Walk slowly uphill, being sure to take in the old buildings that bracket the plaza. Plaques in French and English tell about some of them: the Vandelac House (no. 433), the del Vecchio House (nos. 404 to 410), and the Cartier House (no. 407). All these houses were well suited to the rigors of life in the raw young settlement. Their steeply pitched roofs shed the heavy winter snows rather than collapsing under the burden, and small windows with double casements let in light while keeping out wintry breezes. When shuttered, the windows were almost as effective as the heavy stone walls in deflecting hostile arrows or the antics of trappers fresh from bibulous evenings in nearby taverns.

At the upper, northern, end of the plaza stands a monument to Horatio Nelson, hero of Trafalgar, erected in 1809. Originally, this monument preceded the much larger version in London by several years. However, after years of being subjected to vandalism, presumably by Québec separatists, the original statue was removed and replaced by the current one, an obvious fake.

At the top of the plaza, turn right. In a few steps, on the right, is:

6. Château Ramezay, built by Claude de Ramezay between 1705 and 1706 in the French regime style of the period. This was the home of the city's French governors, starting with de Ramezay, for four decades before being taken over and used for the same purpose by the British.

In 1775 an army of American "rebels" invaded and held Montréal, using the château as their headquarters. Benjamin Franklin was sent to persuade Montréalers to join the American revolt against against British rule. He stayed in the château but failed to sway Québec's leaders to join his cause.

The house has had other uses over the years. It was a courthouse, government office building, teachers' college, and headquarters for Laval University before becoming a museum in 1895. Inside are furnishings, tools, oil paintings, costumes, and other objects related to the economic and social activities of the 18th century and the first half of the 19th century.

Across rue Notre-Dame from the Château Ramezay stands the impressive:

7. Hôtel de Ville, built between 1872 and 1878 in the florid French Second Empire style. The city's administrative offices moved here from Bonsecours Market, where they had been for 25 years. In 1922 the building barely survived a disastrous fire. Only the exterior walls remained, and after substantial rebuilding and the addition of another floor, it reopened in 1926.

Take a minute to look inside at the generous use of Italian marble, the art deco lamps, and the bronze-and-glass chandelier. The sculptures at the entry are *Woman with a Pail* and *The Sower*, both by Alfred Laliberté.

Alongside City Hall is:

8. Place Vauquelin, a public square since 1858, with a splashing fountain and a view of the Champ-de-Mars park, which lies behind and beneath the city hall. The statue is of Jean Vauquelin, commander of the French fleet in New France. It stares across rue Notre-Dame at his counterpart, Nelson, two symbols of Montréal's duality. On the opposite corner is a small but helpful:

9. Tourist information office, with many useful brochures and maps and a bilingual staff ready to answer questions. On this site once stood the famed Silver Dollar Saloon, long since torn down. The tavern got its name from 350 silver dollars embedded in its floor.

To the left of place Vauquelin stands the imposing:

10. Vieux Palais de Justice (Old Court House), most of which was built in 1856. The third floor and dome were added in 1891, as can be discerned on closer examination. The Organizing Committee for the 1976 Olympic Games resided inside, and the city's civil cases continued to be tried here until a new courthouse, the Palais de Justice, was built next door in 1978. Civic departments for the city of Montréal are housed here now. The statue beside the Old Court House, called *Hommage to Marguerite Bourgeoys*, is by sculptor Jules LaSalle.

Continue along rue Notre-Dame five more blocks, crossing rue St-Sulpice, to the magnificent neo-gothic:

11. Basilique Notre-Dame (1829), designed by James O'Donnell, an Irish architect living in New York. Transformed by his experience in building the church, he later converted to Roman Catholicism and is one of only a few people buried here. The main altar is made from a hand-carved linden tree. Behind the altar is the Chapel of the Sacred Heart (1982), a perennially popular choice for weddings. The chapel's altar, 32 bronze panels by Montréal artist Charles Daudelin, represents birth, life, and death. The church can seat 4,000 people, and its bell, one of the largest in North America, weighs 12 tons. There's a small museum (open only on Saturday and Sunday) beside the chapel.

The basilica faces:

12. Place d'Armes, the centerpiece of which is a monument to city founder Paul de Chomedey, sieur de Maisonneuve (1612–76). It marks the spot where the settlers defeated the Iroquois fighters in bloody hand-to-hand fighting, with Maisonneuve himself locked in combat with the Iroquois chief. Maisonneuve won and remained here 23 years. The inscription on the monument reads "You are the buckwheat seed which will grow and multiply and spread throughout the country." The sculptures at the base of the monument represent three prominent citizens of early Montréal—Charles Lemoyne (1626–85), a farmer; Jeanne Mance, the founder of the first hospital in Montréal; Raphael-Lambert Closse, a soldier and the mayor of Ville-Marie—and an Iroquois warrior. Closse is depicted with his dog, Pilote, whose bark once warned the early settlers of an impending Iroquois attack.

On the opposite corner of the square from the basilica is the 23-story art deco:

13. Edifice Aldred, 507 place d'Armes, which may look somehow familiar. There's a reason: It was built in 1931 to resemble the Empire State Building in New York. The building's original tenant was Aldred and Co. Ltd., a New York–based multinational finance company with offices in New York, London, and Paris. Beside it stands the eight-story, red sandstone:

14. Edifice New York Life Insurance, 511 place d'Armes, a Richardson romanesque building with a striking wrought-iron door and clock tower. This was Montréal's first skyscraper back in 1888, and it was equipped with a technological marvel, an elevator.

Directly across the square from the statue of Maisonneuve and the basilica is the domed, colonnaded:

15. Banque de Montréal, Montréal's oldest bank building (1847). Besides being impressively proportioned and lavishly appointed inside and out, it houses a small banking museum that illustrates its early operations. Admission is free. From 1901 to 1905, American architect Stanford White was in charge of extending the original building beyond ruelle des Fortifications to what is now rue St-Antoine. In this enlarged space he created a vast chamber with high, green-marble columns topped with golden capitals. The public is welcome to stop in for a look.

Opposite the square from the bank and adjacent to the basilica on rue Notre-Dame is the:

16. Vieux Séminaire de St-Sulpice, a seminary in the city's oldest building, which is surrounded by equally ancient stone walls. It was erected by the Sulpician priests in 1658, a year after they arrived in Ville-Marie. (The Sulpicians are part of an order founded in Paris by Jean-Jacques Olier in 1641.) The clock on the facade dates from 1701 and has a movement made almost entirely of wood. Unfortunately, the seminary is not open to the public.

Walk past the seminary, heading west on rue Notre-Dame, and turn left at rue St-François-Xavier. At rue de l'Hôpital, to the left, is the stately:

17. The Centaur Theater, home to Montréal's principal English-language theater housed in a former stock exchange building. The Beaux Arts architecture is interesting in that the two entrances are on either side rather than in the center of the facade. The building, erected in 1903, was designed by American architect George Post, who was also responsible for the New York Stock Exchange. It served in its original function until 1965, when it was redesigned as a theater with two stages.

Continue down rue St-François-Xavier. At rue St-Paul, turn left. L'Air du Temps, one of the city's most enduring jazz clubs, is on the corner, at no. 191.

Walk the short distance to 150 rue St-Paul and the neoclassical:

18. **Vieille Douane (Old Customs House)**, erected from 1836 to 1838. The building was doubled in size in 1882 to what you'll see today by extending it to the south; walk around to the other side of the building for a look. The Old Customs House faces the north side of place Royale, the first public square in the early settlement of Ville-Marie. Europeans and Amerindians used to come here to trade their wares.

Across the way, the new, roughly triangular building is the:

19. **Pointe-à-Callière**, which houses the Museum of Archaeology and History, the repository of artifacts unearthed here during more than 10 years of excavation. This was the site where Ville-Marie (Montréal) was founded in 1642. The museum also incorporates, via an underground connection, the Old Customs House just passed.

A fort stood on this spot in 1645, and 30 years later, the château of a monsieur de Callière, from whom the building and triangular square take their names. At that time, the St. Pierre River separated this piece of land from the mainland; it was made a canal in the 19th century and later filled in.

🌀 **TAKE A BREAK** One possibility for lunch or an afternoon pick-me-up is the casual, second-floor **L'Arrivage café** at the museum. Another is the moderately priced **Stash Café** at 200 rue St-Paul ouest, at rue St-François-Xavier, which specializes in Polish fare and is open from 11am until late in the evening.

West of Pointe-à-Callière, near rue St-François-Xavier, stands an:

20. **Obelisk** commemorating the founding of Ville-Marie on May 18, 1642. The obelisk was erected here in 1893 by the Montréal Historical Society and bears the names of the city's early pioneers, including Maisonneuve and Jeanne Mance.

Continuing west from the obelisk two blocks, look for the:

21. **Ecuries d'Youville (Youville Stables)**, on the left at 296–316 place d'Youville. The rooms in the iron-gated compound, built in 1825 on land owned by the Gray Nuns, were used mainly as warehouses. Like much of the waterfront area, the U-shaped Youville building (the actual stables, next door, were made of wood and disappeared long ago) was run-down and forgotten until the 1960s, when a group of enterprising businesspeople decided to buy and renovate the property. Today the compound contains offices and a popular restaurant, Gibbys. Go inside the courtyard and take a look if the gates are open, as they usually are.

Continue another block west to 335 rue St-Pierre and the Dutch-style:

22. **Centre d'Histoire de Montréal (Montréal History Center)**. Built in 1903 as Montréal's Central Fire Station, it now houses exhibits, including many audiovisual ones, about the city's past and present. Visitors learn about the early routes of exploration, the fur trade,

architecture, public squares, the railroad, and life in Montréal from 1920 to 1950.

Less than a block away, on the left at 138 rue St-Pierre, pass the former:

23. Hôpital des Soeurs Grises (Gray Nuns Hospital), in operation from 1693 to 1851 and now the administrative offices and a novitiate for future nuns. Officially known as the Sisters of Charity of Montréal, the order was founded by the widow Marguerite d'Youville in 1737. The present building incorporates several additions and was part of the city's General Hospital, run by the Charon Brothers but administered by d'Youville, who died here in 1771. The wing in which she died was restored in 1980. The wall of the original chapel remains. Visits inside must be arranged in advance. Call 514/842-9411 to arrange.

From here, look down rue St-Pierre for the brown awning at no. 118 that marks the entrance to the:

24. Musée Marc-Aurèle Fortin, a museum devoted to a single Canadian artist. Fortin, who died in 1972, was well known for his watercolors of the Québec countryside, including Charlevoix and the Laurentian Mountains. His depictions of elms recall the time when giant Dutch elms lined rues Sherbrooke and St-Joseph in Montréal, before blight decimated them.

Continue past the museum and cross rue de la Commune and the railroad tracks to enter the:

25. Vieux-Port (Old Port), Montréal's historic commercial wharves. Now recycled as a waterfront park, it's frequented by cyclists, in-line skaters, joggers, walkers, strollers, lovers, and picnickers in good weather. This is the entry to parc des Ecluses (Locks Park), where the first locks on the St. Lawrence River are located.

☕ **TAKE A BREAK**　Enjoy a cafeteria-style snack at the **Maison des Ecluses Café** (Locks House Café), open in summer only, in the new structure near the entry to parc des Ecluses. Any time of year, for a snack in an informal atmosphere, and a trip down memory lane, go to **Il Etait Une Fois. . .** (Once Upon a Time), a memorabilia-filled café housed in an old train station, at 600 rue d'Youville.

From there, stroll back north along rue McGill to reach Square Victoria and its Métro station. Or pick up the beginning of the path along the Lachine Canal at parc des Ecluses and follow it for an hour or so to arrive at Montréal's colorful indoor/outdoor Atwater Market.

WALKING TOUR 2
DOWNTOWN

Start: Dorchester Square.
Finish: McCord Museum of Canadian History.
Time: 1¹/₂ hours.

Best Times: Weekdays in the morning or after 2pm, when the streets hum with big-city vibrancy but aren't too crowded.

Worst Times: Weekdays from noon to 2pm, when the streets, stores, and restaurants are crowded with businesspeople on lunch-break errands; and on Sunday, when most stores are closed and the area is virtually deserted. (Museums, however, are open.)

After a tour of Vieux Montréal, a look around the heart of the new 20th-century city provides ample contrast. To see the city at its contemporary best, take the Métro to the Bonaventure stop. Emerging from that station, the dramatic skyscraper immediate to the west is:

1. **1000 rue de la Gauchetière,** a recent contribution to the already-memorable skyline. Easily identified by its copper-and-blue pyramidal top, it rises to the maximum height permitted by the municipal building code. Inside, past an atrium planted with live trees, is the Bell Amphitheatre, a huge indoor skating rink bordered with cafés with seating for over 1,500 spectators.

   Walk west on rue de la Gauchetière. In one block, on the left, is:

2. **Le Château Champlain,** a hotel with a distinctive facade of half-moon windows, which have given it the nickname "cheese grater."

   Turn right next on rue Peel, walking north. In another block, this arrives at:

3. **Dorchester Square,** with its tall old trees and benches that invite lunchtime brown-baggers. This used to be called Dominion Square, but was renamed for Baron Dorchester, an early English governor, when the adjacent street, once named for him, was changed to boulevard René-Lévesque. Along the east side of the square is the Sun Life Insurance building, built in three stages between 1914 and 1931, and the tallest building in Québec until the skyscraper boom of the post–World War II era. This is also another gathering point for calèches (horse-drawn carriages). In winter, the drivers replace their carriages with sleighs and give rides around the top of Mont-Royal.

   At the northeast corner of the square is the main office of:

4. **Infotouriste,** where it's possible to obtain many useful maps and brochures, ask questions of bilingual attendants, change money, make hotel reservations, or even rent a car.

   From that office, go back to the other end of the square and turn left (east) on:

5. **Boulevard René-Lévesque,** formerly Dorchester Boulevard, renamed in 1988 following the death of the Parti Québécois leader who led the movement in favor of Québec independence and the use of the French language. Boulevard René-Lévesque is the city's broadest downtown thoroughfare, and the one with the fastest traffic.

   On the right is an only marginally successful copy of St. Peter's Basilica in Rome, built to roughly one-quarter scale, the:

6. **Cathédrale Marie-Reine-du-Monde (Mary Queen of the World Cathedral),** built between 1875 and 1894 as headquarters for

Walking Tour—Downtown Montréal

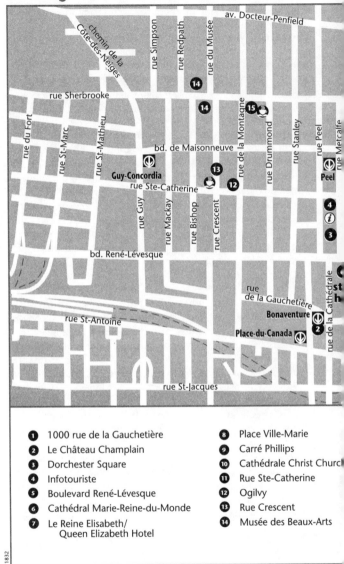

1. 1000 rue de la Gauchetière
2. Le Château Champlain
3. Dorchester Square
4. Infotouriste
5. Boulevard René-Lévesque
6. Cathédral Marie-Reine-du-Monde
7. Le Reine Elisabeth/
   Queen Elizabeth Hotel
8. Place Ville-Marie
9. Carré Phillips
10. Cathédrale Christ Churc
11. Rue Ste-Catherine
12. Ogilvy
13. Rue Crescent
14. Musée des Beaux-Arts

Montréal's Roman Catholic bishop. The statue in front of the cathedral is of Bishop Ignace Bourget (1799–1885), the force behind the construction of the basilica. It was sculpted in 1903 by Louis-Philippe Hébert, who was also responsible for the statue of Maisonneuve in place d'Armes.

Continuing past the cathedral and crossing rue Mansfield is the:

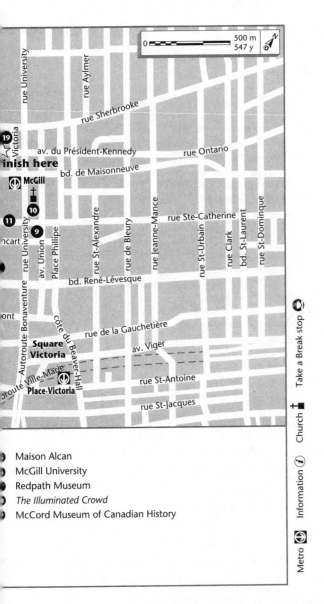

- Maison Alcan
- McGill University
- Redpath Museum
- *The Illuminated Crowd*
- McCord Museum of Canadian History

Metro ⬥   Information ⓘ   Church ✝■   Take a Break stop ⬥

7. La Reine Elisabeth/Queen Elizabeth Hôtel. Opened in 1958, Montréal's largest hotel stands above Central Station, making it incredibly convenient for people arriving by train. It also has direct access to the Underground City, and buses leave for Dorval and Mirabel airports from here.

Across boulevard René-Lévesque from the Queen Elizabeth is:

8. Place Ville-Marie, keystone of the postwar urban redevelopment efforts in Montréal. The cross-shaped skyscraper, designed by I. M. Pei, recalls Cartier's cross, planted to claim the island for France, and Maisonneuve's first little settlement, Ville-Marie. The complex, completed in 1962, has a fountain in its plaza called *Feminine Landscape* (1972), executed by Toronto artist Gerald Gladstone. Place Ville-Marie is known as "PVM" to Montrealers.

At the end of the hotel, turn left along rue University, crossing boulevard René-Lévesque and walking two blocks to rue Ste-Catherine. On the right is:

9. Carré Phillips, a plaza with a statue of Edward VII, and, much of the time, a farm stand. Over to the left, across rue Ste-Catherine, is:

10. Cathédrale Christ Church. Built from 1856 to 1859, the neo-gothic building is the seat of the Anglican bishop of Montréal. The cathedral's 127-foot aluminum-covered steel steeple replaced a heavier stone original that was threatening to collapse. Its garden is modeled on a medieval European cloister. The cathedral donated the land on which place de la Cathédrale and the shopping complex underneath it, Promenades de la Cathédrale, were built, in return for eventual ownership of the skyscraper and the underground complex. All those subterranean corridors and levels have caused some to dub it the "floating" or "flying" church.

Turn left on:

11. Rue Ste-Catherine and head west, through the center of Montréal's shopping district. Most of the remaining department stores are along here, including Eaton and, right of the church, La Baie (or "The Bay," short for Hudson's Bay Company, successor to the famous fur-trapping firm). Movie houses, cafés, and shops line rue Ste-Catherine for several blocks.

At the corner of rue de la Montagne is:

12. Ogilvy, the most vibrant of a breed of store that appears to be fading from the scene. Founded in 1866, it strives to maintain its upmarket stature by blending tradition with tasteful marketing strategies. Its Christmas windows are eagerly awaited each year and a bagpiper announces openings, closings, and high noon. Note that Québec's language laws have rendered Eaton and Ogilvy apostrophe-less.

Continue one more block to:

13. Rue Crescent. This and nearby streets are the locus of the center-city social and dining district, largely Anglo-yuppie in character, if not necessarily in strict demographics. Pricey boutiques, inexpensive pizza joints, upscale restaurants, and dozens of bars and dance clubs draw enthusiastic, stylish consumers looking to spend money and find love or undemanding lust. This center of gilded youth and glamour was once a run-down slum area slated for demolition. Luckily, buyers with a good aesthetic sense saw the possibilities these late 19th-century rowhouses had and brought them back to life.

Turn right on rue Crescent and:

☕ **TAKE A BREAK**   For a quiet spot to munch on a croissant or sip some strong coffee, choose **Café Via Crescent,** on the left-hand side, on the ground floor of the Château Royal Hotel. Walkers who prefer a livelier setting can choose **Thursdays,** opposite, or walk a little farther up rue Crescent and get a sidewalk table at **Sir Winston Churchill Pub.**

Continue up rue Crescent, past boulevard de Maisonneuve, to the corner of rues Crescent and Sherbrooke. On this left-hand corner, and on the opposite side of Sherbrooke, is the:

14. Musée des Beaux-Arts (Museum of Fine Arts), Canada's oldest and Montréal's most prominent museum. The modern annex on this side was added in 1991 and is connected to the stately Beaux Arts original building (1912) across the way by an underground tunnel that doubles as a gallery. Both buildings are made of Vermont marble.

Turn right on rue Sherbrooke, passing, at the next corner, Holts department store, formerly known as Holt Renfrew. Continue on rue Sherbrooke, soon passing, on the right, the:

15. Maison Alcan, which has been frequently lauded for its incorporation of 19th-century houses into its late 20th-century facade. Step inside the lobby to see the results, especially over to the right.

If it's time for a rest, walk through the lobby, bearing left to:

☕ **TAKE A BREAK**   Open from early morning to late evening, **La Tulipe Noire** is a café-pâtisserie serving anything from plain coffee to chocolate cake to light meals. In good weather, it sets tables out on a small terrace on rue Stanley.

In four more blocks, on the opposite side of rue Sherbrooke, is the entrance to:

16. McGill University, probably Canada's most prestigious university. The gate is usually open. Step inside and see, just to the left, a large stone that designates the site of the native Horchelaga settlement that existed here before the arrival of the Europeans.

Also on the campus is the:

17. Redpath Museum, The building dates from 1882, and the museum's main draw is the Egyptian antiquities collection, the second largest of its kind in Canada.

Opposite the university, and just half a block south of rue Sherbrooke, on the left, is a gleaming-white sculpture called:

18. *The Illuminated Crowd* (1979), by Toronto artist Raymond Mason. Although it's frequently photographed and widely admired for its evocation of the human condition, its detractors find it sentimental and obvious. Circle it at leisure and then return to rue Sherbrooke, turning right.

One block east is the:

19. **McCord Museum of Canadian History,** 690 rue Sherbrooke, which first opened in 1921 and was substantially renovated and expanded in 1992. The private museum has an eclectic and often eccentric collection of 80,000 artifacts. It's named for its founder, David Ross McCord (1844–1930). Furniture, clothing, china, silver, paintings, photographs, and folk art reveal elements of city and rural life from the 18th to the 20th century. Amerindians are represented in the First Nations room.

WALKING TOUR 3
PLATEAU MONT-ROYAL

Start: The corner of avenue du Mont-Royal and rue St-Denis.
Finish: Square St-Louis.
Time: At least two hours, but allow longer to explore this fascinating neighborhood at length.
Best Times: Monday through Saturday during the day, when the shops are open. Boulevard St-Laurent is at its liveliest on Saturday. Many shops close on Sunday.
Worst Times: Sunday, when most stores are closed, if shopping is important to you. But for bar-hopping, evenings are fine, too.

This is essentially a browsing and grazing tour, sampling the sea of ethnicities known as Plateau Mont-Royal, north of downtown Montréal and due east of Mont-Royal Park. The neighborhood, which in recent years has seen an explosion of restaurants, cafés, clubs, and shops, is bounded on the south by rue Sherbrooke, on the north by boulevard St-Joseph, on the east by avenue Papineau, and on the west by rue St-Dominique. Monuments and obligatory sights are few along these commercial avenues and the residential side streets whose rowhouses are home to students, young professionals, and immigrants old and new. The point of this walk is to get to know established and freshly minted Montréalers and the way they live and amuse themselves.

To begin, take the Métro to the Mont-Royal station. There's a fruit stand out front. Turn left, walking west on avenue du Mont-Royal to St-Denis. Turn left. In the block between rues Mont-Royal and Marie-Anne, there's much to discover. Some highlights follow, with the caveat that things change: Stores and bistros open and close frequently; businesses do change hands.

On the left-hand side of the street is:

1. **Quai des Brumes,** 4481 rue St-Denis, a popular gathering spot for jazz, blues, and beer. There's live music most evenings, and even some afternoons. Its name means "Foggy Dock." Nearby is:

2. **Tintin,** 4419 rue St-Denis, filled with memorabilia related to the popular Belgian cartoon character from whom the shop takes its name. Across the street is:

3. **Requin Chagrin,** 4430 rue St-Denis, a retro shop with a good selection of secondhand clothing. Farther along is:

Walking Tour—Plateau Mont-Royal

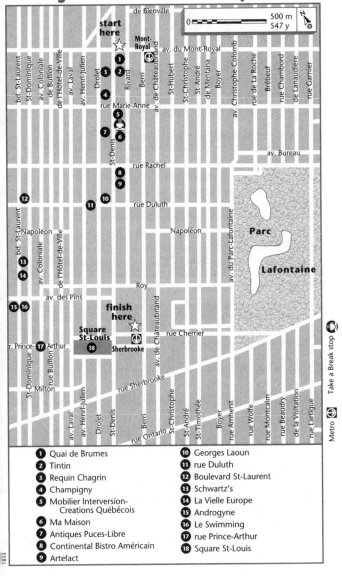

Legend:
1. Quai de Brumes
2. Tintin
3. Requin Chagrin
4. Champigny
5. Mobilier Interversion-Creations Québécois
6. Ma Maison
7. Antiques Puces-Libre
8. Continental Bistro Américain
9. Artefact
10. Georges Laoun
11. rue Duluth
12. Boulevard St-Laurent
13. Schwartz's
14. La Vielle Europe
15. Androgyne
16. Le Swimming
17. rue Prince-Arthur
18. Square St-Louis

4. **Champigny,** 4380 rue St-Denis, a large bookstore with mostly French stock. They do carry travel guides and literature in English, as well as magazines and newspapers in many languages from all over the world. It's open seven days.

Cross rue Marie-Anne. On the left-hand corner is:

5. **Mobilier Interversion–Creations Québécois,** 4349 rue St-Denis, a showroom that displays and sells contemporary Québécois furniture.

☕ **TAKE A BREAK**   At 4325 rue St-Denis, **Fondumentale** specializes in what it says—fondues as appetizers, as main courses, as desserts. Excess is not without its virtues. The turn-of-the-century house has a terrace in front and a garden.

Continue south on rue St-Denis to:

6. **Ma Maison,** 4279 rue St-Denis, with two stories of household items from around the world, including place settings, fondue sets, wind chimes, glasses, and coffeemakers.

On the right-hand side of rue St-Denis, look for the wonderfully cluttered shop called:

7. **Antiques Puces-Libre,** 4240 rue St-Denis, with three floors of 19th-century French-Canadian country collectibles—pine and oak furniture, lamps, clocks, vases, and much more.

From here, cross rue Rachel. On the left-hand side of the street is the:

8. **Continental Bistro Américain,** 4169 rue St-Denis, which is no more American than the Café Deux Magots on the Left Bank. It's populated with people who look as if they read *Le Monde*, smoke Gauloises, and see no point in shaving more than twice a week. There's often music here, if only at the upright piano in front. Just down the street is:

9. **Artefact,** 4117 rue St-Denis, with clothing and paintings by Québécois designers and artists.

On the opposite side of the street, at the corner of rue Duluth and rue St-Denis, is:

10. **Georges Laoun,** 4012 rue St-Denis, selling glasses and contact lenses. The shop carries imaginative frames that range from $160 to $2,000.

Turn right (west) along:

11. **Rue Duluth,** which is dotted with eateries that purvey Greek, Portuguese, Italian, Algerian, and Vietnamese cooking.

Continue along rue Duluth until it ends at a north-south thoroughfare so prominent in the cultural history of the city that it's known to Anglophones, Francophones, and Allophones alike simply as "The Main."

Turn left on:

12. **Boulevard St-Laurent.** Traditionally a beachhead for immigrants to Montréal, it has increasingly become a street of chic bistros and clubs. The late-night section of boulevard St-Laurent runs for several miles, roughly from avenue Viger to rue Fairmount. This trend has been fueled by low rents and the large number of industrial lofts in this area, a legacy of St-Laurent's heyday as a garment-manufacturing center. Today these cavernous spaces have been

converted into restaurants and clubs, many of which have the lifespans of fireflies, but some of which pound on for years.

Soon, there is:

13. Schwartz's, at 3895 bd. St-Laurent, as it is known by nearly everyone but the language police, who insisted on the exterior sign with the French mouthful "Chez Schwarz Charcuterie Hébraïque de Montréal." This narrow, no-frills deli serves the smoked meat against which all other versions must be measured. Vegetarians and those who require more distance from their neighbors' elbows will hate it.

Next, a few steps along, is:

14. La Vieille Europe, at 3855 bd. St-Laurent, a delicatessen selling aromatic coffee beans from many nations, sausages and meats, cheeses, and cooking utensils.

Continuing south, notice, on the other side:

15. Androgyne, at 3636 bd. St-Laurent. This gay, lesbian, and feminist bookstore is one of the best places to connect with activities in Montréal's gay community.

Opposite, on this side, is:

16. Le Swimming, 3643 bd. St-Laurent, with a bar downstairs and an upstairs hall with a dozen pool tables.

Continue down boulevard St-Laurent to:

17. Rue Prince-Arthur. Named after Queen Victoria's third son, who was governor-general of Canada from 1911 to 1916, it's a pedestrian street filled with bars and restaurants, most of which add more to the liveliness of the street than to the gastronomic reputation of the city. Establishments go by such names as La Caverne Grecque, La Cabane Grecque, Casa Grecque—no doubt visitors will discern an emerging pattern. Their owners vie constantly with gimmicks to haul in passersby, including two-drinks-for-the-price-of-one and dueling table d'hôte prices that plummet to $5 or lower for three courses. Beer and sangría are the popular drinks at the white resin tables and chairs set out along the sides of the street. Mimes, vendors, street performers, and caricaturists also compete for the tourist dollar.

Five blocks along, rue Prince-Arthur ends at:

18. Square St-Louis, a public garden framed by attractive rowhouses that were erected for well-to-do Francophones in the late 19th and early 20th centuries. On occasional summer days, there are impromptu concerts. The Square ends at rue St-Denis.

From here, bear left on rue Cherrier to catch the Métro at the Sherbrooke station, less than half a block away.

WALKING TOUR 4
MONT-ROYAL

Start: At the corner of rue Peel and avenue des Pins.
Finish: At the cross on top of the mountain.

Time: Two hours, allowing for some dawdling. If you're pressed for time, it's possible to get to the lookout in a little more than half an hour and back down the mountain in 15 minutes.

Best Times: Spring, summer, and autumn mornings.

Worst Times: Winter, when snow and slush make a sleigh ride to the top of the mountain much more enticing than a hike.

The most enjoyable way to explore Parc Mont-Royal is simply to walk up from downtown. Joggers, cyclists, in-line skaters, and anyone in search of a little greenery and space heads here in warm weather. In winter, cross-country skiers follow the miles of paths within the park, and snowshoers tramp along trails laid out especially for them. The 494-acre (200-hectare) park was created in 1876 to a plan by American landscape architect Frederick Law Olmsted, who designed Central Park in New York City as well as parks in Philadelphia, Boston, and Chicago.

Start this tour at the corner of rue Peel and avenue des Pins, at the:

1. **Downtown park entrance,** where a handy map helps to set bearings. From here, it's possible to ascend the mountain by several routes. Fit and hearty souls can choose the quickest and most strenuous approach—scaling the steep slope directly to the lookout at the top. Those who prefer to take their time and gain altitude slowly can take one short set of stairs followed by a switchback bridle path (turn left onto it) leading to the top. The approach outlined here falls somewhere in between, but points out the other alternatives as they arrive.

   Take the gravel path to the right (facing the map of the park). It has intervals of four to six steps, and parallels the wall that separates the park from the outside world. When the path dead-ends, turn left (away from the steep steps seen beside a small lookout).

   Those who have chosen the athletic route can take the next:

2. **Stairs on the right.** Fair warning: There are more than 250 steps in all, and the last 100 go straight up. For the less taxing route, stay on the wide:

3. **Chemin Olmsted (Olmsted Road),** named for the park's designer and actually the only part of his design that became a reality. Following this road will bypass a few of this tour's stops and get to the next stop (no. 6) in about 45 minutes.

   Frederick Law Olmsted designed the road at such a gradual grade not only for pedestrians, but also for horse-drawn carriages (calèches). Horses could pull their loads up the hill at a steady pace, and on the way down would not be pushed from behind by the weight of that carriage. Chemin Olmsted is closed to automobiles. Early on, it passes some beautiful stone houses off Redpath Circle, to the left. A couple of paths lead up the mountain to the right. They'll get walkers to their destination more quickly, but aren't as strenuous as the steps recently bypassed. So if the road begins to seem a little too slow, take the:

Walking Tour—Mont-Royal

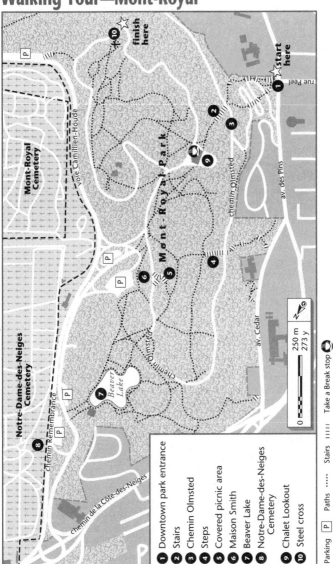

start here

finish here

rue Peel

voie Camillien-Houde

Mont-Royal Cemetery

Notre-Dame-des-Neiges Cemetery

Mont-Royal Park

chemin Olmsted

av. des Pins

chemin Olmsted

chemin Remembrance

av. Cedar

Beaver Lake

chemin de la Côte-des-Neiges

1. Downtown park entrance
2. Stairs
3. Chemin Olmsted
4. Steps
5. Covered picnic area
6. Maison Smith
7. Beaver Lake
8. Notre-Dame-des-Neiges Cemetery
9. Chalet Lookout
10. Steel cross

Parking   P   Paths ·····   Stairs ||||| Take a Break stop ●

250 m
273 y

0

1834

4. Steps that eventually appear on the right, leading to an old pump station, to the right. From here, continue in an uphill direction until you arrive at a:

5. Covered picnic area, an open-air stone-and-wood structure with a copper roof. Walk around behind the shelter and take the stairway behind it down the hill, which descends again to chemin Olmsted, minus a couple of big loops edited out of the walk. Up ahead is the back of the:

6. Maison Smith (Smith House), which was built in 1858 and has been used as a park rangers' station and park police headquarters. From 1983 to 1992 it served as a small nature museum. Nearby is the 300-foot-high Radio Canada Tower.

From the house, walk through the field of sculptures, away from the radio tower, until you reach:

7. Lac des Castors (Beaver Lake). The name refers to the once-profitable fur industry, not to the actual presence of the famously absorbed animals. In summer it's surrounded by sunbathers and picnickers and filled with boaters. In the cold winter months before the snow sets in it becomes an ice-skater's paradise. Once the pond is covered with snow, the small ski tow starts operation, tugging novice skiers up the gentle slope for practice runs down and across the pond's face.

There's a small concession stand in the pavilion here, but if you're planning to have something to eat or drink on the mountain, wait for the snack bar at the chalet at the nearby lookout. Both the chalet and the pavilion have restrooms and telephones.

Walk across the road, called chemin de la Remembrance (Remembrance Road), behind the pavilion, to enter:

8. Notre-Dame-des-Neiges Cemetery, the city's Catholic cemetery. A day of exploring cemeteries can be made moving from here to the adjacent Protestant cemetery, and then on behind it to the small Jewish, Spanish, and Portuguese cemetery, but that would be a challenging and time-consuming walk. Notre-Dame-des-Neiges Cemetery reveals some of the strata of the ethnic mix in Montréal. There are headstones, some with likenesses in photos or tiles, for Montréalers with surnames as diverse as Zagorska, Skwyrska, De Ciccio, Sen, Lavoie, Barrett, O'Neill, Hammerschmid, Fernandez, Muller, Giordano, Haddad, and Boudreault.

After wandering through this part of the cemetery, return to chemin Olmsted, pass the Smith House again, and continue along the road for a few minutes until you arrive at a water spigot embedded in a granite slab. Take the narrow, blacktopped path (not the dirt one) below it through the trees. Along the way, look for a tree trunk carved by artist Jacques Morin in 1986; part of the inscription explains—an "old, sick tree, sculpted and transformed, neither male nor female. . ."

The path leads to the:

9. Chalet Lookout. The chalet was constructed in 1931–32 at a cost of $230,000, and has been used over the years for receptions and concerts. Inside the chalet, note the 17 paintings hanging just below the ceiling, starting to the right of the door that leads into the snack bar. They tell the history of the region as well as of the French explorations in North America.

The exhibit inside is provided by the Environmental Education Center on Mont-Royal. The front terrace offers a panoramic view of the city and the river. In winter, there's a warming room for skiers here.

☕ **TAKE A BREAK** The concession stand in the chalet, usually open daily from 9am to 5pm, sells sandwiches, muffins, apples, ice cream, milk, juice, tea, and coffee. Heed the signs that ask patrons to refrain from feeding the squirrels seen begging so adorably. These cute scavengers can find plenty to eat on the mountain, but they're not above snatching food right out of people's hands.

Facing the chalet from the terrace is a path running off to the right. Follow it for about eight minutes to a giant:

10. Steel cross, seen from most vantages in the city below. Tradition has it that Maisonneuve erected a wooden cross here in 1642. The present incarnation, erected in 1924, is lighted at night, making it visible from all over the city. Beside the cross is a plaque marking the spot where a time capsule was placed in August 1992, during Montréal's 350th-birthday celebration. Some 12,000 children ages 6 to 12 filled the capsule with messages and drawings depicting their visions for the city in the year 2142, when Montréal will be 500 years old and the capsule will be opened.

To return to downtown Montréal, return along the path to the chalet terrace. On the left, just before the terrace, is another path. It leads to the 250 or so steps that descend to where this tour began, at the entrance to the park. Or catch bus no. 11 at Beaver Lake, hop off at chemin de la Remembrance and Côte-des-Neiges, and pick up bus no. 165, which goes to the Guy Métro station.

If your tour ends at the park entrance, walk down the hill on rue Peel, turn right onto rue Sherbrooke, and head one block to La Tulipe Noire pâtisserie, in the Alcan building on rue Sherbrooke at rue Stanley, for dessert and coffee or a sandwich. Enter on rue Stanley or Sherbrooke. The café is in the back of the building's lobby and has a nice terrace.

8

Montréal Shopping

Whether you view shopping as an elemental necessity or just a diversion, you won't be disappointed in Montréal. It ranks right up there with dining out as a prime activity among the natives. Most of them are of French ancestry, after all, and believe that impeccable taste bubbles through the Gallic gene pool. This state of affairs has produced a thriving fashion industry, from couture to ready-to-wear, with a history that reaches back to the earliest trade in furs and leather. In any event, it is unlikely that any reasonable consumer need—and some outlandish fantasies—cannot be met here. After all, there are over 1,500 shops in the Underground City alone, and many more than that at street level and above.

1 The Shopping Scene

Major shopping streets include Sherbrooke for international and domestic designers, art galleries, and the Holt Renfrew department store. Luxury items, including furs and jewelry, are most likely to be found along Sherbrooke. Crescent has a number of scattered upscale boutiques and numerous cafés for a break from shopping. St-Laurent covers everything from budget practicalities to off-the-wall handmade fashions. Look along Laurier between St-Laurent and de l'Epée for French boutiques, home accessories shops, and young Québécois designers. St-Paul in Vieux-Montréal has a growing number of galleries, a few jewelry shops, souvenir stands, and even shops that sell kites. At least 35 antique stores line Notre-Dame between Guy and Atwater. Ste-Catherine is the home of the city's four top-of-the-line department stores and myriad satellite shops, while Peel is known for its men's fashions and some crafts. Avenue Greene in Anglophone Westmount has some decidedly English stores. And don't forget the reliable museum shops, especially the one in the Musée des Beaux-Arts, for tasteful and unusual gifts and souvenirs. Most of Montréal's big department stores were founded when Scottish, Irish, and English families dominated the city's mercantile class, and most of their names are identifiably English, albeit shorn of their apostrophes. The principal exception is La Baie, French for "The Bay," itself a shortened reference to an earlier name, the Hudson Bay Company.

American visits have the advantage of a markdown on all prices encountered in Montréal shops due to the contrast in exchange rates between the Canadian and United States dollars (recently holding at about a 28% difference). When traveling with U.S. dollars, go to a bank to exchange U.S. cash or traveler's checks for Canadian currency. Banks usually give the best rate, and the transaction takes only a few minutes. While stores typically accept U.S. money, in dollars or traveler's checks, the exchange is likely to be less than the amount obtained in a bank. There are exceptions, however, as some stores, in an attempt to attract customers carrying U.S. funds, put out signs offering better exchange rates.

Note that when making purchases with a credit card, the charges are automatically converted at the going bank rate before appearing on the following monthly statement. In most cases, this is the best deal of all for visitors. Visa and MasterCard seem to be the most popular bank cards in this part of Canada. Discover is rarely accepted by shops, and American Express reluctantly.

BEST BUYS

Most items are priced at approximately the same cost as in their countries of origin, including such big international names as Polo and Ralph Lauren.

Exceptions are British products, including tweeds, porcelain, and glassware, which tend to cost less. Inuit sculptures and 19th- to early 20th-century country furniture are not cheap, but are handsome and authentic. Québec's daring clothing designers produce some appealing fashions at often reasonable prices. Less expensive crafts than the intensely collected Inuit works are produced, including quilts, drawings, and carvings by Amerindian and other folk artists.

STORE HOURS

Most stores are open Monday through Wednesday from 9:30am to 6pm, Thursday and Friday from 10am to 9pm, and Saturday and Sunday from 10am to 5pm. Department stores downtown tend to open at 10am and are closed on Sundays.

TAXES & REFUNDS

Save your sales receipts from any store in Montréal or the rest of Québec, and ask shopkeepers for tax refund forms. After returning home, mail the originals (not copies) to the specified address with the completed form. Refunds usually take a few months, but are in the currency of the applicant's home country. A small service fee is charged. For faster refunds, follow the same procedure, but hand in the receipts and form at a duty-free shop designated in the government pamphlet, *Goods and Services Tax Refund for Visitors*, available at tourist offices and in many stores and hotels.

BEST SHOPPING AREAS

Concentrations of prime boutiques are found on rue Crescent between Sherbrooke and Maisonneuve, while haute couture is around the corner, on Sherbrooke, notably on the blocks adjacent to the Ritz-Carlton Hotel. Antiques can be found along Sherbrooke near the Musée des Beaux-Arts, and on the little side streets near the museum.

More antiques and collectibles, one tempting shop after another, can be found on the several blocks of rue Notre-Dame between Guy and Atwater.

Upscale boutiques and a couple of art galleries can be found near place Jacques-Cartier and along rue St-Paul in Vieux-Montréal. Artists display and sell their largely undistinguished but nevertheless competent works along compact rue St-Amable, just off place Jacques-Cartier. From it, meander into a walkway called Le Jardin Amable, to find a courtyard filled with kiosks stocked with eye-catching costume jewelry and items crafted in silver and gold. Rue St-Denis north of Sherbrooke has strings of shops filled with items that are fun or funky.

With conscientious digging, there may be worthwhile items in the vast accumulation of T-shirts, collectibles, and junk in the large flea market, Marché aux Puces, at the Old Port.

Some of the best shops in Montréal are in its museums, tops among them Pointe-à-Callière, the Montréal Museum of Archeology and History in Vieux-Montréal, and the Museum of Fine Arts and the McCord Museum of Canadian History, both on rue Sherbrooke in center city.

2 Shopping A to Z

ANTIQUES

The best place to find numerous antiques shops clustered together is along rue Notre-Dame between rues Guy and Atwater. Or visit:

Antiques Puces Libres

4240 rue St-Denis (near Rachel). ☎ 514/842-5931.

Three fascinatingly cluttered floors are packed with pine and oak furniture, lamps, clocks, vases, and more, most of it 19th- and early 20th-century French-Canadian art nouveau.

ARTS AND CRAFTS

The Canadian Guild of Crafts

2025 rue Peel (at Maisonneuve). ☎ 514/849-6091.

A small but choice collection of craft items is displayed in a meticulously arranged gallery setting. Among the objects are blown glass, paintings on silk, pewter, tapestries, ceramics. The stock is particularly strong in avant-garde jewelry and Inuit sculpture. A small carving might be had for for $100–$200, but the larger, more important pieces go for hundreds, even thousands, more.

Dominion Gallery

1438 rue Sherbrooke ouest (Bishop). ☎ 514/845-7471.

Founded more than 50 years ago, this prominent gallery features both international and Canadian painting and sculpture in 14 rooms spread out over four floors.

La Guilde Graphique

9 rue St-Paul ouest, Vieux-Montréal. ☎ **514/844-3438.**

Over 200 contemporary artists are represented here, working in a variety of media and techniques, but producing primarily works on paper, including drawings, seriographs, etchings, lithographs, and woodcuts. Some of the artists can often be seen working in the upstairs studio.

L'Empreinte

272 rue St-Paul est, Vieux-Montréal. ☎ **514/861-4427.**

This is a coopérative artisane, a craftpersons' collective, a block off place Jacques-Cartier at the corner of rue du Marché Bonsecours. The ceramics, textiles, glassware, and other items on sale often occupy that vaguely defined borderland between art and craft. Quality is uneven, but usually tips toward the high end.

BOOKS

Centre Canadien d'Architecture Bookstore

1920 rue Baile (rue du Fort). ☎ **514/939-7028.**

This bookstore may be the most engrossing department of the centre, featuring a comprehensive selection of books on architecture, with emphasis on Montréal in particular and Canada in general. Volumes are also available on landscape and garden history, photography, preservation, conservation, design, and city planning.

Champigny

4380 rue St-Denis (rue Marie-Anne). ☎ **514/844-2587.**

For those who know the language or want to brush up, this two-level French bookstore is a valuable resource. It also sells tapes, CDs, and newspapers and magazines from all over the world. Authors read here on Saturday and Sunday.

Coles

1171 rue Ste-Catherine ouest (Stanley). ☎ **514/849-8825.**

This is the flagship store of a chain with many branches, stocking both French and English volumes on both general and specialized subjects.

Ulysses

480 bd. René Lévesque (near Bleury). ☎ **514/843-9882.**

This travel bookstore keeps a good stock of guidebooks, many in English, as well as travel accessories, including maps, day packs, money pouches, electrical adapters, sewing kits, coffeemakers, and pill cases. There are two smaller locations downtown, at 560 av. du Président-Kennedy at Aylmer (☎ 514/843-7222), and on the lower level of Ogilvy department store, on Ste-Catherine at rue de la Montagne (☎ 514/842-7711, ext. 362).

CLOTHING
FOR MEN

America
1101 Ste-Catherine ouest (Stanley). ☎ **514/289-9609**.

One of the many links in a popular Canadian chain, it carries casual and dressy clothes for men, including suits, jackets, and slacks. There's a women's section upstairs. Among several other local outlets is the one at Place Montréal Trust.

Brisson & Brisson
1472 rue Sherbrooke ouest (near Mackay). ☎ **514/937-7456**.

Apparel of the nipped-and-trim British and European cut fill three floors, from makers as diverse as Burberry, Brioni, and Valentino.

Club Monsieur
1407 rue Crescent (near Maisonneuve). ☎ **514/843-5476**.

Armani and Hugo Boss styles prevail, for those with the fit frames to carry them and the required discretionary income.

L'Uomo
1452 rue Peel (near Ste-Catherine). ☎ **514/844-1008**.

Largely Italian menswear by such forward-thinking designers as Valentino, Cerruti, Versace, and Salvatore Ferragamo.

FOR WOMEN

Ambre
201 rue St-Paul ouest (place Jacques-Cartier). ☎ **514/982-0325**.

Sonia Kozma designs the fashions here—suits, cocktail dresses, and dinner and casual wear made of linen, rayon, and cotton. And to go with the clothes, there are bold but complementary accessories.

Artefact
4117 rue St-Denis (near rue Rachel). ☎ **514/842-2780**.

Browse here among articles of clothing and paintings by up-and-coming Québécois designers and artists.

Giorgio Femme
1455 rue Peel (near Maisonneuve). ☎ **514/282-0294**.

Hyper-chic designer wear from Italy is not for everyone, but the ideas first promulgated here are bound to be seen on the streets not long after, if in modified form.

Kyoze
World Trade Center, 282 rue St-Jacques ouest, second floor. ☎ **514/847-7572**.

The eye-catching creations of Québécois and other Canadian designers are featured, including jewelry and accessories.

FOR MEN AND WOMEN

Felix Brown
1233 rue Ste-Catherine ouest (Drummond). ☎ **514/287-5523**.

A diverse selection of designers and manufacturers, mostly Italian, makes choices difficult. Among them are Bruno Magli, Moschino, Casadel, and Vicini.

Marks & Spencer

Place Montréal Trust, 1500 av. McGill College (Ste-Catherine). ☎ **514/499-8558.**

The British origins of this store grow less obvious as the mother chain continues to spread over several continents, but the clothing still represents a favorable price-to-value ratio.

Polo Ralph Lauren

1290 rue Sherbrooke (near Montagne). ☎ **514/288-3988.**

As he has elsewhere, the international designer has set up shop in a townhouse in the poshest part of town, near the Ritz-Carlton. Apparel for the well-heeled family, plus house accessories.

COFFEES & TEAS

Brulerie St-Denis

3967 rue St-Denis (near Duluth). ☎ **514/286-9158.**

This enticingly aromatic shop has an international selection of coffees, whole or ground to order. There are tables at which to try a cup of a likely selection, and some desserts to go with it.

DEPARTMENT STORES

Montréal's major shopping emporia stretch along rue Ste-Catherine (except for Holt Renfrew), from rue Guy eastward to Carré Phillips at Aylmer. An excursion along this 12-block stretch can keep a diligent shopper busy for hours, even days. Most of the stores mentioned below have branches elsewhere, including the Underground City.

Eaton

677 rue Ste-Catherine ouest (Alymer). ☎ **514/284-8484.**

Brought to the city in 1925, Eaton offers a conventional range of middle-of-the-road goods at reasonable prices. It is also Montréal's largest store, and it is connected to the 225-shop Eaton Centre, a shopping mall that is part of the Underground City. There is an Art Deco dining room on the ninth floor with a nautical flavor.

Henry Birks et Fils

1240 Carré Phillips (Union). ☎ **514/397-2511.**

Across from Christ Church Cathedral stands Henry Birks et Fils, a highly regarded jeweler since 1879. This beautiful old store, with its dark-wood display cases, stone pillars, and marble floors is a living part of Montréal's Victorian heritage. Valuable products displayed go beyond jewelry to encompass pens and desk accessories, watches, ties, leather goods, belts and other personal accessories, glassware, and china.

Holt Renfrew

1300 rue Sherbrooke ouest (Montagne). ☎ **514/842-5111.**

This showcase for international style focuses on fashion for men and women. On offer are such prestigious names as Giorgio Armani, Gucci,

Karl Lagerfeld, and Birger Christensen Furs, as well as sophisticated menswear from the world's top designers, quality ready-to-wear and private-label clothing, accessories, and cosmetics and fragrances. The firm began as a furrier in 1837.

La Baie

Rue Ste-Catherine ouest(near Aylmer). ☎ **514/281-4422.**

No retailer has an older or more celebrated name than that of the Hudson's Bay Company, a name shortened in recent years to The Bay, then transformed into La Baie by the language laws. The company has done business in Canada for the better part of 300 years. Its main store is a full-selection operation with an emphasis on clothing, but also offering crystal, china, and Inuit carvings. Its Canadiana Boutique features historical souvenir items and wool merchandise, including their famous Hudson's Bay blankets.

Ogilvy

1307 rue Ste-Catherine ouest (Montagne). ☎ **514/842-7711.**

Ogilvy was established in 1856 and has been at this location since 1912. Besides having a reputation for quality merchandise, the store is known for its eagerly awaited Christmas windows. Once thought of as hidebound with tradition—a bagpiper still announces the noon hour—it now contains a collection of high-profile boutiques, including Jaeger, Aquascutum, and Rodier Paris. Wide aisles and glowing chandeliers make the experience a pleasure.

GIFT ITEMS

La Cerf-Volanterie

224 rue St-Paul ouest (at St-Pierre). ☎ **514/845-7613.**

This corner shop in Vieux-Montréal is filled with dazzling kites created by the owner, who is often seen at his workbench in back. He has flown or hung kites in many of the city's public places, including Eaton Center.

Les Artisans du Meuble Québécois

88 rue St-Paul est (near place Jacques-Cartier). ☎ **514/866-1836.**

A mix of crafts, jewelry, and other objects, some noteworthy, others mediocre, make this an intriguing stop in Old Montréal. Among the possibilities are clothing and accessories for women, greeting cards, woven goods, items for the home, and handmade quilts.

McCord Museum of Canadian History Shop

690 rue Sherbrooke ouest (at Victoria). ☎ **514/398-3142.**

Part of the newly expanded museum that tells the history of the province, this shop has a small, carefully chosen selection of cards, books with an emphasis on history, coloring books, jewelry, and handcrafts.

Museum of Fine Arts Boutique

380 rue Sherbrooke ouest (Bishop). ☎ **514/285-1600,** ext. 342.

Next to the new annex of the Museum of Fine Arts, this unusually large and impressive shop sells everything from folk art to furniture. The expected art-related postcards and prints are at hand, along with ties, jewelry, watches, scarves, address books, toys, games, clocks, and even designer napkins and paper plates. The boutique is to the right of the museum entrance, a large bookstore to the left.

Pointe-à-Calliere, Montréal Museum of Archeology and History Shop

350 place Royale (rue de la Commune). ☎ **514/872-9150.**

This fully-stocked shop in the Old Customs House sells collectibles for the home, gift items, paper products, toys, and books (in French). Some are worthwhile, some not.

Tintin

4419 rue St-Denis (near av. du Mont-Royal). ☎ **514/843-9852.**

Paraphernalia related to the popular Belgian cartoon character are on sale—key rings, buttons, T-shirts, books, and postcards.

A MARKET

Marché aux Puces

Old Port, end of bd. St-Laurent. ☎ **514/843-5949.**

Montréal's largest flea market is located in the Vieux-Port (Old Port), in a cavernous dockside warehouse. It is divided into stalls where vendors sell collectibles, knickknacks, jewelry, odd lots, furniture new and used and antique, clothing both old and new, souvenirs, tools, and junk. Diligent picking through the heaps of merchandise may unearth a desirable item or two. It's open daily from 10am to 5pm, early May to mid-September. Admission is free.

MUSIC

Archambault Musique

500 rue Ste-Catherine est. ☎ **514/849-6201.**

Some French-Canadian singers are gaining fans across the border—Céline Dion among them—and their music can be found here, along with recordings by the Montréal Symphony Orchestra, Ensemble I Musici, and others, some of which may be hard to find outside of Québec. The store is across the park from the Voyageur bus terminal.

SHOPPING COMPLEXES

A unique facet of Montréal, the Underground City is a warren of hidden passageways connecting over 1,500 shops in 10 shopping complexes that have levels both above and below street level. One of the largest malls is **Centre Eaton,** 705 Ste-Catherine ouest at Aylmer (☎ 514/288-3708), next door to Eaton department store. **Complexe Desjardins** is bounded by rues Jeanne-Mance, Ste-Catherine, St-Urbain, and boulevard René-Lévesque (☎ 514/281-1870). It has waterfalls and fountains, trees and hanging vines, music, lanes of shops going off in every direction, and elevators whisking people up to one of the four tall office towers or into the Meridien hotel. **Les Cours Mont-Royal,** 1455 rue Peel at Maisonneuve (☎ 514/842-7777), a recycling of the old Mount Royal Hotel. **Place Bonaventure,** at de la Gauchetière and University (☎ 514/397-2325), is perhaps the city's largest shopping center, with 125 boutiques beneath the Bonaventure Hilton International. **Place Montréal Trust,** at 1500 McGill College and Ste-Catherine (☎ 514/843-8000), is a five-story shopping complex. **Place Ville-Marie,** opposite the Queen Elizabeth hotel on René-Lévesque, between boulevard René-Lévesque and Cathcart (☎ 514/861-9393) was Montréal's first major postwar shopping complex, called simply "PVM." **Promenades de la Cathédrale,** at the corner of rue University and rue Ste-Catherine (☎ 514/849-9925), has 255 shops on the levels below the Cathédrale Christ Church. The new **Ruelle des Fortifications,** on rue St-Pierre between St-Antoine and St-Jacques (☎ 514/982-9888), is in the World Trade Center. There are 80 upscale boutiques, centered on two fountains, one modern and one traditional. **Westmount Square,** at rue Wood and rue Ste-Catherine (☎ 514/932-0211), combines a shopping center, office complex, and condominium designed by Mies van der Rohe.

WINES

Maison des Vins de Montréal

505 av. du Président-Kennedy. ☎ **514/873-2274.**

A virtual supermarket for wines and liquors, this has a bottle to suit every need and occasion, with over 3,000 labels from 55 countries. Prices run from $10 to close to $1,000 for some prized Bordeaux vintages. It is, of course, a member of the Société des Alcools du Québec. The excellent Cheese Shoppe (☎ 514/849-1232) is located in the same building.

9

Montréal Nights

Montréal's reputation for effervescent nightlife stretches back to the 13-year experiment with Prohibition south of the border. Fortunes were made by Canadian distillers and brewers—not all of them legal— and Americans streamed into Montréal for temporary relief from alcohol deprivation. That the city enjoyed a both sophisticated and slightly naughty reputation as the Paris of North America added to the allure. Nightclub and bar-hopping remain popular activities, with much later hours than those of archrival Toronto, still in thrall to Calvinist notions of propriety and early bedtimes.

Montréalers' nocturnal pursuits are often as cultural as they are social. The city boasts its own outstanding symphony, French- and English-speaking theater companies, and the incomparable Cirque du Soleil (Circus of the Sun). It's also on the standard concert circuit that includes Chicago, Boston, and New York, so internationally known entertainers, rock bands, orchestra conductors and virtuosos, and ballet and modern-dance companies pass through frequently. A decidedly French enthusiasm for film, as well as the city's shifting reputation as a movie-production center, ensure support for cinemas showcasing experimental, offbeat, and foreign films, as well as the usual Hollywood blockbusters.

And in summer, the city becomes livelier than usual with several enticing events: the **International Jazz Festival** (early July), the **Just for Laughs Festival** (late July), the **Festival de Théâtre des Amériques** (late May), and the flashy **Benson & Hedges International Fireworks Competition** (mid-June). And every year, in late September or early October, a **Festival International de Nouvelle Danse** is held, attracting modern-dance troupes and choreographers from around the world.

For details of current performances or special events, pick up a free copy of **Montréal Scope**, a weekly ads-and-events booklet, at any large hotel reception desk, or the free weekly newspapers **Mirror** (in English) or **Voir** (in French). Place des Arts puts out a monthly calendar of events (*Calendrier des Spectacles*) describing concerts and performances to be held in the various halls of the performing-arts complex. Pick one up in most large hotels, or near the box offices in Place des Arts. Montréal's newspapers, the French-language **La Presse** and the English **Gazette,** carry listings of films, clubs, and performances in their Friday and Saturday editions.

Concentrations of pubs and discos underscore the city's linguistic dichotomy, too. While there's a great deal of crossover mingling, the parallel blocks of **rue Crescent,** rue Bishop, and rue de la Montagne north of rue Ste-Catherine have a pronounced Anglophone character, while Francophones dominate the **Latin Quarter,** with college-age patrons most evident along the lower reaches of rue St-Denis and their yuppie elders gravitating to the nightspots of the slightly more uptown blocks of the same street. **Vieux-Montréal,** especially along rue St-Paul, has a more universal quality, where many of the bars and clubs feature live jazz, blues, and folk music. In the **Plateau Mont-Royal** area, boulevard St-Laurent, parallel to St-Denis and known locally as "The Main," has become a miles-long haven of chic restaurants and clubs, roughly from avenue Viger to rue St-Viatur. Boulevard St-Laurent is a good place to end up in the wee hours, as there's always some place with the welcome mat still out.

1   The Performing Arts

PERFORMING ARTS COMPANIES
THEATER

The annual **Festival de Théâtre des Amériques** (☎ 514/842-0704) is an opportunity to see dramatic and musical stage productions that are international in scope, not simply North American, as the name suggests. In 1995 there were works from Vietnam and China as well as from Canada, the United States, and Mexico. The plays are performed in the original languages, as a rule, with simultaneous translations in French and/or English, when appropriate. Call for information.

Centaur Theatre

453 rue St-François-Xavier (near rue Notre-Dame). ☎ **514/288-3161.** Tickets $20–$30 adults, $16 students, $12 seniors. Métro: Place d'Armes.

The former Stock Exchange building (1903) is now home to Montréal's principal English-language theater. A mix of classics, foreign adaptations, and works by Canadian playwrights are presented, including such past productions as *Anthony and Cleopatra, The Visitor, The Substance of Fire, Winter in Westmount, The Search for Signs of Intelligent Life in the Universe, Dancing at Lughnasa,* and *Cabaret.* Off-season, the theater is rented out to other groups, both French- and English-speaking. Performances are held October to June, Tuesday through Saturday at 8pm and on Sunday at 7pm, with Saturday (and most Sundays) matinees at 2pm.

Saidye Bronfman Centre for the Arts

5170 Côte-Ste-Catherine (near bd. Décarie). ☎ 514/739-2301 for information, or 514/739-7944 or 514/739-4816 for tickets. Tickets $15.50–$45 adults, $15 seniors. Métro: Côte-Ste-Catherine. Bus: 129 ouest.

Montréal's Yiddish Theatre was founded in 1937 and is housed in the Saidye Bronfman Centre for the Arts, not far from St. Joseph's Oratory. It stages two plays a year in Yiddish. They run three to four weeks, usually in June and October. At other times during the year, the 300-seat theater hosts dance and music recitals, a bilingual puppet festival, occasional lectures, and three English-language plays. There's also an art gallery on the premises, with exhibits that change almost monthly. Across the street, in the Edifice Cummings House, is a small Holocaust museum and the Jewish Public Library. The center takes its name from philanthropist Saidye Bronfman, widow of Samuel Bronfman, who was a founder of the Seagram Company. She died in 1995 at the age of 98. The box office is usually open Monday through Thursday from 11am to 8pm and on Sunday from noon to 7pm—call ahead. Performances are held Tuesday through Thursday at 8pm and on Sunday at 1:30 and 7pm.

DANCE

Frequent appearances by notable dancers and troupes from other parts of Canada and the world augment the accomplished native company, among them Paul Taylor, the Feld Ballet, and Le Ballet National du Canada. During the summer, they often perform at the outdoor Théâtre de Verdure in Parc Lafontaine. In winter, they're scheduled at various venues around the city, but especially in the several halls at the Place des Arts. The fall season is kicked off by the inevitably provocative **Festival International de Nouvelle Danse,** in early October.

Les Grands Ballets Canadiens

Salle Wilfrid-Pelletier, Place des Arts, 200 bd. de Maisonneuve ouest. ☎ **514/ 849-8681.** Tickets $12–$40. Métro: Place-des-Arts.

This prestigious company has developed a following far beyond national borders over more than 35 years, performing both classical and modern repertory. In the process, it has brought prominence to many gifted Canadian choreographers and composers. It tours internationally and was the first Canadian ballet company to be invited to the People's Republic of China. The troupe's production of *The Nutcracker* is always a big event in Montréal the last couple of weeks in December. The box office is open Monday through Saturday from noon to 8pm. Performances are held from late October to early May at 8pm.

CLASSICAL MUSIC & OPERA

L'Opéra de Montréal

Salle Wilfrid-Pelletier, Place des Arts, 260 bd. de Maisonneuve ouest. ☎ **514/ 985-2222** for information, or 514/985-2258 for tickets. Tickets $23.50–$86. Métro: Place-des-Arts.

Founded in 1980, this outstanding opera company mounts seven productions a year in Montréal, with artists from Québec and abroad participating in such productions as *Madame Butterfly, Carmen, Fedora,* and *The Magic Flute.* Video translations are provided from the original languages into French and English. The box office is open Monday through Friday from 9am to 5pm. Performances are held from September to June, usually at 8pm.

Orchestre Métropolitan de Montréal

Maisonneuve Theatre, Place des Arts, 260 bd. de Maisonneuve ouest. ☎ **514/ 598-0870.** Tickets $15–$30. Métro: Place-des-Arts.

This orchestra, conducted by Agnès Grossmann, has a regular season at Place des Arts but also performs in St-Jean-Baptiste Church and tours regionally. Most of the musicians are in their mid-30s or younger. The box office is open Monday through Saturday from noon to 8pm. Performances are held from mid-October to early April, usually at 8pm. Outdoor concerts are given in Parc Lafontaine in August.

Orchestre Symphonique de Montréal

Salle Wilfrid-Pelletier, Place des Arts, 260 bd. de Maisonneuve ouest. ☎ **514/ 842-9951.** Tickets $10–$50. Métro: Place-des-Arts.

This world-famous orchestra, under the baton of Swiss conductor Charles Dutoit (and Zubin Mehta before him), performs at Place des Arts and the Notre-Dame Basilica, as well as around the world, and may be heard on numerous recordings (see "Recommended Books, Films & Recordings," in Chapter 1). In the well-balanced repertoire are works from Elgar to Rabaud to Saint-Saëns, in addition to Beethoven and Mozart. The box office is open Monday through Saturday from noon to 8pm. Performances are usually at 8pm, during a full season that runs from September to May, supplemented by Mozart concerts in Notre-Dame Basilica in June and July, interspersed with performances at three parks in the metropolitan region.

CONCERT HALLS & AUDITORIUMS

Forum de Montréal

2313 rue Ste-Catherine ouest (at Atwater). ☎ **514/790-1245.** Métro: Atwater.

Big-name rock bands and pop stars on the order of the Rolling Stones, Madonna, and R.E.M are booked into Montréal's Forum, which is also home to the Montréal Canadiens hockey team. If a concert is scheduled, printed flyers, posters, and radio and TV ads make certain that everyone knows. The Forum, which can seat up to 16,500, will move to a new, more central downtown location in 1996. The box office is open Monday through Friday from 10am to 6pm, to 9pm on days of events. Performances are at 7:30 or 8pm. Ticket prices vary greatly, depending on the attraction.

Place des Arts

260 bd. de Maisonneuve ouest. ☎ **514/285-4200** for information, 514/842-2112 for tickets, or 514/285-4275 for guided-tour reservations. Métro: Place-des-Arts.

Founded in 1963 and in its striking new home in the heart of Montréal since 1992, Place des Arts mounts performances of musical concerts, opera, dance, and theater in five halls: **Salle Wilfrid-Pelletier** (2,982 seats), where the Montréal Symphony Orchestra often performs; the **Maisonneuve Theatre** (1,460 seats), where the Orchestre Métropolitan de Montréal and the McGill Chamber Orchestra perform; the **Jean-Duceppe Theatre** (755 seats); the new **Cinquième Salle**, which opened in 1992 (350 seats); and the small **Studio-Théâtre du Maurier Ltée** (138 seats). Noontime performances are often scheduled. The Museum of Contemporary Art moved into the complex in 1992. The box office is open Monday through Saturday from noon to 8pm, and performances are usually at 8pm. Ticket prices vary according to hall and the group performing.

Pollack Concert Hall

On the McGill University campus, 555 rue Sherbrooke ouest. ☎ **514/398-4547.** Métro: McGill.

In a landmark building dating from 1899 that's fronted by a statue of Queen Victoria, this hall is in nearly constant use, especially during the university year. Among the attractions are concerts and recitals by professionals, students, or soloists from McGill's music faculty. Recordings of some of the more memorable concerts are available on the university's own label, McGill Records. Concerts are also given in the campus's smaller **Redpath Hall,** 3461 rue McTavish (☎ **514/398-4547**). Performances are at 8pm, and are usually free.

Spectrum de Montréal

318 rue Ste-Catherine ouest (at rue de Bleury). ☎ **514/861-5851.** Métro: Place-des-Arts; then take the Bleury exit.

A broad range of Canadian and international performers, usually of a modest celebrity unlikely to fill the larger Forum, use this converted movie theater. Alternative rock bands of less wattage than Pearl Jam often book nights here, for example. The space also hosts segments of the city's annual jazz festival. Seats are available on a first-come, first-served basis. The box office is open Monday through Saturday from 10am to 9pm and on Sunday from noon to 5pm. Performances are at 8:30 or 9pm.

Théâtre de Verdure

In Lafontaine Park. ☎ **514/872-2644.** Métro: Sherbrooke.

Nestled in a quiet city park, this open-air theater presents free music and dance concerts and theater, often with well-known artists and performers. Sometimes they show outdoor movies. Many in the audience pack picnics. Performances are held from June to August; call for days and times.

Théâtre St-Denis

1594 rue St-Denis (at Emery). ☎ **514/849-4211.** Métro: Berri-UQAM.

Recently refurbished, this theater in the heart of the Latin Quarter hosts a variety of shows, including pop singers and groups and comedians, as well as segments of the Just for Laughs Festival in summer. It's actually two theaters, one seating more than 2,000 people, the other almost 1,000. The box office is open daily from noon to 9pm. Performances are usually at 8pm.

A CIRCUS EXTRAORDINAIRE

Cirque du Soleil

Old Port, quai Jacques-Cartier. ☎ **514/522-2324** or 800/361-4595. Tickets $12–$39 adults, $6–$27 children. Métro: Champ-de-Mars.

Through the exposure generated by its frequent tours across North America, this circus is enjoying an ever-multiplying following. One reason, curiously, is the absence of animals in the troupe, which means that no one need be troubled by the possibility of mistreated lions and elephants. What is experienced during a Cirque du Soleil performance is nothing less than magical, a celebration of pure skill and theater, with plenty of clowns, trapeze artists, tightrope walkers, and contortionists. In Montréal from late April to early June during odd-numbered years only, the show goes on the road throughout North America during even-numbered years. Look for the yellow-and-blue tent at the Old Port. The box office is open Tuesday through Sunday from 9am to 9pm. Performances are Tuesday through Friday at 8pm, on Saturday at 4 and 8pm, and on Sunday at 1 and 5pm.

2 The Club & Music Scene

COMEDY

Last decade's explosion in comedy venues across North America has cooled. Montréal still has places to sample the fading phenomenon, perhaps because it's the home to the **Just for Laughs Festival** every summer (for information, call 514/845-2322). Those who have so far eluded the comedy club experience should know that profanity, scatological references, and assorted ethnic slurs are common fodder for performers. If patrons wish to avoid being objects of the comedians' barbs, it's wise to sit well away from the stage.

Comedy Nest

In the Hôtel Nouvel, 1740 bd. René-Lévesque (at rue Guy). ☎ **514/932-6378.** Cover $9. Métro: Guy-Concordia.

This club, newly relocated in the Hôtel Nouvel, features mostly local talent, with occasional appearances by better-known visiting comics. Shows are held Wednesday through Sunday at 8:30pm, with added shows on Friday and Saturday at 11:30pm. Drinks cost $3.75 to $6.25. The dinner-and-show package costs $18 Wednesday, Thursday, and Sunday, $24 on Friday and Saturday; dinner starts at 6:30pm.

Comedyworks

1238 rue Bishop (at rue Ste-Catherine). ☎ **514/398-9661.** Cover $3–$10, plus a one-drink minimum. Métro: Guy-Concordia.

There's a full card of comedy at this long-running club, up the stairs from Jimbo's Pub on a jumping block of rue Bishop south of rue Ste-Catherine. Monday is open-mike night, while on Tuesday and Wednesday improvisation groups usually work off the audience. Head-liners of greater or lesser magnitude—usually from Montréal, Toronto, New York, or Boston—take the stage Thursday through Sunday. No food is served, just drinks. Reservations are recommended, especially on Friday, when early arrival may be necessary to secure a seat. Shows are daily at 8:30pm, and also 11:15pm on Friday and Saturday. Drinks cost $3.75 to $6.50.

FOLK/ROCK/POP

Scores of bars, cafés, theaters, clubs, and even churches present live music on at least an occasional basis, if only at Sunday brunch. The performers, local or touring, traffick in every idiom, from metal to funk to grunge to unvarnished Vegas. In most cases they only stay in one place for a night or two. Here are a few selections that focus their energies on the music.

Café Campus

57 rue Prince-Arthur est (near bd. St-Laurent). ☎ **514/844-1010.** Cover $10 and up. Métro: Sherbrooke.

When anyone over 25 shows up inside this bleak club on touristy Prince-Arthur, it's probably a parent of one of the musicians. Alternative rock prevails, but metal and retro-rock bands also make appearances. Followers of the scene may be familiar with such groups as Bootsauce, Come, and Elastica, all of whom have appeared.

Club Soda

5240 av. du Parc (near Bernard). ☎ **514/270-7848.** Cover $15 and up. Métro: Parc.

Here, in one of the city's larger venues for attractions below the megastar level, performers are given a stage before a hall that seats several hundred. Three bars lubricate audience enthusiasm. Musical choices hop all over the charts—folk, rock, blues, country, Afro-Cuban, heavy metal—you name it. Acts for the annual jazz and comedy festivals are booked here, too.

Déjà Vu

1224 rue Bishop (near rue Ste-Catherine). ☎ **514/866-0512.** No cover. Métro: Guy-Concordia.

Upstairs, over a club called Bowser & Blue, this casual room puts on live music every night of the week. The management has eclectic tastes, hiring bands that specialize in old-time rock 'n' roll, country, blues, and whatever else takes their fancy. They run a loose, fun place with three floors and two small dance floors, and keep it relatively inexpensive.

Nuit Magique

2 rue St-Paul (at place Jacques-Cartier). ☎ **514/861-8143.** No cover. Métro: Place d'Armes.

The pumped-up Vieux Montréal night scene hasn't swamped this long-time fave, probably because it doesn't suffer delusions of consequence. No big names, a decidedly scruffy non-decor—just a pool table in back and energetic bands in front nightly. It fits like an old pair of motorcycle boots.

Le Pierrot/Les Deux Pierrots

114 & 104 rue St-Paul est (west of place Jaques-Cartier). ☎ **514/861-1686.** Cover: Le Pierrot, $2 Fri–Sat, none other nights; Aux Deux Pierrots, $3 Thurs, $5 Fri–Sat. Métro: Place d'Armes.

Perhaps the best known of Montréal's *boîtes-à-chansons*, Le Pierrot is an intimate French-style club. The singer interacts animatedly with the crowd, often bilingually, and encourages them to join in the lyrics. Le Pierrot is open only during the warmer months, with music late into the wee hours of the morning. Its sister club next door, the larger Les Deux Pierrots, features live bands playing rock 'n' roll songs year round, half in French and half in English. The terrace joining the two clubs is open on Friday and Saturday nights in summer. Le Pierrot is open only May to September, nightly. Les Deux Pierrots is open year round, Thursday through Sunday from 8pm to 3am. Drinks cost $3 to $4.50.

JAZZ & BLUES

The respected and heavily attended **Festival International de Jazz** held for 10 days every summer in Montréal sustains interest in the most original American art form. (For information, call **514/871-1881**). Scores of events are scheduled, indoors and out, many of them free. "Jazz" is broadly interpreted, to include everything from Dixieland to reggae to world beat to the unclassifiable experimental. Artists represented in the past have included Thelonious Monk, Cleo Laine, Pat Metheny, Jimmy Smith, Joe Williams, John Mayall, and B. B. King. Piano legend Oscar Peterson grew up here and often returns to perform in his hometown. There are many more clubs than the sampling that follows. Pick up a copy of *Mirror* or *Hour,* distributed free everywhere, or buy the Saturday edition of the *Gazette* for the entertainment section. These publications have full listings of the bands and stars appearing during the week.

L'Air du Temps

191 rue St-Paul ouest (at rue St-François-Xavier). ☎ **514/842-2003.** Cover $5–$25. Métro: Place d'Armes.

A Montréal jazz tradition since 1976, L'Air du Temps is an ardent jazz emporium of the old school—a little seedy and beat-up, and no gimmicks or frippery to distract from the music. The main room and an upper floor in back can hold over 135, and the bar stools and tables fill up quickly. Get there by 9:30pm or so to secure a seat. The bands go on at 10:30pm or thereabouts. L'Air du Temps doesn't serve food, just a wide variety of drinks, but there are several good mid-priced restaurants nearby. The club doesn't take reservations. It's open Thursday through Monday from 9pm to 3am. Drinks cost $2.75 to $7.75.

Les Beaux Esprits

2073 rue St-Denis (at rue Sherbrooke). ☎ **515/844-0882.** No cover. Métro: Sherbrooke.

Blues gets a wide hearing in this musical city, as demonstrated here in the thumping heart of the youthful Latin Quarter. Simple and unpretentious, the place attracts avid fans of the music, mostly of university age. Local musicians perform nightly from 8pm to 3am. Drinks cost $3 to $5.

Berri Blues

1170 St-Denis (at bd. René-Lévesque). ☎ **514/287-1241** or 800/503-4448. No cover. Métro: Berri-UQAM.

This used to be a barnlike Bavarian bierstube called Vieux Munich, with oompah bands and waitresses in dirndls. It's too early to tell whether it will flourish with its new music format, but they rotate gifted blues belters on one- or two-night stands Thursday through Saturday nights. They add a gospel brunch on Sunday. Call for starting times. Drinks are $5 to $9.

Biddle's

2060 rue Aylmer (north of rue Sherbrooke). ☎ **514/842-8656.** No cover, but a $6.50-per-person minimum Fri–Sat. Métro: McGill.

Right downtown, where there isn't much other after-dark action, this longtime stalwart is a club-restaurant with hanging plants and faux art nouveau glass that fills up early with lovers of barbecued ribs and jazz. The live music starts around 5:30pm (at 7pm on Sunday and Monday) and continues until closing time. Charlie Biddle plays bass Tuesday through Friday nights when he doesn't have a gig elsewhere. He and his stand-ins favor jazz of the swinging mainstream variety, with occasional digressions into more esoteric forms. It's open Sunday from 4pm to 12:30am, Monday through Thursday from 11:30am to 1:30am, and on Friday and Saturday from 11:30am to 2:30am. Drinks cost $5 to $6.50, and there's a mandatory paid coat check.

Le Grand Café

1720 rue St-Denis (near Ontario). ☎ **514/849-6955.** Cover up to $10. Métro: Berri-UQAM.

The French of Canada are as enthusiastic about jazz as their European brethren. As evidence, this funky joint deep in the Francophone Latin Quarter. The stage is upstairs, big enough to hold large combos and small bands. Sometimes the management brings on blues or rock as a change of pace. When it's chilly out, they stoke up the fireplace. The big windows in front give a preview of what's going on inside, and they open out in summer. It's open daily from 11am to 3am. Drinks cost $3.50 to $4.50.

Le Quai des Brumes

4481 rue St-Denis (at av. du Mont-Royal). ☎ **514/499-0467.** No cover. Métro: Mont-Royal.

Loosely translated, the name means "foggy dock," a reference of elusive significance. But it's an atmospheric place in which to listen to jazz, blues, and rock. Jazz gets lots of play upstairs in the Central Bar. The crowd has been described as "a fairly uniform group of post-sixties francophone smokers." Open daily from 2pm to 3am. Drinks cost $2.75 to $4.75.

DANCE CLUBS

As elsewhere, Montréal's dance clubs change in tenor and popularity in mere eyeblinks, and new ones open and close with dizzying frequency. For the latest fever spots, quiz concierges, guides, waiters—all those who look as if they might follow the scene by inclination or professional obligation. Here are a few that appear more likely to survive the whims of night owls and landlords. Expect to encounter steroid abusers with funny haircuts guarding the doors. Usually, they'll let you enter.

Batalou

4372 bd. St-Laurent (at rue Marie-Anne). ☎ **514/845-5447.** No cover. Métro: Mont-Royal.

An infectiously sensual tropical beat issues from this club-with-a-difference on "The Main," a hot, happy variation from the prevailing grunge and murk of what might be described as mainstream clubs. Although most of the patrons revel in their ancestral origins in the Caribbean and Africa, the sources of the live and recorded music, an ecumenical welcome is extended to all comers. Admittedly, the hip-waggling expertise of the dancers might be intimidating to the uninitiated. Things get going about 10pm every night but Monday. Drinks cost $3.50 to $7.

Hard Rock Café

1458 rue Crescent (near bd. de Maisonneuve). ☎ **514/987-1420.** No cover. Métro: Guy-Concordia.

No surprises here, now that clones have sprouted all across North America. The hamburgers are good enough and not too expensive, guitars and costumes and other rock memorabilia decorate the walls, and the usual Hard Rock Café souvenirs are available. The formula continues to work, and it gets crowded at lunch and weekend evenings. Open daily from 11:30am to 3am; the disco starts up at 10pm. Drinks cost $3.45 to $6.

Métropolis

59 rue Ste-Catherine est (near bd. St-Laurent). ☎ **514/288-5559.** Cover $5 Thurs–Fri, $8 Sat. Métro: Berri-UQAM.

Housed in a handsome old theater dating from the 1890s is this monster club that can accommodate 2,200 gyrating bodies at a time. The sound system and the light show are state-of-the-art, and there are six bars on three levels. The neighborhood is scruffy but not especially worrisome, and not far from the campus of the Université du Québec. It's open only Thursday through Saturday from 10pm to 3am. Drinks cost $3 to $5.50.

3 The Bar & Café Scene

An abundance of restaurants, bars, and cafés masses along the streets near the downtown commercial district, from rue Stanley to rue Guy between rue Ste-Catherine and boulevard de Maisonneuve. Rue Crescent, in particular, hums with activity from late afternoon until far into the evening, especially after 10pm on a cool summer weekend night, when the street swarms with people careening from club to bar to restaurant. Boulevard St-Laurent, another nightlife hub, abounds in bars and clubs, most with a distinctive European—particularly French—personality, as opposed to the Anglo flavor of the rue Crescent area. Increasingly active rue St-Paul, west of place Jacques-Cartier in Vieux Montréal, falls somewhere in the middle on the Anglophone-Francophone spectrum. It's also a little more likely to get rowdy on late weekend nights. In all cases, bars tend to open around 11:30am and go late. Last call for orders is 3am, but patrons are often allowed to dawdle over those drinks until 4am.

Le Continental Bistro Américain

4169 rue St-Denis (at rue Rachel). ☎ **514/845-6842.** No cover. Métro: Mont-Royal.

The after-curtain crowd from the Théâtre St-Denis gathers here for drinks or late meals, which range far enough afield to be called "international." A guy with a cigarette dribbling from his lips sits down at the upright piano when the mood strikes, sometimes spelled by a guitarist or two. Their music is often submerged beneath the high buzz of conversation. Designer Jacques Sabourin fashioned the revivalist deco decor, including the bar, which doubles as a display counter. It's open Monday through Friday from 11:30am to midnight and on Saturday and Sunday from 6pm to midnight. Drinks cost $4 to $7.

Lutetia Bar

In L'Hôtel de la Montagne, 1430 rue de la Montagne (north of rue Ste-Catherine). ☎ **514/288-5656.** Métro: Guy-Concordia.

Within sight of the trademark lobby fountain with its nude bronze sprite sporting stained-glass wings, this appealing bar draws a standing-room-only crowd of youngish to middle-aged professionals after 5:30pm. Later on, there's often music by jazz duos. In summer the hotel opens the terrace bar on the roof by the pool.

Lux

5220 bd. St-Laurent (near av. Laurier). ☎ **514/271-9272.** Métro: Laurier.

Lux is a favorite gathering spot for young Montréalers, in part because it never closes, not even at 5am on Christmas morning. Clients get wilder and weirder in dress and attitude as the night wears on. The converted textile mill has a circular main room with a steel floor. With two metal staircases spiraling up to a glass-domed second floor, the comings and goings arouse quite a clatter. The bar's on the ground floor, behind the café, which is surrounded by racks displaying more than 1,000 magazines.

Ritz Bar

In the Ritz-Carlton Kempinski Hôtel, 1228 rue Sherbrooke ouest (at rue Drummond). ☎ **514/842-4212.** Métro: Peel.

A mature, prosperous crowd seeks out the quiet Ritz Bar in the Ritz-Carlton Kempinski Hôtel, adjacent to its semi-legendary Café de Paris restaurant. Anyone can take advantage of the tranquil room and the professionalism of its staff, but men should wear jacket *and* tie to be sure they'll be allowed entrance. Piano music tinkles just above the level of consciousness during cocktail hour Monday through Friday from 5 to 8pm and at the dinnertime (5 to 11pm) from September to mid-May. The bar is just off the hotel lobby, to the right.

Shed Café

3515 bd. St-Laurent (north of rue Sherbrooke). ☎ **514/842-0220.** Métro: Sherbrooke.

It looks as if the ceiling is caving in on the bar, but that's intentional. There are local beers on tap, as well as good fries and oversize portions of cake on the newspaper-style menu. The crowd skews young.

Sir Winston Churchill Pub

1459 rue Crescent (near rue Ste-Catherine). ☎ **514/288-0623.** Métro: Guy-Concordia.

The twin upstairs/downstairs bar-cafés are rue Crescent landmarks. One reason is the sidewalk terrace, open in summer, enclosed in winter, and a vantage for checking out the pedestrian traffic all the time. Inside and down the stairs, the pub attempts to imitate a British public house, with marginal success. The mixed crowd is dominated by questing young professionals whose skin has cleared up—just. They mill around a total of 17 bars and two dance floors. Winnie's, on the second floor, is a restaurant with a terrace of its own. During the 5 to 8pm happy hour, they take $1 off wine and beer prices.

Le Swimming

3643 bd. St-Laurent (north of rue Sherbrooke). ☎ **514/282-7665.** Métro: Sherbrooke.

A nondescript entry and a stairway that smells of stale beer leads to a trendy pool hall that attracts as many men and women who come to drink and socialize as to play pool. Many Montréal bars have a pool table, but this one has 13, along with nine TVs and a terrace. Two people can play pool for an hour for $8, three play for $9, and four for $10.

Thursday's

1441–1449 rue Crescent (near rue Ste-Catherine). ☎ **514/288-5656.** Métro: Guy-Concordia.

Thursday's is a prime watering hole of Montréal's young professional set, who are ever alert to the possibilities of companionship among its habitués. The pubby bar spills out onto the terrace that hangs over the street. There's a glittery disco in back connected to a restaurant called Les Beaux Jeudis, in the same building. Thursday's presumably takes its name from the Montréal custom of prowling nightspots on Thursday evening in search of the perfect date for Friday. The disco opens at 9pm.

Whisky Café

5800 bd. St-Laurent (at rue Bernard). ☎ **514/278-2646.** Métro: Outremont.

Those who enjoy scotch, particularly single-malt imports like Cragamore and Glenfiddich, find 30 different labels to sample here. Trouble is, the Québec government applies stiff taxes for the privilege, so 70% of the patrons stick to beer. The decor is sophisticated, with exposed beams and vents, handmade tiled tables, and large wood-enclosed columns, but the real decorative triumph is the men's urinal, with a waterfall for a *pissoir*. Women are welcome to tour it.

4 Gay & Lesbian Bars & Clubs

L'Exit II

4297 rue St-Denis (near rue Rachel). ☎ **514/843-8696.** Métro: Mont-Royal.

A lesbian bar, welcoming women of all ages, it has pool tables and a dance floor that's put to heavy use on Friday and Saturday. The (usually) friendly staff and customers are good sources for information about lesbian and gay activities and events in the city. Occasionally there's live music, and in summer drinks are served on the terrace.

K.O.X.

1450 rue Ste-Catherine (near Amherst). ☎ **514/523-0064.** Cover $2–$4. Métro: Beaudry.

Despite the arch name, this dance space has survived and prospered, drawing an enthusiastic mixed crowd of men and women. House music in retro and progressive forms is the beat of choice, blended by

DJs who take their job seriously. Drinks and admission prices are reasonable, and there's no cover for the Sunday tea dance. The disco is open Tuesday and Friday through Sunday. Drinks cost $2.25 to $4.

5 More Entertainment

CINEMA

In Montréal, English-language films are usually presented with subtitles in French. However, when the initials "VF" (for *version française*) follow a movie title, they mean that the movie has been dubbed into French. Besides the many first-run movie houses that advertise in the daily newspapers, Montréal is rich in "ciné-clubs," which tend to be slightly older and show second-run, foreign, and art films at reduced prices. A downtown ciné-club that shows English-language films is the **Conservatoire d'Art Cinématographique,** at 1400 bd. de Maisonneuve ouest (☎ **514/848-3878**); the price of admission is $3. Old movies are also shown at no charge at the unique eatery, **Café Ciné-Lumière,** 5163 bd. St-Laurent (☎ **514/495-1796**), where headsets are provided for individual listening while dining.

In first-run movie houses, admission is $8 for adults in the evening, $5 for adults in the afternoon, and $4.50 for seniors and children all the time. Some cinemas offer $5 tickets all day on Tuesday. The **Centre Eaton,** 705 rue Ste-Catherine ouest, near the corner of rue McGill, has a complement of six modern cinemas. The female half of the moviegoing public will be interested to know that the **Palace 6** cinema, at 698 rue Ste-Catherine ouest (☎ **514/866-6991**), part of the Famous Players chain, provides 14 stalls in the women's restroom.

The **National Film Board of Canada** (Cinema ONF), 1564 rue St-Denis (☎ **514/496-6895**), shows Canadian and international films, primarily in English and French, particularly film classics. Showings are Tuesday through Sunday; call for times.

Imposing images surround viewers of the seven-story screen in the **IMAX theater** in the Old Port, at rue de la Commune and boulevard St-Laurent (☎ **514/496-4629**). Available productions are limited, so efforts are made to create films suitable for the entire family.

GAMBLING

In autumn 1993 the **Montréal Casino** (☎ **514/392-2746** or 800/665-2274), Québec's first, opened on Ile Notre-Dame in the former French Pavilion, which was left over from the world's fair called Expo '67. The casino has 65 gaming tables, including roulette, blackjack, and midi-baccarat, and 1,200 slot machines (no craps tables, though). It can accommodate 5,300 people, most of whom come to try their luck, of course, but the two restaurants have been getting good notices, and there are several bars, live shows, and two shops selling gifts and souvenirs. Gambling hours are 11am to 3am daily. No alcoholic beverages are served in the gambling areas. Patrons must be 18 or over. The relatively strict dress code prohibits such casual attire as shorts, T-shirts, sweatpants, running shoes, and denim pants of any color. To get to the casino, take the Métro to the Ile Ste-Hélène stop, which is adjacent to Ile Notre-Dame, and walk or take the shuttle bus from there.

10

Excursions from Montréal

For respite from urban stresses and demands, Montrealers need drive only 30 minutes or so to the north or east of the city to find themselves in the hearts of the resort regions of the Laurentides (the Laurentians) or Estrie. An amplitude of lakes and mountains have invited development of year-round vacation retreats and ski centers in both areas. The pearl of the Laurentides is Mont-Tremblant, at 3,175 feet (968m) the highest peak in eastern Canada. Bucolic Estrie, long known as the Eastern Townships when it was a haven for English Loyalists and their descendents, is blessed with a trio of memorable country inns on beautiful Lake Massawippi and four seasons of outdoor diversions.

1 The Laurentides (The Laurentians)

34–80 miles (55–130km) N of Montréal

Expect no spiked peaks or high ragged ridges. The rolling hills and rounded mountains of the Laurentian Shield are among the oldest in the world, worn down by wind and water over eons. They average between 980 and 1,700 feet (300m and 520m), with the highest being Mont-Tremblant, at 3,175 feet (968m). In the lower precincts, nearest Montréal, the terrain resembles a rumpled quilt, its folds and hollows cupping a multitude of lakes large and small. Farther north the summits are higher and craggier, with patches of snow persisting well into spring, but these are still not facsimiles of Alps or Rockies. They're welcoming and embracing rather than awe-inspiring.

Half a century ago the first ski schools, rope tows, and trails began to appear, and today there are 19 ski centers within a 40-mile radius, and cross-country skiing has as enthusiastic a following as downhill (the best cross-country trails are at Far Hills in Val-Morin and L'Esterel in Ville d'Esterel, and on the grounds of a monastery called Domaine du St–Bernard near Villa Bellevue in Mont-Tremblant). Sprawling resorts and modest lodges and inns are packed each winter with skiers, some of them through April. Trails for advanced skiers typically have short pitches and challenging moguls, with broad, hard-packed avenues for beginners and the less experienced.

But skiing is only half the Laurentians' story. As transportation improved, people took advantage of the obvious opportunities for water sports, golf (courses in the area now number 30), tennis, mountain biking, hiking, and every other kind of summer sport. Before long the region had gained a widespread and often-deserved reputation for fine dining and a convivial atmosphere that survives to this day. Birdwatchers of both intense and casual bent are fully occupied. Loon lovers, in particular, know that the lakes of Québec province's mountains are home to an estimated 16,000 of the native waterfowl that gives its name to the dollar coin. Excellent divers and swimmers, the birds are unable to walk on land, which makes nesting a trial, and they're identified by a distinctive call that might be described as an extended mournful giggle.

Winter or summer, a visit to any of the villages and resorts in the Laurentians is sure to yield pleasant memories. The busiest times are in February and March, in July and August, and during the Christmas–New Year's holiday period. Other times of the year, reservations are easier to get, prices of virtually everything are lower, and crowds are less dense. May and September are often characterized by warm days, cool nights, and just enough people so that the streets don't seem deserted. In May and June, it must be said, the indigenous black flies can seem as big and as ill-tempered as buzzards, so prepare for them with Cutter, Off, or Avon Skin So Soft. Some of the resorts, inns, and lodges close down for a couple of weeks in the spring and the fall. A handful are open only for a few winter months.

March and April are the season when the maple trees are tapped, and *cabanes à sucre* ("sugar shacks") open up everywhere, some selling only maple candies and syrup, others serving full meals featuring the principal product and even staging entertainments.

In mid-July, the region's annual **Fete de Vins** (Wine Festival) is held for two days in Saint-Jérôme, and the emphasis is on gastronomy and wine tasting; a dozen restaurants in the area participate.

July and August usher in glorious summer days in the Laurentians, and the last two weeks in September the leaves put on an unrivaled show of autumnal color. Skiers can usually expect reliable snow from early December to mid-April.

As for prices, they can be difficult to pin down: The large resorts have so many various types of rooms, cottages, meal plans, discounts, and packages that a travel agent may be needed to pick through the thicket of options. In planning, remember that Montréalers fill the highways when they "go up north" on weekends, particularly during the top skiing months of February and March, so plan ahead when making reservations.

Pet owners, take note: Few Laurentian resorts accept animals.

ESSENTIALS
GETTING THERE

BY CAR   The fast and scenic Autoroute des Laurentides (Laurentian Autoroute), also known as Autoroute 15, goes straight from Montréal to the Laurentian mountains. Just follow the signs to St-Jérôme. The exit numbers are actually the distance in kilometers the village is from Montréal. One likely stop, for instance, is the Laurentian Tourism House at Exit 39 in St-Jérôme, and St-Jérôme is 39km (24 miles), from Montréal. This is a comely drive, once out of the clutches of the tangle of expressways surrounding Montréal. The Autoroute des Laurentides gives a sweeping, panoramic introduction to the area, from the rolling hills and forests of the lower Laurentians to the mountain drama of the upper Laurentians.

Those with the time to meander, can exit at St-Jérôme and pick up the older, parallel Route 117, which plays tag with the autoroute all the way to Sainte-Agathe-des-Monts, where the highway ends. Most of the region's more appealing towns are strung along or near Route 117. Approaching each town, signs direct drivers to the local tourism information office, where attendants provide helpful tips on lodging, restaurants, and things to do. North of Ste-Agathe, Route 117 becomes the major artery for the region, continuing deep into Québec's north country and finally ending at the Ontario border hundreds of miles from Montréal.

Be aware that Québec's equivalent of the Highway Patrol maintains a strong presence along the stretch of Autoroute 15 between St-Faustin and Ste-Adèle, and remember that radar detectors are illegal in the province and subject to confiscation.

BY BUS   Limocar Laurentides buses depart Montréal's Terminus Voyageur, 505 bd. de Maisonneuve est, stopping in the larger Laurentian towns, including Ste-Agathe, Ste-Adèle, and St-Jovite; call 514/842-2281 for schedules. An express bus can make the run to St-Jovite and Mont-Tremblant in less than 2 hours, while a local bus, making all the stops, takes almost 3. From Montréal to Ste-Adèle takes about $1^1/_2$ hours, 15 minutes more to Val-Morin and Val-David. Some of the major resorts provide their own bus service at an additional charge.

BY LIMOUSINE   Taxis and limousines await arrivals at both Dorval and Mirabel airports in Montréal, and will take them to any Laurentian hideaway—for a price. While the fare for the one-hour trip by limo from Dorval is steep, four or five people can share the cost and dilute the pain. Mirabel is actually in the Laurentians, five minutes south of St-Antoine and 35 minutes from the slopes. Ask the standard fare to your inn or lodge when calling to make reservations. The inn usually will take responsibility for seeing that a taxi or limo is indeed waiting at the airport and may even help to find other guests arriving at the same time to share the cost.

VISITOR INFORMATION

For an orientation to the entire region, stop at **La Maison du Tourisme des Laurentides,** 14142 rue de la Chapelle (R.R. 1), St-Jérôme, PQ J7Z 5T4 (☎ **514/436-8532,** or 514/476-1840 in Montréal, or 800/ 561-6673; fax 514/436-5309), a regional tourist information office located in St-Jérôme at Exit 39 off the Laurentian Autoroute 15. Perhaps most important to the traveler, the staff can make reservations for lodging throughout the Laurentides, either by phone or in person. The service is free. The red-roofed stone cottage is off the highway to the east; take Route 158 and follow the signs. It's open daily: from late June to the end of August from 9am to 8:30pm; the rest of the year, from 9am to 5pm.

The Laurentides (The Laurentians)

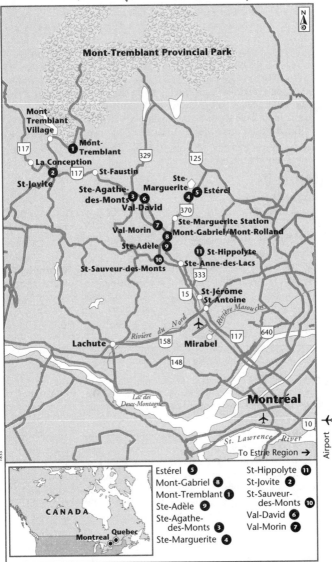

Estérel ⑤
Mont-Gabriel ⑧
Mont-Tremblant ①
Ste-Adèle ⑨
Ste-Agathe-des-Monts ③
Ste-Marguerite ④

St-Hippolyte ⑪
St-Jovite ②
St-Sauveur-des-Monts ⑩
Val-David ⑥
Val-Morin ⑦

ST-SAUVEUR-DES-MONTS

Only 37 miles (60km) north of Montréal, St-Sauveur-des-Monts (pop. 5,864) can easily be visited on a day trip. The village square is dominated by a handsome church, and the streets around it bustle with activity much of the year, so be prepared to have difficulty finding a parking place in season. Dining and snacking on everything from crêpes to hot dogs are popular activities here, evidenced by the many beckoning cafés. In season, there's a tourist kiosk on the square. Pick up some bread or pastries at nearby Page, as do the locals and Montréalers who have weekend cottages in the area.

The area is well known for its night skiing—23 well-lit trails, only three fewer than those available during the day. The mountain is wide, with a 700-foot vertical drop and a variety of well-groomed trails, making it a good choice for families. In summer, St-Sauveur-des-Monts becomes Canada's largest water park, featuring a wave pool and a mountain slide where you go up in chair lifts and come down in tubes.

The **Bureau Touristique de la Vallée de St-Sauveur,** in Les Galeries des Monts, 75 av. de la Gare (☎ **514/227-2564**), is open year-round, daily from 9am to 5pm.

WHERE TO STAY

Auberge St-Denis

61 rue St-Denis, St-Sauveur-des-Monts, PQ J0R 1R4. ☎ **514/227-4602** or 800/ 361-5724. Fax 514/227-8504. 18 rms, 24 suites. A/C TEL. $94 double; $123 suite. Additional person $10 extra. Meal plans with breakfast and/or dinner available. AE, DC, ER, MC, V.

Set back from the road, surrounded by birch and evergreens, the Auberge St-Denis looks much like a country club, complete with a heated outdoor pool and an aloof attitude at the front desk. The rooms in the old section are comfortable enough, with fireplaces and large baths. Those in the new wing are larger and more polished, with queen-size beds, fireplaces, TVs, minibars, and whirlpools. Ski and golf packages are available, and, appropriately, therapeutic massages. Reception is in the building with the green awning.

L'Auberge Victorienne

119 rue Principale, St-Sauveur-des-Monts, PQ J0R 1R0. ☎ **514/227-2328** or 514/ 667-9985. 5 rms (none with bath). $70–$80 double. Rates include full breakfast. No credit cards.

From the street this looks like a narrow brick doll's house, with a steeply pitched roof. Inside, floral touches are employed with abandon. The five bedrooms share four bathrooms, almost as good as having a private bath. There's a patio at the side for guests' use. Breakfast may include muesli, pancakes, Cheddar bread, muffins, waffles, and/or eggs. One of owners is French Canadian and a teacher; the other is Egyptian, a former banker and retired teacher.

Manoir St-Sauveur

246 chemin du Lac-Millette, St-Sauveur-des-Monts, PQ J0R 1R3. ☎ **514/227-1811** or 800/361-0505. Fax 514/227-8512. 163 rms, 37 suites. A/C MINIBAR TV TEL. Mid-June to mid-Oct, $99–$118 single or double; from $180 suite. Mid-Oct to mid-June, $89–$108 single or double; from $160 suite. Additional person $10 extra; children 17 and under stay free in parents' room. Packages available. AE, DC, ER, MC, V. Take Exit 60 off Autoroute 15.

This is one of the region's several large resort hotels, with a monster outdoor pool and a comprehensive roster of four-season activities: Its facilities include a fitness center with weight machines and a sauna, an indoor pool, racquetball, squash, tennis, in-house movies, and a shop.

An Important Note on Prices

Unless stated otherwise, **the prices cited in this guide are given in Canadian dollars,** which is good news for visitors from the States because the Canadian dollar is worth about 25% less than the American dollar, but buys just about as much.

As we go to press, $1 Canadian is worth 75¢ U.S., which means that a $100-a-night hotel room will cost only $75 U.S. a night (the tax on it is refundable), a $50 dinner for two costs only $37.50 U.S., and a $5 breakfast, only $3.75 U.S.

For a conversion chart, see "Information, Entry Requirements & Money," in Chapter 2.

A warm personality isn't included. It isn't really necessary, considering that the rooms are commodious and comfortable, blandly modern with light-wood furnishings that hint vaguely of 19th-century Gallic inspirations, both provincial and royal. The main building is easily spotted from the road, with its green roof and many dormers.

WHERE TO DINE
Les Berges

129 rue Principale. ☎ **514/227-3695.** Reservations recommended. Main courses $11.50–$22. MC, V. Daily 5–10pm. FONDUES.

It's only open for dinner, and the specialty is fondues. Name it and dip it at Les Berges: cheese, beef, chicken, seafood. One filling, reasonably priced special includes a Swiss fondue main course with a salad. The restaurant, in a house a bit out of town, has a terrace and a glass-enclosed porch. It's particularly popular in winter as a place to stop in and take the chill off. Licensed.

Les Prés

231 rue Principale. ☎ **514/227-8580.** Main courses $5.50–$13. MC, V. Mon–Thurs 11am–9pm, Fri 11am–2am, Sat 9am–11pm, Sun 9am–10pm. LIGHT FARE.

Utilizing a well-preserved Victorian house in the middle of town, Les Prés is only one of a number of fetching casual eateries clustered near the village square. Several of them are units of Montréal chains, as is this one, whose name means "the meadows." Daily lunch specials offer soup, a main course, and coffee, while à la carte main courses come with a vegetable and fries. In summer, the front porch has prized tables for watching the street activity.

MONT-GABRIEL

Mont-Gabriel is only 2¹/₂ miles (4km) from St-Sauveur-des-Monts. To get there, follow Autoroute 15 to Exit 64 and turn right at the stop sign. There's no tourist office in Mont-Gabriel, but the staff at the Auberge Mont-Gabriel and at nearby tourist bureaus can answer your questions.

Popular as a resort destination and convention spot in summer, Mont-Gabriel comes into its own each winter when guests schuss down its 21 trails and slopes and then slide back up again on the seven T-bar lifts, the triple-chair, or the quadruple-chair lift. Snowmaking equipment keeps the slopes in condition, and eight of them are lit for night skiing. Cross-country trails girdle the mountain and range through the surrounding countryside. For variety, after Mont-Gabriel's challenging trails, several other mountains are within short drives.

WHERE TO STAY & DINE

Auberge Mont-Gabriel

Mont-Rolland, PQ J0R 1G0. ☎ **514/229-3547,** 514/861-2852 in Montréal, or 800/668-5253 in Canada. Fax 514/229-7034. 126 rms. TV TEL. $100 double; $120 triple. Rates include breakfast. Children 6–12 are charged $7.50. Packages available. AE, ER, MC, V. Take Exit 64 from Autoroute 15.

Perched atop Mont-Gabriel, above highways and the valley and look-ing like the rambling log "cottages" of the turn-of-the-century wealthy, this desirable hotel is a scant 20 miles from Montréal's Dorval Airport. Set on a 1,200-acre forest estate, the resort complex features golf and tennis programs in summer, ski packages in winter. The spacious rooms in the Tyrol section are the most desirable, many with views of the surroundings hills, while those in what they call the Old Lodge are older, more rustic. Some rooms have air conditioning and minibars, but a specific request must be made for them. With the Club Package comes three meals and unlimited access to all sports facilities, and prices include tax and service charge. Rates drop for stays of two to five nights.

Dining/Entertainment: Meals are served in the resort's dining rooms and at poolside. Evenings, there's dancing in the main lodge.

Services: In summer, activity programs for children.

Facilities: Indoor facilities include a pool, sauna, whirlpool, and exercise room. The outdoor swimming pool (summer only) is heated, and there's a par-71 golf course, six tennis courts, and basketball. In summer, tobogganlike thrills can be had on the "Superglissoire" (Super Slide), a half-mile track down the mountainside that's descended on a one-person sled.

STE-ADÈLE

Highway 117 swings directly into Ste-Adèle to become its main street, boulevard Ste-Adèle, or take Exit 67 off Autoroute 15 North. The village of Ste-Adèle (pop. 7,800), only 42 miles (67km) north of Montréal, is a near-metropolis compared to the other Laurentian villages that line the upper reaches of Hwy. 117. What makes it seem big is not so much its population as its services: police, doctors, ambulances, shopping center, art galleries, and a larger collection of places to stay and dine than are found elsewhere in the Laurentians. As rue Morin mounts the hill to Lac Rond, Ste-Adèle's resort lake, it's easily seen why the town is divided into a lower part ("en bas") and an upper part ("en haut").

The **Bureau Touristique de Ste-Adèle,** at 333 bd. Ste-Adèle (☎ **514/229-2921** ext. 207), is open daily: in July and August from 9am to 7pm; the rest of the year, from 9am to 5pm.

WHAT TO SEE & DO

The main street of Ste-Adèle, **rue Valiquette,** is a busy one-way thoroughfare lined with cafés, galleries, and bakeries. But **Lac Rond** is the center of activities during the Ste-Adèle summer. Canoes, sailboats, and "pédalos" (pedal-powered watercraft), rented from several docks, glide over the placid surface, while swimmers splash and play near shoreside beaches.

In winter the surrounding green hills are swathed in white, and the **ski trails** descend to the shores of the frozen lake. Downhill ski equipment can be rented and lessons obtained at Le Chantecler resort, which has 22 trails served by six chair lifts and two T-bars. Some of the trails end right by the main hotel. At the town's **Centre Municipal,** Côtes 40/80, 1400 rue Rolland (☎ **514/229-2921**), the trails are good for beginners: three T-bar lifts carry up the slopes for the run down five different trails.

Ste-Adèle has a **theater** showing English-language movies all year.

Musée Village de Séraphin

Montée à Séraphin, off Hwy. 177 (Exit 72), Ste-Adèle. ☎ **514/229-4777.** $8.75 adults, $6.75 children 12–17, $5.75 children 5–11, children under 5 free. Mid-May to mid-June and mid-Sept to mid-Oct, Sat–Sun 10am–5pm; mid-June to mid-Sept, daily 10am–5pm. Closed mid-Oct to mid-May. Drive 1 mile north of Ste-Adèle on Hwy. 117.

This re-creation of a 19th-century Laurentian village is a mild diversion from the prevailing activities, at least for a short visit. Among the 20 structures are log cabins and slightly more refined public buildings set along dirt streets that hint at what life was like 100 years ago. Children usually enjoy the park's old-time atmosphere, and they can ride a miniature train on a 20-minute run through the village and the forest. The on-site Bar Chez Ti-Père serves old-time Québec favorites like "caribou," "ti-blanc" (highly alcoholic), and cider.

WHERE TO STAY

Auberge Champêtre

1435 bd. Ste-Adèle (Hwy. 117), Ste-Adèle, PQ J0R 1L0. ☎ **514/229-3533** or 800/ 363-2466. Fax 514/229-3534. 48 rms. A/C TV TEL. $54–$94 single or double. Rates include continental breakfast. Additional person $10 extra; children 12 and under stay free in parents' room. Lower rates for stays longer than one night and in off-season spring and fall. Packages available. Discounts and full breakfast available for stays longer than two nights. AE, DC, ER, MC, V.

Budgets can be stretched by choosing lodging places that offer accommodations alone, without the sports and meal packages promoted by the region's comprehensive resorts. A case in point is this unpretentious auberge, which is somewhere between a motel and a condominium block. Of the several different kinds of accommodations, the most appealing are the mid-priced rooms called "Chalet Nest" and "Whirlpool Nest." The least expensive for two people are the "Champêtre" rooms, equipped with a queen-size or two twin beds, cable color TV, and AM/FM radio. Besides the Franklin fireplace (with firewood) in each room, the auberge has a breakfast room with a small pool surrounded by a hedge.

Auberge Spa Excelsior

3655 bd. Ste-Adèle (Hwy. 117), Ste-Adèle, PQ J0R 1L0. ☎ **514/229-7676** or 800/363-2483. Fax 514/229-8310. 105 rms. A/C TV TEL. Old section, from $50 double. New section, $78 double including breakfast, $115 double including half board (breakfast and dinner). AE, MC, V. Coming from Montréal, take Exit 67 off the autoroute.

A number of motel units are scattered along a slope beside Hwy. 117 south of the central structure, which is about a mile north of town. They used to constitute a Days Inn, which explains the Auberge Spa Excelsior's no-frills aspect and the aesthetic differences from its more attractive main building. Architectural distinctions aside, the management maintains high standards of housekeeping, and all rooms have cable color TVs and share indoor and outdoor pools, a tennis court, squash courts, exercise room, sauna, whirlpool, and Amadéus restaurant and bar. Many rooms have balconies and some are reserved for nonsmokers.

Le Chantecler

1474 rue de Chantecler (C.P. 1048), Ste-Adèle, PQ J0R 1L0. ☎ **514/229-3555** or 800/363-2420. Fax 514/229-5593. 280 rms, 20 suites. MINIBAR TV TEL. $172–$212 double; from $292 suite. Rates include half board (breakfast and dinner). Room only (spring and fall), from $89. Children 7–12 are charged $22 extra; children 6 and under stay free in parents' room. Packages available. AE, DC, ER, MC, V. Take Exit 67 off Autoroute 15, turn left at the fourth traffic light onto rue Morin, then turn right at the top of the hill.

Sprawled across the sides of four mountains, this resort is composed of several stone buildings of varying heights, with roofs bristling with steeples and dormers. It has 22 slopes for all levels of skiers, including a 622-foot vertical drop, and a ski school, making it a logical family-vacation choice. The rooms are decorated with pine furniture made locally; most have air conditioning. Many of the suites have fireplaces, and most have whirlpool baths. A bountiful buffet breakfast is served in the glass-enclosed dining room, which overlooks the active slopes and the lake with its small beach.

Dining/Entertainment: Dining room with terrace, piano bar, disco (winter only), movies in the projection room, summer-stock theater.

Services: Babysitting, dry cleaning, ski lockers.

Facilities: Ski school, 22 runs on four mountains (including 13 night-lit runs), ski chalet (with cafeteria and bar), cross-country trails, ice skating, indoor sports complex (with a pool, sauna, Jacuzzi, squash, racquetball, badminton, and some fitness equipment), 18-hole and lit 9-hole golf courses, six lit tennis courts, windsurfing, canoeing, paddleboats, rowboats, mountain bikes.

L'Eau à la Bouche

3003 bd. Ste-Adèle (Hwy. 117), Ste-Adèle, PQ J0R 1L0. ☎ **514/229-2991** or 800/363-2582 from Montréal. Fax 514/229-7573. 23 rms, 2 suites. A/C TV TEL. $135 double; $220 suite. Rates include breakfast. Packages available. AE, DC, ER, MC, V.

L'Eau à la Bouche started as a roadside restaurant and the chef-owners later added the separate hotel. It's a member of the international Relais & Châteaux consortium of inns and small hotels, an organization that places its emphasis on gastronomy rather than physical exertion. That it does here, and admirably, as my separate recommendation of its restaurant suggests (see "Where to Dine," below). However, the hotel faces the Mont-Chantecler ski trails, is across the road from a golf course, and has a heated outdoor pool. Inside is a large living room with a brick fireplace and bar and sofas set about in conversation groups. Substantial breakfasts are served there, at tables with bentwood chairs and green-and-white checkered cloths. The bedrooms are comfortably forgettable, with queen- or king-size beds, ceiling fans, and reproductions of Québec country furniture. The large bathrooms have hairdryers and robes. All rooms are large enough for sitting areas, and six also have fireplaces and balconies or patios. No elevator and no porters, but help with luggage can be obtained if necessary.

A Bed & Breakfast

Bonne Nuit, Bonjour

1980 bd. Ste-Adèle (Hwy. 117; C.P. 2168), Ste-Adèle, PQ J0R 1L0. ☎ **514/229-7500.** 6 rms, 4 with bath. Sun–Thurs, $65 double with or without bath; Fri–Sat and holidays, $75 double. Rates include breakfast. Weekend packages available. MC, V. Driving north on Hwy. 117, watch for the stone fence with a sign on the left.

Almost hidden in a stand of cedar beside Hwy. 117 stands this stone house with two dormer windows and pink shutters. Inside is a sitting room with a rock fireplace, a small TV room, and a breakfast solarium looking out on a garden with a brook running through it. Two of the simply furnished rooms share a large bath, while the others have private baths. Room 5 has its own balcony. The outdoor swimming pool is unusual for a small B&B.

WHERE TO DINE

✪ L'Eau à la Bouche

3003 bd. Ste-Adèle (Hwy. 117). ☎ **514/229-2991** or 800/363-2582 from Montréal. Reservations recommended. Main courses $19.50–$29.50; fixed-price lunch from $15; fixed-price five-course dinner $54. AE, MC, V. Sun–Fri 11:30am–2pm and 6–9pm, Sat 6–9pm. FRENCH.

Owners Anne Desjardins and Pierre Audette leave no doubt where their priorities lie. Their nearby hotel (see above) is entirely satisfactory, but this, the restaurant, is their love child, and it has the glow-in-the-dark reviews to prove it. False modesty isn't a factor—*l'eau à la bouche* means "mouth-watering," and the kitchen delivers. The faux Provençal interior employs heavy ceiling beams, white plaster walls, and pine paneling to set the mood. On one occasion, the pre-appetizer was a dollop of salmon tartare laced with flecks of ginger and sweet red pepper. It provided an interlude to appreciate the generous martinis that exceed the skimpy Québec norm and to study the carefully assembled wine list. The captain proves to be a trustworthy guide to the formidable cellar. A good deal is the three glasses of vintage clarets for $30, which can accompany a choice of four different fixed-price meals that range from $45 to $80. Native ingredients and hefty portions are meshed with nouvelle presentations, as with the fanned leaves of rosy duck breast garnished with slivered broccoli and a timbale of puréed sweet potato. Fiddleheads appear in their short spring season paired with baby asparagus heads; game dishes arrive in fall. Desserts are impressive, but the cheese plate—pungent nubbins of French and Québec varieties delivered with warm baguette slices—is special. The young staff contrives to be both efficient and unintrusive. A meal here might well be the most memorable—and pricey—dining experience of a Laurentian visit.

Restaurant La Bruyère

173 rue Morin (at rue de Chantecler). ☎ **514/229-4417.** Main courses $14–$20. AE, MC, V. Tues–Fri 4:30–11pm, Sat 3–11pm, Sun noon–10pm. INTERNATIONAL.

A favorite dining place in Ste-Adèle, the outdoor patio bar is first in view. There's plenty of room there and in the L-shaped dining room, which sports linen tablecloths. The chef-owners perform behind the semi-open counter inside the front door, sending out unsurprising but generally successful versions of onion soup, seafood crêpes, and garlicky escargots. These are followed by surf and turf, rabbit, or shrimp provençal. Fondues are both main courses and desserts, with 10 different versions. Don't make a special trip, but this place is entirely satisfactory when you're in the neighborhood.

STE-MARGUERITE & ESTÉREL

To get to Ste-Marguerite (pop. 2,000) or the even less populous Estérel, only two miles apart, follow Autoroute 15 north to Exit 69. Or if driving from Ste-Adèle, look for a street heading northeast named chemin Ste-Marguerite. It becomes a little road that crosses the Laurentian Autoroute (at Exit 69), bridges the Rivière du Nord, and leads into an area of many lakes bordered by upscale vacation properties.

Ste-Marguerite and Estérel are 53 miles (85km) and 55 miles (88km) north of Montréal, respectively. In summer, information about the area is available from Pavillon du Parc, 74 chemin Masson, in Ste-Marguerite-du-Lac-Masson (☎ 514/228-3525); year-round, go to the nearby tourist bureau of Ste-Adèle (see above).

WHERE TO STAY & DINE IN ESTÉREL

Hôtel L'Estérel

Bd. Fridolin-Simard (C.P. 38), Ville d'Estérel, PQ J0T 1E0. ☎ **514/228-2571** or 800/363-3623 from Montréal. Fax 514/228-4977. 135 rms. A/C TV TEL. $252–$309 double. Rates include half board (breakfast and dinner), use of all indoor facilities and the outdoor tennis courts, and service. Lower rates Dec 23–May. Discounts for stays of three or five nights. Packages available. AE, DC, ER, MC, V. Take the Limocar bus from Montréal into Ste-Adèle; the hotel picks up guests there.

One of the most prominent Laurentian resorts lies a few miles past Ste-Marguerite in the town of Estérel. Almost a town in itself, this year-round complex is capable of accommodating 300 guests on a 5,000-acre estate with three linked lakes, and offers most of the outdoor activities that might be wished. Occupying an expanse of otherwise vacant lakeshore, with an unnecessarily large illuminated sign on its side, L'Estérel offers conventional rooms with private bath and color TV. Those with a view of the lake are more expensive than those looking into the surrounding trees. For a special winter experience, inquire about the dogsled trips through the woods and over the frozen lake.

Facilities: 53 miles (85km) of cross-country ski trails, nearby downhill skiing, ice skating on a rink, 18-hole golf course and a golf school, tennis, racquetball, nature trails, horseback riding, sailing, parasailing, waterskiing, canoeing, pedalboats, badminton, volleyball, hot-air ballooning, snowshoeing, ice fishing, dog sledding.

WHERE TO DINE IN STE-MARGUERITE

✪ Le Bistro à Champlain

75 chemin Masson. ☎ **514/228-4988.** Reservations recommended. Main courses $15–$25; fixed-price three-course dinner $23; *menu dégustation* $52. AE, MC, V. Summer, Tues–Sat 6–10pm, Sun noon–10pm; the rest of the year, Thurs–Sat 6–10pm, Sun noon–10pm. FRENCH.

On the shore of Lac Masson is one of the most honored restaurants in the Laurentians. Its 1864 building used to be a general store, and it retains the original rough-hewn board walls, exposed beams, wooden ceiling, and cash register. Gastronomy, not hardware, is now the motivation for customers who routinely motor up from Montréal for dinner. The 35,000-bottle cellar is a big reason, and 20 of the stocked wines can be sampled by the glass. Superior guidance is provided by sommelier François Chartier, who in 1994 was named the best in his profession in an international competition hosted in Paris. Tours of the cellar are often conducted by Chartier or his equally enthusiastic boss, a practicing radiologist. They will gladly recommend a claret to complement a main course of fresh lamb from the region, lightly smoked in the restaurant. The crusty baguettes served at every meal are baked on site.

VAL-DAVID & VAL-MORIN

Follow Hwy. 117 north to Exit 76 or 78, respectively, to reach Val-David or Val-Morin.

To those who know it, the faintly bohemian enclave of **Val-David** (pop. 3,225), 50 miles (80km) north of Montréal, conjures up images of chalet and cabin hideaways set among abruptly rising hills rearing above ponds and lakes, and laced with creeks tumbling through fragrant forests. The village celebrates its 75th anniversary in 1996.

Val-Morin (pop. 1,400) has its own special lure: the Far Hills Inn. The neighboring villages, only 2 miles apart, together sponsor an annual arts festival during the first two weeks of August.

There's no **tourist office** in Val-Morin, but Val-David has one, on the main drag at 2501 rue de l'Eglise (☎ **819/322-1515**). It's open daily: June 20 to Labor Day from 9am to 7pm; September 5 to June 19th from 10am to 4pm. Another possibility for assistance is **La Maison du Village,** a cultural center in a two-story wooden building at 2495 rue de l'Eglise (☎ **819/322-3660**).

Note that this far north into the Laurentians, the telephone area code changes to 819.

In Val-Morin
Where to Stay & Dine
Far Hills Inn

Val-Morin, PQ J0T 2S0. ☎ **819/322-2014** or 800/567-6636 from Montréal. Fax 819/322-1995. 72 rms. TEL. $198 double. Rates include half board (breakfast and dinner). Children 11 and under stay for half price in parents' room. Packages available. AE, ER, MC, V. Leave the autoroute at Exit 76, go through Val-Morin, and follow the signs up into the hills for almost 3 miles.

Well away from main roads, this stone-and-clapboard inn is set in the midst of a lavish botanic garden that keeps two gardeners employed full-time. The inn has a large public room with picture windows and two sitting areas. A large outdoor pool is cut into the hillside below the main building. The bedrooms are comfortable enough, but not fancy, and guests who are adrift without cable television or computer ports had best seek other accommodation. Some rooms have air conditioning.

Dining/Entertainment: The pine-paneled dining room with beamed ceiling and picture windows is the setting for meals that employ local produce whenever possible. The wine list features French bottlings, and several are available by the glass. When making reservations, ask for a table overlooking the grounds. Diners who aren't overnight guests can expect to pay about $35 for a five-course dinner. Patio brunches in summer are enjoyable, and the Panorama piano bar has music several nights a week.

Facilities: A cross-country ski school and 62 miles of cross-country trails; motor-free lake and indoor and outdoor pools; sauna; tennis, squash, and racquetball courts; Ping-Pong; hiking and mountain climbing; canoeing, sailing, and paddleboating. Golf courses and horse trails nearby.

In Val-David
What to See & Do

Val-David is small, so park anywhere and meander at leisure. A favorite activity here is visiting the studios of local artists, including the pottery workshop of **Kinya Ishikawa,** at 2435 rue de l'Eglise (☎ 819/322-6868), where you can view the eponymous artist's work and discuss it with him.

Or have a picnic beside the North River in the **Parc des Amoureax.** It has plenty of benches, and some parking spaces on the approach to the park, which is 2¹/₂ miles (4km) from the main road through town. Watch for the sign SITE PITTORESQUE and turn at chemin de la Rivière.

Val-David sits astride a 124-mile (200km) parkway that's a trail for cycling in summer and for cross-country skiing in winter.

The first two weeks of August herald Val-David's annual **Village d'Art festival,** when painters, sculptors, ceramicists, jewelers, pewtersmiths, and other craftspeople display their work. There are concerts and other outdoor activities.

Le Village du Père Noël

Hwy. 117. ☎ **819/322-2146**. Admission $7, free for children 12 and under. Mid-May to mid-June, Sat–Sun 10am–6pm; mid-June to Labor Day, daily 10am–6pm. Closed Labor Day to early May.

Younger children may be diverted by a visit to this "summer home of Santa Claus," located in Val-David since 1954. Besides Kris's house, set in a mock alpine village painted in blazing colors, there are animals, games, boats, a picnic area, fast food, and a room filled with 38,000 balls meant for plunging.

Where to Stay

Auberge du Vieux Foyer

3167 chemin Doncaster, Val-David, PQ J0T 2N0. ☎ **819/322-2686** or 800/567-8327 in Canada. Fax 819/322-2687. 22 rms, 3 chalets. $148–$190 double; $230 chalet for two. Rates include half board (breakfast and dinner). Additional person $65 extra. Weekly rates, off-season rates, and packages available. MC, V. Follow the signs through the town about 1 1/2 miles (3km) to the Swiss-style inn, which stands beside its own private pond.

In the tidy main living room, armchairs are drawn up to the big fireplace. The guest rooms are smallish and plain vanilla, with views of the surrounding forested hills. Some have whirlpools. There are also three chalets that hold up to eight people. With the auberge's popularity and limited number of rooms, advance reservations are a necessity at most times of the year; in winter, at least two months in advance, if possible.

Dining/Entertainment: The dining room features French fare, serving Sunday brunch, a buffet, or dinner to both guests and non-guests. A small bar is attached.

Facilities: Pool, table tennis, and indoor shuffleboard; bicycles, pedalboats, and whirlpool; a heated outdoor pool; cross-country skiing; skating rink.

La Maison de Bavière

1472 chemin de la Rivière, Val-David, PQ J0T 2N0. ☎ **819/322-3528**. 4 rms. $65, $75, or $110 double. No credit cards. Take Exit 76 off Autoroute 15; turn right at the first traffic light, then turn left at the first street.

This bed-and-breakfast has an excellent location beside both the North River and the new cycling and cross-country ski trail that spans the entire Laurentian chain. The owners strive for a homey atmosphere, from the soft duvets on the beds to the hand-painted doors reminiscent of Bavaria. Guests eat in the dining nook under a skylight and share a reading room with a wood-burning stove. The guest rooms are named after German composers. The Beethoven Room has five windows overlooking the river, a free-standing bathtub in the bedroom, and a private deck. Smoking is not permitted in the house.

Where to Dine

Au Petit Poucet

1030 Hwy. 117. ☎ **819/322-2246**. Reservations recommended for weekends. Sandwiches $5.65–$9.20; main courses $5.65–$13; buffet (Sat–Sun) $15.40, half price for children 12 and under. AE, MC, V. Sun–Thurs 8am–10pm, Fri–Sat 8am–1am. QUÉBÉCOIS.

If you're driving north on Hwy. 117, this roadside restaurant is a possible lunch stop, on the right-hand side just before the Val-David turnoff. Large windows provide a pleasant vista while awaiting meals that center around maple-smoked ham, served a variety of ways, including sandwiches. Other offerings include meat pies, barbecued chicken, or pigs' knuckles with mashed potatoes and gravy. A buffet is served on Saturday and Sunday. Breakfast is a good bet too, with ample portions of simple foods.

Le Grand Pa

2481 rue de l'Eglise. ☎ **819/322-3104.** Pizzas and sandwiches $4–$14; main courses $16–$26. MC, V. Sun and Tues–Thurs noon–11pm, Fri–Sat noon–midnight. ITALIAN/CANADIAN.

In the middle of the town, near the tourist information office, an open deck reaches out to the sidewalk. It's crowded with white resin chairs and tables, where locals dig into a dozen varieties of pizzas, baked in the brick oven inside. With their puffy crusts and fresh ingredients, in 8-inch and 12-inch sizes, they're the star attractions, often taken with pitchers of beer or sangría. Full meals are also available, and in summer they fire up a barbecue pit. Friday and Saturday nights they lay on live music by small combos.

STE-AGATHE-DES-MONTS

With a population approaching 10,000, Ste-Agathe-des-Monts, 53 miles (85km) north of Montréal, is the largest town in the Laurentians. Follow Autoroute 15 north to Exit 83 or 86. Ste-Agathe marks the end of the autoroute.

Early settlers and vacationers flocked here in search of lakefront footage on Lac des Sables, and business and industry followed the crowds. Ste-Agathe's main street, rue Principale, is the closest to citification in these timeless mountains, but it's only a touch of urbanity. Follow rue Principale from the highway through town and end up at the town dock on the lake. Watch out for four-way stops along the way.

The dock and surrounding waterfront park make Ste-Agathe a good place to pause for a few hours. One possibility is renting a bicycle from **Jacques Champoux Sports,** 74 rue St-Vincent, for the 3-mile ride around the lake. Summer waterskiing and lake cruises lure many visitors into lingering for days. The motels near town on Hwy. 117 are convenient for a night or two, but for longer stays, consider a lakeside lodge.

The **Bureau Touristique de Ste-Agathe-des-Monts,** 190 rue Principale est (☎ **819/326-0457**), is open daily: from 9am to 8:30pm in summer, 9am to 5pm the rest of the year.

WHAT TO SEE & DO

Get your bearings by taking an **Alouette cruise** (☎ **819/326-3656**), which departs from the dock at the foot of rue Principale from mid-May to late October. It's a 50-minute, 12-mile voyage on a boat equipped with a bar and running commentary of the sights that observes, among other things, that Ste-Agathe and the Lac des Sables are famous for waterski competitions and windsurfing. The cost for the

Alouette cruise is $10 for adults, $9 for seniors with ID, and $5.50 for children 5 to 15. Children under 5 are free. There are half a dozen departures a day; call for exact times.

WHERE TO STAY

Auberge du Comte de Watel

250 rue St-Venant, Ste-Agathe, PQ J8C 2Z7. ☎ **819/326-7016** or 800/363-6478. Fax 819/326-7556. 21 rms. A/C TV TEL. $118 double. Rates include breakfast in high and shoulder season. Additional person $20 extra; children 15 and under stay free in parents' room. Prices drop 17% or more off-season. AE, DISC, MC, V. Free parking.

A stone's throw from the auberge recommended below, the three-story Watel is across the road from the lake, beach, and docks. Some of the otherwise ordinary rooms have double whirlpool baths and refrigerators. The Watel has an outdoor swimming pool with a deck, some exercise equipment, and a TV lounge. The licensed dining room welcomes the public for lunch or dinner. Overnight guests, however, are charged only $22 beyond the price of the room for the four-course dinner.

Auberge du Lac des Sables

230 rue St-Venant, Ste-Agathe, PQ J8C 2Z7. ☎ **819/326-3994** or 800/567-8329. Fax 819/326-7556. 19 rms. A/C TV. $78–$118 double. Rates include breakfast. Additional person $15 extra. AE, DISC, MC, V.

All the rooms in this small lakefront inn have whirlpool baths, their chief distinguishing feature. Those with double Jacuzzis and a view of the lake are slightly more expensive. There's a small terrace overlooking the lake, a good vantage for watching the sunset. Downstairs is a games room with a pool table and pinball machine. The auberge is about $1^{1}/_{2}$ miles from the village center and within walking distance of the beach and boating. English is spoken by the hosts, who also own the Auberge du Comte de Watel (see above).

Auberge La Sauvagine

1592 Rte. 329 nord (R.R. 2), Ste-Agathe, PQ J8C 2Z8. ☎ **819/326-7673**. 9 rms, 7 with bath. $75–$130 double with or without bath. MC, V.

For something a little different, check this out—an auberge housed in a deconsecrated chapel. (An order of nuns added the chapel when they ran the property as a retirement home.) Antiques and semi-antiques are scattered through the public and private spaces. Only two rooms share a bath. A TV is available to guests in the living room. The restaurant, open Wednesday through Sunday for dinner only, offers a three-course table d'hôte for $37. Make reservations even if you're staying overnight. The inn is $1^{1}/_{4}$ miles (2km) north of Ste-Agathe, on the road to St-Donat.

WHERE TO DINE

Chez Girard

18 rue Principale Ouest, St-Agathe-des-Monts, PQ J8C 1A3. ☎ **819/326-0922**. Reservations recommended. Main courses $14.50–$29.50; three-course table d'hôte lunch $7.50–$13; four-course table d'hôte dinner $20–$32. AE, ER, MC, V. July–Aug, Tues–Sun 10am–11pm; Sept–June, Mon–Sat 5–10pm, Sun 10am–2pm (brunch) and 5–10pm. FRENCH.

Head toward the town dock and near the end of rue Principale, on the left, is a Québec-style house with a crimson roof. That's Chez Girard. In good weather diners can sit on the terrace overlooking the lake. Game is a central interest of the kitchen; it can be heavy on warm days, but tasty on cool nights as summer fades. Among the possibilities are guinea hen with fragrant pheasant sausage, escargots and mushrooms in a pastry shell, and venison tournedos with wild-grape sauce.

The auberge also has lodgings, five rooms and three suites, in two village houses. Some units have fireplaces. They go for $100 to $120 double with breakfast, $125 to $170 double with half board (breakfast and dinner); suites are $110 with breakfast.

ST-FAUSTIN

St-Faustin, which lies 16 miles (25km) north of Ste-Agathe and 71 miles (115km) north of Montréal, is not a tourist town, just a commonplace mountain village with a church. The main attraction is over on the left when driving north: Mont-Blanc, the second-highest peak in the Laurentians. To get here, follow Hwy. 117 north from Ste-Agathe. It's just south of St-Jovite.

The **Bureau Touristique de St-Faustin,** 1535 Rte. 117 (☎ **819/ 688-3738**), is open daily: from 9am to 8pm in summer, 9am to 5pm the rest of the year.

WHERE TO STAY & DINE

Hôtel Mont-Blanc

Rte. 117 (C.P. 122), St-Faustin, PQ J0T 2G0. ☎ **819/688-2444** or 800/567-6715. Fax 819/688-6112. 53 rms, 3 suites. TV. Mid-Mar to early Apr and late Nov to mid-Feb, $180–$272 double. Mid-Feb to mid-Mar, $198–$286 double. Suites: Mid-Mar to early Apr and late Nov to mid-Feb, $269, mid-Feb to mid-Mar, $280. Rates include half board (breakfast and dinner) and two lift tickets. Lower rates for stays of two or more days. Weekend specials and packages available. AE, MC, V. Closed mid-Apr to late Nov.

Open only in winter, Mont-Blanc ski resort, beside the highway at the base of Mont-Blanc, has 35 ski trails and eight ski lifts, including one quad chair lift, and snowmaking equipment to cover 80% of the trails. The lodge suffers from heavy traffic during the ski season, and looks it, especially in the public areas. This has been offset, in part, by new rugs and furnishings in many of the bedrooms. The rooms on the third floor may be the best, with duvets on the beds and scatterings of country antiques. Most rooms have a sofa bed. The suites have marble fireplaces and Jacuzzis. Check in by 4:30pm or risk losing the room.

Dining/Entertainment: Le Chamonix dining room, cafeteria, bar.
Services: Babysitting.
Facilities: Ski school, ski shop, indoor and outdoor pools, exercise room, Jacuzzis, steam baths, saunas.

ST-JOVITE & MONT-TREMBLANT

Follow Hwy. 117 some 23 miles (37km) north from Ste-Agathe to the St-Jovite exit. It's 76 miles (122km) north of Montréal. To get to Mont-Tremblant, turn right on Route 327, just before the church in St-Jovite; most vacationers make their base at one or another of the resorts or lodges scattered along Route 327. Mont-Tremblant is 28 miles (45km) north of Ste-Agathe and 80 miles (130km) north of Montréal.

Tourist information, including maps of local ski trails, is available at the **Bureau Touristique de Mont-Tremblant,** rue du Couvent at Mont-Tremblant (☎ 819/425-2434), open daily, from 9am to 9pm in summer, and 9am to 5pm the rest of the year; and from the **Tourist Bureau of Saint-Jovite/Mont-Tremblant,** 305 chemin Brébeuf in St-Jovite (☎ 819/425-3300), open daily, from 9am to 7pm in summer, and 9am to 5pm the rest of the year.

St-Jovite (pop. 4,118) is the commercial center for the most famous and popular of all Laurentian districts, the area surrounding Mont-Tremblant, at 2,135 feet (650m) the highest peak in the Laurentians.

In 1894 the provincial government set aside almost 1,000 square miles of wilderness as **Mont-Tremblant Park,** and the foresight of this early conservation effort has yielded outdoor enjoyment to skiers and four-season vacationers ever since.

In summer, water-sports lovers come to revel in the region's lakes and rivers; in winter, the ski centers of Mont-Tremblant and Gray Rocks lure snow bunnies to their miles of cross-country trails and snowmobile terrain. The autumn spectacle of brilliant foliage in the Laurentians can be seen to great advantage from the many chair lifts at Mont-Tremblant.

The mountain's name comes from a legend of the area's first inhabitants. When the first Amerindians arrived here early in the 17th century, they named the peak after their god, Manitou. When humans disturbed nature in any way, Manitou became enraged and made the great mountain tremble—*montagne tremblante.*

St-Jovite, a pleasant community, provides all the expected services, and its main street, rue Ouimet, is lined with cafés and shops, including Le Coq Rouge, which sells folk art and country antiques. The village of Mont-Tremblant, though several miles nearer the large resorts and the mountain itself, has only the most basic services, including a market and post office but no pharmacy.

WHAT TO SEE & DO

Water sports in summer are as popular as the ski slopes and trails in winter, because the base of Mont-Tremblant is surrounded by no fewer than 10 lakes: Lac Tremblant, a gorgeous stretch of water 10 miles long; and also Lac Ouimet, Lac Mercier, Lac Gelinas, Lac Desmarais, and five smaller bodies of water, not to mention rivers and streams. From June to mid-October, **Grand Manitou Cruises,** chemin Principale, in Mont-Tremblant (☎ 819/425-8681), offers a 75-minute narrated tour of Lac Tremblant, focusing on its history, nature, and legends.

Mont-Tremblant, which has the same vertical drop—3,175 feet— as Mont-Ste-Anne near Québec City, draws the biggest downhill ski crowds in the Laurentians. Founded in 1939 by Philadelphia millionaire Joe Ryan, **Station Mont-Tremblant** is one of the oldest ski areas in North America, and the first to create trails on both sides of a mountain. It was the second in the world to install a chair lift. There are higher mountains with longer runs and steeper pitches, but something about Mont-Tremblant compels people to return time and again.

By the late 1980s the resort was in need of refurbishment and, under new management since 1991, it's on its way to becoming a world-class resort year-round. Today Mont-Tremblant has the snowmaking capability to cover 328 acres, making skiing possible from early November to late May, with more than 30 trails open at Christmastime (as opposed to 9 in 1992). Station Mont-Tremblant now has 43 downhill runs and trails, including the recently opened Dynamite and Verige trails, with 810-foot (245m) and 745-foot (225m) drops, respectively, and the Edge, a peak with two gladed trails. The several lifts are for gondolas and chairs, no T-bars.

On nearby Lac Ouimet stands **Gray Rocks** resort, the first resort built in the Laurentians. It actually was established in 1896, by George Wheeler of Chazy, New York, as a sawmill, but by 1906, and a quirk of destiny, had become better known as an inn. Its low mountain slopes make it particularly popular with families.

The Laurentians region, however, is known for more than its down-hill skiing. It also sees plenty of cross-country action on 56 miles (90km) of maintained trails. And in summer there's no lack of things to do. Choose from championship golf, tennis, horseback riding, boating, swimming, biking, and hiking—for starters.

Rivers run through it too, connecting all those lakes. An organization called **Escapade Nature** in Sainte-Agathe-des-Monts (☎ **819/ 326-3799**) conducts canoe trips along the Rivers Diable and Rouge, from a few hours in duration to made-to-measure expeditions of up to two weeks, from June through September. The $3^1/_2$-hour trip is $37 for adults, $18.50 for children 11 to 17; the $4^1/_2$-hour version is $49 for adults, $24.50 for children 11 to 17. Children 10 and under are free when accompanied by an adult. Canoes, equipment, and guides are part of the package.

WHERE TO STAY

The area has a number of large resorts, but there are smaller, convivial establishments that offer welcome at lower prices. That simply means that it may be necessary to drive to Gray Rocks or Mont-Tremblant for a golf game, seaplane ride, or ski lift, a small cost in inconvenience.

Resorts

✪ Club Tremblant

Av. Cuttle, Mont-Tremblant, PQ J0T 1Z0. ☎ **819/425-2731,** or 800/363-2413 in the U.S., 800/567-8341 in Canada. Fax 819/425-9903. 37 rms, 73 suites. TV TEL. $121–$205 per person double; from $125 per person suite. Rates include half board (breakfast and dinner). Children 6–12 are charged $29. Rates lower for stays of two days or more. Packages available. AE, DC, ER, MC, V. Turn off Hwy. 327 near the Auberge Sauvignon and follow the signs less than a mile.

Terraced into a hillside sloping steeply to the shore of Lac Tremblant, this handsome property consists of several lodges in blessedly muted alpine style. Essentially a concentration of privately owned condominium apartments operated by a single management, the accommodations represent excellent value and that greatest of luxuries—space. Most of the 110 rental units are suites of one to three bedrooms, for the price of a single room at many other resorts in the region. A typical suite has a fireplace, balcony, sitting room with cable TV and dining table, full kitchen with cookware and dishwasher, one or two bathrooms with Jacuzzi, clotheswasher and dryer. Nearly all have views of the lake and Mont-Tremblant, which rises from the opposite shore.

Dining/Entertainment: The dining room employs a largely French menu, with a five-course table d'hôte. A woody bar, with a stone fireplace and picture windows, is an inviting spot any evening, and there's usually piano music Thursday through Saturday nights.

Services: Day-care program for children 3–13, lifeguarded swimming areas. During ski season, a 22-passenger bus shuttles between the lodge and the slopes.

Facilities: Indoor and outdoor pools, Jacuzzi, workout room (with weight machine, Exercycles, and rowing machines), four tennis courts; six nearby golf courses.

Gray Rocks

525 chemin Principal, Mont-Tremblant, PQ J0T 1Z0. ☎ **819/425-2771** or 800/567-6767. Fax 819/425-3474. 150 rms, 50 condos. A/C TEL. $198–$360 double or condo. Rates include full board (breakfast, lunch, and dinner). Children 11–16 stay in parents' room at 40% discount; children 5–10, at 50% discount; children 4 and under, free. Meals optional in condos. Ski-school packages available. AE, MC, V.

The area's dowager resort has been under new management since 1993. The accommodations—rooms and condos—are in a huge rambling main lodge, in the cozier Le Château lodge, or in one of the resort's four-person cottages. Only the condos have TVs. That minor deficiency aside, the resort covers most other recreational bases, including golf, tennis, a spa, horseback riding, and boating. And not only is there a private airport for guests who fly in, but also a seaplane base on Lac Ouimet. There's a complete playground with attendants to provide child care, as well as a program of free swimming lessons.

Dining/Entertainment: There's a dining room serving three meals a day, and a bar with piano and other music for dancing.

Services: Room service, child-care program, same-day dry cleaning and laundry, junior and adult tennis school.

Facilities: Par-72 golf course, indoor pool and fitness center, 22 tennis courts, horseback riding, sailboat rentals, shuffleboard, croquet; skiing, lifts, ski school, and access to 56 miles (90km) of cross-country skiing.

Tremblant

3005 chemin Principal, Mont-Tremblant, PQ J0T 1Z0. ☎ **819/681-2000** or 800/461-8711. Fax 819/681-5999. 185 condos, 5 chalets. TV TEL. Two-night minimum, $220–$315 per person, double occupancy. Rates include half board (breakfast and dinner) and a lift ticket. Meals for children 6–12 are $45–$80; for children 3–5, $45. Special packages, rates without meals, and occasional one-night specials available. AE, MC, V. Drive 3 miles north of St-Jovite on Hwy. 117; then take Montée Ryan and follow the blue signs for about 6 miles. Bus: The Limocar bus from Montréal stops at the front door; there's door-to-door transport from Dorval and Mirabel airports Fri–Sun.

Not merely a hotel with a pool, Tremblant is a complete and growing resort village stretching from the mountain's skirts to the shores of 10-mile-long Lac Tremblant. At recent count, there were 14 shops, including a liquor store, as well as nine eating places and bars. The four-story Le Saint-Bernard, at the base of the mountain, is a new but historic-looking condominium hotel, with 113 condos with one or two bedrooms, ski-in/ski-out underground parking for 200 cars, and boutiques. The building is the creation of Cote, Leahy & Associates, the firm that restored the Hôtel Victoria and the Quartier Petit Champlain in Québec City. When the snow is deep, skiers here like to follow the sun around the mountain, making the run down slopes with an eastern exposure in the morning and down the western-facing ones in the afternoon.

Dining/Entertainment: At the base of the South Side, the Chalet des Voyageurs cafeteria serves meals and snacks; and the Octo Bar handles après-ski. At the base of the North Side, you can get short orders from La Fourchette du Diable and Pizzatinni. On the summit of the mountain is Le Rendez-vous café, with a circular fireplace; and the 1,000-seat Le Grand Manitou restaurant, with a dining room called La Legende, plus a bistro and cafeteria.

Services: Supervision for children 2–6 at Kids' Kamp, ski rentals and repair, a gondola to take visitors and residents from the parking lot to the village.

Facilities: In winter, 61 slopes and trails in all, served by 10 ski lifts, including two base-to-summit high-speed quads, triple-chair lifts, double-chair lifts; ski school; ski shop; access to cross-country ski trails. In summer, lake swimming, boat cruise (extra fee), chair-lift rides to the top of Mont-Tremblant (extra fee), 11 lighted Har-Tru tennis courts, 18-hole St. Andrews Golf Club, and a dozen other indoor and outdoor amusements.

Villa Bellevue

845 chemin Principale, Mont-Tremblant, PQ J0T 1Z0. ☎ **819/425-2734** or 800/567-6763. Fax 819/425-9360. 130 rms. TV TEL. $60–$258 double without meals, $130–$328 double with half board (breakfast and dinner). Children 17 and under stay free in parents' room. Condos for four to eight people available. Weekly rates and ski weekend packages available. DC, ER, MC, V.

The two-level, shingled Villa Bellevue sits at the edge of Lac Ouimet. The rooms look somewhat worn, but have large, sunny windows; some have air conditioning. Choices are between those in the lodge and deluxe units in a newer building. A few rooms even have kitchenettes— of interest to families. There's an indoor swimming pool, augmented by sauna, steam baths, and weight room. In summer, staff members can take children off their parents' hands during the afternoon and evening at an extra charge. The Villa Bellevue has been run by the Dubois family for three generations. Cross-country skiing is nearby. A shuttle bus carries guests to and from the lifts.

A Laurentian Inn

ⓢ Château Beauvallon

616 Montée Ryan (Box 138), Mont-Tremblant, PQ J0T 1Z0. ☎ **819/425-7275.**
Fax 819/425-7275. 12 rms, 6 with bath. $32 per person for room with or without
bath. Rates include full breakfast. Children 12 and under stay for half price in parent's
room. Winter packages available. No credit cards. Free parking.

An antidote to the impersonal bustle of Mont-Tremblant's big resorts
is this modest inn, a white gambrel-roofed and gabled structure with
yellow shutters set back from the road and bordered by a log fence.
The château's own lake beach is a short stroll away on Lac Beauvallon, and
its boats are moored nearby. Built in 1942, it was once part of the
Mont-Tremblant Lodge resort. Today this seclusion is much of its
appeal, along with the low tariffs, and little happens to disturb the
tranquillity.

The rustic rooms have knotty-pine paneling. Up to 30 guests can be
seated in the dining room, and meals can be preceded or followed by
drinks beside the fireplace in the lounge.

Motel-like Inns

Several motels near Mont-Tremblant and St-Jovite offer the routine
advantages of reasonable prices and predictable comforts. Bonuses
sometimes include kitchenettes—great money-savers for groups of
skiers willing to do their own cooking—and private swimming pools
open in the summer months. They may lack the spacious grounds and
rosters of activities found at the larger resorts, but these amenities are
accessible nearby.

Auberge du Coq de Montagne

2151 chemin Principal (C.P. 208), Mont-Tremblant, PQ J0T 1Z0. ☎ **819/425-3380**
or 800/595-3380. Fax 819/425-7846. 15 rms, 11 with bath; 2 suites. $60 double with
or without bath; $80–$90 suite. Weekend packages and meal plan available. AE,
MC, V. Free parking.

On the shores of Lac Moore, the auberge is less than a mile from the
center of Mont-Tremblant village. Italian meals are served in the
dining room six nights a week, and there's a bar. The two suites have
two double beds, sofa, color TV, and private bath.

Auberge La Porte Rouge

Chemin Principale, Mont-Tremblant, PQ J0T 1Z0. ☎ **819/425-3505.** 14 rms. A/C TV.
$110 double; $47 per person triple; $43 per person quad. Rates include half board
(breakfast and dinner). Rates without meals are about 25% less. Five-night ski or summer
packages available. Chalets, with kitchen and fireplace, available for 3–10 people. MC, V.

The closest motel to everything, this is in the village right across the
road from the Hôtel de Ville (City Hall). Wake to a view of Lake
Mercier through the picture window or from the little balcony. Later
in the day, take lunch on the terrace facing the lake or wind down in
the cocktail lounge. The dining room serves all three meals, including
a four-course table d'hôte. A pool is positioned by the lake. Rowboats
and paddleboats are available.

Auberge Mountain View

Rte. 327 (C.P. 817), St-Jovite, PQ J0T 2H0. ☎ **819/425-3429** or 800/561-5122. Fax 819/425-9109. 44 rms. A/C TV TEL. $68–$89 double. Additional person $14 extra. Packages and off-season discounts available. AE, MC, V.

Just over a mile from the center of St-Jovite stands the Auberge Mountain View. The motel is perpendicular to the highway, minimizing traffic noise. Some rooms have fireplaces and refrigerators. There's a small heated pool. In the slack periods, when many other Laurentian lodgings are closed, its rates are lowered by 20% to 40%. Snowmobiles are available for rent.

WHERE TO DINE

Although most Laurentian inns and resorts have their own dining facilities, and often require that guests use them, especially in winter, Mont-Tremblant and vicinity have several decent independent dining places for the odd night out, casual lunches, or snacks en route. Here is a quartet of local favorites:

L'Abbé du Nord

112 rue Deslauriers, Mont-Tremblant. ☎ **819/425-8394.** Reservations recommended, especially on weekends. Main courses $15–$25; fixed-price meals $15–$25. AE, MC, V. Winter, Tues–Sat and holidays 6–9pm; the rest of the year, Wed–Sat and holidays 6–9pm. ITALIAN/CONTINENTAL.

The Abbé du Nord, in a historic house on the top of a hill in the middle of the village, is particularly popular in winter because of its hearty fare in generous servings and the supportive decor of dark paneling, antiques, and stained glass. Among the house specialties are ribs and rack of lamb, but meat-avoiders can have fish. Breads and desserts are homemade. No one leaves hungry.

Antipasto

855 rue Ouimet, St-Jovite. ☎ **819/425-7580.** Main courses $8–$18. MC, V. Daily 4–11pm. ITALIAN.

Antipasto is housed in an old train station moved to this site, so there's the expected railroad memorabilia on the walls, but the owners have resisted the temptation to play up the theme aspect to excess. Captain's chairs are drawn up to big tables with green Formica tops with paper placemats. Almost everyone orders the César salad (their spelling), which is dense and flavorful, perhaps a little too strong for some tastes—the half portion is more than enough as a first course. Individual pizzas come in 30 versions, on a choice of regular or whole-wheat crust. Pastas are available in even greater variety, those with shellfish among the winners. The sauces are savory, if a bit thin. There are outdoor tables in summer.

Petite Europe

804 rue Ouimet, St-Jovite. ☎ **819/425-3141.** Most items $2.50–$10. MC, V. Summer, daily 8am–11pm; winter, daily 8am–6pm. DELI.

Charcuterie once meant a pork shop, but today it signifies a delicatessen—in this case, with a small bistro and terrace attached. For a picnic, stop by to choose among five dozen varieties of cold meat, three dozen cheeses, two cold cases full of various pastries, and racks of jams and condiments. Petite Europe has a few small booths and tables too, for eating in on sandwiches made from any of these good things, or assorted salads, pâtés, omelets, and pasta dishes. The café au lait is a treat, and they have *bières en fût* (beer on tap). Petite Europe is conveniently located downtown, near the busiest part of the town's main street.

La Table Enchantée

Hwy. 117 nord, Lac Duhamel. ☎ **819/425-7113.** Reservations usually required. Main courses $14.50–$22.50. Table d'hôte $15.50–$24.50. AE, MC, V. Tues–Sun 5–10pm. Closed mid-Oct to mid-Nov and two weeks in May. QUÉBÉCOIS.

The tables in this small, tidy restaurant support some of the most carefully prepared dishes in the region. The kitchen adheres to the traditional Québec repertoire with an occasional detour—their Frenchified médaillons of red deer, for instance. Clam chowder is a favored starter, or, in the short spring, fiddlehead greens. Then, perhaps, the pâté called cretons, followed by Québécois cipaille, a pot pie layered with pheasant, guinea hen, rabbit, veal, and pork. Dessert might be grand-pères au sirop d'érable (dumplings in maple syrup).

2 The Estrie Region

48 miles (80km) SE of Montréal

Estrie serves, in part, as Québec's breadbasket, a largely pastoral region marked by billowing hills and by the 2,600-foot (792 m) peak of **Mont-Orford,** centerpiece of a provincial park and the region's premier downhill ski area. Only a short distance from Mont-Orford is **Sherbrooke,** the industrial and commercial capital of the Estrie (also known as the Eastern Townships), and throughout the Mont-Orford–Sherbrooke area are serene glacial lakes that attract summer fishing enthusiasts, sailors, and swimmers from all around. Touristically, Estrie is Québec's best-kept secret, so it's mostly Montrealers and Québécois who occupy rental houses to ski, fish, cycle, or launch their boats.

Follow their lead: Once out of Montréal, drive east along arrow-straight Autoroute 10 past silos and fields, clusters of cows, meadows strewn with wildflowers. As you crest the hill at km 100, there's an especially beguiling view of mountains and countryside stretching toward New England, not far over the horizon.

Unlike the Laurentians, which virtually close down in "mud time" when spring warmth thaws the ground, Estrie kicks into gear as crews penetrate every "sugar bush" (stand of sugar maples) to tap the sap and "sugar off." Autumn, likewise, has its special attraction here, for in addition to the glorious autumn foliage (usually best in the weeks fore and aft of the third weekend in September), Estrie orchards sag under the weight of apples of every variety, and cider mills hum day and night to produce what has been described as the "wine" of Québec. It's not unusual for visitors to help with the autumn apple harvest, paying a low price for the baskets they gather themselves. The cider mills throw open their doors for tours and tastings.

Estrie towns and villages often have maple-sugar festivals, and numerous farms host "sugaring parties" at which guests partake of considerable country repasts and claim their dessert out by the sugar house. Hot maple syrup is poured on the fast-melting winter snow and cooled instantly to produce a form of maple-sugar candy. Montréal newspapers and local tourist offices and chambers of commerce keep current lists of what's happening where and when.

Although town names such as Granby, Waterloo, and Sherbrooke are obviously English, Estrie is now about 90% French-speaking. Tidy little towns along the roads through apple country are filled with houses kept neat as a pin and surrounded by carefully tended orchards and farmland.

On the drive from Montréal, one of the first Estrie towns of interest is **Rougemont,** at Exit 37 off Autoroute 10 and 13^1/$_2$ miles (22 km) along Route 112, known for its orchards and cider mills. The main street is dotted all year with little stands selling various sorts of apples, apple products, vegetables, and homemade bread. At **St-Césaire,** a few miles farther along 112, small stands and shops specialize in locally made handicrafts. The next town, **St-Paul-d'Abbotsford,** was founded in the late 1700s by Scottish settlers. Abbotsford became the name of the town in 1829, the "St-Paul" added later by the French inhabitants. It was here in 1896 that the local apple-growers cooperative, Société de Pomologie du Québec, was founded.

Another possible detour is 17 miles (27 km) south of Autoroute 10. Take Exit 55 onto Rte. 233 sud to Rte. 104 est (briefly) to Rte. 235 sud. This soon becomes the main street of **Mystic.** Some 64 people live in this community, a wide spot in a side road which enjoyed a short-lived prosperity from 1868 to 1880, when an ironworks was located here and the railroad passed through town. Among its landmarks are a gothic-inspired brick church (1882) in the center of town and an unusual 12-sided barn on the south side. Mystic is also home to a fetching little enterprise called **L'Oeuf** (☎ **514/248-7529**), a combination B&B, restaurant, chocolatier, and gift and food shop. While most travelers are unlikely to stay the night in Mystic, they should give L'Oeuf a look, if only for a snack or light meal. It's open Wednesday through Sunday for lunch and dinner.

From Mystic, it's a short drive south to **Stanbridge East.** The regional Missiquoi Museum, open in summer only, stands beside the Aux Brochets River. It's housed in the photogenic 1860 Cornell Mill with a waterwheel. There's a picnic area beside it.

For extended stays in the region, consider making base in sprightly **Magog** or smaller, more bucolic **North Hatley,** both to the south of Sherbrooke, and take day trips from there.

ESSENTIALS
GETTING THERE

BY CAR   Leave the island of Montréal by the Champlain Bridge, which leads to Autoroute 10, heading for Sherbrooke. People in a hurry can remain on Autoroute 10—and plenty of express buses do this, too—but to get to know the countryside, turn off the autoroute at Exit 37 and go north the short distance to join Hwy. 112.

BY BUS   Local buses leave Montréal to follow Hwy. 112 over a dozen times a day, arriving in Sherbrooke, 100 miles (160 km) away, 3¹/₄ hours later. Express buses use Autoroute 10, making a stop in Magog and arriving in Sherbrooke in 2 hours and 10 minutes (2¹/₂ hours from Québec City). Call 514/842-2281 at the Terminus Voyageur in Montréal for information.

VISITOR INFORMATION

The **Regional House of Tourism for the Estrie Region,** at Exit 68 off Autoroute 10 (☎ **514/375-8774** or 800/263-1068; fax 514/ 375-3530), is open daily, from 10am to 6pm during the summer and from 9am to 5pm the rest of the year; or contact **Tourisme Estrie,** 25 rue Bocage, Sherbrooke, PQ J1L 2J4 (☎ **819/820-2020** or 800/ 355-5755; fax 819/566-4445), for more information. The **Sherbrooke Tourist Information Bureau** is at 48 rue Depot (☎ **819/564-8331**), open daily: late June to Labor Day from 8:30am to 7:30pm, and the rest of the year from 9am to 5pm.

The **telephone area code** is 514 or 819, depending on the part of the region called (towns with a 514 area code are closer to Montréal).

GRANBY

Industrial Granby (pop. 41,500), at Exit 68 off Autoroute 10, has a surprise—the second most important zoological garden in Québec province. The **Granby Zoo** at 347 rue Bourget (☎ **514/372-9113**), is 70 wooded acres harboring more than 1,000 mammals, exotic birds, reptiles, and amphibians from all over the world. Founded in 1953, the zoo has an educational program for children and presents shows every day in summer. New exhibits include a nocturnal cave, "Bear Mountain," and a display of robotized whales. There are restaurants, picnic areas, gift shops, and free rides. The zoo is open from late May to early September only, daily from 9:30am to 5pm (but closing times vary). Admission is $15 for adults, $13 for seniors, $6 for students 5 to 17, and $3 for children 1 to 4. Parking is $3. You'll spot signs for the zoo after taking Exit 68 off Autoroute 10. The visitors' entrance is on boulevard David-Bouchard nord.

Granby also has **Yamaska Park,** with a 2-mile (3km) hiking trail, 25 miles (40km) of cross-country ski trails, and 13¹/₂ miles (22km) of cycling trails along an old railroad track between Granby and the towns of Bromont and Waterloo. Another attraction is **Boivin Fountain,** with its 150-foot plume of water in Lake Boivin.

Tourisme Granby is at 650 rue Principale, Granby, PQ J2G 8L4 (☎ **514/372-7273** or 800/567-7273; fax 514/372-7782). It's open daily: in summer from 10am to 6pm, and the rest of the year from 8am to 5pm.

BROMONT

Take Exit 78 off Autoroute 10 to reach Bromont (pop. 5,000), a popular area for day and night skiing, mountain biking (rent bikes at the entrance to the town opposite the tourist office), golf, horseback riding, hiking, zipping down alpine and water slides, and shopping in the two largest **factory outlets** in Canada—Versants de Bromont and Les

Manufacturiers de Bromont—and at the area's largest **flea market,** with 350 stalls set up in the local drive-in from 9am to 5pm the first Sunday in May to the second Sunday in November.

WHERE TO STAY & DINE

Château Bromont

90 rue Stanstead, Bromont, PQ J0E 1L0. ☎ **514/534-3433** or 800/363-0363. Fax 514/534-0514. 154 rms. A/C MINIBAR TV TEL. $100–$135 per person double. Additional person $10 extra. Spa, ski, and other packages available. AE, ER, DISC, MC, V.

All the rooms at the château have rocking chairs and loft beds, and half have fireplaces. Some no-smoking rooms are available. A landscaped terrace and two hot tubs look up at the mountain. The staff is young and bilingual. Les Quatre Canards restaurant serves lunch and dinner, and there's a bistro bar, L'Equestre, and the Château Terrasse Bar-BBQ. In addition to indoor and outdoor pools and Jacuzzis, a sauna, a small gym, and squash and racquetball courts, there's a European spa featuring mud and algae baths (use of the spa facilities costs extra).

KNOWLTON

Those who shop for amusement, not mere necessity, will want to make this a destination. Knowlton is compact, but its two main shopping streets are chockablock with stores and **discount outlets,** including Liz Claiborne, Ralph Lauren, Ben & Jerry, and others.

Knowlton is on the southeast corner of **Lake Brome,** and is part of the five-village municipality known as Lac Brome (pop. 4,824). The first settler here, Paul Holland Knowlton, a Loyalist from Vermont, arrived in 1815 and established a farm where the golf course is now. By 1834 he had added a sawmill, a blacksmith shop, a gristmill, and a store. He also founded the first high school.

Another Knowlton resident, Reginald Aubrey Fessenden, invented a wireless radio in 1906, a year ahead of Marconi, and relayed a message from Brant Rock, Massachusetts, to ships in the Caribbean. Large mansions overhang the lake on either side of town. The town hosts a **Blue Grass Festival** in June, and the **Brome Fair** is held over Labor Day weekend.

The **tourist information office** is in the local museum (see "What to See and Do," below).

WHAT TO SEE & DO

Musée Historique du Comté de Brome
(Brome County Historical Museum)

130 Lakeside St. (Rte. 243). ☎ **514/243-6782.** $2.50 adults, $2 seniors, $1 students. Mon–Sat 10am–4:30pm, Sun 11am–4:30pm. Closed late Aug to May.

This museum fills five historic buildings, including the town's first school, established by Paul Holland Knowlton. Exhibits focus on the various aspects of town life, with re-creations of a schoolroom, bedroom, parlor, and kitchen. The Martin Annex (1921) is dominated by the 1917 Fokker single-seat biplane, the foremost German aircraft in World War I. It also houses a collection of guns from the 18th to the early 20th century. There's also a collection of old radios. The museum sells books about the area.

WHERE TO STAY

⑤ L'Abri'cot

562 Knowlton Rd. (Rte. 104 ouest), Knowlton, PQ J0E 1V0. ☎ **514/243-5532.** 4 rms, 2 with bath. $60–$80 double with or without bath. Rates include full breakfast. Discounts for stays of two or more nights. No credit cards.

Set in a pine grove 1¹/₂ miles west of town, L'Abri'cot, built in 1889, has a light, airy downstairs, with wide-board floors, a sun room, breakfast room, patio, and living room with a stone fireplace. The bedrooms, each named for an animal, are upstairs. The Cat Room, with a skylight in the bath, is appealing. Two smaller rooms share a large bath. Outside, there's a swimming pool in the garden. Owner Denise Goyer often spoils guests with cheese, pâté, fruit, or sherry.

SUTTON

A pleasant outing from Knowlton, or anywhere in the vicinity, Sutton (pop. 1,587) is a town with a number of promising cafés and perhaps the best bookstore in the region, **The Book Nook,** at 14 rue Principale sud (☎ **514/538-2207**). Nearby **Mont-Sutton** is known in summer for its 33 miles (54km) of hiking trails that link up with the Appalachian Trail, and for its glade skiing in winter. The surrounding country roads are popular with bikers.

For more information about the town and the area, drop by the **Sutton Tourist Association** (☎ **514/538-2646**), opposite the bookstore.

MONT-ORFORD

Mont Orford Provincial Park is among Québec's loveliest and most popular for camping and hiking. In high summer season, campsites fill up quickly, especially on weekends. From mid-September to mid-October the park blazes with autumn color, and in winter visitors come for the more than 20 miles of ski trails and slopes, with a vertical drop of 1,500 feet, or for the extensive network of cross-country ski and snowshoe trails.

Mont-Orford is a veteran ski area compared to Mont-Bromont (see above), and has long provided slopes of choice for the monied families of Estrie and Montréal. The other two mountains in the area, Owl's Head and Mont-Sutton, are more family-oriented, less glitzy. These four ski centers have banded together to form **Ski East,** enabling skiers to purchase an all-inclusive five-day ticket good at all four areas anytime. Similarly economical lesson plans are available.

Orford has another claim to fame in the **Centre d'Arts Orford** (☎ **819/843-3981**), set on a 222-acre estate within the park and providing music classes for talented young musicians every summer. From the end of June to the end of August, a series of classical and chamber-music concerts is given in connection with **Festival Orford.** Prices usually are $11 to $21, or free to $19 for student performances, which are held on Wednesday, Thursday, and Friday at 8pm and on Sunday at 11am. A complete luncheon is served outside following the Sunday concert. Visual arts exhibitions at the center are open to the public, and walking trails connect it to a nearby campground.

The **Bureau d'Information Touristique Magog-Orford** is at 55 rue Cabana (via Rte. 112), Magog, PQ J1X 2C4 (☎ **819/ 843-2744** or 800/267-2744).

WHERE TO STAY

Cheribourg

2603 Rte. 141 nord (C.P. 337), Magog, PQ J1X 3W9. ☎ **819/843-3308,** or 800/ 567-6132 in Québec. Fax 819/843-2639. 97 rms, 90 chalets. A/C MINIBAR TV TEL. $92 per day double; from $435 per week chalet. Additional adult $12 extra; children

---

The Estrie Wine Country?

Canada is known more for its beers and ales than its wines, and rightly so. That hasn't stopped a few stouthearted agriculturists from attempting to plant vines and transform the fruit into approximations of drinkable clarets, chardonnays, and sauternes. So far, the most successful efforts have blossomed along the Niagara Frontier in southern Ontario and in the relatively warmer precincts of British Columbia. But Estrie enjoys the mildest microclimates in Québec, and where apples grow—and they do in abundance in these parts—so will other fruits, including grapes. Inevitably, a few hardy entrepreneurial sorts decided to give winemaking a go.

Their efforts are concentrated around **Dunham,** a farming village about 18 miles west of Sutton, with several nearby vineyards along Rte. 202. They've only been at it for about 14 years, so their vines and the end product are still maturing. No winemaker in the valleys of Napa or the Gironde—nor, for that matter, the Hudson—is feeling the hot breath of competition from the vintages of Estrie. Still, a stop for a snack or a tour of vineyard facilities makes for a pleasant break from driving, and those demonstrating such daring deserve to be encouraged.

One possibility is the family-owned and -run **Les Blancs Coteaux,** at 1046 Rte. 202 (☎ **514/295-3503**), which opened in 1990. They serve lunch and give tours in summer, but they welcome visitors anytime from June to November. The vineyard's shop sells its white wines, hard cider, apple syrup, strawberry vinegar, relish, cider jelly, and dried wreaths and wildflower arrangements. The area's oldest vineyard, **l'Orpailleur,** 1086 Rte. 202 (☎ **514/295-3112**), opened in 1982. Look, too, for **Domaine des Côtes d'Ardoise,** at 879 Rte. 202 (☎ **514/295-2020**), and **Les Trois Clochers,** at 341 Rte. 202 (☎ **514/295-2034**). L'Orpailleur serves meals and all three have picnic tables, offer wine tastings, and conduct tours, but call ahead to determine schedules and hours, which vary by the season.

11 and under stay free in parents' room. Discounts and packages available. AE, DC, DISC, ER, MC, V. Take Exit 118 from Autoroute 10.

These clusters of attached structures with sharply angled orange roofs are easy to spot on the way to Mont-Orford and Lac Memphremagog. Founded only in 1971, it is nevertheless one of the area's oldest resorts, set on 200 acres in Mont-Orford Park. Guests have access to clay tennis courts, two outdoor pools, an exercise room, sauna, Jacuzzi, mountain bikes, a children's playground, and a disco in summer. The rooms, most of which have two queen-size beds, are decorated with bleached pine furniture. Two- or three-room chalets are a frugal choice for families or groups of up to six friends. All are equipped with a fireplace, kitchenette, and utensils. Reasonable prices and the good location offset the heavily used look of the interiors and the harried demeanor of the staff. The Cheribourg is open year-round.

MAGOG & LAC MEMPHRÉMAGOG

Orford is where people visit but Magog (pop. 14,500) is where people live. As with countless other North American place names, Magog came by its handle through corruption of a Native Canadian word. The Abenaki name Memrobagak (Great Expanse of Water) somehow became Memphremagog, which was eventually shortened to Magog (pronounced *May*-gog). The town is positioned at the northernmost end of Lac Memphrémagog (pronounced Mem-*phree*-may-gog), *not* on Lac Magog, which is about 8 miles north of Magog. Memphrémagog straddles the U.S.-Canadian border into Vermont.

The **Magog-Orford tourist information office,** at 55 rue Cabana, Magog, PQ J1X 2C4 (☎ **819/843-2744** or 800/267-2744; fax 819/847-4036), is open daily: in summer from 8:30am to 7:30pm, and in winter from 9am to 5pm.

WHAT TO SEE & DO

Magog has a well-used waterfront, and in July each year the **International Crossing of Lac Memphrémagog** creates a big splash. Participants start out in Newport, Vt., at 6am and swim 24 miles to Magog, arriving in midafternoon around 3:30 or 4pm. To experience the lake without such damp exertion, take a $1^3/_4$-hour **lake cruise** aboard the *Aventure I* or *Aventure II* (☎ **819/843-8068**). The cost is $10.75 for adults, $5.50 for children 11 and under; a day-long cruise is $40. The boats leave from Point Merry Park, the focal point for many of the town's outdoor activities. And Memphrémagog has its own legendary sea creature, nicknamed Memphre, which supposedly surfaced for the first time in 1798. It will come as no surprise that other sightings have been claimed since then.

An 11-mile (18.5 km) bike path links the lake with Mont-Orford; in winter it is transformed into a **cross-country ski trail,** and a $1^1/_2$-mile-long (2.5 km) **skating rink** is created on the shores of the lake. Snowmobiling trails crisscross the region.

Other popular activities in the area include golf, tennis, and horseback riding. A **Vintage Festival** is held the last couple of weekends in September.

Benedictine Abbey of Saint-Benoît-du-Lac

Chemin Fisher. ☎ **819/843-4080**. Free admission, but donations accepted. Daily 6am–8pm; mass with Gregorian chant at 11am, vespers with Gregorian chant at 5pm (7pm on Thurs). No vespers on Tues in July–Aug. Shop, Mon–Sat 9–10:45am and 2–4:30pm. Driving west from Magog on Route 112, watch for the first road on the left on the far side of the lake; take chemin Bolton est 12 miles (19km) south to the turnoff to the abbey.

No mistaking the abbey, with its granite steeple that thrusts into the sky above the lake, its backdrop Owl's Head Mountain. Although Saint-Benoît-du-Lac dates only from 1912, the serenity of the site is timeless. Some 40 monks help keep the art of Gregorian chant alive in their liturgy, which can be attended by outsiders. For the 45-minute service (times above), walk to the rear of the abbey and down the stairs; follow signs for ORATOIRE, and sit in back to avoid a lot of otherwise obligatory standing and sitting. The abbey receives 7,000 pilgrims a year, 60% of them between the ages of 16 and 25. It maintains separate hostels for men and women. (Make overnight arrangements in advance; figure $35 or so per person.) A bleu cheese known as L'Ermite, among Québec's most famous, and a tasty Swiss-type cheese, are produced at the monastery, and are on sale in the little shop. It also sells chocolate from Oka, honey, a nonalcoholic cider, and tapes of religious chants. Do visit the tiny stone chapel to the left at the entrance to the property, opposite the small cemetery. Visitors during the last two weeks of September or the first two weeks of October may want to help pick apples in the orchard.

WHERE TO STAY

Auberge L'Etoile sur le Lac

1150 rue Principale ouest, Magog, PQ J1X 2B8. ☎ **819/843-6521,** or 800/567-2727 in Québec. Fax 819/843-5007. 26 rms. A/C TV TEL. $78–$121 double. Golf, sailing, and other packages available. AE, CB, DC, DISC, ER, MC, V. Take Exit 115 from Autoroute 10 and follow Route 112 into Magog; the hotel is on the right soon after passing the Tourist Information Bureau.

Its name means "star on the lake," not exactly hyperbole, given the unremarkable state of Magog lodgings. Primary virtues are its lakeside location and ready access to Mont-Orford, 3½ miles (6 km) away. All the rooms overlook Lac Memphrémagog and have patios or balconies. Upstairs is a TV room with a fireplace, a rustic lounge, and a glass-enclosed Jacuzzi overlooking the lake. The hotel rents bicycles and ice skates. A dining room and bar occupy much of the ground floor, with terrace dining in summer. A small outdoor pool is available, if not especially inviting.

GEORGEVILLE

Georgeville, established in 1797 on the eastern shore of Lac Memphrémagog, was once a stop along the stagecoach route from Montréal to Brome, then a five-day trip. Today the town has just enough houses to shelter 845 residents, a general store, a little church, and a nine-hole golf course with views of the lake. It's also a summer home of actor Donald Sutherland.

The 14-mile (22 km) drive along Hwy. 247 south from Georgeville to Beebe (see below) is pleasant, not stunning. Owl's Head is the name of the prominent mountain off to the right, and just before entering Beebe Plain, watch for the whimsical wood carvings of bears, in a yard to the left.

WHERE TO DINE

Auberge Georgeville

71 chemin Channel, Georgeville, PQ J0B 1T0 (Rte. 247). ☎ **819/843-8683.** Reservations recommended. Fixed-price dinner $30. MC, V. Daily 6–10pm. Closed Oct 30–Dec 16 and Sun–Mon off-season. Take Hwy. 247 10 miles south from Magog.

Built in 1890 as an inn to serve stagecoach traffic, this auberge is known primarily for its dining room, although there are a dozen small bedrooms upstairs. The nightly five-course table d'hôte typically features fish, beef, or duck according to the chef-owner's whim. She favors the use of fruit in much of her cooking, rarely to the point of redundancy. Vegetarian meals, composed of organic ingredients, are available to those who make advance requests. The three dining areas have board floors and fresh flowers, pottery, and hand-woven placemats on the tables. A pink house with white trim, the inn has a somewhat dispirited air from the outside that dissipates upon entry. The bedrooms, eight with showers, go for $88 to $93 double, including full breakfast. Note that lunch isn't served.

LAKE MASSAWIPPI

Southeast of Magog, reachable by Route 141 or 108, east of Autoroute 55, is Lake Massawippi, easily the most desirable resort area in Estrie. Set among rolling hills and fertile farm country, the 12-mile-long lake with its scalloped shoreline was discovered in the early years of this century by people of wealth and power, many of whom were American Southerners trying to escape the sultry summers of Virginia and Georgia. They built grand "cottages" on slopes in prime locations along the lakeshore, with enough bedrooms to house their extended families and friends for months at a time. Some of these have now been converted to inns. For a few days' escape from work or intensive travel, it's difficult to do better than Lake Massawippi.

In winter, the lands around the lake have 35 miles (56 km) of cross-country ski trails, and a special three- or six-night package, called **Skiwippi,** allows any takers to spend brisk days skiing between the exemplary Auberge Ripplecove, Manoir Hovey, and Auberge Hatley (see "North Hatley," below), reveling each night in the varied accommodations and accomplished kitchens of the three. In summer, there's a comparable golf version. For the less athletically inclined, a similar package (*sans* skis), called **A Moveable Feast,** is also available. Book either package through any of the inns.

NORTH HATLEY

The jewel of Lake Massawippi, this town of 704, only half an hour from the U.S. border and 85¹/₂ miles (138 km) from Montréal, has a river meandering through it. Old photographs show flocks of people coursing along the one main village street. Apart from impressive sunsets over the lake, it has a variety of lodgings and places to dine, shops, golf, horseback riding, a marina, post office, launderette, and general store. An English-language theater, the **Piggery,** on a country road outside town (☎ **819/842-2431**), presents plays of an often-experimental nature during the summer.

WHERE TO STAY & DINE
✪ Auberge Hatley Inn

325 rue Virgin (P.O. Box 330), North Hatley, PQ J0B 2C0. ☎ **819/842-2451.** Fax 819/842-2907. 25 rms. A/C TEL. $250–$360 double. Rates include half board (breakfast and dinner) and gratuities. AE, MC, V. Take Exit 29 from Autoroute 55 and follow Route 108 east, watching for signs.

This acclaimed gastronomic resort occupies a hillside above the lake, not far from the town center. All rooms have bath with tub or shower, and over half have Jacuzzis and/or fireplaces. An abundance of antiques, many of them sizeable Québécois country pieces, are joined by complementary reproductions. There's a swimming pool, and the staff will advise on nearby activities, including riding, hiking, fishing, skiing, and hunting.

There's no uncertainty where owners Liliane and Robert Gagnon place their priorities: the pleasures of the table. The dining room has a bank of windows looking over the lake. Tables with pink coverings are set with Rosenthal china, fresh flowers, and candles. It's a necessarily soothing environment, since dinner can easily extend over three hours. Updated but essentially classical French techniques are applied to such ingredients as salmon, bison, and wild boar. Most herbs and some vegetables come from the Gagnons' hydroponic farm, and the ducks and pheasants come from their 100-acre game island. A particular treat is the meal-ending selection of cheeses, served with the waiter's careful description and not a little ceremony.

✪ Manoir Hovey

Chemin Hovey (P.O. Box 60), North Hatley, PQ J0B 2C0. ☎ **819/842-2421** or 800/661-2421. Fax 819/842-2248. 35 rms. A/C TEL. $200–$350 double. Rates include full breakfast, dinner, tax, gratuities, and use of most recreational facilities. AE, MC, V. Take Exit 29 off Autoroute 55 and follow Route 108 east, watching for signs.

Named for Capt. Ebenezer Hovey, a Connecticut Yankee who came upon the lake in 1793 and was the first white settler, the columned manor was built in 1899. Encompassing 20 acres and 1,600 feet of lakefront property, it's one of eastern Canada's most complete resort inns, a member of the international Romantik Hotels group. Many of the guest rooms have fireplaces, balconies, and whirlpool baths; most have TV sets. Eight new no-smoking rooms were added in 1994. The library adjoining the reception area has floor-to-ceiling bookshelves and a stone fireplace. A lighted tennis court, touring bikes, modestly equipped exercise room, heated outdoor pool, and two beaches add to its appeal. In winter, they push a heated cabin out onto the lake for ice fishing. The dining room serves updated French cuisine, with a menu that changes with the seasons and features fresh herbs, vegetables, and edible flowers from the kitchen garden. "Heart-healthy" dishes are featured. All are fragrant and full-bodied, in attractive presentations. Steve and Kathy Stafford are the gracious hosts.

Manoir Le Tricorne

50 chemin Gosselin, North Hatley, PQ J0B 2C0. ☎ **819/842-4522.** Fax 819/842-2692. 11 rms. $95–$160 double. Rates include full breakfast. MC, V. Take Route 108 west out of North Hatley and follow the signs.

While the core of this house is 125 years old, it looks as if it were erected 5 years ago. The exterior is shocking-pink and white, the interior decked out in best middle-brow *Good Housekeeping* manner, with lots of duck decoys, birdcages, and tartans. The decorative scheme won't be to everyone's taste, but all is immaculately kept and there is ample room to move about. Three rooms have fireplaces; five have Jacuzzis. No phones or TVs, but those are available in the common room. New guests are welcomed with mimosas or glasses of port. Menus of the substantial breakfasts are changed regularly, with fruit omelets one day, eggs Benedict the next. Up the hill is a pool, and one of the two ponds is stocked for fishing. There are spectacular views of Lake Massawippi from all over the hilltop property.

WHERE TO DINE

Pilsen

55 rue Principale. ☎ **819/842-2971.** Reservations recommended on weekends. Main courses $7–$23. MC, V. Wed–Sun 11:30am–9pm. (The bar stays open until 3am Fri–Sat). INTERNATIONAL.

All drives through North Hatley pass the Pilsen, a pub and restaurant in the center of town. A narrow deck overhangs the river that feeds the lake. The place fills up quickly on warm days, the better to watch motorboats and canoes setting out or returning. Inside or out, patrons snaffle up renditions of the usual suspects: nachos and burgers, pastas, and lobster bisque. Vegetarian plates are available. There's an extensive choice of beers, including local microbrews Massawippi Blonde and Townships Pale Ale. Park behind the restaurant.

WHERE TO STAY & DINE IN AYER'S CLIFF

✪ Auberge Ripplecove

700 rue Ripplecove (P.O. Box 26), Ayer's Cliff, PQ J0B 1C0. ☎ **819/838-4296.** Fax 819/838-5541. 21 rms and cottages, 4 suites. TEL. $184–$318 double or cottage for two; $290–$358 suite. Rates include half board (breakfast and dinner), recreational facilities, and gratuities. AE, MC, V. Take Hwy. 55 to Exit 21; follow Route 141 east, watching for signs.

An exceptionally warm welcome is extended by the staff of this handsome inn, and impeccable housekeeping standards are observed throughout. The core structure dates from 1945, but subsequent expansions have added rooms, suites, and cottages. About half have gas fireplaces, cable TV, balconies, and whirlpool tubs, while the suites add stocked minibars. The 12-acre property beside Lake Massawippi has a private beach and a heated outdoor pool. Instruction and equipment are available for sailing, sailboarding, waterskiing, canoeing, fishing, and cross-country skiing. Golf courses and riding stables are a short drive away. The inn's award-winning lakeside restaurant fills up most nights in season with diners drawn to the kitchen's contemporary French creations, many of which sing with Thai spicings. Such exotica as wapiti and caribou appear on the card. Recent renovations included installation in the lobby of an ornate 14-foot-high breakfront built in 1880 and the hull of a fishing dory recycled as a buffet table in the dining room. Innkeeper Jeffrey Stafford is the brother of the owner of the Auberge Hovey in North Hatley.

SHERBROOKE

Seat of an archbishopric and home to 76,500 people and about 150 different manufacturing firms, Sherbrooke is the metropolis of the Estrie region. Some of Canada's increasingly elusive trains actually still stop here. Truth to tell, that may be one of the few reasons the average leisure traveler will make much note of the city, a largely commercial and industrial center of undisciplined aspect.

It's set on hilly terrain, beside the point where the Magog and Saint-François rivers meet. Sherbrooke is 16 miles (26 km) northeast of North Hatley and 99 miles (160 km) east of Montréal.

Rue King, the city's main artery, is 7^1/$_2$ miles (12 km) long, and most of the hotels, restaurants, bars, and shops line it. The **tourist office** is near the intersection of King and Wellington, in the old train station, at 48 rue Depot, Sherbrooke, PQ, J1H 5G1 (☎ **819/564-8331** or 800/561-8331).

The city has a **fine-arts museum (Musée des Beaux-Arts de Sherbrooke)** downtown at 174 rue du Palais, and a **natural sciences museum** at 195 rue Marquette. In **Parc Jacques-Cartier,** there are 12^1/$_2$ miles (20 km) of bike trails. The French-speaking **University of Sherbrooke,** with 10,000 students, is here. (Its English counterpart, Bishop's University, built by one of the architects of Oxford University in England, is a few miles south, in Lennoxville.)

Every year in mid-May, Sherbrooke, which despite its name is 90% French-speaking, hosts the **Festival des Harmonies du Québec,** a popular music festival, followed by the **Fête du Lac des Nations** (Environmental Festival) in July and an **Exposition Agricole** (Agricultural Fair) in August.

WHERE TO STAY

Le Mitchell

219 rue Moore, Sherbrooke, PQ J1H 1C1. ☎ **819/563-8636.** Fax 819/562-1516. 4 rms, 1 with bath. TEL. $95 double without bath, $115 double with bath. Rates include breakfast. AE, MC, V.

The Tudor-style Le Mitchell became a bed-and-breakfast in 1991. Guests have use of the TV room, and can warm themselves in front of three fireplaces. There's some noise from the street, so the room in the back of the house is quietest. Afternoon and evening refreshments are offered, in addition to breakfast. Le Mitchell is a five-minute walk from downtown. A fax and photocopier are available for those business travelers who need to stay in touch but prefer lodging less predictable than the chain hotels that loom over rue King.

WHERE TO DINE

Le Devinière

17 rue Peel (at rue King). ☎ 819/822-4177. Reservations recommended. Main courses $16–$22. MC, V. Tues–Fri 11am–2:30pm and 5–11pm, Sat 5–11pm. FRENCH.

Sherbrooke has many eating places, few of them worth a significant detour. That makes this snug, centrally located, 44-seat spot a top local choice by default. The cuisine is thoroughly Gallic-bistro in inspiration and execution, and the specialty is lamb. They aren't licensed to serve wine or liquor, but patrons are welcome to *apportez votre vin*—bring your own.

STANSTEAD PLAIN, ROCK ISLAND & BEEBE PLAIN

For a unique day or half-day trip from North Hatley, follow Hwy. 143 as far south as possible without actually crossing into the United States and turn west to explore these three French border towns. If you should cross the border accidentally—which is easy to do—just report to the inspectors and come back across. There may not even be anyone on duty.

The first town is **Stanstead Plain** (pop. 1,059), some 30 miles (49km) south of North Hatley and only 9 miles (15km) north of Newport, Vt. With a modest reputation for distinctive architecture, Stanstead Plain offers the Centenary United Church, with a unique clock face that bears the name of the person who donated the granite to build the church; the Victorian Butler House (1866), at 10 rue Dufferin; and the 1859 Italianate **Musée Colby Curtis,** 35 rue Dufferin (☎ 819/876-7322), displaying collections of antique toys and dolls and 19th-century tools and furnishings and portraits by Québec artist Orson Wheeler. It's open Tuesday through Friday from 10am to 5pm, and on Saturday and Sunday from 1 to 5pm (closed weekends October to March); admission is $3 for adults, $2 for seniors, and 50¢ for children.

Stanstead East runs into the village of **Rock Island** (pop. 1,067), which is the commercial center of the area. Follow Stevens Street (uphill) on entering Rock Island; it's a cul-de-sac, but the reward is a great view.

Collectors of geographical oddities will love the **Haskell Opera House.** Dating from 1901, it's literally and logistically half Canadian and half American: The stage and performers are in Canada and the audience is in the United States.

About 2¹/₂ miles (4km) west of Rock Island, **Beebe Plain** (pop. 975) is a center for quarrying granite. The Catholic church here (enter through the side door) has outstanding wood sculptures, and that's a portrait of St. Teresa behind the altar. But what makes this town unique is half-mile-long **Canusa Street,** the north side of which is in Canada, the south side in the United States—thus its name, CAN-USA. Check the car license plates on either side. Here, it's long-distance to call a neighbor across the street, and while they're free to walk across the street for a visit, they are expected, at least technically, to report to the authorities if they decide to drive.

11

Getting to Know Québec City

Québec City is the soul of New France. It was the first settlement in Canada, and today is the capital of politically prickly Québec, a province larger than Alaska. The old city, a tumble of granite, slate-roofed houses clustered around the dominating Château Frontenac, is a haunting evocation of a coastal town of the motherland, as romantic as any on the continent. The St. Lawrence makes a majestic sweep beneath the palisades on which the capital stands, as gray as gunmetal under dark skies, but silvered by sunlight when the clouds pass. Because of its history, beauty, and unique stature as the only walled city north of Mexico, the historic district of Québec was named a UNESCO World Heritage site in 1985.

Québec City is almost solidly French in feeling, in spirit, and in language; 95% of its population speaks French. But many of its 648,000 citizens speak some English, especially those who work in hotels, restaurants, and shops where they deal with Anglophones every day. This is also a college town, and thousands of young people study English as a second language. So while it is often more difficult in Québec City than in Montréal to understand and be understood, the average Québécois goes out of his or her way to communicate—in halting English, sign language, simplified French, or a combination of all three. Admitting exceptions, most of the Québécois are an uncommonly gracious lot, and it is a pleasure to spend time in their company and in their city.

In the following chapters are tips on where to stay, where to dine, and what to do in the city itself. After exploring Québec City, consider a trip to the Île d'Orléans, an agricultural and resort island within sight of the Château Frontenac, then a drive along the northern coast past the shrine of Ste-Anne-de-Beaupré to the provincial park and ski resort at Mont Ste-Anne, or perhaps the southern bank of the St. Lawrence, where often picturesque riverside villages reward lingering.

1 Orientation

Almost all of a visit to Québec can be spent in the Old City, as many hotels and lodging places, restaurants, and tourist-oriented services are based there. The colonial city was first built right down by the St. Lawrence at the foot of Cape Diamond. It was here that merchants, traders, and boatmen earned their livelihoods, but due to unfriendly fire in the 1700s, this Basse-Ville—Lower Town—became primarily a wharf and warehouse area, and residents moved to safer houses atop the steep cliffs that form the rim of Cap Diamant—Cape Diamond.

Haute-Ville, or Upper Town, the Québécois later discovered, was not immune from cannon fire either, as the British General Wolfe was to prove. Nevertheless, the division into Upper and Lower Towns persisted for obvious topographical reasons. The Upper Town remains enclosed by fortification walls, and several ramplike streets and a cliffside elevator (funiculaire) connect it to the Lower Town.

For a panoramic look at the city, seek out the Québec government's office building, called Edifice "G," 1033 rue de la Chevrotière (☎ 418/644-9841). Enter the tower at the corner of de la Chevrotière and René-Lévesque, and look for signs and special elevators labeled "Anima G, 31e Etage." On the 31st floor, an observatory with an information desk is open from 10am to 4pm weekdays, 1 to 5pm on Saturday, Sunday, and holidays. Entrance is free. It's closed from mid-December to mid-January.

Another place for an overall view is L'Astral, the revolving restaurant atop Loews Le Concorde Hotel. It isn't necessary to plan a meal there, since the bar is as good a vantage point as any.

ARRIVING

BY PLANE   Jean-Lesage International Airport is small, despite the grand name. Buses into town are operated by Maple Leaf Sightseeing Tours, Inc. (☎ 418/649-9226). The 12-mile trip costs $8.75. Buses leave at variable times, depending on the season. A taxi into town costs about $25.

BY TRAIN   The train station in Québec City, Gare du Palais, 450 rue de la Gare-du-Palais (☎ 418/524-4161), was designed by Bruce Price, who designed the fabled Château Frontenac. Handsome though it is, the Lower Town location isn't central. Plan on a moderately strenuous uphill hike or a $6 cab ride to the Upper Town. That's $6 per ride, incidentally, not per passenger, as an occasional cabbie may pretend.

BY BUS   The bus station, Terminus d'Autobus Voyageur, at 320 rue Abraham-Martin (☎ 418/525-3000), is near the train station. As from the train station, it is an uphill climb or quick cab ride to Château Frontenac and the Upper Town. A taxi should cost about $6, the same as from the train station. To save money take another bus: Walk out the front door of the bus station, turn right, and walk to the end of the block. Turn right again to the bus stop. The no. 3 bus heads up the hill to the Upper Town every 15 minutes and goes directly to the Château Frontenac for $1.80 in exact change. It is, however, far more convenient and not much more expensive to take a taxi.

BY CAR   From New York City, follow I-87 to Autoroute 15 to Montréal, picking up Autoroute 20 to Québec City. Take 73 Nord across the Pont Pierre-Laporte and exit onto boulevard Champlain immediately after crossing the bridge. This skirts the city at river level. Turn left at Parc des Champs-de-Bataille (Battlefields Park) and right

Impressions

Québeck was surveyed and laid out by a gentleman who had been afflicted with the delirium tremens from childhood, and hence his ideas [sic] of things was a little irreg'ler. The streets dont [sic] lead anywhere in partic'ler, but everywhere in gin'ral.
—Charles F. Browne, "Artemus Ward," in *Canada* (1865)

onto the Grande-Allée. For a slower but more scenic route, follow Hwy. 132 from Montréal along the south shore of the St. Lawrence River to Québec City. Or, follow the north shore from Montréal, along Autoroute 40.

From Boston, take I-89 to I-93 to I-91 in Montpelier, Vt., which connects with Autoroute 55 in Québec to link up with Autoroute 20. Or, follow I-90 up the Atlantic coast, through Portland, Maine, to Route 201 west of Bangor, then Autoroute 173 to Lévis, where there is a car-ferry to Québec City, a 10-minute ride across the St. Lawrence River. The ferry runs every hour on the hour during the day from Lévis (slightly less often at night), and costs $3 for the car and $1.25 per person.

VISITOR INFORMATION

The Greater Québec Area Tourism and Convention Bureau operates two useful provincial information centers in and near the city. One is in the old part of Québec City at 60 rue d'Auteuil (☎ **418/ 692-2471**), another in suburban Ste-Foy, at 3005 bd. Laurier, near the Québec and Pierre-Laporte bridges (☎ **418/651-2882**). The information center in the Upper Town is open daily 8:30am to 8pm from early June to Labor Day, from 8:30am to 5:30pm from Labor Day to October 10, and 9am to 5pm Monday to Friday the rest of the year.

The Québec Government's Tourism Department operates a city information office on place d'Armes, down the hill from the Château Frontenac, at 12 rue Ste-Anne (☎ **418/873-2015** or 800/363-7777 from other parts of Québec, Canada, and the United States). It's open from 8:30am to 7:30pm from mid-June to early September, from 9am to 5pm the rest of the year. The office has many brochures, cruise and bus tour operators, a souvenir shop, a 24-hour ATM, a currency exchange office, and a free accommodations reservation service.

Parks Canada operates an information kiosk in front of the Château Frontenac; it's open daily from 9am to noon and 1 to 5pm.

CITY LAYOUT

MAIN AVENUES & STREETS   Within the walls of the **Upper Town** the principal streets are rues St-Louis (which becomes the Grande-Allée outside the city walls), Ste-Anne, and St-Jean, and the pedestrians-only terrasse Dufferin, which overlooks the river. In the **Lower Town,** major streets are St-Pierre, Dalhousie, St-Paul and, parallel to it, St-André.

FINDING AN ADDRESS   If it were larger, the historic district, with its winding and plunging streets, might be confusing to negotiate. As compact as it is, though, most visitors have little difficulty finding their way around. Most streets are only a few blocks long, so when the name of the street is known, it is fairly easy to find a specific address.

STREET MAPS   There are good maps of the Upper and Lower Towns and the metropolitan region in the *Greater Québec Area Tourist Guide,* provided by any tourist office.

NEIGHBORHOODS IN BRIEF

Haute-Ville   The Upper Town, surrounded by thick ramparts, occupies the crest of Cap Diamant and overlooks the St. Lawrence River. It includes many of the sites for which the city is famous, among them the Château Frontenac, place d'Armes, Basilica of Notre-Dame, Québec Seminary and museum, and the terrasse Dufferin. At a higher elevation, to the south of the Château, is the Citadelle, a partially star-shaped fortress begun by the French in the 18th century and augmented often by the English well into the 19th. Since most of the buildings of the Haute-Ville are at least a hundred years old, made of granite in similar styles, it enjoys a harmonious visual aspect, with few jarring modern intrusions. When they added a new wing to the château a few years ago, they modeled it with considerable care after the original. That is a standing policy. The Dufferin pedestrian promenade attracts crowds in all seasons for its magnificent views of the river and the land to the south, ferries gliding back and forth, cruise ships, and Great Lakes freighters putting in at the harbor below.

Basse-Ville   Linked to the Upper Town by the funicular on terrasse Dufferin and by several streets and stairways, including one near the entrance to the funicular, it encompasses place Royale, the restored quartier du Petit-Champlain, including pedestrian-only rue du Petit-Champlain, the small Notre-Dame-des-Victoires church, and nearby, the impressive Museum of Civilization, a highlight of any visit. Petit-Champlain is undeniably touristy, but not too unpleasantly so. It contains several agreeable cafés and shops, and the T-shirt vendors have been held in check, if not entirely banned. Restored place Royale is perhaps the most attractive of the city's many squares, upper or lower.

Grande-Allée   This boulevard is the eastern extension of rue St-Louis, from the St-Louis Gate in the fortified walls to avenue Taché. It passes the stately Parliament building, in front of which Winter Carnival takes place every year (the ice sculptures are installed across the street), as well as the numerous terraced bars and restaurants that line both sides from

Impressions

I wish I could give a picture of this extraordinary mass of confusion, which is quite as irregular in shape, height, position and colour as many of the extravagant parts of the Old town of Edinburgh. . . . The whole effect is very lively.
                                    —Capt. Basil Hall, *Travels in North America* (1829)

rue de la Chevrotière to rue de Claire-Fontaine. Later, it skirts the Museum of Fine Arts and the Plains of Abraham, where one of the most important battles in the history of North America took place. The city's large contemporary hotels are also on or near the Grande-Allée.

2 Getting Around

Once within or near the walls of the Haute Ville, virtually no place of interest nor hotel or restaurant is out of walking distance. In bad weather, or when traversing between opposite ends of Lower and Upper Towns, a taxi might be necessary, but in general, walking is the best way to explore the city.

March of the Tongue Troopers

When the separatist Parti Québécois took power in the province in 1976, they wasted no time in undertaking to make Québec unilingual. They promptly passed Bill 101, which made French the sole official language of government and sharply restricted the use of language in education and commerce. Since about 20% of the population had English as a primary language, one out of five Québecers felt themselves declared instant second-class citizens. Francophones responded that it was about time *les Anglais,* a.k.a. *les autres* (the others), knew what that felt like and set about enforcing the new law.

The vehicle was *L'Office de la langue française.* Its agents fanned out across the province, scouring the landscape for linguistic insults. No offense was too slight for their stern attention. "Merry Christmas" signs were removed from storefronts, and any merchant who put up a "Going Out of Business" poster faced the possibility of a fine. Department stores had to come up with a new name for Harris Tweed. By fiat and threat of punishment, hamburgers became *hambourgeois,* a hot dog was now *le chien chaud,* a funeral parlor was a *salon funéraire,* and Schwartz's Montreal Hebrew Delicatessen became *Chez Schwartz Charcuterie Hebraïque de Montréal.* Particular scrutiny was accorded the Eastern Townships, on the south side of the St. Lawrence River. They had been settled by United Empire Loyalists, Americans who were faithful to the British Crown and fled to Canada at the time of the Revolution. The region, known henceforth as Estrie, had a Tea Table Island and a Molasses Lake, now called Île Table à Thé and Lac à Mélasse.

Eventually, it might be assumed, there would be no more words to conquer. But bureaucrats will be bureaucrats. Definitions were required, describing every object in the known world. One is a *petit gâteau de forme rectangulaire, aromatisé au chocolat, dont la texture se situe entre le biscuit sec et le gâteau spongieux.*

Or, in a word, a brownie.

BY PUBLIC TRANSPORTATION   Although there are streets and stairs between the Château Frontenac on the top of the cliff and place Royale in the Lower Town, there is also a **funicular,** which operates along an inclined 210-foot track between the terrasse Dufferin and the quartier du Petit-Champlain. The fare is $1, and the car operates daily from 8am to midnight in summer. It closes at 11:30pm in winter. The **upper station** is near the front of the Château Frontenac and place d'Armes, while the **lower station** is actually inside the Maison Louis-Jolliet, on rue du Petit-Champlain. Local **buses** run quite often and charge $1.80 in exact change. No. 7 travels up and down rue St-Jean. No. 11 shuttles along Grande-Allée/rue St-Louis, and, along with nos. 7 and 8, also goes well into suburban Ste-Foy, for those who want to visit the shopping centers there. **One-day bus passes** are available for $3.50.

BY TAXI   They're everywhere, cruising and parked in front of the big hotels and in some of the larger squares of the Upper Town. In theory, they can be hailed, but they are best obtained by finding one of their ranks, as in the place d'Armes or in front of the Hôtel-de-Ville (City Hall). Restaurant managers and hotel bell captains will also summon them. Fares are expensive, in part to compensate for the short distances of most rides. To call a cab, try Taxi Coop (☎ 418/525-5191) or Taxi Québec (☎ 418/525-8123).

BY CAR   See "Getting Around"—"By Car" in Chapter 3 for information on gasoline and driving rules in Canada.

Rentals   Car-rental companies include **Avis,** at the airport (☎ **418/872-0409** or 800/879-2847) and in the city (☎ 418/523-1075); **Budget,** at the airport (☎ **418/872-9885** or 800/268-8900) and in the city (☎ 418/692-3660); **Hertz Canada,** at the airport (☎ **418/871-1571** or 800/654-3131) and in the city (☎ 418/694-1224); **Thrifty,** at the airport (☎ **418/877-2870** or 800/367-2277) and in the city (☎ 418/683-1542); and **Tilden,** at the airport (☎ **418/871-1224**).

Parking   On-street parking is very difficult in the cramped quarters of old Québec. When a rare space on the street is found, be sure to check the signs for hours that parking is permissible. When meters are in place, the charge is 25¢ per 15 minutes up to 120 minutes. Metered spots are free on Sundays, before 9am and after 6pm Monday through Wednesday and on Saturday, and before 9am and after 9pm Thursday and Friday.

Many of the smaller hotels have special arrangements with local garages, resulting in discounts for their guests of three or four dollars less per day than the usual $10 or so. Check at the hotel first before parking in a lot or garage.

If a particular hotel or auberge doesn't have access to a lot, there are plenty available, clearly marked on the foldout city map available at tourist offices. Several convenient ones include the one next to the Hôtel-de-Ville (City Hall), where parking is free in the evening and on weekends; Complexe G, off the Grande-Allée on rue St-Cyrille, with twice-daily in-and-out privileges at no extra charge; and in the Lower

Town across the street from the Museum of Civilization, on rue Dalhousie, where discounts are often offered on weekends.

BY BICYCLE   Given the hilly topography of the Upper Town, cycling isn't a particularly attractive option. But pedal and motorized bicycles are available at a shop in the flatter Lower Town, near the lighthouse. Bikes are about $6 an hour or $30 a day, mopeds, about $50 per day. The shop, Location Petit-Champlain, at 94 rue du Petit-Champlain, also rents strollers, and it's open daily from 9am to 11pm (☎ 418/692-2817). Bikes can also be rented on relatively flat Ile d'Orléans, across the bridge from the north shore at the gas station (☎ 418/828-9215).

FAST FACTS: Québec City

Airport   See "Orientation" in this chapter.

American Express   There is no office right in town, but for lost traveler's checks, call ☎ 800/221-7282. American Express keeps a customer service desk in two shopping centers in Ste-Foy, a bus or taxi ride away: Les Galeries de la Capitale, 5401 bd. des Galeries (☎ 418/627-2580); and place Laurier, 2740 bd. Laurier, (☎ 418/658-8820).

Area Code   Québec City's area code is 418.

Babysitters   Check at the hotel concierge or front desk.

Bookstores   Most of Québec City's bookstores cater to the solidly French-speaking citizenry and the horde of students at the university, but a few shops carry some English books. One such is **Librairie Garneau,** 24 côte de la Fabrique (☎ 418/692-4262). **Librairie du Nouveau Monde,** 103 rue St-Pierre in Old Québec (☎ 418/694-9475), features titles dealing with Québec history and culture, including books in English. **Librairie Pantoute,** 1100 rue St-Jean (☎ 418/692-9748), sometimes carries copies of Berlitz's *French for Travellers.* For travel books, visit **Ulysses,** 4 bd. St-Cyrille est (☎ 418/529-5349).

Business Hours   Banks are open from 10am to 3pm, with most also having hours on Thursday and Friday evenings. Several banks have Saturday hours, but the ones that do are mostly located outside of the Old Town.

Car Rentals   See "Getting Around" in this chapter.

Consulate   The U.S. Consulate is near the Château Frontenac, facing Jardin des Gouverneurs at 2 place terrasse-Dufferin (☎ 418/692-2095).

Currency   See "Information, Entry Requirements & Money" in Chapter 2.

Currency Exchange   Conveniently located near the Château Frontenac, the bureau de change at 19 rue Ste-Anne and rue des

Jardins is open Monday, Tuesday, and Friday from 10am to 3pm, and Wednesday and Thursday from 10am to 6pm. (On weekends, change money in hotels and shops.)

Dentists   Call ☎ **418/653-5412** Monday 9am to 8pm; Tuesday and Wednesday 8am to 8pm; Thursday 8am to 6pm; and Friday 8am to 4pm; for weekend emergencies, call ☎ 418/656-6060.

Doctors   For emergency treatment, call Info-Santé (☎ **418/648-2626**) 24 hours a day, or the Hôtel-Dieu de Québec Hospital emergency room (☎ 418/691-5042).

Drugstores   Caron & Bernier, in the Upper Town, 38 côte du Palais, at rue Charlevoix, is open from 8:15am to 8pm Monday through Friday, and 9am to 3pm on Saturday (☎ **418/692-4252**). In an emergency, it's necessary to travel to the suburbs to Pharmacie Brunet, in Les Galeries Charlesbourg, 4266 Première Avenue (1ère or First Avenue), in Charlesbourg (☎ 418/623-1571), open 24 hours, 7 days.

Electricity   What works in the United States works in Québec.

Emergencies   For police, call 911. Marine Search and Rescue (Canadian Coast Guard), 24 hours a day, ☎ 418/648-3599 (Greater Québec area) or 800/463-4393 (St. Lawrence River). Poison Control Center, ☎ 418/656-5412. For pets, Vet-Medic (☎ 418/647-2000), 24 hours a day.

Holidays   See "When to Go" in Chapter 2.

Information   See "Visitor Information" in the "Orientation" section earlier in this chapter.

Liquor & Wine   A supermarket-sized Société des Alcools store is located on av. Cartier. Another attractive possibility is the Maison des Vins, on place Royale in the Lower Town. The ground floor of this old Québec house is a liquor store, with a good choice of wines. But down in the cellar ("les caves") is their collection of rare and special wines and champagnes. The cellars are worth a visit even if there is no intention of buying.

Lost Property   Call the police (☎ **418/691-6911**).

Luggage Storage and Lockers   Luggage storage is available in the train station, Gare du Palais, 450 rue de la Gare-du-Palais, in the Lower Town.

Newspapers and Magazines   Québec City's English-language newspaper, the *Chronicle-Telegraph*, is the equivalent of a small-town newspaper, published weekly on Wednesday. The content is local news and advertisements, of marginal interest to visitors. Major Canadian and American English-language newspapers and magazines are available in the newsstands of the large hotels and at vending machines placed around tourist corners in the old town. The leading French-language newspapers are *Le Soleil* and *Le Journal de Québec*.

Photographic Needs Film can be purchased or developed at Librairie Garneau, 24 côte de la Fabrique (☎ 418/692-4262).

Police For the Québec City police, call 911. For the Sûreté du Québec, comparable to the state police, call ☎ **418/623-6262.**

Post Office The main post office (bureau de poste) is in the Lower Town, at 300 rue St-Paul near rue Abraham-Martin, not far from carré Parent (Parent Square) by the port (☎ **418/694-6176**). Hours are 8am to 5:45pm Monday through Friday. A convenient branch in the Upper Town, half a block down the hill from the Château Frontenac at 3 rue Buade (☎ **418/694-6102**), keeps the same hours.

Radio and TV Most broadcasts on radio and TV are in French, but FM 104.7 is in English. In the large hotels, cable TV is standard, with some English-language stations. Channel 5 offers English-language programming.

Restrooms Find them in the tourist offices and on the ground floor of the commercial complex at 41 rue Couillard, just off rue St-Jean (it's wheelchair accessible). Many cafés situate their restrooms near the telephone.

Safety Canadian cities are far safer than most of their U.S. counterparts. Still, tourists are particular targets of street criminals, so the usual caveats pertain. A moneybelt or pouch worn under clothing is a good idea, as are staying aware of the behavior of people nearby and keeping a close eye on your possessions.

Time Québec City is on the same time as New York, Boston, Montréal, and Toronto. It's an hour behind Halifax.

Tipping Waiters, waitresses, and cabbies should be given 10% to 15% tip, depending upon the quality of service they provide. Bellhops get $1 per bag, slightly more if they are heavy or must be carried a long distance. The doorman who hails a cab deserves some coins, up to a dollar. Many hotel guests leave a dollar per night for the chambermaid.

Transit Information Call ☎ **418/627-2511.**

Useful Telephone Numbers For Alcoholics Anonymous, ☎ **418/529-0015,** daily 8am to midnight. Health Info, a 24-hour line answered by nurses, ☎ **418/648-2626.** Tel-Aide, for emotional distress including anxiety and depression, ☎ **418/683-2153.** Tides, ☎ **418/648-7293,** 24 hours daily.

Water It's safe to drink.

Weather For the forecast, call ☎ **418/640-2736,** 24 hours a day.

3 Networks & Resources

FOR STUDENTS

A favorite gathering spot for coffee and conversation is Café **Chez Temporel,** 25 rue Couillard (☎ **418/694-1813**). Folk music is the attraction **at Chez Son Père,** 24 rue St-Stanislas at rue St-Jean

(☎ 418/692-5308). These are convivial spots, where it's often easy to strike up a conversation. When looking for a dance partner, head to the Grande-Allée and the club **Chez Dagobert,** no. 600 (☎ 418/522-0393), opposite Loews Hotel Le Concorde. Many museums offer discounted admissions to students.

FOR GAYS & LESBIANS

Gay haunts in Québec City change frequently, but they can be found at the west end of rue St-Jean, around and past place d'Youville and the St-Jean Gate.

FOR WOMEN

Women, particularly those traveling alone, feel comfortable in Café Chez Temporel, 25 rue Couillard (☎ 418/694-1813), and the more upscale Saint Alexandre Pub, 1087 rue St-Jean (☎ 418/694-0015), which has dozens of foreign and domestic brews on draft and in bottles.

FOR SENIORS

Senior travelers can often get—and should always ask about—discounts in hotels and museums. An ID with proof of age may be requested.

12

Québec City Accommodations

Staying in one of the small hotels or auberges within the walls of the Upper Town can be one of Québec City's memorable experiences. That isn't to imply that it will necessarily be enjoyable. Standards of comfort, amenities, and prices fluctuate so wildly from one small hotel to another—even within a single establishment—that it is wise to shop around and examine any rooms offered before registering. From rooms with private baths, minibars, and cable TVs to walk-up budget accommodations with linoleum floors and toilets down the hall, Québec has a wide variety of lodgings to suit most tastes and wallets.

If cost is a prime consideration, note that prices drop significantly from November through April. On the other hand, if you want luxury and the Château Frontenac is fully booked, you will need to go outside the ancient walls to the newer part of town. Most of the high-rise chain hotels out there are within walking distance of the attractions in the Old City, or are only a quick bus or taxi ride away.

CATEGORIES The prices given in the listings below are rack rates. "Expensive" rooms range from $125 to $185 for a double room in summer. Although Québec City has many fewer luxury and first-class hotels than Montréal, there are still enough of them to provide for the crowds of businesspeople and well-heeled tourists who flock to the city year-round. A city that combines tourism and governmental functions with a pronounced four-season climate studded with festivals and special events inevitably produces complex and rapidly changing rate structures for its lodgings. Simply delaying a trip or moving it up by a week or even a few days can make a significant difference in cost. To save, skip Christmas or Winter Carnival or summer and ask about weekend stays, honeymoon specials, and senior citizen or corporate discounts. Remember also that families with children can often share a room for the cost of the parents alone.

"Moderate" establishments listed below are those that charge $80 to $125 for a double room in summer. "Inexpensive" establishments, which charge $45 to $80 for a double room in summer or even less, are generally smaller, often converted residences or carved out of several row houses. They offer fewer of the usual electronic gadgets—air-conditioning and TV are far from standard at this level—and may be several floors high, without elevators. Even with an advance reservation, always ask to see two or three rooms before making a choice in this price category. Unless otherwise noted, all rooms in the lodgings listed below have baths. Remember that prices are given in Canadian dollars.

In addition to guesthouses, many owners of private homes make one to five rooms available for guests, providing them also with breakfast. This kind of bed-and-breakfast doesn't have a sign out front. The only way to locate and reserve one is through one of the umbrella organizations that maintain listings. One such, in a shifting field, is **Bonjour Québec,** 3765 bd. de Monaco, Québec G1R 1N4, ☎ **418/527-1465.** Rooms are generally in the $35 to $65 range for double occupancy. When calling to make arrangements, be very clear about your needs and requirements. Some hosts don't permit smoking or children or pets. They may have only one or two bathrooms to be shared by four or five rooms, or all their rooms may be fourth-floor walkups, or they may be located far from the center of things. As with the inexpensive lodging choices listed below, TVs and air-conditioning are exceptions, not regular features. A deposit is typically required, and minimum stays of two nights are common. Credit cards may not be accepted.

1 Best Bets

- **Best Historic Hotel:** The Château Frontenac is over a century old, one of the first hotels built to serve railroad passengers and to encourage tourism at a time when most people stayed close to home. It's still worth a visit. Château Frontenac, 1 rue des Carrières (St-Louis), Québec, PQ G1R 4P5. ☎ **418/692-3861** or 800/828-7447. Fax 418/692-1751.
- **Best for Business Travelers:** A tie. Both the Hilton and the Radisson Gouverneurs are as central as can be found, with good fitness centers and executive floors with concierges and business services. Hilton International Québec, 3 place Québec, Québec PQ G1K 7889. ☎ **418/647-2411** or 800/445-8667. Fax 418/847-6488. Radisson Gouverneurs, 690 bd. René-Lévesque est, Québec, PQ G1R 5A8. ☎ **418/647-1717** or 800/463-2820 from eastern Canada and Ontario, 800/333-3333 from elsewhere. Fax 418/647-2146.
- **Best for a Romantic Getaway:** It's hard to beat curling up with a glass of wine beside the fire in the country-chic great room of the Auberge St-Antoine. Auberge St-Antoine, 10 rue St-Antoine (Dalhousie), Québec, PQ G1K 4C9. ☎ **418/692-2211** or 800/267-0525. Fax 418/692-1177.
- **Best Trendy Hotel:** The Auberge St-Antoine again, which is spurring a trend in boutique hotels in the Old City. See "Best for a Romantic Getaway" above for address, phone, and fax numbers.
- **Best Location:** Where else? For tourists, nothing can beat the Château Frontenac for proximity to all the sights. The Château

is one of the sights. See "Best Historic Hotel" above for the hotel's address, phone and fax numbers.

• **Best Health Club and Hotel Pool:** At the Radisson Gouverneurs, they have weights, exercycles, and a workout room with instructors, as well as a whirlpool and sauna to ease out the kinks. When it's snowing outside, slipping into the heated water inside and swimming out to the open air is quite a sensation. Radisson Gouverneurs, 690 bd. René-Lévesque est, Québec, PQ G1R 5A8. ☎ **418/647-1717** or 800/463-2820 from eastern Canada and Ontario, 800/333-3333 from elsewhere. Fax 418/647-2146.

2 Upper Town

EXPENSIVE

Château Frontenac

1 rue des Carrières (St-Louis), Québec, PQ G1R 4P5. ☎ **418/692-3861** or 800/828-7447. Fax 418/692-1751. 611 rms, 24 suites. A/C MINIBAR TV TEL. Mid-May to mid-Oct, $190–$285 double, $385–$685 suite. Mid-Oct to mid-May, $125–$190 double, $300–$600 suite. AE, CB, DC, DISC, ER, MC, V. Parking garage: $12.25 per day.

Québec's magical "castle" turned 100 years old in 1993. To celebrate, the management added a new, 66-room wing, and since the hotel serves as the very symbol of the city, spent the money to replicate the original architectural style. Added to the facilities were a new indoor pool and a large gym overlooking Governor's Park. Fitness swimmers may find the pool monopolized by youngsters much of the day. In the past, the hotel hosted Queen Elizabeth and Prince Philip, and during World War II, Churchill and Roosevelt had the entire place to themselves for a conference. The hotel was built in phases, following the land line, so the wide halls follow crooked paths. The price of a room depends on its size, location, view or lack thereof, and on how recently it was renovated. The fare in the dining rooms is yet to measure up to the grandeur of the physical spaces.

Dining/Entertainment: The main dining rooms are the upscale Le Champlain dining room and the more casual Café de la Terrasse, which offers a buffet dinner and dancing on Saturday nights. Two bars overlook the terrace Dufferin. Le Bistro is the lower level snackbar.

Services: Concierge, room service (6:30–11:30pm), dry cleaning, laundry service, babysitting, limo service, secretarial services.

Facilities: Large indoor pool, business center, children's pool, Jacuzzi, health club with massage, shops, no-smoking rooms.

MODERATE

Many of the hotels and auberges recommended below are on or near the Jardin des Gouverneurs, immediately south of the Château Frontenac.

Au Jardin du Gouverneur

16 rue Mont-Carmel (rue Haldimand), Québec, PQ G1R 4A3. ☎ **418/692-1704.** Fax 418/692-1713. 16 rms, 1 suite. A/C TV. $65–$90 double. Rates include continental

breakfast. Extra person over 12 years $15, under 12, $5. AE, DC, ER, MC, V. Parking in nearby garage.

Identified by its white stucco front and blue-gray trim, the building at the upper corner of the park is over 150 years old, a former home of prominent Québec politicians. Rooms are serviceable rather than memorable, but comfortable enough to represent good value. About half the rooms have views of the park. The Château Frontenac and terrasse Dufferin are at the downhill end of the park.

Cap Diamant Maison de Touristes

39 av. Ste-Geneviève (near de Brébeuf), Québec, PQ G1R 4B3. ☎ **418/694-0313.** 9 rms. A/C TV. Summer, $54–$100 double. Winter, $45–$70 double. Rates include morning coffee and juice. Extra person $10. MC, V. Parking $6 in nearby lot.

Every room is different in this amiable guesthouse, its assortments of furniture including brass beds, Victorian memorabilia, and nonspecific retro pieces retrieved from attics. All the rooms have small refrigerators, air-conditioning, color TV, and private bath. In back of the house, which dates from 1826, there's an enclosed porch and a garden. The Cap Diamant is only 2^1/$_2$ blocks from the Jardin des Gouverneurs. The grassy lawns of the Plains of Abraham are right behind it, leading up to the Citadelle. Rooms overlook the rooftops of the Old City. The view from no. 2 is particularly captivating.

⑤ Château Bellevue

16 rue Laporte (Laporte), Québec, PQ G1R 4M9. ☎ **418/692-2573** or 800/ 463-2617. Fax 418/692-4876. 57 rms. A/C TV TEL. $74–$99 double. Extra person $10. Packages available Oct–May. AE, CB, DC, ER, MC, V. Valet parking free.

Occupying several row houses at the top of the Parc des Gouverneurs, this mini-hotel has a pleasant lobby with leather couches and chairs and helpful staff as well as the creature comforts that many of the smaller auberges in the neighborhood lack. While some of the rooms suffer from unfortunate decorating choices, they are quiet for the most part and have private baths. A few higher-priced units look out onto the

---

🏨 Family-Friendly Hotels

Château Frontenac *(see p. 202)*   It's a fairy-tale castle posing as a hotel.

Hôtellerie Fleur-de-Lys *(see p. 204)*   The Old City's only motel, it provides a 24-hour laundry and rooms with kitchenettes and TVs, three things that make travel with kids more comfortable.

L'Hôtel du Vieux Québec *(see p. 205)*   Popular with families and school groups, it's in a good location for exploring Upper or Lower Town.

Radisson Gouverneurs *(see p. 209)*   The rooftop swimming pool is a treat, with its indoor water route to the outside. It's especially fun in winter, when snow covers everything but the pool itself. Winter Carnival activities are a quick and easy walk away.

Québec City Accommodations

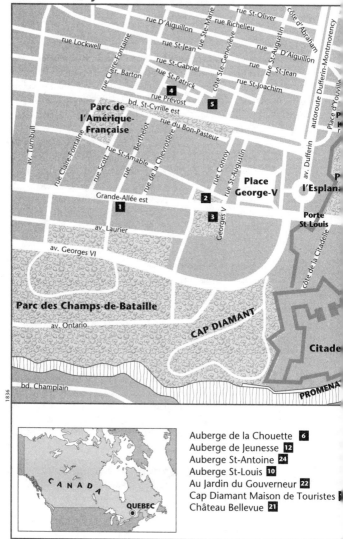

Auberge de la Chouette **6**
Auberge de Jeunesse **12**
Auberge St-Antoine **24**
Auberge St-Louis **10**
Au Jardin du Gouverneur **22**
Cap Diamant Maison de Touristes **❚**
Château Bellevue **21**

park. The hotel's private parking is directly behind the building, a notable convenience in this congested part of town.

Hôtellerie Fleur-de-Lys

115 rue Ste-Anne (near Ste-Ursule), Québec, PQ G1R 3X6. ☎ **418/694-0106** or 800/567-2106. Fax 418/692-1959. 36 rms. A/C TEL TV. $85–$120 double. Extra adult $12. Children 6–15 $6. Continental breakfast in room $4. AE, MC, V. Parking $7.25.

This motel with its brick front tucked into the midst of the Old City is a bit jarring visually, but it's away from the major sites on a quiet side

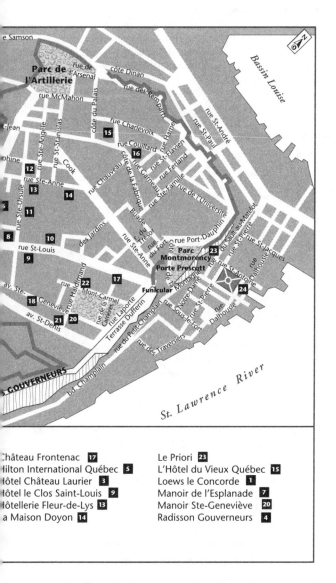

Parc de l'Artillerie

rue de l'Arsenal
côte Dinan
rue McMahon
rue des Remparts
côte du Palais
rue Charlevoix
rue Ste-Angèle
rue St-Stanislas
Cook
rue Couillard
rue Ferland
rue St-Flavien
rue Ste-Famille
rue de l'Université
rue Ste-Anne
rue Ste-Ursule
rue du Trésor
rue des Jardins
rue St-Louis
rue St-André
rue St-Paul
Bassin Louise
rue St-Antoine
rue St-Pierre
rue Dalhousie
Parc Montmorency
Porte Prescott
Funicular
rue Haldimand
Mont-Carmel
av. Ste-Geneviève
av. St-Denis
Terrasse Dufferin
rue du Petit-Champlain
rue des Traversiers
bd Champlain
DES GOUVERNEURS

St. Lawrence River

15 **16** **12** **13** **14** **11** **8** **10** **9** **17** **22** **18** **21** **20** **23** **24** **5**

Château Frontenac **17**
Hilton International Québec **5**
Hôtel Château Laurier **3**
Hôtel le Clos Saint-Louis **9**
Hôtellerie Fleur-de-Lys **13**
La Maison Doyon **14**

Le Priori **23**
L'Hôtel du Vieux Québec **15**
Loews le Concorde **1**
Manoir de l'Esplanade **7**
Manoir Ste-Geneviève **20**
Radisson Gouverneurs **4**

street and has its soothing virtues. These include the enclosed parking lot and a laundry room available to guests 24 hours a day. In addition, every room has a refrigerator, a dining table and chairs. Some rooms have kitchenettes.

L'Hôtel du Vieux Québec

8 rue Collins (near St-Jean), Québec, PQ G1R 4J2. ☎ **418/692-1850.** Fax 418/692-5637. 28 rms and suites. TV TEL. May to mid-Oct, Christmas holidays, and Winter Carnival, $89–$119 double. Mid-Oct to Dec (except Christmas period), $50–$79 double. Jan–Apr $60–$79. Extra person $10. AE, ER, MC, V. Parking $6.

The century-old brick building has been carefully renovated and modernized. Guest rooms are equipped with sofas, two double beds, kitchenettes, cable color TVs, and modern bathrooms. With those homey layouts, it's understandably popular with families, skiers, and the groups of visiting high-schoolers who descend upon the city in late spring. Some rooms have air conditioning. Many moderately priced restaurants and nightspots are found on nearby St-Jean.

Manoir Ste-Geneviève

13 av. Ste-Geneviève (Laporte), Québec, PQ G1R 4A7. ☎ and fax **418/694-1666.** 9 rms. A/C TV. May–Oct, $87–$100 double, Nov–Apr, rates 30% lower. Extra person $10. No credit cards. Parking $6.

The front of the Manoir Ste-Geneviève, at the upper corner of the Parc des Gouverneurs, hints at the gentility that awaits you inside, with its leaded-glass doorway and flower boxes in the windows in summer. Six of the rooms, most of them somewhere between compact and cramped, have full bath, while three have shower only. A couple have rudimentary kitchenettes. The second-story terrace is for guests' use.

INEXPENSIVE

Auberge de la Chouette

71 rue d'Auteuil (near St-Louis), Québec, PQ G1R 4C3. ☎ **418/694-0232.** 10 rms. A/C TV TEL. Summer, $70 double. Winter, $55 double. AE, MC, V. Parking $6 a day.

Across the street from Esplanade Park and near the Porte St-Louis, this auberge has an accomplished Asian restaurant, Apsara, on the main floor. A spiral stairway leads up to the rooms, all of which have full bath. The tourist office, Citadelle, and Winter Carnival or Québec Summer Festival activities are only minutes away.

Auberge St-Louis

48 rue St-Louis (near Ste-Ursule), Québec, PQ G1R 3Z3. ☎ **418/692-2424** or 800/ 663-7878 in Canada. Fax 418/692-3797. 27 rms (13 with bath). June–Oct, $40–$55 double without bath, $61 double with private shower and sink and shared toilet, $76–$85 with bath. Nov–May, $39 double without bath, $49 with shower and sink only, $59 with bath. MC, V. Rates include breakfast. Extra person $10. MC, V. Parking nearby $6 a day.

Guest rooms here come in a variety of configurations, with occasional features adding visual interest, such as a carved-wood fireplace or a

---

An Important Note on Prices

Unless stated otherwise, **the prices cited in this guide are given in Canadian dollars,** which is good news for visitors from the U.S. because the Canadian dollar is worth about 25% less than the American dollar, but buys just about as much.

As of this writing, $1 Canadian is worth 75¢ U.S., which means that a $100-a-night hotel room costs only about $75 (U.S.) a night.

For a conversion chart, see "Information, Entry Requirements & Money" in Section 1, Chapter 2.

stained-glass window. But the reasons to stay here are low prices combined with a good location. Some rooms only have a sink and shower, but no toilet, and some have a color or black-and-white TV. Only two units have air-conditioning, the rest have fans.

Hôtel le Clos Saint-Louis

71 rue St-Louis (near place d'Armes), Québec, PQ G1R 3Z2. ☎ **418/694-1311** or 800/461-1311 in Canada. Fax 418/694-9411. 30 rms (13 with bath). Summer, $58 double without bath; $98-$118 double with bath. Winter, $40 double without bath; $56-$65 double with bath. Rates include continental breakfast. Special packages from $40 per person Nov–May. MC, V. Parking $6.

Housed in a pair of converted 19th-century houses near the Château Frontenac, the guest rooms at no. 71 are the more desirable. Most of the rooms have TVs, and some have nonworking marble fireplaces. As is true of most of the lodging places in this category, price and location are the primary considerations.

La Maison Doyon

109 rue Ste-Anne (near place de l'Hôtel-de-Ville), Québec PQ G1R 3X6. ☎ **418/694-1720.** Fax 418/694-1164. 16 rms (14 with bath). TV. May–Oct and Winter Carnival, $50 double without bath; $70–$80 double with bath. MC, V. Rates include continental breakfast. Extra person $10. Children under 12 free. Rates drop about 40% Nov–Apr (except during Winter Carnival). MC, V. Parking nearby $6.

An informal guesthouse, this is clean and presentable, if pared down to the basics. Rooms are small, but all have ceiling fans and TVs. The breakfast room has a map of the city on the wall, and the backyard garden is open to guests.

✪ Auberge de Jeunesse

19 Ste-Ursule (at rue Dauphine), Québec, PQ G1R 4E1. ☎ **418/694-0755** or 800/461-8585 from elsewhere in the province except Montréal or 514/252-3117 from Montréal or outside the province. Fax 418/694-2278 or 514/251-3119 from Montréal and outside the province. 281 beds. $12.75–$16.75 members, $15.75–$19.75 nonmembers. Half price for children 9–13; free for children 8 and younger. AE, MC, V.

Officially a youth hostel, this two-story brick building up the hill from rue St-Jean has some rooms with two beds and a few with double beds, but most units have four beds. There are also dorms with 10 to 12 beds. The cafeteria is open most of the year, and breakfast costs about $3.50. Lockers are available for luggage, skis, and bicycles. There is a laundry, a lounge with a pool table, and a backyard with picnic tables. Guests can use the common kitchen. There's no curfew.

3 On or Near the Grande-Allée

EXPENSIVE

✪ Hilton International Québec

3 place Québec, Québec, PQ G1K 7889. ☎ **418/647-2411** or 800/445-8667. Fax 418/847-6488. 565 rms, 39 suites. A/C MINIBAR TV TEL. $166–$226 double, from $335 suite. Extra person $22. Children of any age stay free in parents' room. Special rates and ski and weekend packages available. AE, CB, DC, DISC, MC, V. Parking $13.50.

Superior on virtually every count to the other mid-rise contemporary hotels outside the Old Town, this Hilton is the clear choice for visiting executives and for those leisure travelers who can't bear to live without their gadgets. The location, across the street from the city walls and near the Parliament building, is excellent. It is also connected to the place Québec shopping complex, where there are 75 shops and two cinemas, and the Convention Center. The public rooms are big and brassy, Hilton-style, while the guest chambers are in need of freshening, looking outdated and uninspired. Most have one or two large beds. Upper-floor views of the St. Lawrence River, Old Québec, and the Laurentian Mountains are grand. The staff is generally efficient and congenial. Non-smoking rooms available. To get there, head east along Grande-Allée, and just before the St-Louis Gate in the city wall, turn left on rue Dufferin, then left again, passing the Parliament building. The hotel is ahead one block.

Dining/Entertainment: Le Caucus restaurant and bar serves a buffet as well as à la carte for all meals. Friday and Saturday evenings are theme nights, with live entertainment.

Services: Airport shuttle, room service, dry cleaning, laundry service, babysitting, car rental.

Facilities: In-room movies, heated outdoor pool (summer only), health club with sauna and massage, whirlpool.

Loews Le Concorde

1225 place Montcalm (at Grande-Allée), Québec, PQ G1R 4W6. ☎ **418/647-2222** or 800/235-6397 from the U.S., 800/463-5256 from Canada. Fax 418/647-4710. 400 rms, 22 suites. A/C MINIBAR TV TEL. $135–$180 double, from $195 suite. AE, DC, ER, MC, V. Extra person over 17, $20. Special off-season rates available, along with weekend and ski packages. AE, DC, ER, MC, V. Parking garage $12.50.

From outside, the building that houses the hotel is an unforgivable insult to the skyline, blighting a neighborhood of late Victorian townhouses. Enter, and the affront might be forgotten, at least by those who have business to do and can't be bothered with aesthetics. Standard rooms have marble bathrooms with hairdryers, prints of Québec City street scenes, and three telephones. They bestow spectacular views of the river and the Old City, even from the lower floors. It's about a 10-minute walk to the walls and then another 10 minutes to the center of the Haute-Ville. Since this is the farthest away of the hotels recommended here, that's not too distant.

Dining/Entertainment: L'Astral is the city's only revolving rooftop restaurant. It has a bar and piano music Tuesday to Sunday nights. Le Café serves light lunch or dinner. La Place Montcalm offers buffet or à la carte breakfasts until 11:30am (noon on weekends).

Services: Concierge, room service (6am to midnight), dry cleaning, laundry service.

Facilities: In-room movies, seven non-smoking floors, seven business-class floors, a small fitness facility with sauna and some exercise equipment, outdoor heated pool (April to November, access to pool in private club the rest of the year).

Radisson Gouverneurs

690 bd. René-Lévesque est, Québec, PQ G1R 5A8. ☎ **418/647-1717** or 800/
463-2820 from eastern Canada and Ontario, 800/333-3333 from elsewhere. Fax 418/
647-2146. 377 rms, 14 suites. A/C TV TEL. $140–$160 double, from $195 suite.
Extra adult $15; children free. AE, DC, DISC, ER, MC, V. Parking $11, with in/out
privileges.

Part of place Québec, a multiuse complex similar to those in Montréal,
the hotel is also connected to the city's convention center. It is also a
block from the Hilton, two blocks from Porte Kent (Kent Gate) in the
city wall, and not far from the Québec Parliament building, a location
likely to fit almost any businessperson's needs. It is, however, an uphill
climb from the Old City, as is true of all the hotels and inns along or
near the Grande-Allée. While the decor of the hotel is outspoken and
ultramodern, it is the most successful and tasteful of Québec City's
large hostelries. Some rooms have minibars. An indoor waterway leads
to the heated outdoor pool, a rare treat to swim through when snow
is falling. Reception is two levels up. Québec's Gouverneurs chain
of hotels and motels joined forces with the American Radisson
group in 1992. To get there, turn left off Grande-Allée, then left again
onto Dufferin, just before the St-Louis Gate in the city wall. Once you
pass the Parliament building, take the first left. The hotel is two blocks
ahead.

   Dining/Entertainment: Le Café serves buffet and à la carte meals.
   Services: Room service, dry cleaning, laundry service, babysitting.
   Facilities: In-room movies, three nonsmoking floors, two executive
floors, fully-equipped and staffed health club with exercycles and sauna,
Jacuzzi, outdoor heated pool (year-round).

MODERATE

Hôtel Château Laurier

695 Grand-Allée est (at Georges V), Québec, PQ G1R 2K4. ☎ **418/522-8108** or
800/463-4453. Fax 418/524-8768. 55 rms. A/C TV TEL. Summer, $89–$119 double.
Winter, $69 double. Extra person $10. AE, DC, ER, MC, V. Parking free, behind the
hotel.

Just a few blocks from the St-Louis Gate and next to the Plains of
Abraham, this century-old stone structure has a Victorian parlor with
a grandfather clock. Rates depend on room size, fixtures, and view. An
elevator serves the several floors, and a sauna is available. Le Patrimoine
restaurant, on the ground floor, is open from early morning to late
evening. When booking, ask about the availability of the package that
covers two nights' lodging, two breakfasts, and two dinners for $139
per person, double.

INEXPENSIVE

Manoir de L'Esplanade

83 rue d'Auteuil (at rue St-Louis), Québec, PQ G1R 4C3. ☎ **418/694-0834.** Fax
418/692-0456. 37 rms. A/C TV TEL. Summer, $65–$90 double. Winter, 45% less.
Extra person $10. AE, MC, V. Parking $6 a day.

Though not as well appointed as some of the other places around the Grande-Allée, it's clean and all rooms have private baths, not something one can generally assume at this rate level. Some have double beds. Students like this place, which used to be a nunnery. The tourist office is right across the street.

☉ Relais Charles-Alexander

91 Grande-Allée est (av. Galipeault), Québec, PQ G1R 2H5. ☎ **418/523-1220.** Fax 418/523-9556. 17 rms (14 with bath). A/C TV. $70–$80 double. Rates include breakfast. No credit cards. Parking nearby $6.

On the ground floor of this charming brick-faced bed-and-breakfast is an art gallery, which also serves as the breakfast room. That stylish use of space extends to the bedrooms, crisply maintained with eclectic choices of antique pieces and reproductions. They are quiet, for the most part, since the inn is just outside the orbit of the sometimes raucous Grande-Allée terrace bars. Yet the St-Louis Gate is less than a 10-minute walk.

4 Lower Town

EXPENSIVE

✪ Auberge St-Antoine

10 rue St-Antoine (Dalhousie), Québec, PQ, G1K 4C9. ☎ **418/692-2211** or 800/ 267-0525. Fax 418/692-1177. 22 rms, 7 suites. A/C TV TEL. $129–$269 double, $439 suite. Rates include buffet breakfast. Extra person $10. Children under 12 free. AE, DC, MC, V. Parking free.

The centerpiece of this uncommonly attractive boutique hotel is the 1830 maritime warehouse that contains the lobby and meeting rooms, with the original dark beams and stone floor. Buffet breakfasts and afternoon wine and cheese are set out in the lobby, where you can relax in wing chairs next to the hooded fireplace. Canny mixes of antique and reproduction furniture are found in both public and private areas. The bedrooms, in an adjoining modern wing, are spacious, in many different color schemes, with such extra decorative touches as custom-made iron bedsteads and tables. The big bathrooms have robes and hairdryers. Three rooms have private terraces, and thirteen have river views, but a large parking lot intervenes. The eight new suites have kitchenettes, fax machines, and computer jacks. To get there, follow rue Dalhousie around the Lower Town to rue St-Antoine. The hotel is next to the Musée de la Civilisation.

Le Priori

15 rue Sault-au-Matelot (at rue St-Antoine), Québec, PQ G1K 3Y7. ☎ **418/ 692-3992.** Fax 418/692-0883. 20 rms, 5 suites. TV TEL. $90–$120 double, $135– $210 suite. AE, MC, V. Parking $8 a day.

A second newcomer to the emerging Lower Town hotel scene, two blocks behind the Auberge St-Antoine, this has a playful postmodern ambience behind the somber facade of a 1766 house. Hot French designer Phillipe Starck inspired the owners, who deployed versions of his conical stainless-steel sinks in the bedrooms and sensual multinozzle showers in the small bathrooms. Queen-size beds have black tubular frames and soft duvets. The dim lighting doesn't help readers and in some rooms, a clawfoot tub sits beside the bed. Suites have sitting rooms with wood-burning fireplaces, a kitchen, and a bath with Jacuzzi. The hotel houses the admirable Laurie Raphaël restaurant, which focuses on nouvelle cuisine québécois. At last visit, there were rumors of an impending sale, perhaps to the owners of the restaurant.

13

Québec City Dining

Once you are within these ancient walls, walking along streets that look like they've been transplanted intact from Brittany or Provençe, it is understandable if you imagine that you have one supernal dining experience after another in Québec City in store. Unfortunately, it isn't true. If that French tire company with the red guidebook decided to cast its hotly contested stars upon Québec restaurants, they might grudgingly part with three or four. Hype and expectations aside, the truth is that this gloriously scenic city has no temples de cuisine comparable to those of Paris or Manhattan or even Montréal. While it is easy to eat well in the capital—even, in a few isolated cases, *quite* well— the remembered pleasures of a stay will lie in other areas, with other senses.

But that's not to imply that you're in for barely edible meals served by sullen waiters. By sticking to any of the many competent bistros, the handful of Asian eateries, and one or two of the emerging nuovo Italiano trattorias, you will be content. Another step up, two or three ambitious enterprises tease the palate with hints of higher achievement. Even the blatantly touristic restaurants along rue St-Louis and around the place d'Armes can produce decent meals, despite the fact that they aren't obliged to satisfy demanding regular clienteles. The less extravagant among them, in fact, are entirely satisfactory for breakfast or simple lunches, a useful fact to keep in mind if you're staying in one of the many Old Town guesthouses that serve no meals.

As throughout the province, the best dining deals are the table d'hôte—fixed-price—meals. Virtually all full-service restaurants offer them, if only at lunch. They rarely require significant sacrifice, assuming you don't expect beluga, foie gras, and the pricier cuts of meat. As a rule, they include at least soup or salad, a main course, and a dessert. Some places add in an extra appetizer and/or a beverage, all for the approximate à la carte price of the main course alone.

Curiously, for a city standing beside a great waterway and a day's sail from some of the world's best fishing grounds, seafood is not given much attention. Mussels and salmon are on most menus, but cherish those places that go beyond those staples. Game is popular, however, and everything from venison, rabbit, and duck to more exotic quail, goose, caribou, and wapiti is available.

At the better places, and even some of those that might seem inexplicably popular, reservations are all but essential during traditional holidays and the festivals that pepper the social calendar. Other times, it's usually necessary to book ahead only for weekend evenings. In the listings below, where no mention is made of reservations, they aren't necessary. Dress codes are only required at a few restaurants, but Quebecers are a stylish lot. "Dressy casual" works almost everywhere. Remember that for the Québécois, "dinner" is lunch, and "supper" is dinner, though for the sake of consistency, I have used the word "dinner" below in the traditional American sense. They tend to have the evening meal earlier than Montréalers, at 6 or 7 rather than 8pm.

CATEGORIES   The restaurants recommended below are arranged by location and price category. Those listed as "expensive" charge $20 to $30 à la carte for most of their main courses at dinner (supper); "moderate," $10 to $20; and "inexpensive," $10 or less. When figuring costs, add the 15% in federal and provincial taxes, and a tip, usually 10% to 15%. Prices shown are in Canadian dollars.

1   Best Bets

- **Best Spot for a Romantic Dinner:** Stars above, tables illuminated by the flutter of candlelight and gas lamps, service both skillful and unobtrusive, and even the name, Le Saint-Amour, speaks of romance. Le Saint-Amour, 48 rue Ste-Ursule (near St-Louis). ☎ **418/694-0667.**
- **Best Spot for a Celebration:** There are other candidates, certainly, but for a grownup, rather sedate celebration that doesn't involve helium balloons, consider Le Saint-Pierre for its graceful manner, luxurious spaces, and nightly show tunes on the grand piano. Le Saint-Pierre, 54 rue St-Pierre (at Montagne). ☎ **418/ 694-6194.**
- **Best View:** Revolving rooftop restaurants rarely dish out food of a standard to match their lofty venues, and L'Astral in the Loews Le Concorde hotel doesn't challenge that perception. Go for the views and a drink and you shouldn't be disappointed. L'Astral at Loews Le Concorde, 1225 place Montcalm (at Grande-Allée), Québec, PQ G1R 4W6. ☎ **418/647-2222.**
- **Best Contemporary Cuisine:** Laurie Raphaël is named for the owners' children, a choice which isn't lost on those diners who devote great care to things they hold important—family, friends, and the tables around which they gather. Reservations recommended. Laurie Raphaël, 17 rue du Sault-au-Matelot (at St-Antoine). ☎ **418/692-4555.**
- **Best Seafood:** The owner of Le Marie-Clarisse makes a weekly round-trip to Montréal to choose the just-off-the-boat ingredients served at this, his comfortable bistro. Le Marie-Clarisse, 12 rue du Petit-Champlain (Sous-le-Fort). ☎ **418/692-0857.**
- **Best Pizza:** For conventional and unusual toppings on crispy-thin crusts that work better with knife and fork than fingers, hit Les Frères de la Côte. Reservations recommended. Les Frères de

la Côte, 1190 rue St-Jean (near côte de la Fabrique). ☎ **418/ 692-5445.**

- **Best People-Watching:** Perched at the last level of Breakneck Stairs, above the main pedestrian intersection of le quartier Petit-Champlain, the few outdoor tables of Le Marie-Clarisse monopolize an unsurpassed observation point. See "Best Seafood" above for the address and phone number of this bistro.
- **Best Place to Take a Teenager:** Tasty pizzas and inventive pastas coupled with a thumping stereo and the noise level of a 20-lane bowling alley make Les Frères de la Côte a logical choice for parents with teens who usually communicate only with members of their own tribe anyway. See "Best Pizza" above for the address and phone number of this establishment.

2 Restaurants by Cuisine

BISTRO/FRENCH
L'Ardoise (Lower Town, M)

BISTRO/INTERNATIONAL
Le Cochon Dingue (Lower Town, M)

BISTRO/SEAFOOD
Le Marie-Clarisse (Lower Town, M)

CONTEMPORARY FRENCH
Laurie Raphaël (Lower Town, E)
Le Paris-Brest (On Grande Allée, E)
Le Saint-Amour (Upper Town, E)
Le Saint-Pierre (Lower Town, E)

CONTEMPORARY FRENCH/ ITALIAN
Le Graffiti (Near Grande Allée, M)

CONTEMPORARY ITALIAN
Momento (Near Grande Allée, M)

CRÊPES
Au Petit Coin Breton (On Grande Allée, IE)

Le Casse-Crêpe Breton (Upper Town, M)

ECLECTIC
Serge Bruyère (Upper Town, E)
French/International
Le Café du Monde (Lower Town, M)

INTERNATIONAL
Le Casse-Crêpe Breton (Upper Town, IE)

LIGHT FARE
Chez Temporel (Upper Town, IE)
Le Casse-Crêpe Breton (Upper Town, M)

MEDITERRANEAN
Les Frères de la Côte (Upper Town, M)

QUÉBÉCOIS
Buffet de l'Antiquaire (Lower Town, IE)

SOUTH ASIAN
Aspara (Upper Town, M)
Fleur de Lotus (Upper Town, M)

TRADITIONAL FRENCH
La Ripaille (Upper Town, M)

3 Upper Town

EXPENSIVE

✪ Serge Bruyère

1200 rue Saint-Jean (côte de la Fabrique). ☎ **418/694-0618.** Reservations recommended for dinner. Main courses $9.50–$26.50, table d'hôte lunch $8–$12, dinner $19–$49. AE, DC, MC, V. Mon–Fri 12noon–2pm, 6–10:30pm, Sat–Sun 6–10:30pm. ECLECTIC.

He bought the wedge-shaped building in 1979, and set about creating a multilevel dining emporium that had something for everyone. At ground level, Serge Bruyère renovated and opened a casual café with a cold case displaying salads and pastries, just the place for a leisurely afternoon snack. Up a long staircase at the back is his *La Petite Table,* with a bare wood floor and three semicircular windows looking down on the street. Blue water glasses stand on paper-covered tablecloths. This is meant for lunches, a purpose it serves admirably. Soup and dessert are included in the price of the main course, and come with rounds of crusty chewy bread. Foods are adroitly seasoned, making salt and pepper shakers unnecessary. Finally, another flight up, is the formal *Grand Table.* Overpraised from the outset, its menu is nevertheless highly imaginative and immaculately presented. Gaps between the several courses of the gastronomic extravaganza stretch on . . . and on . . . for an entire evening. Whether the excellent fabrications justify the ecclesiastical tone and pace is an evaluation you must make. Dress well, and arrive with a healthy credit card. Serge Bruyère died young, and tragically. His executive chef carries on, along a similar path.

✪ Le Saint-Amour

48 rue Ste-Ursule (near rue St-Louis). ☎ **418/694-0667.** Reservations recommended for dinner. Main courses $19.50–$28, table d'hôte lunch $9.50, dinner $25–$28, gastronomic dinner $48. AE, CB, DC, ER, MC, V. Tues–Fri noon–2:30pm, daily 6–10:30pm. CONTEMPORARY FRENCH.

Every effort is made to render this a gratifying dining experience, touching all the senses, and the energetic chef-owner tirelessly scours away imperfections. This is a restaurant for adults, many of them coolly attractive and romantically inclined, dressed in designer jeans or silk. They pass a front room with lace curtains and potted greenery into a covered terrace lit by candles and flickering Victorian gas fixtures. Up above, the roof is retracted on warm nights, revealing a splash of stars.

The kitchen has a sure hand with game, featured even on the warm-weather version of the seasonally changed menu. Look for the varying preparations of caribou and wapiti steak, currently trendy items in Québec, as well as boned quail, duck, and rabbit. The long wine list has some not-too-expensive bottlings, and the chocolate desserts are especially tempting. The house, built in the 1820s, is a little off the tourist track, so "I'm With Stupid" T-shirts are not in evidence. There aren't three other restaurants in town that equal Le Saint-Amour.

An Important Note on Prices

Unless stated otherwise, **the prices cited in this guide are given in Canadian dollars,** which is good news for visitors from the U.S., because the Canadian dollar is worth about 25% less than the American dollar, but buys just about as much.

At this writing, $1 Canadian is worth 75¢ U.S., which means that a $50 dinner for two costs only $37.50 (U.S.), and a $5 breakfast will cost only $3.75 (U.S.).

For a conversion chart, see "Information, Entry Requirements & Money" in Chapter 2.

MODERATE

Apsara

71 rue d'Auteuil (near St-Louis Gate). ☎ **418/694-0232.** Main courses $10–$13. AE, MC, V. Mon–Fri 11:30am–2pm, 5:30–11pm, Sat and Sun 5:30–11pm. SOUTH ASIAN.

Near the tourism office and the city walls, this 1845 Victorian row house is home to one of the city's top three Asian restaurants. The interior looks more like the British consulate in Shanghai, an incongruity that doesn't trouble diners who come for a gastronomic tour arcing from Taiwan to Vietnam to Cambodia to Thailand. Head straight for the last stop, since the Thai dishes are clearly masters over the mostly wan alternatives. This *cuisine asiatique* includes satays and *mou sati*—brochettes—breaded shrimp in a zingy sauce, and spicy roast beef. An enticing possibility is the seven-course sampler meal for $36 for two people. House wines aren't expensive, but aren't too good, either. Have beer.

⑤ Les Frères de la Côte

1190 rue St-Jean (near côte de la Fabrique). ☎ **418/692-5445.** Reservations recommended. Main courses $8.25–$10.25, table d'hôte $8.25–$11.50. AE, MC, V. Daily 8am–11pm. MEDITERRANEAN.

At the east end of the Old Town's liveliest nightlife strip, this supremely casual café-pizzeria is as loud as any dance club, all hard surfaces and patrons shouting over the booming stereo music. None of this discourages a single soul, as the packed tables—even on a usually slow Monday night—attest. Chefs in straw hats at the open kitchen in back crank out a dozen different kinds of pizza—thin-crusted, with unusual toppings that work—and about as many pasta versions—not too interesting. Bountiful platters of fish and meats, often in the form of brochettes, make appetizers unnecessary. House wines are available by the glass or carafe. Remember this when kids are in tow. There's no way they can make enough noise to bother other customers.

Fleur de Lotus

38 côte de la Fabrique (opposite the Hôtel-de-Ville). ☎ **418/692-4286.** Main courses $8–$14; table d'hôte lunch $8, dinner $16–$25. MC, V. Mon–Wed 11:30am–10:30pm, Thurs–Fri 1–11pm, Sat 5–11pm, Sun 5–10:30pm. SOUTH ASIAN.

This tiny, spare storefront is busy every midday and evening for all the right reasons—tasty food, efficient service, and low prices. This is another kitchen that skips through the variegated cuisines of Cambodia, Vietnam, and Thailand, and again, the Thai is tops. The more than 20 dishes that crowd the menu include chicken in ginger, pork in sweet sauce, and shrimp in soya purée. Execution is better than good, less than wonderful, but the price is right, and the reception, amiable.

La Ripaille

9 rue Buade (at rue du Fort). ☎ **418/692-2450.** Reservations recommended. Main courses $8.25–$19.95, table d'hôte lunch $8.95–$13.50, dinner $23–$28. AE, DC, DISC, ER, MC, V. Mon–Sat 11:30am–2:30pm, 5–11pm, Sun 5–11pm. TRADITIONAL FRENCH.

This is a place to remember what it was we liked about French food in the first place, back before cholesterol and triglyceride alerts. Here is rack of lamb, meltingly tender and flavorful, and bouillabaise, packed

---

It Helps to Be Born Here

When the first waves of settlers took up residence in New France, they had to subsist on what was available. That meant root vegetables and beans that could be stored over the long winter, what game there was to be caught, and such novelties as the sugar distilled from the sap of maple trees, which grew in abundance along the St. Lawrence Valley. This gave rise to a distinctive Québécois cookery (it was too sturdily humble to be called "cuisine"). It never came close to that invented by their cousins, the Cajuns of Louisiana, but it persists as a comfort food no native Québécois can long resist, no matter how elevated his or her tastes.

Outsiders may wonder how this can be, given the components, but then they didn't take it in with mother's milk. Traditional pea soup is thick and good, shellfish in cider and rabbit braised in beer can be tasty . . . but *poutine?* (Fried potatoes drowned in melted cheese.) *Fève au lard?* (Beans with salt pork.) *Ragoût de pattes de cochon?* (Stew of pigs' feet.) Sure. These are treats of high order compared with *pâté à la râpure,* an Acadian specialty composed of glutinous potatoes encasing bits of meat of uncertain origin. Library paste is more appealing.

Let us not be too unkind. There are winners in the Québécois repertoire, or, depending on the skill of the chef, nonlosers. The meat pies called *tourtières* can be, um, . . . not bad . . . and the pork pâté known as *cretons* is smooth and meaty. But the dish that makes converts of the skeptical is sugar pie. That achingly sweet refutation of the nutrition police is as persistent an object of controversy as the existence of space aliens. It is made either of maple sugar or brown sugar, with or without nuts, *avec* one or two crusts. If only for this, *vive gastronomie habitant!*

with briny morsels of fish, and veal and salmon and duck as those of a certain age remember them, 20 years before Cal-Ital and Nouvelle Southwestern. The room is from memory, too, with lace curtains on the windows, cushy booths, and flowers in vases on pink tablecloths. Service is correct, not stuffy. The restaurant is part of a hotel in an 1835 building situated a block north of the place d'Armes. Valet parking is available after 6pm.

INEXPENSIVE

⑤ Chez Temporel

25 rue Couillard (near côte de la Fabrique). ☎ **418/694-1813.** Most menu items $1.50–$5.25. No credit cards. Sun–Thurs 7:30am–1:30am, Fri–Sat 7:30am–2:30am. LIGHT FARE.

This Latin Quarter café with tile floor and wooden tables attracts denizens of nearby Université Laval. They read *Le Monde*, play chess, swap philosophical insights, and clack away at their laptops from breakfast until well past midnight. It could be a Left Bank hangout for Sorbonne students and their profs. Capture a table and hold it forever for just a cappucino or two. Croissants, jam, butter, and a couple of belts of espresso cost half as much as a hotel breakfast. Later in the day, drop by for a sandwich, quiche, salad, or plate of cheese with a beer or glass of wine. Only 20 people can be seated downstairs, but another 26 can fit upstairs, where the light is filtered through stained-glass windows.

⑤ Le Casse-Crêpe Breton

1136 rue St-Jean (near rue Garneau). ☎ **418/692-0438.** Reservations not required. Most menu items $3–$6.50. No credit cards. Mon–Wed 7:30am–midnight, Thurs–Sun 7:30am–1am. CRÊPES/LIGHT FARE

Eat at the bar and watch the crêpes being made, or attempt to snag one of the five tables. Main-course crêpes come with two to five ingredients of the customer's choice. Dessert crêpes are stuffed with jams or fruit and cream. Soups, salads, and sandwiches are as inexpensive as the crêpes. The name of the café is a play on the word casse-croûte, which means "break crust." It's open more than 16 hours a day, which is useful, but when it gets busy, the service is glacial. Beer is served in bottles or on tap.

4 On or Near the Grande-Allée

EXPENSIVE

Le Paris-Brest

590 Grande-Allée est (at rue de la Chevrotière). ☎ **418/529-2243.** Reservations recommended. Main courses $17.50–$28; table d'hôte lunch $9–$14, dinner $18–$23. AE, CB, DC, ER, MC, V. Mon–Fri 11:30am–2:30pm, Mon–Sat 6–11:30pm, Sun 5:30–11:30pm. CONTEMPORARY FRENCH.

Named for a French dessert, this is a fashionable hideaway with a solid reputation, easily the class of the Grande-Allée. By itself, that is well short of a rave, given the competition. But this is a league ahead, not just a notch, with a polished performance from door to reckoning. The vaguely Art Moderne interior employs mahogany paneling, soft lighting, lush flower arrangements, and a temperature-controlled walk-in wine repository. Game is featured, including caribou steaks, venison, and pheasant. Escargots provençales or au Pernod are savory starters, to be followed by such standards as lamb noisettes, seafood cassoulette, poached Atlantic salmon, steak tartare, and beef Wellington. The staff, and especially the headwaiter, is so alert and attentive even single diners are made welcome, not all but ignored, as is so often the case. Find the entrance around on rue de la Chevrotière, under 200 Grande-Allée. There's a small patio for outdoor dining, and free valet parking is available from 5:30pm.

MODERATE

✪ Le Graffiti

1191 ave. Cartier (near Grand-Allée). ☎ **418/529-4949.** Reservations recommended. Main courses $13–$20, table d'hôte $19. AE, DC, ER, MC, V. Daily 5–11pm. CONTEMPORARY FRENCH/ITALIAN.

These two or three blocks off Grand-Allée are just outside the perimeter of tourist Québec, enough to avoid flashy banality, close enough to remain convenient. This busy establishment blends bistro with trattoria, often on the same plate. Emblematic is the sautéed rabbit with puréed carrot, broccoli florets, and angel-hair pasta powerfully scented with tarragon. One result is a banishment of insipid flavorings, as with a two-fisted consommé afloat with tendrils of crêpe.

Momento

1144 ave. Cartier (near Grande-Allée). ☎ **418/647-1313.** Reservations recommended at dinner. Main courses $8–$14, table d'hôte lunch $8–$10, dinner $13–$18. Mon–Fri 11:15am–11pm, Sat–Sun 5pm–midnight. CONTEMPORARY ITALIAN.

Considering its manic popularity elsewhere on the continent, updated Italian cooking was late arriving in Québec. It had the usual parlors shoveling overcooked spaghetti with thin tomato sauce that afflict most cities, but not the kind of spiffy neo-trattoria that traffics in light-but-lusty dishes meant for lives lived fast. This racy spot is helping to take up the slack, and although it lags somewhat in execution compared to its rival, *Le Graffiti* (above), it is a welcome antidote to prevailing Franco-Italian clichés of the city's tourist troughs. If possible, go with a gang for the "Festino Italiano," and surrender to five courses—from pizza bites to soup to antipasti sampler to family-sized platters of pasta-of-the-day to tastes of three sweets.

INEXPENSIVE

✪ Au Petit Coin Breton

655 Grande-Allée est. ☎ **418/525-6904.** Most menu items $2–$10. AE, MC, V. Summer, daily 10am–midnight. Winter, daily 10am–11pm. CRÊPES.

At this "Little Corner of Brittany," the crêpe's the thing, be it for breakfast, brunch, a light lunch, a snack, or dessert. Stone, brick, and wood set the mood, as do waiters and waitresses in Breton costume—the

😊 Family-Friendly Restaurants

Au Petit Coin Breton *(see p. 219)*   The costumes the waitresses wear are fun. So's the food, especially when it's served outside.

Le Cochon Dingue *(see p. 222)*   It's big so kids can let themselves go here (to a point). And eating in a place called "The Crazy Pig" is something to write home to grandma about.

Le Lapin Sauté   The burgers are tasty, breakfast is good, and "The Jumping Rabbit" is another place grandma will want to hear about.

women in lace cap, long dress, and apron. After onion soup or salad, choose one (or several) of the over 80 varieties of the savory dinner crêpes and sweet dessert crêpes. Ice cream made on the premises is an alternative topper. Often every last seat is taken, especially on the terrace on a sunny day, making a wait inevitable and service slow. A second location, at 1029 rue St-Jean, at the corner of rue Ste-Ursule, has similar hours, menu, and prices (☎ 418/694-0758).

5 Lower Town

EXPENSIVE

✪ Laurie Raphaël

17 rue du Sault-au-Matelot (at rue St-Antoine). ☎ **418/692-4555.** Reservations recommended. Main courses $19.95–$25.95, table d'hôte lunch $8.95–$14.95, dinner $30–$35. AE, DC, ER, MC, V. Daily 8–10:30am, 12noon–2:30pm, 5:30–11pm. Closed Sun and Mon night, Oct–April. CONTEMPORARY FRENCH.

An *amuse-gueule* of wonton with minced pork filling arrives with the special Kir Royale, a sparkling wine laced with blackberry liqueur. After a suitable interlude, the waiter arrives and happily explains every dish on the menu in as much detail as his customers care to absorb. Appetizers aren't really necessary, since the main course comes with soup or a salad, but they're so good, a couple might wish to share one. The carpaccio of Portobello mushrooms, perhaps, spashed with fruity olive oil and showered with frizzled tendrils of sweet potato, paper-thin leaves of Parmesan, and sprigs of fresh thyme. Main courses run to caribou and rack of lamb in unconventional guises, and, unlikely as it might sound, a concern for "healthy" saucing and combinations is evident. In no time, the place ascends to that level of happy babble that is music to a restaurateur's ears. If the kitchen can be faulted, it might be for the identical garnishes appearing on every plate—pea sprouts and nasturtiums on one recent spring evening. But that's quibbling, for this is a restaurant that shares the uncrowded pinnacle of the local dining pantheon.

Le Saint-Pierre

54 rue St-Pierre (at Montagne). ☎ **418/694-6194.** Reservations recommended on weekends. Main courses $10–$35, table d'hôte lunch $7–$12.50, dinner $16–$28.

AE, DC, MC, V. Mon–Fri 11:30–2pm, 5:30–11pm, Sat 5:30–11, Sun 5–10. Closed Sun, Oct–April. CONTEMPORARY FRENCH.

A waiter in apron and black bow tie is often stationed at the door, a living signboard announcing that the former bank is now a place to dine. After all, it had only been open a week when first encountered. Inside, the owners are bidding for a grand elegance not much seen in the city. Big vases with outsized peonies and birds of paradise stand on the bar and over the showy dessert display near the entrance. Greco-Roman structural details frame the large room, whose greatest luxury is the wide-open spaces between tables, another rarity here. The grand piano at one side is put to use every night. With all this, the food has much to accomplish. It comes close, as with the salmon fillet nested with delicate shreds of eggplant, sweet pepper, and zucchini, a spray of asparagus spears and roasted potato balls to one side. Portions are on the skimpy side, however, and some of the combinations are off-kilter. It will be fun to return to see if the promise is being fulfilled.

MODERATE

L'Ardoise

71 rue St-Paul (near Navigateurs). ☎ **418/694-0213.** Reservations recommended. Main courses $9.95–$16, table d'hôte $18 or $24. AE, MC, V. Daily 9am–11pm. BISTRO FRENCH.

Mussels are staples at Québec restaurants, prepared in the Belgian manner, with bowls of frites on the side. Despite their popularity, the chef in this companionable bistro is reluctant to serve them in the warmer months, explaining that the farmed variety available then tend to be mealy.

That he cares about what he sends out of his kitchen is evident. *Haute,* his food isn't, but vibrant and flavorful, it is. His arena is a smallish room on antique row, with banquettes along both walls and wicker-and-iron chairs pulled up to tables with paper placemats. Piaf and Aznavour clones warble laments on the stereo. This is a place to leaf through a book, sip a double espresso, and meet neighbors.

Tourists haven't discovered it. Yet.

✪ Le Café du Monde

57 rue Dalhousie (at côte de la Montagne). ☎ **418/692-4455.** Reservations recommended on weekends. Main courses $7.25–$16, table d'hôte lunch $8–$12, dinner $18–$21. AE, DC, ER, MC, V. Mon–Fri 11:30am–11pm, Sat–Sun brunch 9:30am–11pm. FRENCH/INTERNATIONAL.

Near the Musée de la Civilisation, this relative newcomer is enjoying ever-increasing popularity. While it promotes the roster of world dishes promised in its name, the atmosphere is definitely Lyonnaise brasserie. That is seen in the culinary origins of its most-ordered items—pâtés, quiches, entrecôte, and several versions of mussels with frites—prepared in a kitchen overseen by a chef from Brittany. One of his extravaganzas is a five-course evening meal, called "Le Ciel, La Terre, La Mer" or "Sky, Earth, Sea," a kind of upscale surf 'n' turf. Pastas and couscous are some of the non-French preparations. Imported beers are favored beverages, along with wines by the glass. Look for the striped awnings and bright neon sign out front. Service is friendly, but easily distracted. Waiters and customers sit down at the upright piano for impromptu performances.

Le Cochon Dingue

46 bd. Champlain (rue du Marché-Champlain). ☎ **418/692-2013.** Main courses $6–$12.50, table d'hôte meals $17–$20. AE, ER, MC, V. Daily 7am–midnight. BISTRO/INTERNATIONAL.

This "Crazy Pig" faces the ferry dock and lighthouse in the Lower Town and has some sidewalk tables and several indoor dining rooms with rough fieldstone walls and black-and-white floor tiles. It makes stout efforts to be a one-stop eating center, with long hours to cover every possibility. Choose from mussels, steak frites, hefty plates of chicken liver pâté with pistachios, spring rolls, smoked salmon, half a dozen salads, onion soup, pastas, quiches, sandwiches, pastas, grilled meats, and more than 20 desserts. Wine is sold by the glass, quarter-liter, half-liter, or bottle, at reasonable prices, and there is a children's menu for kids 10 and under. The same people also own the nearby, smaller Le Lapin Sauté (☎ 692-5325) at 52 rue Petit-Champlain.

✪ Le Marie-Clarisse

12 rue du Petit-Champlain (rue Sous-le-Fort). ☎ **418/692-0857.** Reservations not required. Main courses $8–$11.75. AE, DC, ER, MC, V. Mon–Fri 11:30am–2:30pm, 6–11pm. Sat 6pm–11pm. BISTRO/SEAFOOD.

Nothing much beyond sustenance is expected of restaurants stationed at the flooded intersections of galloping tourism. That's why this modest little café is such a happy surprise. There it sits, at the bottom of Breakneck Stairs, a few yards from the funicular terminal, the streets awash with mouthbreathers, daypackers, and shutterbugs. And yet it serves what many consider to be the best seafood in town, selected by a finicky owner said to travel each week to Montréal to make his selections personally at market. A more pleasant hour cannot be passed than here, over a plate of shrimp scented with anise or a selection of terrines and pâtés, out on the terrace on an August afternoon or cocooned by the stone fireplace inside in January. Just skip the vegetables, unless the chef has learned to remove them from the pot while they still have some fiber.

INEXPENSIVE

Buffet de l'Antiquaire

95 rue St-Paul (near rue du Sault-au-Matelot). ☎ **418/692-2661.** Reservations not required. Most menu items under $10. AE, MC, V. Daily 7am–11pm. QUÉBÉCOIS.

Another inhabitant of St-Paul's antique row, this is the humblest of the lot, with exposed brick and stone walls lending what there is of decor. It is the place to go when every other Lower Town café is closed, such as for Sunday breakfast. And, since it caters to homefolks rather than tourists, reliable versions of native Québécois cooking are always available, including, but not limited to, pea soup, poutine, and fèves au lard. Essentially a slightly upgraded luncheonette, it serves sandwiches, salads, and pastries at all hours, backed by full bar service.

6   Picnic Fare & Where to Eat It

Pick up supplies from the bountiful selection at **Epicerie Gaboury,** 27 rue Couillard (☎ **418/692-3748).** It's open daily from 10am to 11pm. A larger selection of wines (2,000, in fact) is available at Maison des Vins, in the Lower Town, at 1 place Royale (☎ 418/643-1214).

The place to enjoy a picnic in the Lower Town is **Parc du Porche,** on rue Notre-Dame half a block north of place Royale. Outside the city walls, pick a site on the expansive Parc des Champs-de-Bataille (Battlefields Park).

14

What to See & Do in Québec City

Wandering at random through the streets of Vieux-Québec is a singular pleasure, comparable to exploring a provincial capital in Europe. On the way, you can happen upon an ancient convent, blocks of gabled houses with steeply pitched roofs, a battery of 18th-century cannon in a leafy park, and a bistro with a blazing fireplace on a chilly day. This is such a compact city it is hardly necessary to plan precise sightseeing itineraries. Start at the terrasse Dufferin and go off on a whim, down Breakneck Stairs to the Quartier Petit-Champlain and place Royale, or up to the Citadel and onto the Plains of Abraham, where Wolfe and Montcalm fought to the death in a 20-minute battle that changed the destiny of the continent.

Most of what there is to see is within the city walls, or in the Lower Town. It's fairly easy walking. While the Upper Town is hilly, with sloping streets, it's nothing like San Francisco, and only people with physical limitations will experience difficulty. If rain or ice discourage exploration on foot, tour buses and horse-drawn calèches are options.

1 Suggested Itineraries

If You Have 1 Day Take the funicular or walk down from the terrasse Dufferin to explore the Lower Town. Use the walking tours in Chapter 15 as a guide.

If You Have 2 Days Spend your first day as suggested above.

On the second day, In the morning visit the Citadelle or the Musée du Québec or both.

If You Have 3 Days Spend the first two days as suggested above.

On the third day, make a short excursion north of the city to visit Montmorency Falls and the shrine of Ste-Anne-de-Beaupré.

If You Have 5 Days or More Spend these days as suggested above.

On Day 4, spend the day circling bucolic Île d'Orléans, isolated from the mainland until a bridge was built in 1935. The island is home to five pleasing hamlets with several middling-good restaurants. It's preferable to drive rather than take a tour.

Spend the fifth and/or sixth day driving the "slow road" along the southern bank of the St. Lawrence River and exploring the small villages along the way. Return to Québec City via Charlevoix and the northern bank. Or vice versa.

2 The Top Attractions

UPPER TOWN

Château Frontenac

1 rue des Carrières (place d'Armes). ☎ **418/692-3861.** Admission free.

Perched atop Cape Diamond, Château Frontenac, built to resemble a monster version of a Loire Valley palace, was opened in 1893 to house railroad passengers and encourage tourism. Additions were completed in 1925 and in 1993, the last in celebration of the hotel's centennial. It's the city's trademark, its Eiffel Tower or Tower Bridge, and can be seen from almost every quarter. Visitors are welcome to enter and wander around the lobby and shops. The greatest pleasure, though, is standing outside and taking in the magnificent facade. (Also see "Walking Tour—Upper Town," in Chapter 15.)

✪ La Citadelle [The Citadel]

1 côte de la Citadelle (enter off rue St-Louis). ☎ **418/648-3563.** Admission $4.50 adults, $4 seniors, $2 children 7–17, free for handicapped persons and children under 7. Guided 55-minute tours, mid-Mar to April, daily 10am–3pm; May–June and Labor Day to Oct, daily 9am–4pm; July to Labor Day daily 9am–6pm. Nov to mid-Mar, group reservations only. Changing of the guard (30 min.), mid-June to Labor Day daily 10am (may be canceled in case of rain); beating the retreat (20 min.) July–Aug, Tues, Thurs, and Sat–Sun (may be canceled in case of rain).

The Duke of Wellington had this partially star-shaped fortress built at the east end of the city walls in anticipation of renewed American attacks after the conclusion of the War of 1812. Some remnants of earlier French military structures were incorporated into it, including a 1750 magazine. Dug into the Plains of Abraham, the fort has a low profile that keeps it all but invisible until walkers are actually upon it. Although it has never exchanged fire with an invader, it keeps its silent vigil from the tip of Cap Diamant. Construction of the fortress, now a national historic site, was begun in 1820 and took 30 years to complete. As events unfolded, it proved an exercise in obsolescence. Since 1920, it has been home to Québec's Royal 22e Régiment, the only fully Francophone unit in Canada's armed forces. That makes it the largest fortified group of buildings still occupied by troops in North America. As part of a guided tour only, the public may visit the Citadel and its 25 buildings, including the regimental museum in the former powderhouse and prison, and watch the changing of the guard or beating the retreat. To get to the Citadel, walk up the côte de la Citadelle from the St-Louis Gate.

LOWER TOWN

✪ Musée de la Civilisation

85 rue Dalhousie (St-Antoine). ☎ **418/643-2158.** Admission $6 adults, $5 seniors, $3 students, $1 12–16, free for children under 12. Tues free to all (except in

Québec City Attractions

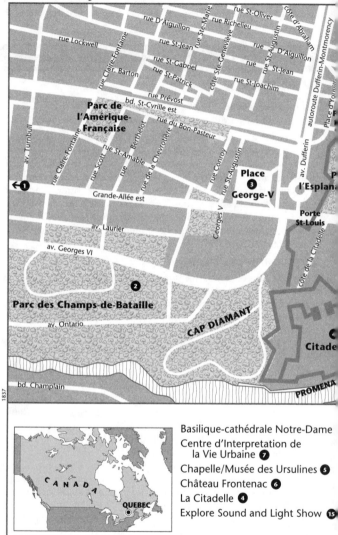

Basilique-cathédrale Notre-Dame

Centre d'Interpretation de
  la Vie Urbaine ➐

Chapelle/Musée des Ursulines ➎

Château Frontenac ➏

La Citadelle ➍

Explore Sound and Light Show ⓯

summer). June 24–Sept 4 daily 10am–7pm, Sept 5 to June 23, Tues–Sun 10am–5pm (to 9pm Wed).

Designed by Boston-based, McGill University–trained Moshe Safdie and opened in 1988, this museum is an innovative presence in the historic Basse-Ville, near place Royale. A dramatic atrium-lobby sets the tone with a massive sculpture rising like jagged icebergs from the watery floor, a representation of the mighty St. Lawrence at spring breakup. Through the glass wall in back can be seen the 1752 Maison Estèbe, now restored to contain the museum shop. It stands above

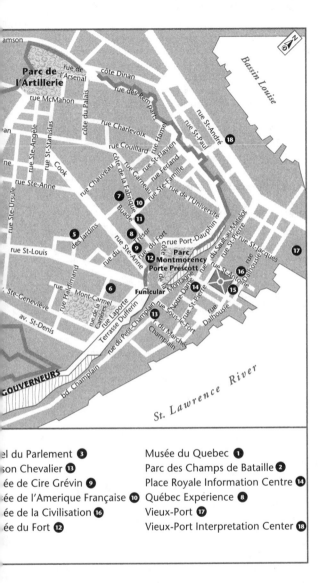

el du Parlement ❸

son Chevalier ⓭

ée de Cire Grévin ❾

:ée de l'Amerique Française ❿

ée de la Civilisation ⓰

ée du Fort ⓬

Musée du Quebec ❶

Parc des Champs de Bataille ❷

Place Royale Information Centre ⓮

Québec Experience ❽

Vieux-Port ⓱

Vieux-Port Interpretation Center ⓲

vaulted cellars, which can be viewed. In the galleries upstairs are four permanent exhibitions, supplemented by up to six temporary shows on a variety of themes. The mission of the museum has never been entirely clear, leading to some opaque metaphysical maunderings in its early years. Never mind. Through highly imaginative display techniques, hands-on devices, computers, holograms, videos, even an ant farm, the curators have assured that visitors will be so enthralled by the experience they won't pause to question intent. Notice, as an example of their thoroughness, how a squeaky floorboard has been installed at the entrance to a dollhouse-size display of Old Québec houses. If time is short, definitely use it to take in "Memoires" (Memories), the permanent exhibit that is a sprawling examination of Québec history, moving from the province's roots as a fur-trading colony to the present. Furnishings from frontier homes, tools of the trappers' trade, old farm implements, religious garments from the 19th century, old campaign posters, and a re-created classroom from the past envelop visitors with a rich sense of Québec's daily life from generation to generation.Exhibit texts are in French and English. There's a café on the ground floor. Try to set aside at least two hours for a visit to this special museum, one of the most engrossing in all Canada.

Place Royale Information Centre

215 rue du Marché-Finlay (Lower Town). ☎ **418/643-6631.** Admission free. June 5–Oct 1 daily 10am–6pm.

Picturesque place Royale is the literal and spiritual heart of the Lower Town. It's a short walk from the lower terminus of the funicular or the Breakneck Stairs, via rue Sous-le-Fort. In the 17th and 18th centuries, it was the town marketplace and the center of business and industry. The église Notre-Dame-des-Victoires dominates the enclosed square. All the buildings have been restored, save one. The stone facade at the northeast corner with metal and painted plywood covering its doors and windows isn't simply abandoned. There is nothing behind that wall but an empty lot. Note the ladders on some of the other roofs, a common Québec device for removing snow and fighting fires. Folk dances, impromptu concerts, and other festive gatherings are often held near the bust of Louis XIV (the roi, or king) in the square.

ON OR NEAR THE GRANDE-ALLÉE

Musée du Québec

1 av. Wolfe-Montcalm (av. George VI). ☎ **418/643-2150.** Admission $4.75 adults, $3.75 seniors, $2.75 students, free for children under 16; Wed free for everyone. Late May (Victoria Day)–early Sept (Labor Day) daily 10am–5:45pm (Wed until 5:45pm); early Sept–late May, Tues–Sun 10am–5:45pm (Wed until 8:45). Bus no. 11.

In the southern reaches of Battlefields Park, just off the Grande-Allée, the Québec Museum now occupies two buildings, one a former prison, linked together by a soaring glass-roofed "Grand Hall" housing the reception area, a stylish cafeteria, and a shop. The original 1933 building houses the permanent collection, the largest aggregation of Québec art in North America, filling eight galleries with works from the beginning of the colony to the present. Traveling exhibitions and musical events are often arranged. The new addition to the museum

Impressions

The old world rises in the midst of the new in the manner of a change of scene on the stage . . .on its rocky promontory sits the ancient town, belted with its hoary wall and crowned with its granite citadel . . .
— Henry James, "Québec" (1871), in *Portraits of Places* (1883)

is the 1871 Baillairgé Prison, which later became a youth hostel nick-named the "Petite Bastille." One cellblock has been left intact as an exhibit. In this building, four galleries house temporary shows, and the tower contains a provocative sculpture called Le Plongeur (The Diver) by David Moore, an Irish artist who lives in Montréal. Also incorporated in the building is the Battlefields Interpretation Centre (below). The museum is just off the Grande-Allée, at the intersection of rue George VI and avenue Wolfe-Montcalm. It's a half-hour walk or a bus ride from the Upper Town.

Parc des Champs de Bataille Interpretation Centre (Battlefields Park)

Av. Wolfe-Montcalm (Musée du Québec). ☎ **418/648-5641.** Admission to park, free. Interpretation center, martello tower no. 1, astronomy tower, and bus tour in summer, $2 for visitors ages 18–64, $1 ages 13–17 and 65 and over, ages 12 and under free, Tues free to all. Late May to Labor Day daily 10am–5:45pm, early Sept–late May Tues–Sun 12am–5:45pm.

Covering more than 250 acres of grassy knolls, sunken gardens, monuments, fountains, and trees, Québec's Battlefields Park stretches over the Plains of Abraham, where Wolfe and Montcalm engaged in their swift but crucial battle, and is a favorite place for all Québécois when they want some sunshine, a jog, or a bike ride. Be sure to see Jardin Jeanne d'Arc (Joan of Arc Garden), just off avenue Laurier between Loews Le Concorde Hôtel and the Ministry of Justice. The statue was a gift from some anonymous Americans, and it was here that "O Canada," the country's national anthem, was sung for the first time. Within the park are two martello towers, cylindrical stone defensive structures built between 1808 and 1812, when Québec feared an invasion from the United States. This sort of tower, which became popular during the Napoleonic Wars, housed supplies on the first floor and troops on the second, and served as forward observation posts.

Today Battlefields Park covers 266 acres and contains almost 5,000 trees representing more than 80 species. Prominent among these are sugar maple, silver maple, Norway maple, American elm, and American ash and hawthorn. There are always special activities, including theatrical and musical events, planned in the park during the summer. Year-round, the park interpretation center provides an in-depth look (for a small fee) at the historical significance of the Plains of Abraham to Québec over the years. In summer, a shuttle bus tours the park in its entirety in 45 minutes with guided narration in French and English for a small fee.

3 More Attractions

UPPER TOWN

Basilique-cathédrale Notre-Dame

16 rue Buade (at côte de la Fabrique). ☎ **418/692-2533.** Admission to Basilica and guided tours, free. "Act of Faith" sound-and-light show, $6 adults, $5 seniors, $3 students 12 and over with ID, children 11 and under free (tickets available from 20 rue

Buade). Basilica, daily 6:30am–5:30pm; guided tours mid-May to mid-Oct daily 9am–4:30pm. "Act of Faith" multimedia sound-and-light show, summer nightly 6:30pm, 7:45pm, and 9pm.

The oldest Christian parish north of Mexico, it has seen a tumultuous history of bombardment, reconstruction, and restoration. Parts of the existing basilica date to the original 1647 structure, including the bell tower and portions of the walls. The interior is flamboyantly Baroque, in the manner of the time in which much of it was built. Shadows waver from the fluttering light of votive candles. Paintings and ecclesiastical treasures still remain from the time of the French regime, including a chancel lamp given by Louis XIV. In summer, the basilica is the backdrop for a multimedia sound-and-light show called "Act of Faith," which dramatically recalls five centuries of Québec's history, and that of this building itself. The basilica is connected to the complex of old buildings that makes up Québec Seminary. To enter that complex, go to 7 rue de l'Université.

Centre d'Interpretation de la Vie Urbaine [Urban Life Interpretation Center]

43 côte de la Fabrique (Hôtel-de-Ville). ☎ **418/691-4606.** Admission free. Late June to early Sept daily 10am–5pm; early Sept to late June Tues–Sun 10am–5pm.

It's in the basement of the City Hall, passed daily and largely ignored by tourists on the way between place d'Armes and the rue St-Jean. Drop in. It's interesting, free, and doesn't take much time to visit. The main attraction is the big model of Québec City as it was in 1975, which is much the same as it was in 1875 or 1775. It provides a closer handle on the topographical layout of the town. Other exhibits focus on urban planning, including a musical video on Québécois life.

Musée du Fort

10 rue Ste-Anne (place d'Armes). ☎ **418/692-2175.** Admission $5.50 adults, $4.50 seniors, $3.50 students and children under 18. June 24–Aug 31 daily 10am–6pm, Apr–May and Sept–Oct 10am–5pm, Nov–Mar Mon–Fri 11am–3pm, Sat–Sun 11am–5pm.

Bordering place d'Armes, not far from the UNESCO World Heritage monument, this commercial enterprise presents a sound-and-light show using a 400-square-foot model of the city and surrounding region. The 30-minute production concerns itself primarily with the six sieges of Québec, including the famous battle on the Plains of Abraham. Commentary is in French or English. Military and history buffs are most likely to enjoy it.

Musée de Cire Grévin [Wax Museum]

22 rue Ste-Anne (du Trésor). ☎ **418/692-2289.** Admission $5 adults, $3 seniors and students, children under 6 free. Summer daily 9am–10pm, winter daily 10am–5pm.

Occupying a 17th-century house, this momentarily diverting wax museum, entirely renovated in 1994, provides a superficial skim of Québec's history and heroes. Generals Wolfe and Montcalm are portrayed, of course, along with effigies of politicians, singers,

Olympic gold medalists, and other newsmakers. Texts are in French and English.

Musée de l'Amerique Française

Québec Seminary, 2 côte de la Fabrique. ☎ **418/692-2843.** Admission $3 adults, $2 seniors, $1.50 students, $1 children 16 and under, $6 families, free to all on Tues. Concerts $10–$15. June 1–Sept 30 daily 10am–5:30pm, Oct 1–May 31, Tues–Sun 10am–5pm. Guided tours of exhibitions and some buildings, daily in summer, rest of the year, Sat–Sun.

Housed in historic Québec Seminary, whose history dates to 1659, the Museum of French America focuses on the beginnings and the evolution of French culture and civilization in North America. Its extensive collections include paintings by European and Canadian artists, engravings and parchments from the early French regime, old and rare books, coins, early scientific instruments, and even mounted animals and an Egyptian mummy. The mix makes for an engrossing visit. The museum is located in three parts of the large seminary complex. In the Guillaume-Couillard wing, adjacent to the Basilique-cathédrale Notre-Dame, is the entrance hall and information desk. In the Jérôme-Demers wing, bordering the rue de l'Université, down the hill, are the exhibition galleries. Third is the beautiful François-Ranvoyze wing, with its trompe-l'oeil ornamentation, which served as a chapel for the seminary priests and students. It is now open only during the summer for guided tours. Concerts are held in the chapel, as well. Other seminary buildings house a private school.

Chapelle/Musée des Ursulines

12 rue Donnacona (des Jardins). ☎ **418/694-0694.** Admission museum $3 adults, $1.50 seniors and students, $6 families; chapel free. Museum, Jan 3–Nov 24, Tues–Sat 9:30am–noon and 1–4:30pm, Sun 12:30–5pm. Chapel, May–Oct, same days and hours as museum.

The chapel, open only from May through October, is remarkable for its sculptures of the pulpit and two retables. They were created by Pierre-Noel Levasseur between 1726 and 1736. Although the present building dates only to 1902, much of the interior decoration is nearly two centuries older. The tomb of the founder of this teaching order, Marie de l'Incarnation, is to the right of the entry. She arrived here in 1639 at the age of 40, and was declared blessed by Pope John Paul II in 1980. The museum, open from January to late November, displays many of the accoutrements of the daily and spiritual life of the Ursulines. On the third floor are exhibits of fine vestments woven with gold thread by the Ursulines. A cape made of drapes from the bedroom of Anne of Austria and given to Marie de l'Incarnation when she left France for New France in 1639 is on display. There are also musical instruments and Amerindian crafts, including the flèche, or arrow sash, still worn during Winter Carnival. Honors for most bizarre object on display is the skull of General Montcalm. The rest of him is interred in the chapel. Some of the docents are nuns of the active order. The Ursuline convent, built originally as a girls' school in 1642, is the oldest one in North America.

LOWER TOWN

Explore Sound and Light Show

63 rue Dalhousie (St-Antoine). 418/692-2175. Admission $5.50 adults, $4.50 seniors, $3.50 children under 18. June 23–Sept 3 daily 1–4:30pm; Sept 4–Oct 15 and Apr 15–June 22 Mon–Sat 10am–5pm, Oct 16–Apr 14 daily Mon–Fri 11am–3pm.

A splashy, 30-minute multimedia production limns the Age of Exploration through the impressions and adventures of Columbus, Vespucci, Verrazano, Cartier, and Champlain. The theater is shaped like an early sailing vessel, complete with rigging. Among the depictions are the difficulties of Champlain and his crew of 28 who came here in 1608. Twenty men died during the first winter, mainly of scurvy and dysentery (one was hanged for mutiny). They lived in the Habitation, near Annapolis Royal, in Nova Scotia, then part of French territory in North America. Some good books about the founding of Québec are sold here. A map on the back wall depicts the world of 1608.

Maison Chevalier

60 rue du Marché-Champlain (at rue Notre-Dame). ☎ **418/643-2158.** Admission free. June 5–Oct 1 daily 10am–5pm.

Built in 1752 for shipowner Jean-Baptiste Chevalier, the existing structure incorporated two older buildings, dating from 1675 and 1695. It was run as an inn throughout the 19th century. The Québec government restored the house in 1960, and it became a museum five years later. Inside, with its exposed wood beams, wide board floors, and stone fireplaces are changing exhibits on Québec history and civilization, especially in the 17th and 18th centuries. While exhibit texts are in French, guidebooks in English are available at the sometimes unattended front desk. The house is managed by the Museum of Civilization.

Vieux-Port Interpretation Center

100 rue St-Andre (at rue Rioux). ☎ **418/648-3300.** Admission May to Labor Day, $3 adults, $1.50 seniors and children; family $6; rest of the year, free. May to Labor Day daily 10am–5pm; schedule varies the rest of the year (call for hours).

Part of Parks Canada, the center reveals the Port of Québec as it was during its maritime zenith in the 19th century. Four floors of

---

❓ Did You Know?

- Québec is the only remaining walled city north of Mexico.
- The city's birds have it made—a high-rise "Pigeon Palace" that's heated in winter.
- The Plains of Abraham are named not for a biblical character but a Scottish farmer who once owned the land.
- The Citadel is the largest fortified group of buildings still occupied by troops in North America.
- Bonhomme Carnaval is the Mickey Mouse of Québec.
- James Fenimore Cooper recounted some of the military exploits of General Montcalm in *The Last of the Mohicans.*

exhibits illustrate that era. The modern port and city can be viewed from the top level, where reference maps identify landmarks. One of these is the Daishowa Pulp and Paper Mill (1927), which sells newsprint and cardboard to international markets, including the *New York Times.* Texts are in French and English, and most exhibits invite touching.

ON OR NEAR THE GRANDE-ALLÉE

Hôtel du Parlement
Grande-Allée est (av. Dufferin). ☎ **418/643-7239.** Admission free. Guided tours, early Sept to May Mon–Fri 9am–4:30pm; June 24 to early Sept daily 9am–4:30pm. No visitors June 1–23.

Since 1968, what the Québécois choose to call their "National Assembly" has occupied this imposing Second Empire château constructed in 1886. It is the center of the Cité Parlementaire, Québec's government complex. Twenty-two bronze statues of some of the most prominent figures in Québec's tumultuous history gaze out from the facade. The fountain in front, the work of Philippe Hébert (1890), was dedicated to Québec's original Native American inhabitants. The sumptuous chambers of the building may be toured with a guide for no charge, but times change without warning. Highlights are the Assembly Chamber, and the Room of the Old Legislative Council, where parliamentary committees meet. Throughout the building, representations of the fleur-de-lys and the initials "VR" (for Victoria Regina) remind visitors of Québec's dual heritage.

4 Especially for Kids

Québec is such a storybook town most children delight in simply walking around in it. As soon as possible, head for terrasse Dufferin, which has those coin-operated telescopes kids like. In decent weather, there are always street entertainers, such as a Peruvian musical group that plays with saws or wine glasses. A few steps away at place d'Armes are the **calèches,** horse-drawn carriages, and not far in the same direction is the **Musée de Cire** (Wax Museum), on place d'Armes at 22 rue Ste-Anne. Also at place d'Armes is the terminal of the **funicular** to the Lower Town. Its glass walls allow a splendid view of the river, and its steady but precipitous drop is a sure thrill. At the bottom, next to the Breakneck Stairs, is a glass-blowing workshop, always intriguing, but especially for youngsters who haven't seen the craft in action. Also in the Lower Town, at 86 rue Dalhousie, the playful **Musée de la Civilisation** keeps kids occupied for hours in its exhibits, shop, and café.

They also get a charge out of the monstrous cannons ranged along the battlements on rue des Remparts. The gun carriages are impervious to the assaults of small humans, so kids can scramble over them at will. Other military sites are usually a hit. The **Citadelle** has tours of the grounds and buildings and a colorful Changing of the Guard ceremony.

The ferry to Lévis across the St. Lawrence is inexpensive, convenient from the Lower Town, pleasant, and exciting for kids. The crossing, over and back, takes less than an hour. Take your camera.

Do the kids need to run off some excess energy? Head for the **Plains of Abraham,** which is also Québec National Battlefields Park. You can get there by rue St-Louis, just inside the St-Louis Gate, or, more vigorously, by the walkway along terrasse Dufferin and the promenade des Gouverneurs. Acres of grassy lawn give children room to roam and provide the perfect spot for a family picnic.

If there's time for a short excursion, drive out to Montmorency Falls, impressive in either summer or winter. They dwarf kids and adults alike (see Chapter 18, "Excursions from Québec City").

For more active pursuits, consider the **Village des Sports** (☎ 418/844-2551) in St-Gabriel-de-Valcartier, about 20 minutes' drive north of downtown. In summer, it's a water park, with slides, a huge wave pool, and diving shows. In winter, those same facilities are put to use for snow-rafting on inner tubes, ice slides, and skating.

5 Organized Tours

Québec City is small enough to get around quickly and easily with a good map and a guidebook, but a tour is helpful for getting background information on the history and culture of the city, grasping the lay of the land, and seeing those attractions that are a bit of a hike or require wheels to reach, such as the Musée du Québec. Here are some agencies and organizations that have proved reliable in the past.

BUS TOURS

Buses are obviously convenient if extensive walking is difficult, especially in the hilly and steeply sloping Upper Town. Among the established tour operators:

Visite **Touristique de Québec,** or VTQ (☎ 418/653-9722), offers English-only tours, preferable because twice as much information is imparted in the same amount of time as on a bilingual tour. VTQ's city tours are in small coaches that carry 24 or fewer people. In the autumn, the company offers an 8-hour whale-watching excursion, its only bilingual tour. Maple Leaf Sightseeing Tours (☎ 418/649-9226) picks up passengers at their hotels in a 25-passenger "trolley bus" and embark on a comprehensive tour of Québec, old and new, Upper and Lower Towns. **Les Tours du Vieux-Québec** (☎ 418/624-0460) and **Gray Line** (☎ 418/622-7420) also offer a variety of city and regional tours.

City tours tend to last two hours and cost about $20 for adults, half price for children 6 to 12. Many of the tour operators also offer half- or full-day (lunch included) tours to Ste-Anne-de-Beaupré, Montmorency Falls, and Île d'Orléans.

For more information about bus tours of the city, read the "City Tours" section of the *Greater Québec Area Tourist Guide,* supplied by the tourist office.

HORSE-DRAWN CARRIAGE TOURS

A romantic—and expensive—way to tour the city is in a horse-drawn carriage, called a caléche. They can be hired at place d'Armes or on rue d'Auteuil, just within the city walls near the tourist information office.

The 45-minute guided tour in either French or English costs about $50 for 30 minutes. Carriages operate all summer, rain or shine.

WALKING TOURS

Points of departure for walking tours change, so to get up-to-date information on when one's leaving and from where, check at the located kiosk on terrasse Dufferin near the Château Frontenac and beside the funicular entrance. Many tours leave from there. **Visite Touristique de Québec** (☎ **418/653-9722**), which also offers bus and boat tours, has walking tours from June 15 to Oct 15 at a cost of $12 per person. The guide escorts his or her charges through the Latin Quarter down to place Royale in the Lower Town. Tours last about 2½ hours and leave from the tourist office at 12 rue St-Anne and place d'Armes daily at 9am and 3pm June to September, the rest of the year by appointment. As an added convenience, buses are made available to pick up guests staying in hotels outside the Old City and give them rides back at the end of the tour. The walking tour costs $12 for adults or children older than 5.

Park rangers lead free 1-hour walking tours of the Citadelle most days. Walking tours of the villages of nearby Île d'Orléans (see Chapter 18) are arranged by **Beau Temps, Mauvais Temps (Rain or Shine) tours** (☎ **418/828-2275**).

RIVER CRUISES

Two vessels sail the St. Lawrence from May to October. The sleek, glass-enclosed, climate-controlled *Le Bateau Mouche* daily has four 90-minute **daytime cruises** with a live commentary and a 3-hour dinner cruise daily from May to October. Prices are $19.75 ($9.75 for children 6 to 12, under 6 free) for the daytime cruises, and $58.75 per person for the dinner cruise. The boat carries 200 passengers and departs from Bassin Louise (☎ **418/692-4949** or 800/361-0130). Weighing in at 900 tons, *MV Louis Jolli* cruises up the river past Ste-Foy or around the tip of Île d'Orléans. Cruises last 1 to 1½ hours in the afternoon, 2 to 4 hours in the evening, when dancing and dining are part of the experience. Guides are on board the 90-minute cruises. The boat is a three-deck 1930s ferry-turned-excursion vessel. Said to be the largest in Canada, it can carry 1,000 passengers. Prices start at $13 for adults, $6.50 for children 6 to 12 during the day, and $21.25 ($10.75 for children) in the evening; $48.75 ($41.75 for children) for the dinner cruise. For more information or tickets, drop by the kiosk beside the funicular on terrasse Dufferin, or call the operator, **Croisières AML** (☎ **418/692-1159** or 800/463-5310). Board the boat at quai Chouinard, 10 rue Dalhousie, near place Royale in the Lower Town. To cruise around Île d'Orléans, stopping at a farm and a crafts shop along the way, contact **Beau Temps, Mauvais Temps (Rain or Shine) tours** (☎ **418/828-2275**).

6   Spectator Sports

The Nordiques, Québec's representatives in the misnamed National Hockey League, departed in 1995 for Denver, leaving the city without a professional team in any of the major sports.

HARNESS RACING

Fans have been coming to the Hippodrome for afternoons or evenings of harness racing since 1916. Le Cavallo clubhouse is open year-round. Hippodrome de Québec, 2205 av. du Colisée, parc de l'Exposition. ☎ **418/524-5283.** Admission to Clubhouse $5, general admission, $2.50 adults, $1.25 seniors and children 12 and older. All year Mon, Wed–Sun at 1:30pm or 7:30pm (times vary season to season, call ahead).

7 Outdoor Activities

The waters and hills around Québec provide countless opportunities for outdoor activities, from swimming, rafting, and fishing to skiing, snowmobiling, and sleighrides. A few are mentioned below. For more possibilities, see the extensive listings in the *Greater Québec Area Tourist Guide.*

DOGSLEDDING   More off-beat adventures beckon those who desire recreation with the tang of the unusual. One such is dogsledding with **Aventure Nord-bec** (☎ **418/889-8001**) at 665 rue Ste-Anne in Saint-Lambert-de-Lévis, about 20 minutes south of the city. While it isn't a week-long mush across Alaska, participants do get a sense of what that experience is like. They get a four-dog sled meant for two and take turns standing on the runners and sitting on the sled. Much of the route is along a trail directly beneath high-tension wires, but it's still a hushed world of snow and evergreens. It's expensive, especially for families, but the memory will stay.

ICE-SKATING   In winter, there's ice skating at place d'Youville and Parc de l'Esplanade in the Old Town, and at Parc de Champs-de-Bataille (Battlefields Park).

SKIING   Parc de Champs-de-Bataille (Battlefields Park) has 10 kilometers (6 miles) of groomed cross-country ski trails, a convenience for those who don't have cars to get out of town.

Skiers and other outdoors enthusiasts who do have transportation should consider **Station Mont-Ste-Anne** (☎ **418/827-4561**), a park only 40 kilometers (24 miles) northeast of the city. They have over 100 kilometers (62 miles) of cross-country trails at all levels of difficulty. Equipment is available for rent. The park has snowshoeing and down-hill slopes as well, and in summer becomes a recreational bonanza, with golf, hiking, rollerblading, paragliding, and mountain biking on 200 kilometers (124 miles) of trails. Thirty minutes from Québec City, off Route 175 north, is **Parc de la Jacques-Cartier** (☎ **418/848-3169**), where rock-climbing, camping, canoeing, and mountainbiking are possibilities. From the end of May until early September, fishing is allowed in the river that runs through the preserve.

15

Québec City Strolls

The manifold pleasures of walks in Old Québec are entirely comparable to those of similar *quartiers* in northern European cities. Carriage wheels creak behind muscular horses, sunlight filters through leafy canopies to fall on drinkers and diners in sidewalk cafés, stone houses huddle close, and childish shrieks of laughter echo down cobblestoned streets. What most cities don't have is the bewitching vista of river and mountains that the Dufferin promenade bestows. In winter the city takes on a Dickensian quality, with lampglow behind curtains of falling snow. The man who should know, Charles himself, described the "splendid views which burst upon the eye at every turn."

WALKING TOUR 1
UPPER TOWN

Start: The Parc des Gouverneurs.
Finish: Hôtel du Parlement
Time: 2 hours.
Best Times: Anytime.
Worst Times: None.

Start the walk at the:

1. **Parc des Gouverneurs (Governors' Park),** right behind—south of—the Château Frontenac. The park takes its name from the site of the mansion built to house the French governors of Québec. It burned in 1834, and the ruins lie buried under the great bulk of the château. The obelisk monument at the lower end of the sloping park is dedicated to both generals in the momentous battle of September 13, 1759, when Wolfe (British) and Montcalm (French) fought it out for what would be the ultimate destiny of Québec, and, quite possibly, all of North America. The British were victorious. Wolfe, wounded in the fighting, lived

Impressions

Is there any city in the world that stands so nobly as Québec?
—Rupert Brooke, *Letters from America* (1913, 1916)

only long enough to hear of his victory. Montcalm died after Wolfe, knowing the city was lost. In summer, the Parc des Gouverneurs is the scene of various shows and musical programs sponsored by the municipal government. Many small hotels and guesthouses are clustered around or near the park. The building near the southeast corner of the park is the American consulate. Cannons were set up at the lower end of the park, as they are today, though these are not original.

Beyond them, stairs lead down to

2. Terrasse Dufferin, the boardwalk promenade with its green-and-white-topped gazebos, looks much as it did 100 years ago, when ladies with parasols and gentlemen with top hats and canes strolled along it on sunny afternoons, with the Frontenac as a backdrop.

From here, a detour might lead along the boardwalk to the right, soon arriving at the

3. Promenade des Gouverneurs. This skirts the sheer cliff wall and up past Québec's Citadel, a 20-minute uphill walk away. Return to the Parc des Gouverneurs and walk up rue Mont-Carmel, which runs between it and the Château Frontenac, and turn right onto rue Haldimand. At the next corner, with rue St-Louis, stands a white house with blue trim called

4. Maison Kent. Built in 1648, it is possibly the oldest building in Québec. Although it is most famous for being the place in which France signed the capitulation to the British forces, its name comes from the Duke of Kent. The duke, Queen Victoria's father, lived here for a few years at the end of the 18th century, just before he married Victoria's mother in an arranged liaison. His true love, it is said, had lived with him in Maison Kent. Today it houses the consulate general of France, as the tricolor over the door attests.

Diagonally across from Maison Kent, at rue St-Louis and rue des Jardins, is

5. Maison Jacquet, a small white house with a crimson roof and trim, dating from 1677. This venerable Québec dwelling now houses the restaurant Aux Anciens Canadiens, which serves traditional Québécois food. Among the oldest houses in the province, it has sheltered some prominent Québécois, including Philippe Aubert de Gaspé, the author of *Aux Anciens Canadiens,* who lived here from 1815 to 1824. The book recounts the history and folklore of Québec and the Québécois.

☕ **TAKE A BREAK** Try Québécois home cooking at **Aux Anciens Canadiens,** 34 rue St-Louis. Consider rabbit braised in beer or duckling baked in maple syrup. Don't forget the sugar pie floating in heavy cream.

From Maison Jacquet, turn left, and walk downhill along attractive, if commercialized, rue St-Louis, to no. 17, the

6. Maison Maillou, the foundations of which date from 1736. The house was enlarged in 1799 and restored in 1959. Note the metal shutters used to thwart weather and unfriendly fire. Now the building houses the Québec Board of Trade and Industry.

The large building across the street from Maison Maillou is the impressive

7. Québec Ministry of Finance. It started out in 1799 as a courthouse, was renovated between 1927 and 1934, and was restored again from 1983 to 1987. Since 1987 it has been Québec's Ministry of Justice, the name on the facade notwithstanding. The architect of the exterior was Eugène-Etienne Tache, Minister of Public Works at that time. The interior of the building is largely Art Deco. The street fronting the Ministry of Finance building is a popular parking spot for calèches, the horse-drawn carriages that tour the city.

Continue down rue St-Louis to arrive at

8. Place d'Armes, once the military parade ground outside the governors' mansion (which no longer exists). In the small park at the center of the square is the Monument to the Faith, which recalls the arrival of Recollets monks from France in 1615. The Recollets were granted a large plot of land by the king of France in 1681 for their church and monastery. Facing the square is the monument to Samuel de Champlain, who founded Québec in 1608. Created by French artists Paul Chevre and Paul le Cardonel, the statue has stood here since 1898. The stone of the statue's pedestal is made from that used in Paris's Arc de Triomphe and Sacré-Coeur Basilica.

Near the Champlain statue is the diamond-shaped monument designating Québec City a UNESCO World Heritage Site, the only city in North America to be so honored. Placed here in 1985, it is made of bronze, granite, and glass. A tourist information center is also at place d'Armes, at 12 rue Ste-Anne.

Again, up to the right, is the

9. Château Frontenac, which defines the Québec skyline. The first, lower part was built as a hotel in 1892–93 by the Canadian Pacific Railway Company. The architect, Bruce Price of New York, raised his creation on the site of the governor's mansion and named it after Louis de Buade, Comte de Frontenac. Monsieur le Comte was the one who, in 1690, was faced with the threat of an English fleet under Sir William Phips. Phips sent a messenger to demand Frontenac's surrender, but Frontenac replied, "Tell your lord that I will reply with the mouths of my cannons." Which he did. Phips sailed away.

Walking Tour—Upper Town

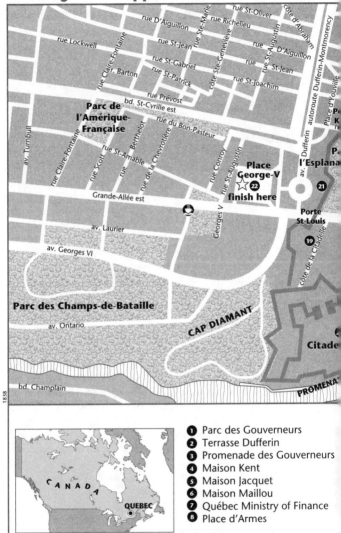

- ❶ Parc des Gouverneurs
- ❷ Terrasse Dufferin
- ❸ Promenade des Gouverneurs
- ❹ Maison Kent
- ❺ Maison Jacquet
- ❻ Maison Maillou
- ❼ Québec Ministry of Finance
- ❽ Place d'Armes

☕ **TAKE A BREAK**   This is a great part of town to sit and watch the world go by. Grab a sidewalk table and enjoy something to drink or a bite to eat at **Au Relais de la place d'Armes,** a red-roofed building with a mock-Tudor facade at 16 rue Ste-Anne.

Leaving there, turn right, then right again on the narrow pedestrian street called

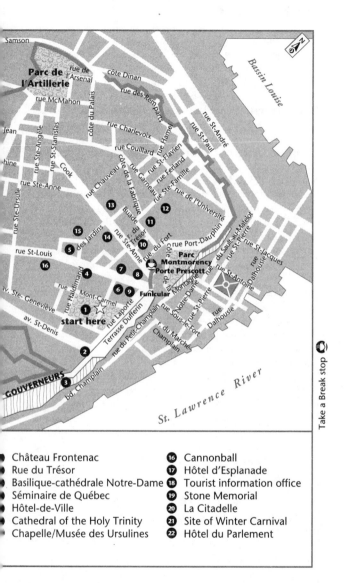

Take a Break stop

- Château Frontenac
- Rue du Trésor
- Basilique-cathédrale Notre-Dame
- Séminaire de Québec
- Hôtel-de-Ville
- Cathedral of the Holy Trinity
- Chapelle/Musée des Ursulines

- **16** Cannonball
- **17** Hôtel d'Esplanade
- **18** Tourist information office
- **19** Stone Memorial
- **20** La Citadelle
- **21** Site of Winter Carnival
- **22** Hôtel du Parlement

10. Rue du Trésor, where artists hang their prints and paintings of Québec scenes. It is busy with browsers and sellers, and most prices are kept within the means of the average visitor. Several of the artists, positioned near adjacent sidewalk cafés, draw portraits or caricatures.

Follow rue du Trésor from rue Ste-Anne down to rue Buade and turn left. On the right, at the corner of rue Ste-Famille is the

11. Basilique-cathédrale Notre-Dame (1647), which has suffered a tumultuous history of bombardment and repeated reconstruction. Its interior is ornate, the air rich with the scent of burning candles. Many artwork remains from the time of the French regime. The chancel lamp was a gift from Louis XIV, and the crypt is the final resting place for most of the bishops of Québec. The rooster atop the basilica is there for religious, not agricultural, reasons.

Downhill from the basilica on rue Ste-Famille, just past côte de la Fabrique, is the historic:

12. Séminaire de Québec, founded in 1663 by Bishop Laval, the first bishop in North America. The seminary had grown into Laval University by 1852, and for many years it occupied the expanded seminary campus. By the middle of the 20th century, however, a new university was constructed west of the city in Ste-Foy. The entire area is still known as the Latin Quarter after the language that once dominated university life. An animated neighborhood at night, many visitors will want to return to participate, especially along rues Couillard, Garneau, and St-Jean. During summer only, tours are given of the old seminary's grounds and some of its stone and wood buildings, revealing a lavish use of stone, tile, brass, and gilt-framed oil paintings. The Musée de l'Amérique Française, housed in the seminary, has an entrance at 9 rue de l'Université. It is open year-round.

From here, head back to the basilica. Take a right on rue Buade and follow it to rue des Jardins to see the

13. Hôtel-de-Ville (City Hall), built in 1883. The building's lower level, with an entrance on côte de la Fabrique, houses the Centre d'Interpretation (Urban Life Interpretation Center), with a large-scale model of Québec City and its suburbs as they were in 1975. It helps strangers to get their bearings, and it might be surprising to see how spread-out the city actually is. While the historic Upper and Lower Towns are compact, the city actually covers 35¹/2 square miles (92 square kilometers).

The park next to the City Hall is often converted into an outdoor show area, and in summer—especially during the Festival d'Eté (Summer Festival)—when concerts, dance recitals, and other programs are staged here.

Continue on rue des Jardins and cross rue Ste-Anne. On the left is the spire of the

Impressions

I think I would rather be a poor priest in Québec than a rich hog-merchant in Chicago.
                    —Matthew Arnold, Letter to Walter Arnold (1884)

14. Anglican Cathedral of the Holy Trinity, which dates from 1804 and is said to be modeled after St-Martin-in-the-Fields in London. The interior of the cathedral is simple but spacious, with pews of solid English oak from the Royal Windsor forest and a latticed ceiling in white with a gilded-chain motif. Visitors may happen upon an organ recital, or at least a rehearsal.

Farther along on rue des Jardins, at rue Donnacona, on the right side of the street, is the

15. Chapelle/Musée des Ursulines. The museum displays the handiwork of the Ursuline nuns from the 17th, 18th, and 19th centuries. There are also Amerindian crafts and a cape made for Marie de l'Incarnation, the reverend mother and a founder of the convent, when she left for New France in 1639.

Be sure to peek into the restored chapel if it's open (May–Oct). It shelters the remains of General Montcalm, who was buried here after he fell in the battle that marked the end of French rule in Québec in 1759. Montcalm's tomb is actually under the chapel and not accessible to the public. His skull, on the other hand, is on display in the Ursuline Museum. The tomb of Marie de l'Incarnation, who died in 1672, is here. The altar, created by sculptor Pierre-Noel Levasseur between 1726 and 1736, is worth a look.

From the museum, turn right on rue Donnacona and walk past to the entrance of the Ursuline Convent, built originally in 1642. The present complex is actually a succession of different buildings added and repaired at various times up to 1836, for frequent fires took their toll. A statue of founder Marie de l'Incarnation is outside. The convent is a private girls' school today and is not open to the public.

Continue left up the hill along what is now rue du Parloir to rue St-Louis. Cross the street and turn right. At the next block, at rue du Corps-de-Garde, note the

16. Cannonball lodged at the base of the tree trunk. It purportedly landed here during the War of 1759 and over the years has become firmly embraced by the tree.

Continue along St-Louis another block and a half to rue d'Auteuil. The house on the corner, over to the right, is now the

17. Hôtel d'Esplanade. Notice that many of the windows in the facade facing rue St-Louis are bricked up. This is because houses were once taxed by the number of windows they had, and the frugal homeowner found a way to get around the law, even though it cut down on his view.

Turn right on rue d'Auteuil and walk to the

18. Tourist information office, set in Parc de l'Esplanade, nestled just inside the city walls. Maps and brochures are available, and bilingual attendants answer questions. A mock snowman called Bonhomme Carnaval, mascot of the city's Winter Carnival, is often positioned out front. Before it became a public space, Parc de l'Esplanade was a military exercise ground. The office faces a row of comely brick and stone houses.

Return to rue St-Louis and turn right, toward Porte St-Louis, a gate in the walls. Next to it is the Esplanade powder magazine, part of the old fortifications. Just before the gate, cross over and turn left along côte de la Citadelle. On the right are headquarters and barracks of a militia district, arranged around an inner court.

Near its entrance is a

19. Stone memorial that marks the resting place of 13 soldiers of General Montgomery's American army, felled in the unsuccessful assault on Québec in 1775. It is a reminder that the conflicts that swirled around Québec for centuries didn't end with the fateful 1759 battle between the British and the French.

Continue up the hill to

20. La Citadelle. The impressive star-shaped fortress keeps watch from a commanding position on a grassy plateau 360 feet above the banks of the St. Lawrence. It took 30 years to complete, by which time it had become obsolete. Since 1920, the Citadel has been the home of the Royal 22e Régiment, which fought in both world wars and in Korea. With good timing, it is possible both to visit the regimental museum and watch the changing of the guard or the ceremony called beating the retreat, weather permitting (see Chapter 14).

Return to rue St-Louis and turn left through Porte St-Louis, which was built in 1873 on the site of a gate dating from 1692.

Here the street broadens to become the Grande-Allée. On the right is a park that runs alongside the city walls. This is the

21. Site of Winter Carnival, one of the most captivating events in the Canadian calendar. The 11-day celebration takes place every year from the first Thursday to the second Sunday of February. A majestic palace of snow and ice, the centerpiece of the festivities, rises on this spot. Colorfully clad Québécois come to admire it, climb on it, and sample some maple syrup candy at the nearby sugar shack set up for the occasion. Across the street, ice sculptures are created by 20 teams of artists from around the world participating in the International Snow Sculpture Competition. Each sculpture illustrates an aspect of the culture of the country it represents.

Fronting the park, on avenue Dufferin, stands Québec's stately

22. Hôtel du Parlement, constructed in 1884. It houses what Québécois are pleased to call their "National Assembly." Someday the label might actually be accurate. Along the facade are 22 bronze statues of the prominent figures in Québec's tumultuous history. The fountain in front of the door, the work of Philippe Hébert (1890), was dedicated to Québec's original Native American, or Amerindian, inhabitants. There are tours of the sumptuous chambers inside, where symbols of the fleur-de-lys and the initials "VR" (for Victoria Regina) are reminders of Québec's dual heritage. If the crown on top is lit, Parliament is in session.

☕ **TAKE A BREAK** Continue along the Grande-Allée a couple more blocks to reach the strip of cafés that supports the frequent comparison of the boulevard with Champs-Elysées. It isn't even close, but there are plenty of places to stop for a drink or a snack, at outdoor tables in summer. One possibility is **Au Petit Coin Breton,** on the south side of the street, at 655 Grande-Allée est.

From the Grande-Allée, walk or take the no. 11 bus back to the Old City. For a longer, but scenic hike, continue along Grand-Allée to visit the Québec Museum, on the left at 1 av. Wolfe-Montcalm, then go into Parc des Champs-de-Bataille (Battlefields Park), picking up the Promenade des Gouverneurs near La Citadelle and proceeding down onto the terrasse Dufferin and the Château Frontenac.

WALKING TOUR 2
LOWER TOWN

Start: On the terrasse Dufferin.
Finish: Place Royal
Time: 1–1¹/₂ hours.
Best Times: Anytime.
Worst Times: None, except the small hours.
Descend to the Lower Town by the

1a. Funicular, on terrasse Dufferin, near the Château Frontenac. As the car descends the steep slope, its glass front provides a broad view. The mammoth grain elevators down by the harbor have a capacity of eight million bushels. Beyond them is the river, with its constant boat traffic, and over to the left, the Laurentian Mountains rise in the distance.

Or, if a more active (and free) means of descent is preferred, use the stairs to the left of the funicular, which link up with

1b. Escalier Casse-Cou, literally "Breakneck Stairs," the name of which will be self-explanatory. A stairway has existed here since the settlement began. But human beings weren't the only ones to use the stairs. In 1698, the town council forbade citizens to take their animals up or down the stairway or face a fine.

Both Breakneck Stairs and the funicular arrive at the intersection of rues Petit-Champlain and Sous-le-Fort. At the corner on the left is the

2. Verrerie la Mailloche. In the front room craftsmen give glass-blowing demonstrations, always intriguing and informative, especially for children who haven't seen that ancient act of legerdemain. The glass is melted at 2,545° Fahrenheit and worked at 2,000°. There are displays of the results and a small shop in which to purchase them.

Exiting, walk down rue Petit-Champlain, passing

3. **Maison Louis Jolliet** (Louis Jolliet House), now the lower terminus for the funicular, and full of tourist trinkets and gimcracks. Built in 1683, it was the home of the Québec-born explorer who, with Fr. Jacques Marquette, was the first person of European parentage to explore the upper reaches of the Mississippi River. Jolliet died in 1700 at the age of 55.

Continue down

4. **Rue du Petit-Champlain,** the oldest street in North America, and usually swarming with restaurantgoers, café sitters, strolling couples, and gaggles of schoolchildren ricocheting from one fetching store to another along the way. (See Chapter 16 for shopping suggestions.)

At the end of the street, turn left onto boulevard Champlain. Across the street stands a transplant from the Gaspé Peninsula

5. **Pointe à la Renommé Lighthouse,** next to the Québec Coast Guard Base at the auto entrance to the Québec-Lévis ferryboat. Erected on the Pointe à la Renommé on the Gaspé Peninsula in 1906, the lighthouse took its name from a point of land, which, in turn, was named for a ship, the *Renommé,* that ran aground there in 1736. A modern lighthouse was erected on Pointe à la Renommé in 1975, and the old one was moved here. Its huge glass lenses represent the height of technology at the turn of the century.

Turn left along boulevard Champlain, past more shops and cafés, following the curve of the street, which soon arrives at

6. **Maison Chevalier** (Chevalier House), once the home of merchant Jean-Baptiste Chevalier and dating from 1752. Note the wealth of windows in the house, more than 30 in the facade alone. In 1763, the house was sold at auction to shipowner Jean-Louis Frémont, the grandfather of Virginia-born John Charles Frémont (1813–90). John Charles was an American explorer, soldier, and politician who mapped some 10 Western and Midwestern territories. This notable workaholic of French-Canadian heritage was also a governor of California and Arizona, a candidate for president of the United States in 1856, and a general during the Civil War.

The Chevalier House was sold in 1806 to an Englishman, who, in turn, rented it to a hotelier, who transformed it into an inn. From this time to the end of the century it was known, under various owners, as the London Coffee House. In 1960 the Québec government restored the house, and it became a museum about five years later, overseen by the Museum of Civilization, which mounts temporary exhibitions here.

Walking Tour—Lower Town

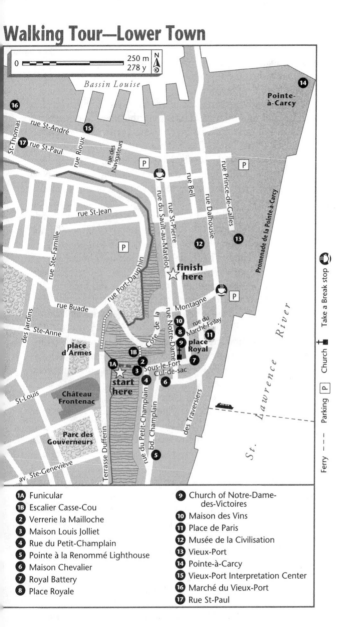

1A Funicular
1B Escalier Casse-Cou
2 Verrerie la Mailloche
3 Maison Louis Jolliet
4 Rue du Petit-Champlain
5 Pointe à la Renommé Lighthouse
6 Maison Chevalier
7 Royal Battery
8 Place Royale
9 Church of Notre-Dame-des-Victoires
10 Maison des Vins
11 Place de Paris
12 Musée de la Civilisation
13 Vieux-Port
14 Pointe-à-Carcy
15 Vieux-Port Interpretation Center
16 Marché du Vieux-Port
17 Rue St-Paul

Turn left after exiting the house, walking up the short block of rue Notre-Dame to rue Sous-le-Fort. Turn right, and walk one more block to the

7. Royal Battery, which was erected in 1691. The cannons were added in 1712 to defend the Lower Town, and they got the chance in 1759, but the English victory silenced them, and the exodus to the Upper Town left them to rust. Sunken foundations were all that remained of the Royal Battery by the turn of the century, and when the time came to restore this area, it had to be rebuilt from the ground up.

From the Royal Battery, return to rue Sous-le-Fort. Here is a good photo opportunity, shooting up the street to capture the Château Frontenac framed between the ancient houses. Go up one block to rue Notre-Dame. Turn right. Half a block up the grade is the heart of the Lower Town,

8. **Place Royale,** at the center of the first permanent colony in New France. In the early days it was the town marketplace, and today it has been restored to very near its old-time appearance. It went into a decline around 1860 and by 1950 had become the derelict, run-down part of town. The prominent bust is of Louis XIV, the Sun King, a gift from the city of Paris in 1928 that was installed here in 1931. The striking 17th- and 18th-century houses around the square once belonged to wealthy merchants. Note the ladders on some of the steep roofs, used to fight snow and fire.

Facing directly onto the square is the small

9. **Church of Notre-Dame-des-Victoires,** the oldest stone church in Québec, built in 1688 and restored in 1763 and in 1969. The paintings, altar, and large model boat suspended from the ceiling were votive offerings brought by early settlers to ensure a safe voyage. The church usually is open to visitors during the day, unless a wedding is under way.

Across the square from the church stands the

10. **Maison des Vins** (House of Wines), the proudest wineshop of the Québec Société des Alcools. In addition to the wines on sale, the store invites the public to examine the cool subterranean vaults of the old stone house, even if they have no intention of making a purchase.

From place Royale, walk down rue du Marché-Finlay (in the far right corner from the church) to reach

11. **Place de Paris,** with its uninspired abstract sculpture Dialogue with History (1987), by French sculptor Jean-Pierre Raynard, which commemorates the first French settlers in Québec.

Continue ahead to rue Dalhousie and turn left.

☕ **TAKE A BREAK** The relatively new but immensely popular restaurant, **Le Café du Monde,** 57 rue Dalhousie, at rue de la Montagne, is known for its imported beers, large selection of wines by the glass, and substantial servings of mussels. It's fun, with ingratiating waiters who sometimes sit down at the upright piano to play.

Leaving the café, turn left on rue Dalhousie and walk to the

12. **Musée de la Civilisation,** 86 rue Dalhousie, just past rue St-Antoine. The museum, which opened in 1988, may be situated among the cobblestoned streets in the historic Basse-Ville, but there is nothing traditional about it. Spacious and airy,

with ingeniously arranged multidimensional exhibits, it is one of the most innovative museums in Canada, if not in all of North America. If there is no time now, put it at the top of the must-see list for a later visit.

Across the street from the Museum of Civilization is the

13. Vieux-Port (Old Port), a 72-acre riverfront area, which in the 17th century was the touchdown for European ships bringing supplies and settlers to the new colony. With the decline of shipping and the shifting of economic power to Montréal by the early 20th century, the port fell into precipitous decline. But since the mid-1980s, it has experienced a rebirth, becoming the summer destination for international cruise ships.

Walk across and turn left at water's edge on the port promenade, soon passing the Naturalium, a privately owned museum of natural sciences that celebrates the biodiversity of the planet, from beetles to bison. Then comes the Agora, an impressive 6,000-seat outdoor theater with a clamshell-shape stage, and behind it, the city's Customs House, built between 1830 and 1839.

Continue walking along the promenade, past the Agora, to the landscaped

14. Pointe-à-Carcy. From here, look out across Louise Basin to the Bunge of Canada grain elevator, which stores the wheat, barley, corn, and soybean crop produced in western Canada before it is shipped to Europe. The bridge to rural Île d'Orléans can also be seen, the island that supplies Québec with much of its fresh fruits and vegetables.

Follow the walkway from Pointe-à-Carcy along the Louise Basin. If it is closed, as it was at this writing because of construction, follow the brick walkway toward the Customs House. On the right is the city's new Navy School.

Walk around the Customs House to rue St-André. From here, walk four not-especially-scenic blocks to rue Rioux. On the right, at rue St-André and rue Rioux (or the left, if the pedestrian walkway along the Louise Basin was the route chosen), is a modern three-story building with blue trim, the

15. Vieux-Port Interpretation Center, at 100 rue St-André. The museum illustrates what the Port of Québec was like in the 19th century, during its heyday. Be sure to see the view of the port and the city from the top level of the Interpretation Center. Useful reference maps identify prominent landmarks. The Interpretation Center charges a small admission in summer,

Impressions

Québec . . . ranks by herself among those Mother-cities of whom none can say. "This reminds me."

—Rudyard Kipling, *Letters to the Family* (1907)

but at other times it's free. Texts are in English and French, and visitors are invited to touch most of the exhibits.

From the Old Port Interpretation Center, go to rue St-André, turn right, and walk one block to the

16. **Marché du Vieux-Port,** a market with jaunty green roofs and blue banners. From here look west to see the 1916 train station, designed by New York architect Bruce Price, who designed the Château Frontenac in 1893.

The colorful farmers' market has rows of booths heaped with fresh fruits and vegetables, relishes, jams, handicrafts, flowers, and honey from local hives. Above each booth hangs a sign with the name and telephone number of the seller. A lot of them bear the initials I.O., meaning they come from Île d'Orléans, 10 miles outside the city. The market is enclosed, and the central part of it, with meats and cheeses for sale, is heated. There's a little café inside at which to order a cup of coffee or a meal, and an ice-cream stand and a bakery.

Leaving the market, cross rue St-André at the light and walk ahead one short block to

17. **Rue St-Paul,** home to burgeoning numbers of antiques shops and cafés. Turn left onto it. Most of the shops stretch from rue Rioux, opposite the Interpretation Center, to rue du Sault-au-Matelot. There's a real sense of neighborhood here.

☕ **TAKE A BREAK**   The busy **Restaurant-Café de Saint-Malo,** at 75 rue St-Paul and rue du Sault-au-Matelot, has low ceilings, rough stone walls, and storefront windows that draw patrons inside. Come for a full meal or, on sunny days, a drink or coffee and dessert at a sidewalk table. From here, meander back toward place Royale and the funicular along rue du Sault-au-Matelot or rue St-Pierre.

If this walking tour has piqued interest in Québec's history, the Librairie du Nouveau Monde (New World Bookstore), at 103 rue St-Pierre, can provide an English-language copy of the illustrated and highly readable *An Historical Guide to Québec,* by Yves Tessier.

16

Québec City Shopping

The compact size of the Old Town, with its upper and lower sections, make it especially convenient for browsing and shopping. Though similar from one place to the next, the merchandise is generally of high quality. There are several art galleries deserving of attention, including an outdoor one in the Upper Town. Antiques shops are proliferating along rue St-Paul in the Lower Town.

1 The Shopping Scene

In the Upper Town, wander along rue St-Jean, both within and outside the city walls, and on rue Garneau and côte de la Fabrique, which branch off the east end of St-Jean. There's a shopping concourse on the lower level of the Château Frontenac. For T-shirts, postcards, and other souvenirs, myriad shops line rue St-Louis.

Côte de la Montagne, which leads from the Upper Town to the Lower Town as an alternative to the funicular, has a gallery specializing in crafts and folk art. The Lower Town itself, particularly the quartier du Petit-Champlain, just off place Royale and encompassing rue du Petit-Champlain, boulevard Champlain, and rue Sous-le-Fort (opposite the funicular entrance), offers many possibilities—clothing, souvenirs, gifts, household items, collectibles—and is avoiding so far the trashiness that often afflicts heavily touristed areas.

Outside the walls, just beyond the strip of cafés that line Grande-Allée, av. Cartier is blossoming with shops and eating places of considerable variety, from clothing and ceramics to housewares and gourmet foods. The four or five blocks attract crowds of generally youngish locals, activity that revs up on summer nights and weekends. It remains outside the tourist orbit.

BEST BUYS

Indigenous crafts, handmade sweaters, and Inuit art are among the desirable items that aren't seen everywhere else. An official igloo trademark identifies authentic Inuit (Eskimo) art, although the differences between the real thing and the manufactured variety become apparent with a little careful study. Inuit artwork, usually carvings in stone or bone, are "best buys" not because of low prices, but because of their high quality. Expect to pay hundreds of dollars for even a relatively small piece. Apart from a handful of boutiques, Québec City does not have the high-profile designer clothing often showcased in Montréal.

SHOPPING COMPLEXES

In the Upper Town, there's a small complex filled with upscale shops called Les Promenades du Vieux Québec, at 43 rue Buade. Here are a perfumery, Inuit carvings, and clothing for men and women, including a Liz Claiborne factory outlet, along with cafés and a currency exchange. Just outside the city walls at Porte Kent, Place Québec incorporates dozens of shops, a cinema, restaurants, a convention center, and the Hilton hotel, an easy-to-spot landmark. Place Québec is accessible from bd. Réne-Lévesque and the Hilton. Shopping malls on a grander scale aren't found in or near the Old Town. For those, it is necessary to travel to a neighboring municipality, Ste-Foy. The malls there differ little from their cousins throughout North America, in layout or available products. For sheer size, however, Place Laurier, at 2700 bd. Laurier, has 350 stores.

THE ANTIQUES DISTRICT

Dealers in antiques have gravitated to rue St-Paul in the Lower Town. To get there, follow rue St-Pierre from the place Royale, then head west on rue St-Paul. So far there are about a dozen shops, with more likely to open, filled with old brass beds, knickknacks, Québec furniture, candlesticks, old clocks, Victoriana, Art Deco and Art Moderne objects, and even the increasingly sought-after kitsch and housewares of the early post–World War II period. To lend piquancy to the search for objects bearing histories, reflect that it was here that Benedict Arnold and his band of Americans were defeated at the hands of Québec defenders (at the corner of rues St-Pierre and St-Jacques, to be exact).

STORE HOURS

Stores tend to keep similar hours, opening and closing in tandem. With some exceptions, they are open Monday through Wednesday from 9:30am to 5:30pm, Thursday and Friday from 9:30am to 9pm, and Saturday from 9:30am to 5pm. Many shops, including Simons department store, stay open on Sunday from noon to 5pm. In the busy summer months, it's not unusual for stores to keep much longer hours—from 9am to 9pm daily, especially in the more obvious tourist districts.

TAXES & REFUNDS

Sales taxes on goods total 15%—7% federal tax and 8% provincial tax. (The Québec tax on lodgings is only 4%.) To get most of that tax money back, ask for and keep all receipts, and pick up a copy of the pamphlet titled "Goods and Services Tax Refund for Visitors," available in many stores, in tourist offices, and at the front desks of most hotels. Inside the pamphlet is a refund application. After returning home, mail the *original* receipts with the completed application to the address specified on the form. The refund takes a few weeks or months, but eventually arrives in the currency of the applicant's home country, minus a small service charge.

2 Shopping A to Z

ARTS & CRAFTS

Abaca
38 rue Garneau (near St-Paul). ☎ **418/694-9761.**

The owners gather their own merchandise on buying trips abroad. Their inventory includes masks, jewelry, musical instruments, sculpture, and related pieces from Africa, India, Afghanistan, Japan, Korea, and China, and a score of other countries. Some jewelry and handcrafts by Québec artists are also sold here. The store takes its name from a tree that grows in the Philippines. Two other stores carry the owners' products: Origènes, filled with jewelry and sculpture, around the corner at 54 côte de la Fabrique, and Magasin Général, at 1196 rue St-Jean.

Aux Multiples
69 rue Ste-Anne (opposite the Hôtel-de-Ville). ☎ **418/692-1230.**

Inuit, vernacular, and modern Canadian art are on offer in this small gallery. The most appealing items, and those given prominence in display are the native carvings in stone, bone, and tusk. The shop ships purchases. Prices are high, but competitive for merchandise of similar quality. Check out its siblings, Galerie Brousseau, on the lower level of the Château Frontenac, and Galerie aux Multiples at 43 rue Buade.

Galerie d'Art du Petit-Champlain
88 rue de Petit-Champlain (near bd. Champlain). ☎ **418/692-5647.**

This new shop features the superbly detailed wood carvings of Roger Desjardins, who applies his skills to meticulous renderings of waterfowl.

Galerie Zanettin
28 côte de la Montagne (near escalier Casse-Cou). ☎ **418/692-1055.**

Whimsical primitive carvings and paintings by folk artists from Québec, the Maritime Provinces, and Alberta are joined with works by schooled artists and craftspeople.

Outdoor Gallery
Rue du Trésor (between rue Ste-Anne and rue Buade). No phone.

Sooner or later, everyone passes this alley near the place d'Armes. Artists gather along here much of the year to exhibit and sell their work, much like the artists on St-Amable Lane in Old Montréal. While none of them are likely ever to find their etchings and seriographs collected by major art museums, neither do they produce the equivalent of tigers and Elvis paintings on black velvet. Most of the prints on view are of Québec scenes, and one or two might make attractive souvenirs. The artists seem to enjoy chatting with interested passersby.

Les Trois Colombes
46 rue St-Louis (at du Parloir). ☎ **418/694-1114.**

Upstairs are handmade hats, coats, sweaters, high-top boots, moccasins, and rag dolls. Downstairs, crafts by Québec artisans include wood carvings, snowshoes, duck decoys, and soapstone sculptures (some by non-Inuits). They ship worldwide.

BOOKS AND MAGAZINES

Librairie Garneau

24 côte de la Fabrique (near Garneau). ☎ **418/692-4262.**

The English-language books are in a small section to the right just inside the entrance. Also in stock are cards, stationery, gift items, coloring books, and film.

Librairie Ulysses

4 bd. René Lévesque est (near av. Cartier). ☎ **418/529-5349.**

Specializing in travel, with guidebooks, travel accessories, and related items, it has a smaller branch in the same building as the tourist information office at 12 rue Ste-Anne, opposite place d'Armes.

Librairie du Nouveau Monde

103 rue St-Pierre (behind the Musée de la Civilisation). ☎ **418/694-9475.**

In the Lower Town, this store has a wide variety of books, mostly in French, including the fascinating *Historical Guide to Québec,* by Yves Tessier, a good read about the city's past, filled with illustrations, photographs, and a foldout map.

Maison de la Presse Internationale

1050 rue St-Jean (near St-Stanislas). ☎ **418/694-1511.**

As the name says, this large store in the midst of the St-Jean shopping and nightlife bustle stocks magazines, newspapers, and paperbacks from around the world, in many languages. It stays open late, and they'll often accept reservations for future editions of the *New York Times,* say, or the *Wall Street Journal.*

CHRISTMAS ITEMS

La Boutique de Noel de Québec

47 rue Baude (near Hôtel-de-Ville). ☎ **418/692-2457.**

The ubiquity of year-round Christmas stores is a mystery to those who find December frantic enough. Nevertheless, the holiday is observed in July at this successful shop, which has just moved to this location. In the interest of diversification, they now also sell products related to observances of Halloween and Easter.

CLOTHING

America

1147 rue St-Jean (near St-Stanislas). ☎ **418/692-5254.**

A link in the popular chain, it offers dependably good quality and style in casual and dress clothes for men.

Boutique le Fou du Roi

57 Petit-Champlain (near the Funiculaire). ☎ **418/692-4439.**

This diminutive shop halfway along Petit-Champlain in Basse-Ville carries an array of sturdy children's toys and games and some attractive clothes for toddlers.

François Cote
35 rue Buade (near Hôtel-de-Ville). ☎ **418/692-6016.**

The menswear in this upscale shop is carefully constructed and eye-catching without being odd. Suits, jackets, slacks, and accessories.

La Maison du Hamac
91 rue Ste-Anne. ☎ **418/692-1109.**

While this shop does indeed carry a wide selection of hammocks, it also has clothing from Latin America—colorful hats, shirts, belts, vests, bags, and jewelry from Mexico, Guatemala, and Brazil . . . and kites, too.

La Maison Darlington
7 rue Baude (near the Hôtel-de-Ville). ☎ **418/692-2268.**

A new enterprise, this comes on strong with both tony and traditional clothing for men and women produced by such makers as Burberry, Gant, and Salty Dog. Better still are the hand-smocked dresses for babies and little girls produced by Helene Gourdeau and her mother.

Oke
40 côte de la Fabrique (near Hôtel-de-Ville). ☎ **418/692-0102.**

This is the one shop in Québec City that comes close to those provocative showcases for the up-and-coming designers of Montréal. The environment is pleasant, the clothes comfortably casual, with easy, flowing lines.

Zazou
31 Petit Champlain (near the funiculaire). ☎ **418/694-9990.**

This little shop focuses primarily on the casual and dressy fashions of Québécois designers.

DEPARTMENT STORE

Simons
20 côte de la Fabrique (near the Hôtel-de-Ville). ☎ **418/692-3630.**

The only department store in the Old City, it opened here in 1840 and has expanded to two other locations. Small by modern standards, Simons has two floors for men's and women's clothing, much of it sportswear, and for household linens. It's all pretty basic, not daring. They'll make alterations.

FOOD

Alimentation Petit-Cartier
1191 av. Cartier (near Fraser).

In effect, this is a mall for foodies, containing a collection of merchants in open-fronted shops purveying fresh meats and fish, cheeses, pâtés and terrines, glistening produce, pastries, confections, and fancy picnic items. There are a few fast-food counters, and delis that make up sandwiches to order. The second floor features nonfood merchandise, lingerie, glasses, a hairdresser, a pharmacy.

GIFTS

La Corriveau

30 côte de la Fabrique. ☎ **418/692-2109.**

Crafts and kicky handknits predominate, all a little on the expensive side but distinctive. Duck decoys and burly sweaters for adults and kids are among the most engaging items, supplemented by lots of hats, gloves, mittens, headbands, moccasins, and lumberjack coats. All the wool items are made by Adrien Racine.

Claude Berry, Inc.

6 côte de la Fabrique. ☎ **418/692-2628.**

Find here hand-painted porcelains from Limoges, jacquard replicas of medieval tapestries, Inuit carvings, religious articles—a grab bag that might produce that elusive gift.

Geomania

59 rue Dalhousie (near St-Antoine). ☎ **418/692-2773.**

They muster shiny arrays of agate, quartz, fossils, Canadian jade, some of it merely in polished chunks, much of it fashioned into jewelry and small carvings. There's another branch at 70 rue St-Pierre (☎ 418/692-1400).

WINES

Société des Alcools de Québec

1059 av. Cartier (near rue Fraser). ☎ **418/643-4334.**

A virtual supermarket of wines and spirits, with thousands of bottles in stock.

Maison des Vins

1 place Royale (opposite Église Notre-Dame-des-Victoires.) ☎ **418/643-1214.**

Over 2,000 labels are in stock here. Visit the historic cellar, even if not planning to make a purchase.

17

Québec City After Dark

While Québec City can't pretend to match the volume of nighttime diversions of exuberant Montréal, there is more than enough to do to occupy every evening of an average stay. And apart from theatrical productions, almost always in French, a knowledge of the language is rarely necessary.

Drop in at the tourism information office for a list of events, such as the annual **Festival d'Eté** (Summer Festival) in July, when free concerts and shows are staged all over town in the evenings and the upper portion of rue St-Jean is closed to cars to become a pedestrian promenade. The same holds true for the **Carnaval d'Hiver** (Winter Carnival) in February, when the city salutes the season with a grand ice palace, ice sculptures, and parades.

Check the "Night Life" section of the Greater Québec Area Tourist Guide for suggestions. A weekly information leaflet called *L'Info-Spectacles,* listing headline attractions and the venues in which they are appearing, is found at concierge desks and in many bars and restaurants, as is the tabloid-sized giveaway *Voir,* which provides greater detail. Both are in French, but salient points aren't difficult to decipher.

Concerts and theatrical performances usually begin at 8:00pm. Most bars and clubs stay open until 2 or 3am, closing earlier if business doesn't warrant the extra hour or two. A clear advantage of a night out in Québec is that cover charges and drink minimums are all but unknown in the bars and clubs that provide live entertainment. Highballs aren't unusually expensive, but neither are they generously poured, which is the reason most people stick to beer, usually Canadian. Some popular brands brewed in Québec are Belle-Gueule, Saint-Ambroise, and Boréale.

1 The Performing Arts

CLASSICAL MUSIC, OPERA & DANCE

Many of the city's churches host **sacred and secular music concerts,** as well as special **Christmas festivities.** Among them are the Cathedral of the Holy Trinity, église St-Jean-Baptiste, historic chapelle Bon-Pasteur, and, on Île d'Orléans, the église Ste-Pétronille. Outdoor performances in summer are staged beside City Hall in the Jardins de l'Hôtel-de-Ville, in the Pigeonnier at Parliament Hill, on the Grande-Allée, and at place d'Youville.

The **Québec Symphony Orchestra,** Canada's oldest, performs at the Grand Théâtre de Québec from September to May; the **Québec Opéra** mounts performances in the spring and fall, at the Grand Théâtre. **Danse-Partout** also performs at the Grand Théâtre.

Agora

120 rue Dalhousie (Vieux-Port). ☎ **418/692-1515** or 418/692-2633.

This 5,800-seat amphitheater at the Old Port is the scene of classical and contemporary music concerts and a variety of other shows in the summer. The city makes a dramatic backdrop. The box office, located in the adjacent Naturalium, is open daily 10am to 5pm.

Grand Théâtre de Québec

269 bd. René-Lévesque est (av. Turnbull). ☎ **418/643-8131.**

Classical music concerts, opera, dance, and theatrical productions are performed in two halls, one of them housing the largest stage in Canada. Visiting conductors, orchestras, and dance companies often perform here when resident organizations are away. The Trident Theatre troupe performs in French in the Salle Octave-Crémazie. Québec's Conservatory of Music is underneath the theater. The box office is open Monday to Friday 10am to 6pm.

2 The Club & Music Scene

For night life, there are three principal streets to choose among—the Grande-Allée, rue St-Jean, and the emerging av. Cartier. During the Summer Festival, the upper portion of rue St-Jean, near Porte St-Jean, is closed to cars and made into a pedestrian promenade.

NIGHTCLUBS & CABARETS

Théâtre du Petit-Champlain

68 rue du Petit-Champlain (near the funiculaire). ☎ **418/692-2631.**

Québécois and French singers fill this roomy café theater with cabarets and revues. Buy tickets down the street at 76 rue du Petit-Champlain, and have a drink on the patio before the show. The box office is open Monday to Friday from 1 to 5pm, to 7pm the night of a show. Performances are usually Tuesday to Saturday.

Les Yeux Bleus

1117 rue St-Jean. ☎ **418/694-9118.** No cover.

Tucked at the end of an alleyway off rue St-Jean, Les Yeux Bleus looks tumbledown from the outside, but is altogether inviting on the inside. The music is 75% Québécois, 25% American.

ROCK

Colisée de Québec

2205 av. du Colisée (parc de l'Exposition). ☎ **418/691-7211.**

Rock concerts are generally held in this arena, located in a park on the north side of the St-Charles River. The box office is open in summer Monday through Friday from 9am to 4pm, in winter from 10am to 5pm.

Bulldog Haute-Ville

598 rue St-Jean (near côte de la Fabrique). ☎ **418/523-7803.** No cover.

Rock prevails, often performed by "hommage" groups playing the songs of famous bands, but with occasional detours into blues. Billiards and a deejay provide diversion at slack times.

Le d'Auteuil

35 rue d'Auteuil (near Porte Kent). ☎ **418/692-2263.** No cover.

Patrons of university age and sartorial preferences play pool downstairs in the bar until the bands start twanging and thumping upstairs. As a rule, live performers are booked Tuesday through Saturday. Sometimes, they are semi-familiar names in rock or blues, more often they are alternative bands or "hommage" groups.

JAZZ & BLUES

Café Blues

1018 rue St-Jean (near St-Stanislas). ☎ **418/692-0001.** No cover.

Upstairs, according to an erratic schedule that defies prediction, blues artists start belting out their laments and popping a sweat at 11pm or thereabouts. Patrons can pass the time at a pool table until the show starts.

L'Emprise

57 rue Ste-Anne (at des Jardins). ☎ **418/692-2480.** No cover.

Listening to jazz, usually of the mainstream or fusion variety, is a long-standing tradition in this agreeable room. The bar, off the lobby of the once-elegant Hôtel Clarendon, has beamed ceilings, large windows, and Art Deco touches. Seating is at tables and around the bar. It has a mellow atmosphere, with serious jazz fans who come to listen. Music is nightly, from about 10:15pm.

FOLK

Chez Son Père

24 rue St-Stanislas (near St-Jean). ☎ **418/692-5308.** No cover.

A musical institution in Québec since 1960, this is the place where French Canadian folk singers often get their start. The stage is on the second floor, with the usual brick walls and sparse decor. A young, friendly crowd is in attendance. The club is a few steps uphill from bustling rue St-Jean.

D'Orsay

65 rue Baude (opposite Hôtel-de-Ville). ☎ **418/694-1582.**

Visitors whose complexion has cleared up and are well into their mortgages will want to keep this chummy pub-bistro in mind. Most of the clientele is on the far side of 35, and they start up conversations easily. There's a small dance floor with a deejay, and in summer, a folk singer perches on a stool on the terrace out back.

Le Saint-James

1110 rue St-Jean (côte du Palais). ☎ **418/692-1030.** No cover.

For decent food teamed with a pretty good show, this large restaurant/cabaret turns the mike over to mostly folk performers, sometimes blues shouters. A plate of pasta goes for $7.95, with soup, dessert, and coffee thrown in. The show starts around 10. Go, if only to hear the singer announce his next tune in his native French and go on to sing it in Deep South English.

DANCE CLUBS & DISCOS

Le Bistro Plus

1063 rue St-Jean (near St-Stanislas). ☎ **418/694-9252**.

A dance floor in back with a light show is full of writhing young bodies—*very* young, in many cases. During the week, the music is recorded, with live groups on some weekends. It gets raucous and messy, especially after the 4–7pm happy hour, but it's fun, too, with a pool table and TVs tuned to sports to keep people entertained.

Chez Dagobert

600 Grande-Allée (near Turnbull). ☎ **418/522-0393**. No cover.

The top disco in Québec City, this three-story club has an arena arrangement on the ground floor for live bands, with raised seating around the sides. Upper floors have a large dance floor, more bars, TV screens to keep track of sports events, and video games. Sound, whether live or recorded, is a hair short of bedlam, and more than a few habitués are seen to use earplugs. Things don't start kicking into gear until well after 11. The crowd divides into students and their more fashionably attired older brothers and sisters. A whole lot of eyeballing and approaching goes on.

Vogue/Sherlock Holmes

1170 d'Artgny (off Grande-Allée). ☎ **418/529-9973**. No cover.

This pair of double-decked bars is far less frenetic than Chez Dagobert, with a small disco upstairs in Vogue, and the pubby eatery Sherlock below, with a pool table and dart board. Grad students and Gen-Xers in their first jobs make up most of the custom.

3 The Bar & Café Scene

The strip of Grande-Allée between place Montcalm and place George V, near the St-Louis Gate, has been compared to the boulevard St-Germain in Paris. That's a real stretch, but it is lined on both sides with cafés, giving it a passing resemblance. Many have terraces abutting the sidewalks, so café-hopping is an active pursuit. Eating is definitely not the main event. Meeting and greeting and partying are, aided in some cases by glasses of beer so tall they require stands to hold them up. This leads, not unexpectedly, to a beery frat-house atmosphere that can get sloppy and dumb as the evening wears on. But early on, it's fun to sit and sip and watch. Discovery is probably best left to individuals, depending upon their moods and predilections. The following bars are away from the Grande-Allée melée.

The Major Concert & Performance Halls

Auditorium Joseph-Lavergne 350 rue St-Joseph est. ☎ **418/ 529-0924** for information, 418/691-7400 box office.

Colisée de Québec 205 av. du Colisée (parc de l'Exposition). ☎ **418/691-7211.**

Grand Théâtre de Québec 269 bd. René-Lévesque est (rue de Claire-Fontaine). ☎ **418/643-8131.**

Palais Montcalm 995 place d'Youville (next to Porte Kent). ☎ **418/691-2399** for information, 418/670-9011 for the box office.

Théâtre Capitole 972 rue St-Jean (near Porte St-Jean) ☎ **418/ 694-4444.**

L'Astral
1225 place Montcalm (at the Grande-Allée). ☎ **418/647-2222.**

Spinning slowly above a city that twinkles below like tangled necklaces, this restaurant and bar in the Hôtel Loews Le Concorde unveils a breathtaking 360-degree panorama. Many people come for dinner. Make it for drinks and the view.

Aviatic Club
Gare-du-Palais (near rue St-Paul, Lower Town.) ☎ **418/522-3555.**

A local favorite with the after-work crowd since 1945, it's in the front of the city's train station. The theme is aviation (which may seem odd given the venue), signaled by two miniature planes hanging from the ceiling. Food is served, along with local and imported beers. Behind the bar, the Pavillon, a casual Italian restaurant with pizza, pasta, and pool tables, is under the same ownership.

Le Pape-Georges
8 rue Cul-de-Sac (bd. Champlain, Lower Town). ☎ **418/692-1320.**

This cozy wine bar features jazz or a French singer on Thursday through Sunday at 10pm. Light fare is served during the day.

Saint Alexandre Pub
1087 rue St-Jean (near St-Stanislas). ☎ **418/694-0015.**

Roomy and sophisticated, this is the handsomest bar in town. It's done in a non-clichéd British pub mode, with polished mahogany and exposed brick and a working fireplace that's a particular comfort eight months a year. It claims to serve over 200 beers from around the world, 20 of them on tap, along with hearty victuals that complement the brews. Sometimes they present jazz duos, usually when other clubs and bars are dark. Large front windows provide easy observation of the busy St-Jean street life.

Au Café Suisse
26 rue Ste-Anne (place d'Armes). ☎ **418/694-1321.**

The location is prime at this congenial sidewalk café opposite the Château Frontenac and beside the colorful artist alleyway, rue du Trésor. An easygoing atmosphere facilitates meeting people or just relaxing with a coffee or a drink, any time of day or night.

GAY & LESBIAN BARS

The gay community in Québec City is a small one, centered in the Upper Town just outside the city walls, on rue St-Jean between av. Dufferin and rue St-Augustin, and also along rue St-Augustin and nearby rue d'Aiguillon, which runs parallel to rue St-Jean. One popular bar and disco, frequented by both men and women (and by men who look like women), is **Le Ballon Rouge,** at 811 rue St-Jean (☎ 418/647-9227).

4   More Entertainment

AN EVENING CRUISE

MV Louis Jolliet

Quai Chouinard, at the port. ☎ **418/692-1159.**

Dancing and cruising are the pursuits of passengers on the *MV Louis Jolliet*'s four-hour evening cruise from 7 to 11pm. Snack food and a complete bar lubricate the evening. The fare is $48.75.

Le Bateau-Mouche

Bassin Louise, at the port. ☎ **418/692-4949** or 800/361-0130.

The sleek *Bateau-Mouche* has arrived in Québec, following in the footsteps of its sister vessel in Montréal. Dinner cruises cost $58.75 and last three hours, from 7 to 10pm. Board at 6:15pm.

MOVIES

First-run English-language films are shown with French subtitles at the **Cinéma Place Québec,** in the place Québec shopping mall, under the Hilton hotel (☎ 418/525-4524), and the **Cinéma Galeries de la Capitale,** in the Galeries de la Capitale shopping mall (☎ 418/628-2455). Check the listings in the entertainment section of the *Québec Chronicle-Telegraph,* published on Wednesday.

ONLY IN QUÉBEC

The Basilique Notre-Dame schedules son-et-lumière (sound-and-light) shows inside the city's loveliest church four times daily Tuesday through Friday, and twice on Saturday. Tickets are $6.

An after-dinner stroll and a lounge on a bench on **terrasse Dufferin,** the boardwalk above the Lower Town, may well be the most memorable night on the town. Ferries glide across the river burnished by moonglow, and the stars haven't seemed that close since childhood.

18

Excursions from Québec City

The first four of the excursions described below can be combined and completed in a day. Admittedly, it will be a breakfast-to-dark undertaking, especially if much time is taken to explore each destination, but the farthest of the four destinations is only 25 miles from Québec City.

The famous shrine of Ste-Anne-de-Beaupré and the Mont Ste-Anne ski area are only about half an hour from the city by car. Bucolic Île d'Orléans, with its maple groves, orchards, farms, and 18th- and 19th-century houses, is a mere 15 minutes away. With two or more days available, you can continue along the northern shore to Charlevoix, where inns and a new casino invite an overnight, then take the ferry across the river and drive back toward Québec City, exploring the villages along the St. Lawrence's southern bank as you make your way.

While it is preferable to drive this region, tour buses go to Montmorency Falls and the shrine of Ste-Anne-de-Beaupré, and circle the Île d'Orléans. Tours don't go to the southern bank at all, however.

1 Île d'Orléans

16km (10 miles) NE of Québec City

Until 1935, the only way to get to Île d'Orléans was by boat in summer or over the ice in winter. The building of the highway bridge has allowed the fertile fields of Île d'Orléans to become Québec City's primary market-garden. During harvest periods, fruits and vegetables are picked fresh on the farms and trucked into the city daily. In mid-July, hand-painted signs posted by the main road announce "Fraises: cueillir vous-même" (Strawberries: pick 'em yourself). The same invitation is made during apple season, September and October. Farmers hand out baskets and quote the price, paid when the basket's full. Bring along a bag or box to carry away the bounty.

ESSENTIALS
GETTING THERE

BY BUS There are no local buses. For organized bus tours, contact **Visite Touristique de Québec** (☎ 418/563-9722), which offers English-only tours; **Old Québec Tours** (☎ 418/624-0460);

Maple Leaf Sightseeing Tours (☎ 418/687-9226); or **Gray Line** (☎ 418/622-7420).

BY CAR It's a short drive from Québec City to the island. Follow rue Dufferin (in front of the Parliament building) to connect with Autoroute 440 east, in the direction of Ste-Anne-de-Beaupré. In about 15 minutes, the Île d'Orléans bridge is seen on the right.

VISITOR INFORMATION

After arriving on the island, turn right on Rte. 368 east toward Ste-Pétronille. The **tourist information** office (☎ **418/828-9411**) is in the house on the right, and it has a useful, free guidebook for the island. It's open daily 8:30am to 7pm in summer; off-season, Monday through Friday only, 8:30am to 12:30pm and 1:30 to 4:30pm. A good substitute for the Île d'Orléans guide is the Greater Québec guide, which includes a short tour of Île d'Orléans. A driving-tour cassette can be rented or purchased at the tourist office, the Auberge La Goéliche, and other local inns or bed and breakfasts (see "Where to Stay and Dine," below).

Bikes can be rented at the gas station/grocery store, Dépanneur Godbout, right across the road from the bridge (☎ **418/828-9215**). If none is available, check at Le Vieux Presbytère bed and breakfast in St-Pierre (☎ **418/828-9723**). The tourist office supplies cycling maps.

For guided walking tours of several of the island's historical villages, or a nearly 2-hour boat tour visiting an apple orchard and the church in St-Pierre and its craft-filled giftshop, contact **Beau Temps, Mauvais Temps (Rain or Shine) tours** (☎ 418/828-2275).

Three stone churches on the island date back to the days of the French regime, due in part to the island's long isolation from the mainland. There are only seven such churches left in all of Québec, so this is a point of pride for Île d'Orléans. A firm resistance to development has kept many of its old houses intact as well. This could easily have become just another sprawling bedroom community, but it has remained a rural farming area. Island residents work to keep it that way. They have plans to bury their telephone lines and to put in a bike lane to cut down on car traffic.

A coast-hugging road circles the island, which is 21 miles long and 5 miles wide, and another couple of roads bisect it. On the east side of the island are many farms and picturesque houses; on the west side, an abundance of apple orchards.

There are six tiny villages on Île d'Orléans, each with a church as its focal point. It's possible to do a quick circuit of the island in half a day, but a full day can be justified, eating in a couple of restaurants, visiting a sugar shack, skipping stones from the beach, and staying the night in one of the several waterside inns. If you're strapped for time, drive as far as St-Jean, then take Route du Mitan across the island, and return to the bridge, and Québec City, via Rte. 368 west.

STE-PÉTRONILLE

The first village reached on the recommended counterclockwise tour is Ste-Pétronille, only 3 kilometers (2 miles) from the bridge.

Excursions From Québec City

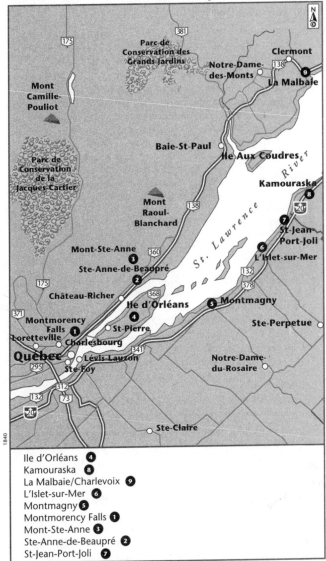

Ile d'Orléans **4**
Kamouraska **8**
La Malbaie/Charlevoix **9**
L'Islet-sur-Mer **6**
Montmagny **5**
Montmorency Falls **1**
Mont-Ste-Anne **3**
Ste-Anne-de-Beaupré **2**
St-Jean-Port-Joli **7**

With 1,050 inhabitants, it's best known for its Victorian inn, La Goéliche (see below), and also claims the northernmost stand of red oaks in North America, dazzling in autumn. The church dates from 1871, and its houses were once the summer homes of wealthy English in the 1800s. Even if you're not planning to stay at the inn, drive down to the water's edge where a small public area with benches is located and stroll or drive down the picturesque rue Laflamme.

WHERE TO STAY & DINE

✪ Auberge La Goéliche

22 av. du Quai, Ste-Pétronille, PQ G0A 4CO. ☎ **418/828-2248.** Fax 418/692-1742. 22 rms (all with bath). TV TEL $90–$120 double. Rates include breakfast. AE, MC, V. Parking free. Closed Nov.

On a rocky point of land at the western tip of the island stands this country house with a wraparound porch and a pool. The river slaps at the foundation of the glass-enclosed terrace dining room, which is a grand observation point for watching cruise ships and Great Lakes freighters steaming past. That location is appropriate, since the 1880 inn takes its name from a type of small cargo boat once used in these parts. Breezes off the river generally make air-conditioning unnecessary, so they don't have any. The dining room of La Goéliche is well-regarded, with updated French cooking, easy on the oils and cream. When ordering à la carte, expect to pay $7.25 to $12 for main courses, while a table d'hôte meal will run $18 to $20.50. A modified American plan is available.

ST-LAURENT

From Ste-Pétronille, continue on Rte. 368 east. In six kilometers (4 miles) is St-Laurent, once a boatbuilding center turning out 400 craft a year. To learn more about that heritage, visit Parc Maritime de St-Laurent (☎ **418/828-2322**), an active wooden-boat yard from 1908 to 1967. Before the bridge was built, it provided islanders the means to get across the river to Québec City. The Maritime Park incorporates the old Godbout Boatworks, and offers demonstrations of the craft. It's open in summer only, daily from 9:30am to 5:30pm.

The town's church was erected in 1860, and there are a couple of picturesque roadside chapels nearby as well. Good views of farmlands and the river are available from the St-Laurent golf course—just follow signs from the main road.

WHERE TO STAY

La Maison sous les Arbres

1415 chemin Royal, St-Laurent, IO, G0A 3Z0. ☎ **418/828 9442.** 3 rms (1 with bath). $60 double. Extra person $20, child $10. Rates include full breakfast. No credit cards.

The name means "the house under the trees," a line taken from a popular French song, and this contemporary bed-and-breakfast fits the description. All the rooms have private entrances, and the two that share one large bath are conveniently close to it. One large room with private bath also has a fireplace and can accommodate up to six people. Breakfast is cereal, homemade bread, fruit, cheeses and pâtés, eggs, french toast, and more in a glass-enclosed room overlooking the river. A swimming pool is available for use after 5pm.

WHERE TO DINE

Le Moulin de Saint-Laurent

754 chemin Royal. ☎ **418/829-3888.** Reservations recommended. Main courses $9.95–$20.95, table d'hôte lunches $10–$17, dinners $23–$35. DC, MC, V. Daily 11:30am–3:30pm and 5–9pm. Closed mid-Oct to May 1. COUNTRY FRENCH.

This former flour mill, in operation from 1720 to 1928, has been transformed into one of the island's most romantic restaurants, tucked behind trees with a stream gurgling past. On a warm day, sit on the terrace beside the waterfall, and be sure to wander upstairs to see the Québécois antiques. Lunch can be light, perhaps an omelet or a plate of assorted pâtés or cheeses. There are at least half a dozen main courses to choose from, only one of them fish, despite all that water out there. On weekends, a small combo plays in the evenings.

ST-JEAN

St-Jean, 6 kilometers (4 miles) from St-Laurent, was home to sea captains, and the homes in the village tend to be more prosperous than others on the island. One indication of that is the yellow-brick facades of several of the houses. The bricks were ballast in boats that came over from Europe. Further, the houses in St-Jean are the only ones on the island whose porches are ornamented with wrought iron. The village church was built in 1732 and the walled cemetery is the final resting place of many fishermen and seafarers. St-Jean, which now has 840 inhabitants, was once considered the de facto capital of the island until the bridge made St-Pierre more accessible.

WHAT TO SEE & DO

Mauvide-Genest Manor

1451 ave. Royale, St-Jean. ☎ **418/829-2630.** Admission $3 adults, $1.50 children 10 to 18, $8 families. Late May–late Aug Sat–Sun 10am–5:30pm, other times by appointment.

On the left when entering the village is the best-preserved and one of the largest houses on the island. Dating from 1752, it is filled with period furnishings, including china and an ornate American chest (1850) with carved flowers and an impressive eagle. A "beggar's bench" on view was so named because a homeless person who appeared at the door late in the day would be offered a bed for the evening (otherwise, he might cast a spell on the house). A small chapel was added in 1930; the altar was made by Huron Indians. The dining room is sometimes open to the public, and its country cooking makes the most of the island's plentiful produce. Next to the manor house, there's an active summer theater.

If you're pressed for time, pick up Route du Mitan, which crosses Île d'Orléans from here to St-Famille on the west side of the island. Route du Mitan, not easy to spot, is on the left past the church in St-Jean. A detour down that road is a diverting drive through farmland and forest. Return to St-Jean and proceed east on Rte. 368 east to St-François.

ST-FRANÇOIS

The 9-kilometer drive (5.5 miles) from St-Jean to St-François exposes vistas of the Laurentian Mountains off to the left on the western shore of the river. Just past the village center of St-Jean, Mont Ste-Anne can be seen, its slopes scored by ski trails. At St-François, home to about 500 people, the St. Lawrence, a constant and mighty presence, is 10 times wider than when it flows past Québec City. Regrettably, the town's original church (1734) burned in 1988.

At St-François, 24 kilometers (15 miles) from the bridge, the road becomes Rte. 368 west.

WHERE TO DINE

Auberge Chaumonot

425 av. Royale, St-François. ☎ **418/829-2735.** Reservations recommended. Main courses $18–$27; table d'hôte lunches $10–$19, dinner $19–$32. AE, MC, V. May–Oct, daily 11am–3pm and 5–9pm (until 10pm July–Aug). Closed mid-Oct–Apr 30. QUÉBÉCOIS.

Traditional regional cooking is especially pertinent on this saltwater-scented rural sojourn. At this riverside inn, the food reflects what farmers have eaten on this island for generations—pork chops, lamb, salmon, tourtière (meat pie), pheasant pâté, tomato-and-onion relish, and plenty of warm bread. The kitchen mixes in such contemporary touches as quiche Lorraine and shrimp and duck pâté. Picture windows look out on the river. The inn has eight tidy and inexpensive bedrooms, but they are not the reason to visit here. It is named for the Jesuit priest Pierre Chaumonot, who led the Hurons to the island in 1651 to protect them from the attacking Algonquins.

STE-FAMILLE

Founded in 1661 at the northern tip of the island, Ste-Famille is the oldest parish on the island. With 1,660 inhabitants, it is 8 kilometers (5 miles) from St-François and 19 kilometers (12 miles) from the bridge. Across the road from the triple-spired church (1743) is the convent of Notre-Dame Congregation, founded in 1685 by Marguerite Bourgeoys, one of Montréal's prominent early citizens. This area supports dairy and cattle farms and apple orchards.

WHAT TO SEE & DO

While in town, visit the **Blouin Bakery**, run by a family that has lived on the island for 300 years, and a little shop called **Le Mitan** that stocks local crafts and books about the island. Anglers might wish to swing by **Ferme Piscicole Richard Boily**, 4739 chemin Royal (☎ **418/829-2874**), where they can wet their lines for speckled or rainbow trout in a stocked pond, daily from 9am to sunset. It isn't *quite* like fishing in a rain barrel. Poles and bait are supplied—no permit is required—and customers pay only for what they catch, about 30¢ per inch; the fish run 9 to 12 inches. They'll clean, cut, and pack what you catch. Some island restaurants can even be persuaded to cook the fish for you. For more passive activity, buy a handful of fish pellets for 25¢, toss them on the water, and watch the ravenous trout jump.

On the same property, the Erablière Richard Boily offers free 15-minute visits to a cabane à sucre, the traditional "sugar shack" where syrup is made. They demonstrate the equipment and explain the process that turns the sap of a tree into maple syrup. Free tastes are offered and several types of products are for sale in a shop on the premises.

WHERE TO DINE

L'Atre

4403 chemin Royal, Ste-Famille. ☎ **418/829-2474.** Reservations required for dinner July–Aug. Main courses $17.50–$23.80, table d'hôte lunch $17.50–$32.75, dinner $29.50–$39.50, special 9–course La Grande Fête $58. July–Aug daily noon–3pm and 5:30–9:30pm, Sept–June, Sat dinner 5:30–9:30pm. QUÉBÉCOIS.

For what might be the most lasting memory of an island visit, park in the lot marked by a sign and wait for the horse-drawn covered carriage to arrive from the restaurant. The 10-minute carriage ride is free, although the driver won't reject a small tip. He deposits diners at a 1680 Québécois house with wide floorboards and whitewashed walls at least two feet thick. Rooms are furnished with rough country antiques and reproductions that look entirely authentic, aided by illumination by oil lamps. "L'Atre" means the fireplace, and the most prominent component is this massive stonework where most of the food served here is cooked. The menu is short but to the point, a paean to the Québécois canon, including such burly standards as soupe aux légumes et fines herbes (vegetables soup flavored with herbs), boeuf au vin rouge (beef stewed in red wine), and tourtière (meat pie). Dessert can be maple-sugar pie or island-grown berries. All this is delivered by servers clothed according to the era they are helping to re-create.

ST-PIERRE

By Île d'Orléans standards, St-Pierre is a big town, with a population of about 2,000. It is only 2 kilometers (1 mile) from the bridge. Its central attraction is the island's oldest church (1717). Thousands of migrating snow geese, Canada geese, and ducks stop by in the spring, a spectacular sight when they launch themselves into the air in flapping hordes so thick they almost blot out the sun.

Services are no longer held in the church. However, it contains a large handicraft shop in the back, behind the altar, which is even older than the church (1695) and open to visitors. The pottery, beeswax candles, dolls, scarves, woven rugs, and blankets they sell aren't to every taste, but are worth a look, nonetheless.

Heading back across the bridge toward Québec City, there is a fine view of the next destination.

2 Montmorency Falls

11 km (7 miles) NE of Québec City

The waterfall for which this town is named is surrounded by a provincial park where visitors can stop to take in the view or have a picnic from early May to late October. At 83 meters (274 feet), the falls, named by Samuel de Champlain for his patron, the Duke of

Montmorency, are 100 feet higher than Niagara, a boast that no visitor is spared. They are, however, far narrower. In winter, the plunging waters contribute to a particularly impressive sight, when the freezing spray sent up by the falls builds a mountain of white ice at the base called the "Sugarloaf." The yellow cast of the waterfall results from the high iron content of the river bed.

ESSENTIALS
GETTING THERE

BY BUS   Programs are subject to frequent change, so check with **Visite Touristique de Québec** (☎ 418/563-9722), which offers English-only tours; **Old Québec Tours** (☎ 418/624-0460); **Maple Leaf Sightseeing Tours** (☎ 418/687-9226); or **Gray Line** (☎ 418/622-7420) to see what's currently available.

BY CAR   Take Autoroute 40, north of Québec City, going east. At the end of the autoroute, where it intersects with Rte. 360, the falls come into view.

VISITOR INFORMATION

A **tourist information** booth is beside the parking area at the falls, just after the turn-off from the highway (☎ **418/663-2877**). It's open early June to early September from 9am to 7pm, and early September to mid-October from 11am to 5pm. Admission to the falls is free.

In 1759, General Wolfe and his army of 4,000 hauled 30 heavy cannon to the heights east of the cataract, aiming them at French troops deployed on the opposite side. The British lost the ensuing firefight, but six weeks later won the decisive battle on the Plains of Abraham. One of the earthen redoubts they constructed survives.

There are a variety of ways to views the falls, including a new cable car (not for the vertiginous), a footbridge that spans the river just where it flows over the cliff, and stairs that descend down one side from the top to near the bottom.

3 Ste-Anne-de-Beaupré

35km (22 miles) NE of Québec City, 24km (15 miles) NE of Montmorency Falls

Legend has it that French mariners were sailing up the St. Lawrence River in the 1650s when they ran into a terrifying storm. They prayed to their patroness, St. Anne, to save them, and when they survived they dedicated a wooden chapel to her on the north shore of the St. Lawrence, near the site of their perils. Not long afterward, a laborer on the chapel was said to have been cured of lumbago, the first of many documented miracles. Since that time pilgrims have come here—over a million a year—to pay their respects to St. Anne, the mother of the Virgin Mary and grandmother of Jesus.

ESSENTIALS
GETTING THERE

BY BUS   An intercity bus to Ste-Anne-de-Beaupré leaves the Québec City bus station three times a day, at around 9:15am, 3pm, and

6:15pm. Return trips are at 2:25pm and 6pm Monday through Saturday and 8pm Sunday. Always call ahead to reconfirm departure times (☎ 418/525-3000). The round-trip fare is $10.25. Also check with **Visite Touristique de Québec** (☎ 418/563-9722), which offers English-only tours; **Old Québec Tours** (☎ 416/624-0460); **Maple Leaf Sightseeing Tours** (☎ 418/687-9226); or **Gray Line** (☎ 418/622-7420).

BY CAR   From Montmorency Falls, it's a 20-minute drive along Rte. 138 east to the little town of Ste-Anne-de-Beaupré. The highway goes right past the basilica, with an easy entrance into the large parking lot.

VISITOR INFORMATION

A reception booth at the southeastern side of the basilica, 10018 av. Royale (☎ 418/827-3781), is open from early May through mid-September daily from 8:30am to 5pm. The basilica itself is open year-round. Masses are held daily but hours vary.

Reactions to the religious complex that has resulted over the years at Ste-Anne-de-Beaupré inevitably vary. To the faithful, this is a place of wonder, perhaps the most important pilgrimage site in North America. To many others, it is perceived as a building that lacks the grandeur its great size is intended to impart, a raw and ponderous structure without the ennobling patina of age. The former group will want to schedule at least a couple of hours to absorb it all, the latter won't need more than fifteen minutes to satisfy their curiosity.

The towering basilica is the most recent building raised on this spot in St. Anne's honor. After the sailors' first modest wooden chapel was swept away by a flood in the 1600s, another chapel was built on higher ground. Floods, fires, and the ravages of time dispatched later buildings, until a larger, presumably sturdier structure was erected in 1887. In 1926, it, too, lay in ruins, gutted by fire.

A lesson finally learned, the present basilica is constructed in stone, following an essentially romanesque scheme. Marble, granite, mosaics, stained glass, and hand-carved wood are employed with a generous hand throughout. The pews, for instance, are of wood with hand-carved medallions at the ends, each portraying a different animal. Behind the main altar are eight side chapels and altars, each different. The conviction that miracles routinely occur here is attested to by the hundreds of crutches, canes, braces, and artificial limbs strapped to columns and stacked on the floor of the vestibule, left behind by those who no longer needed them.

Note that the church and the whole town of Ste-Anne-de-Beaupré are particularly busy on days of significance to the saint: the first Sunday in May, mid- to late July, the fourth Sunday in August, and early in September.

Other attractions in Ste-Anne-de-Beaupré include the Way of the Cross, with life-size cast-iron figures, on the hillside opposite the basilica; the Scala Santa Chapel (1891); and the Memorial Chapel (1878), with a bell tower and altar from the late 17th and early 18th centuries, respectively. More commercial than devotional are the the Historial, a wax museum, and the Cyclorama, a 360° painting of

Jerusalem. Admission to the Historial is $2.50 adults, $1.25 children 6 to 13; to the Cyclorama, it's $5 adults, $3 children 6 to 15.

Driving north on Rte 360 toward Mont Ste-Anne, about two miles from Ste-Anne-de-Beaupré, on the left, is a factory outlet strip mall called Promenades Ste-Anne (☎ 418/827-3555). It has shops selling discounted merchandise from Dansk, Liz Claiborne, Mondi, Marikita (crafts), and Benetton, as well as a vaguely southwestern bistro. The center is open seven days a week.

WHERE TO STAY & DINE

Auberge La Camarine

10947 bd. Ste-Anne-de-Beaupré, PQ G0A 1E0. ☎ **418/827-5703.** Fax 418/827-5430. 31 rooms. TV TEL. $110–$159 double. Table d'hôte dinner $37.95. AE, DC, MC, V.

Why they named it after a bitter Arctic berry is uncertain, but this inn has a kitchen that is equaled by a bare handful of restaurants in the entire province, and that includes Montréal. It bears a resemblance to the fusion cookery of California—essentially French/Italian joined with Asian techniques and ingredients. The menu changes frequently, but anything with duck or salmon is likely to be a winner. They are justly proud of their wine cellar. Bedrooms gracefully blend antique and contemporary notions, some with fireplaces, air-conditioning, and/or exercycles. Two have Jacuzzis.

Overnight guests can have breakfast. Otherwise, the restaurant only serves dinner. The ski slopes of Mount Ste-Anne are a short drive away. You'll find the auberge just past the Promenades Ste-Anne outlet center, off Route 138.

4 Mont Ste-Anne

40km (25 miles) NE of Québec City, about 10km (6 miles) NE of Ste-Anne-de-Beaupré

Like Montréal, Québec City has its Laurentian hideaways. But there are differences: The Laurentians sweep down quite close to the St. Lawrence at this point, so Québécois need drive only about 30 minutes to be in the woods. And since Québec City is much smaller than Montréal, the Québec resorts are more modest in size and fewer in number, but their facilities and amenities are equal to those of resorts elsewhere in the Laurentian range.

Mont Ste-Anne is a four-season getaway that offers the best skiing outside Québec City but also a plethora of outdoor activities during the summer, including golf, mountainbiking, hiking, and paragliding.

ESSENTIALS

GETTING THERE

BY BUS   The Skibus (☎ **418/653-9722**) network serves the slopes at Mont Ste-Anne, making it possible to stay in Québec City and ski the mountain with little inconvenience. The roundtrip fare is $14. Lodging is available.

BY CAR   Continue along Hwy. 360 from Ste-Anne-de-Beaupré to the large ski area.

VISITOR INFORMATION

The park entrance is easy to spot from the highway. For information and rates for mountainbike or ski rentals, call ☎ **418/827-4561** or **418/827-3121.**

Mont-Ste-Anne Park, 30 square miles surrounding a 2,625-foot-high peak, is an outdoor enthusiast's summer paradise. In summer, there's camping, golfing, rollerblading, cycling, hiking, jogging, paragliding, and a 150-mile network of mountainbiking trails (bikes can be rented at the park). An eight-passenger gondola to the top of the mountain operates every day for the benefit of cyclists between late June and early September, weather permitting, at ticket prices of $8 for adults, $6 for ages 14–20, $4.50 for children 7–13, and children under 7 free.

In winter, the park is Québec's largest and busiest ski area. Twelve lifts, including the gondola and three quad chair lifts, transport downhill skiers to the starting points of 50 trails and slopes. Over 130 miles of cross-country trails lace the park, dotted with eight heated rest huts. Cross-country skiers pay day rates of about $10 for an adult, less for students and seniors. Paragliding instruction is available in winter as well as summer.

5 Charlevoix

Baie-St-Paul: 87 km (61 miles) NE of Québec City
La Malbaie: 149 km (92 miles) NE of Québec City
St-Simeon: 182 km (113 miles) NE of Québec City

The Laurentians move closer to the shore of the St. Lawrence as they approach what used to be called Murray Bay at the confluence with the Malbaie River. While it can't be pretended that the entire length of Rte. 138 from Beaupré is fascinating, the Rte. 362 detour from Baie-St-Paul is scenic, with wooded hills slashed by narrow river beds and billowing meadows ending in harsh cliffs plunging down to the river. The air is scented by sea-salt and rent by the shrieks of gulls.

Baie-St-Paul is an artists' colony, and there are several good-to-memorable inns between there and Cap à l'Aigle, a few miles beyond La Malbaie. St-Simeon, where one catches the ferry to the southern shore of the St. Lawrence, affords summer visitors numerous opportunities for whale-watching.

ESSENTIALS

GETTING THERE

BY CAR   Take Route 138 as far as Baie-St-Paul, then pick up Rte. 362 to La Malbaie, merging once again with Rte. 138 to reach the ferry at St-Simeon.

VISITOR INFORMATION

Baie-St-Paul has a year-round tourist office at 4 rue Ambroise-Fafard, open mid-June–Labor Day daily from 9am–9pm, and from Sept to early June daily from 9am–5pm. So does La Malbaie, at 630 bd. de Comporté, with the same hours. St-Siméon has seasonal tourist offices on Rte. 139 and at the ferry landing, open mid-June–Labor Day daily 9am–9pm.

In addition to the country inns dotted from Baie-St-Paul to Cap â l'Aigle to La Malbaie and beyond, nearby Pointe-au-Pic has a new casino, a smaller offshoot of the one in Montréal. The northern end of the region is marked by the confluence of the Saguenay River and the St. Lawrence. These waters attract six species of whales, so many can be seen from shore from mid-June to late October, although whale-watching cruises are increasingly popular. In 1988, Charlevoix was named a UNESCO World Biosphere Reserve. While only one of 325 such regions throughout the world, it was the first so designated to include human settlement.

BAIE-ST-PAUL

The first town of any size reached in Charlevoix via the 138 highway, this attractive community of 6,000 holds on to a reputation as an artists' retreat that started developing back at the start of the century. Over a dozen boutiques and galleries and a couple of small museums show the work of local painters and artisans. Given the setting, it isn't surprising that many of the artists are landscapists, but there are other styles and subjects represented. While some of their production is on the kitchen hobbyist level, much of it is highly professional. To see, check the **Galerie d'Art Iris,** at 30 rue St-Jean-Baptiste (☎ 418/435-5768), which specializes in landscape artists from Québec. Look, in particular, for the works of Louis Tremblay.

WHAT TO SEE & DO

Le Centre d'Exposition

23 rue Amroise-Fafard. ☎ **418/435-3681.** Admission $3 adults, $2 seniors and students, children under 12 free. Sept 5–June 23 daily 9am–5pm, June 24–Sept 4 daily 9am–7pm.

A new (1992) undertaking, the brick-and-glass museum has three floors of work by largely regional artists, both past and present. Inuit sculptures are included, and temporary one-person and group shows are mounted throughout the year.

WHERE TO STAY

La Maison Otis

23 rue St-Jean-Baptiste, Baie-St-Paul, PQ G0A 1B0. ☎ **418/435-2255** or 800-267-2254. Fax 418/435-2464. 30 rms. A/C TV TEL. High season (summer and Christmas–Easter) $130–$250 double, rest of year $130–250. Rates include breakfast and dinner. AE, MC, V.

Prices look steep at first blush but note that with bountiful breakfasts and dinners included, lunch is almost redundant. A wide range of facilities and amenities allows guests who reserve far enough in advance to customize their lodgings. Combinations of fireplaces, whirlpools, stereo systems, VCRs, four-poster beds, and suites that sleep four are all available, distributed through three buildings. Several art galleries are in walking distance. A kidney-shaped indoor pool and sauna are on the premises, as is a jovial piano bar. The required meals are no sacrifice. Housekeeping is meticulous.

ST IRÉNÉE

About 33 kilometers farther along Rte 362, which roller-coasters over bluffs above the river, is this cliff-top hamlet of fewer than 800 year-round residents. Apart from the setting, the two best reasons for daw-dling here are the presence of a convivial inn and an enticing music and dance festival held every summer.

WHAT TO SEE & DO

Domaine Forget

398 chemin les Bains. ☎ **418/452-8111.** Admission $16–$20 adults, children under 12 free. Concerts early June-late Aug Wed, Sat, some Fri 8pm; musical brunches June 18–Aug 27 Sun 11am–2pm.

This performing arts festival was initiated in 1977, with the purchase of a large property overlooking the river. The existing buildings and surrounding lawns were used to stage the concerts and recitals. Their success prompted the construction of a new 600-seat hall, scheduled to be completed in time for the 1996 season. While the program em-phasizes classical music with solo instrumentalists and chamber groups, it is peppered with appearances by jazz combos.

WHERE TO STAY

Auberge des Sablons

223 chemin les Bains, St-Irénée, PQ G0T 1V0. ☎ **418/452-3594** or 800-267-0525. Fax 418/452-3240. 14 rms. May 1–Oct 28 $70–140 double, rest of the year $67–$120. Rates include breakfast and dinner. AE, DC, ER, MC, V.

The front lawn runs down to a rocky beach from a "cottage" built in 1902 and converted to an inn in 1983. Homier in flavor than its slicker compatriot, La Maison Otis (above), this is a place to sleep and eat and feel the stress drain away. No pool, no tennis, and only members of the Polar Bear Club would spend more than 60 seconds in the river. As free of the sounds of civilization as any place mentioned in these pages, birdcalls, wind in the trees, and water folding gently over the shore make excellent accompaniments to a book and a glass of wine on the terrace. Choose to have only breakast and prices drop $25 per person, but dinner at the inn is not to be casually dismissed. The kitchen is adroit in the lightened Québécois mode. Among the packages available is "Le Triangle de Charlevoix," with three or six nights divided among these two inns and the Auberge de Penpliers in Cap-à-l'Aigle.

POINTE-AU-PIC

From St-Irénée, the road starts to bend west after 10 kilometers (six miles) as the mouth of the Malbaie River starts to form. Pointe-au-Pic is one of the trio of villages that are collectively known as La Malbaie, or Murray Bay, as it was known to the wealthy Anglophones who made this their resort of choice from the Gilded Age on through the 1950s. While inhabitants of the region wax poetic about their hills and trees and wildlife "where the sea meets the sky," they have something quite different to preen about now—an upscale casino.

WHAT TO SEE & DO

Casino de Charlevoix

183 av. Richelieu (Rte. 362). ☎ **418/665-5353** or 800-965-5355. Admission free (persons 18 and over only). Daily 11am–3am. Signs are frequent on Rte 362 coming from the south, and on Rtes. 138 and 362 from the north. Round-trip shuttle service from Québec City: $30.

This is the second of Québec's newly approved gambling casinos, the first in Montréal and the third scheduled to open in the Ottawa/Hull region in 1996. It is about as tasteful as such establishments get this side of Monte Carlo. Cherrywood paneling and granite floors enclose the ranks of slot machines, 12 blackjack tables, three roulette wheels, and a lone baccarat table. No craps tables, notice, whose players are more likely to get raucous than other gamblers. Only soft drinks are allowed at the machines and tables, in the hope sober players won't get too stupid about their money. They have to go to an adjacent bar to mourn their losses. And there is a dress code, forbidding such items of apparel as bustiers, cut-off sweaters, blue jeans, shorts, beachwear, motorcycle boots, and "clothing of a violent nature or associated with an organization known to be violent." The adjacent Manoir Richelieu was once the aristocratic haven of swells summering in Murray Bay, who had to meet even more stringent dress codes.

Musée de Charlevoix

1 chemin du Havre (at the intersection with Rte. 362/bd. Bellevue). ☎ **418/665-4411.** Admission $5 adults, $3 seniors and students, children under 12 free. June 26–Sept 4 daily 10am–6pm, Sept 5–June 24 Tues–Fri 10am–5pm, Sat–Sun 1–5pm.

In existence since 1975, the museum moved to these postmodernist quarters in 1990. Folk art, sculptures, and paintings by regional artists figure prominently in the permanent collection, supplemented by frequent temporary exhibitions with diverse themes. It is an edifice and aggregation of uncommon sophistication considering the modest size of the supporting community.

Cap-à-l'Aigle

Rte. 362 rejoins Rte.138 in La Malbaie, the largest town in the area, with almost 4,000 inhabitants. It serves as a provisioning center, with supermarkets, hardware stores, gas stations. Continue through the town center and across the bridge, making a sharp right on the other side. This is Rte. 138, with signs pointing to Cap-à-l'Aigle.

William Howard Taft spent many summers in Murray Bay, starting in 1892 and extending well past his one-term presidency. For much of that time, the only way to get here was by boat, for the railroad didn't arrive until 1919. Given his legendary girth, it can be assumed that Taft knew something about the good life. Had he required it, confirmation of his affection for the region might have been provided by other monied and celebrated summer people. Among them were the Cabots of Boston, the Duke of Windsor, and Charlie Chaplin. Could any of them return, they might well choose what is arguably the premier auberge in Murray Bay (see below).

WHERE TO STAY & DINE

La Pinsonnière

Cap-à-l'Isle, PQ G0T 1B0. ☎ **418/665-4431.** Fax 418/665-7156. 26 rooms, 1 suite. May–Oct 7 and Christmas $130–$275 double, Nov–Apr $100–240 double. AE, DC, ER, MC, V. MAP available, but not required.

In all Canada, this is one of only eight member hostelries in the prestigious Relais & Châteaux organization. As aficionados will know, that means limited size, comfort bordering on luxury in the bedrooms, and an emphasis on food and wine. And despite the presence here of an indoor pool, sauna, tennis, and massages, there is no uncertainty about what aspect of their operation the owners focus their laserlike attention. Seated in the serene dining room beside the picture window, anticipate a dinner that becomes the evening's entertainment. With drinks and menus come the customary pre-appetizers, in one case, a quail leg on a bed of slivered asparagus. Next, perhaps, fettucine tossed with plump mussels, spiked with a spray of pungent tarragon and brightened with an edible pansy. Soup follows, and only then the main event, not infrequently a succulent veal chop, with a nest of shaved carrots, fiddleheads, and purple potatoes. Wines are a particular pride. The twentyish waiter is mastering Winespeak, cradling a bottle that he describes as "young and nervous." His employer needs no urging to conduct tours of his impressive cellar. Bedrooms come in five categories, the pricier of which feature Jacuzzis and gas fireplaces. Little is left to chance, but the lingering memory is of the dining room.

Saint-Simeon

At 33 kilometers (20 miles), the ferry at Saint-Simeon is an easy drive from La Malbaie. The purpose is to cross to Rivère-du-Loup on the other side of the St. Lawrence, returning to Québec City along the south shore. If there is no time, it's only 150 kilometers (93 miles) back to the city.

Once in Saint-Simeon, signs direct cars and trucks down to the ferry terminal. Boarding is on a first-come, first-served basis, and ferries leave on a carefully observed schedule, weather permitting, from late March to early January. Departure times of the five daily sailings vary substantially from month to month, however, so get in touch with the company, Clark Transport Canada (☎ **418/638-2856** or 418/638-5530) to obtain a copy of the schedule. One-way fares are $9.10 adults, $6.05 seniors and children 5–11, $23.20 cars and their passengers. MasterCard and Visa are accepted. Arrive at least 30 minutes before departure, one hour in summer. The boat is equipped with a luncheonette, lounges, and a newsstand. Voyages take 65–75 minutes.

From late June through September, passengers may enjoy a bonus. These are the months during which the whales are most active, and when pelagic (migratory) species join the resident minke and beluga whales. They prefer the northern side of the Estuary, roughly from La Malbaie to Baie-Ste-Catherine, at the mouth of the Saguenay River. Since this is the area the ferry steams through, sightings are an ever-present possibility, especially in summer.

6 The Southern Bank

Montmagny: 50km (31 miles) E of Québec City
St-Jean-Port-Joli: 146km (91 miles) E of Québec City
Kamouraska: 210km (130 miles) E of Québec City

Several towns on the southern bank of the St. Lawrence are within easy range of a day's excursion from Québec City, and in good weather the views of the river and its islands are themselves worth the drive. However, the fact that the tourist office in St-Jean-Port-Joli is closed from October through April says much about the relative desirability of a trip through here in those months. Motels and guesthouses are in sufficient abundance to ensure lodging on short notice, although few of them can be described as memorable. On a day trip, St-Jean-Port-Joli makes a logical turnaround point. But if you're planning to take the ferry across the river and return by the north shore to Québec City, a highly recommended choice, continue to Rivière-du-Loup.

For the first 20 miles of the drive, Île d'Orléans (see above) will be off to the left in midstream, with the Laurentian Mountains on the north bank as a backdrop.

ESSENTIALS
GETTING THERE

BY CAR   Take Autoroute 20 as far as St-Michel, then pick up Rte. 132 east for the only slightly slower scenic road that keeps the river in sight.

VISITOR INFORMATION

The **Montmagny Tourist Office,** in the historic Manoir Couillard-Dupuis, 301 bd. Taché est (☎ **418/248-9196;** fax 248-1436), is open Monday through Friday 8:30am to 4:30pm. It's in a little park with a walkway beside the river. The **St-Jean-Port-Joli Tourist Office,** in the center of town at 7 av. Gaspé est (☎ **418/598-3747**), is open in summer daily 9am to 8pm, in May and early September daily 9am to 5pm, and closed the rest of the year. There is also a summer-only tourist office in the town of **St-Pascal-de-Kamouraska** (☎ **418/492-9552**), adjacent to Kamouraska.

MONTMAGNY

The first big town along the southern shore of the St. Lawrence is Montmagny, a farming and industrial center, with a population of 12,000. From here in summer, you can take a boat out to Grosse Île, the Ellis Island of Canada. Parks Canada is in the process of transforming it into a powerful reminder of one period in the country's history, when 4.5 million people immigrated to Canada via Québec. Thousands with cholera or typhoid fever were quarantined on the island from 1832 to 1937; 4,000 were buried here. Some 300,000 Irish refugees from the potato famines came through here in 1847 and 1848. A small train with a guide carries visitors around the island and makes stops along the way.

Off Montmagny lies the Archipel de l'Île-aux-Grues, islands known for the wildfowl that make it a hunter's destination. There are six islands in all, the largest being Île aux Grues (Cranes' Island) and Île aux Oies (Geese Island). A ferry goes to the Île aux Grues from Montmagny.

Background information on both the immigrants and the birds is provided by the interpretation center at 53 rue du Bassin Nord in Montmagny. Called Théâtre Educatif des Migrations (☎ **418/248-4565**), it is open from 1pm to 5pm from early May to late June, from 10am to 10pm from late June to mid-August, and from 9am to 6pm from mid-August through October.

WHERE TO STAY & DINE

Café Renoir

43 St-Jean-Baptiste ouest. ☎ **418/248-3343.** Main courses $6.50–$18, table d'hôte dinner $19–$27. AE, MC, V. Tues–Sat 11am–2pm; dinner Tues–Sun 5–10pm; brunch Sun 11am–2pm (May–Aug only). FRENCH/QUÉBÉCOIS.

Café Renoir offers large servings of satisfying dishes at reasonable prices. Quiche, pasta, ham-and-cheese croissants, and bagels with smoked salmon and cream cheese are possible lunch choices. Dinners are more ambitious, and Sunday brunch, available only May through August, features enormous omelets and crêpes.

Manoir des Erables

220 bd. Taché est (Rte. 132), Montmagny, PQ G5V 1G5. ☎ **418/248-0100** or 800/563-0200 in Québec. Fax 418/248-9507. Reservations recommended. Main courses $8.95–$13.95; table d'hôte dinners $33–$54. AE, DC, DISC, MC, V. Daily 7:30–10am, 11am–2pm, and 6–9pm. Closed Sun lunch Nov to mid-Apr. CLASSIC FRENCH.

Since 1975, the Cyr family has welcomed guests to their stately 1812 inn, with its glossy reputation for both food and lodging. In the dining room, sterling glints by the light of sparkling chandeliers. The menu changes daily, but among offerings to look for are mussels with anise, a starter, and the ragoût of lobster and scallops. Wines range in price from $20 to $960 (the 1973 Château Pétrus).

Unfortunately, only a few of the large Victorian bedrooms remain, due to a fire in 1982. The rest are modern. Suites have fireplaces and whirlpool baths, and there are eight hotel-style units behind the main house. Eight rooms in a stone house on the property, the Pavillon Collin (1867), are air-conditioned. Rooms start at $90 per double, a good value, and suites are $185. Packages are available on a double-occupancy basis and include breakfast, dinner, tips, and golf or a visit to Grosse Isle National Park.

L'ISLET-SUR-MER

Along Rte 132 on the approach to L'islet-sur-Mer are many roadside farm stands selling honey, fruits, and vegetables. About 17 kilometers (10.5 miles) east of Montmagny, this fishing village produced sailors who roamed the world, among them an Arctic explorer named Joseph-Elzéar Bernier, who claimed the Arctic islands for Canada. Bernier, who became a captain at the age of 17, made 269 voyages and crossed the Atlantic 45 times. In 1874, he did it in 15 days and 16 hours, quite a feat in those days.

WHAT TO SEE & DO

Musée Maritime Bernier

55 rue des Pionniers est. ☎ **418/247-5001.** Admission $4 adults, $1.50 children, $7.50 families. May 20–Sept 29 daily 9am–6pm, Sept 30–May 19 Tues–Fri 9am–noon and 1:30–5pm.

Dedicated to the town's favorite son, the museum relives the area's nautical history from the 17th century forward. The monument in front of the museum illustrates Bernier's explorations on a globe, crowned with the aurora borealis. Housed in a former 19th-century convent, the museum has three floors of exhibits. Particularly captivating are the many large ship models, ranging from fully-rigged galleons to brigantines to Seaway freighters. Most of them were crafted by a former lighthouse keeper, Eugène LeClerc, and his family. Sound, videos, and computers are employed with a degree of sophistication. On the land out back is the hydrofoil Bras d'Or 400 (open to the public only from late June to Labor Day) and the icebreaker *Ernest Lapointe,* which was built in Canada before World War II and used until 1978. Descriptive plaques are in both French and English.

ST-JEAN-PORT-JOLI

This town of 3,400 has gained a measure of fame for the woodcarving that has been done here for generations. It started in the early days when much of the decoration for local churches was carved wood. But in the 1930s, three brothers—Médard, André, and Jean-Julien Bourgault—began carving other things as well: bas-reliefs, statues, figurines, even portraits. As the celebrity of the Bourgault brothers spread, dozens of students were attracted to the town and a wood-sculpture school was established. Today the town has about 100 working craftspeople and is filled with their shops and galleries, showing textiles, pottery, and carvings in stone and wood. Of all the towns along the southern bank, St-Jean-Port-Joli is best organized to welcome travelers and help them find their way around.

WHAT TO SEE & DO

Although such words as "masterful" and "exquisite" are tossed around with abandon in reference to the woodcarvings of these artisans, individual responses vary widely. Just as reactions to Lladró and Hummel figurines tend to fall on either side of a yawning chasm, so are most visitors likely to embrace or reject the works of the St-Jean-Port-Joli carvers rather quickly on first viewing. For that reason, it is probably best to stop by the Museum des Anciens Canadians first for a look at a number of examples to see if you have any interest in pursuing them further.

If that evaluation proves positive, there are ample opportunities to seek out carvings for sale and to meet the people who produced them. Wander into some of the wood-carving shops strung along Rte. 132 for a look at what's being done today. The artists are usually happy to chat and show their studios. Most accept orders for works on commission if something special is desired. A shop with a more diverse inventory of art and handicrafts than the others is Les Enfants du Soleil. Their whimsical melange incorporates used books, jewelry, unusual vests and dresses, folk arts, and primitive objects from Africa and Indonesia. Just across from the church and painted red and orange, this store is hard to miss.

Musée des Anciens Canadiens

332 av. de Gaspé ouest. ☎ **418/598-3392.** Admission $4 adults, $2 children 7–12, under 12 free. May–June daily 9am–6pm, July–Aug daily 9am–9pm, Sept–Oct daily 9am–5pm, Nov–Apr, by reservation only.

"Museum" is too grand a label for this gallery attached to a boutique, but it's a good place to learn about the works of the Bourgault brothers—Médard's religious sculptures and nudes, André's country folk, and Jean-Julien's religious sculptures and furniture. The work of other village artisans is also on display, including that of Nicole Deschênes Duval and Pierre Cloutier, and the model boats carved by members of the Leclerc family (also on display at the Musée Maritime Bernier, see above).

Church of St-Jean-Port-Joli

2 av. de Gaspé ouest. ☎ **418/598-3023.** Admission free. June 27 to Labor Day, daily 9am–5pm; Labor Day to June 26, Mon–Fri 9am–5pm (or by reservation).

The church was built in 1779–81 and later decorated by the early wood-carvers, including the Bourgaults, who created the pulpit in 1937. A more recent addition is the 17-piece crèche, each piece carved by a different local artist and presented to the church in 1987. Buried in the church under the seigneurial pew is the author of *Anciens Canadiens,* Philippe-Aubert de Gaspé, who was the last in a line of lords of the manor (seigneurs) who owned and governed St-Jean since 1633. Look for the nearby plaque that lists all of the town's seigneurs, back to the time when the original land grant was made by the king of France.

Seigneurie des Aulnaies

525 de la Seigneurie, St-Roch-des-Aulnaies. ☎ **418/354-2800.** Admission (including tours) $4 adults, $1.50 children 6–15, $9 families. Late June to early Sept, daily 9am–6pm.

About 14 kilometers (9 miles)east of St-Jean-Port-Joli is this historic farm beside the Ferrée River, with a working flour mill from 1842 and a manor house from 1850. Thanks to a gentle microclimate, the grounds are filled with chestnuts, black locusts, and redwoods—trees not ordinarily found in this area. Tours are given by costumed guides. The fresh-ground flour is for sale. Six tours of mill and manor house are given daily starting at 9:30am.

WHERE TO STAY

Auberge des Glacis

46 route Tortue, C.P. 102, St-Eugène, PQ G0R 1X0. ☎ **418/247-7486.** 8 rms, 2 suites (all with bath). $83–$91 double, $97 and $108 suite. Extra person $16. Parking free. AE, MC, V.

An Important Note on Prices

Unless stated otherwise, **the prices cited in this guide are given in Canadian dollars,** which is good news for visitors from the U.S. because the Canadian dollar is worth about 25% less than the American dollar, but buys just about as much.

As of this writing, $1 Canadian is worth 75¢ U.S., which means that a $100-a-night hotel room will cost only about $75 (U.S.) a night, a $50 dinner for two will cost only about $37.50 (U.S.), and a $5 breakfast will cost only about $3.75 (U.S.).

For a conversion chart, see "Information, Entry Requirements & Money" in Chapter 2.

About 12 kilometers (7.5 miles) west of St-Jean-Port-Joli, this 1841 stone mill-turned-inn sits beside a stream in the woods. The only steady sounds are of crickets and gurgling water. Each room has special touches—a spinning wheel, a brass bed, an antique armoire—that recall the century past. One room has a television, another is perfect for families, with a bedroom, separate sitting area, and loft with two single beds reached by a ladder. Baths in three rooms have both tub and shower, others have showers alone. The innkeepers rent cross-country skis, and have plans to rent bikes. Horseback riding is available a couple of miles away. In the dining room, the French menu is changed daily. An à la carte lunch costs $9 to $14 and a table d'hôte dinner, $21 to $29.

WHERE TO DINE

Café La Coureuse des Grèves

Rte 204 (rue de l'Eglise, near Rte 132). ☎ **418/598-9111.** Reservations not required. Main courses $5.95–$13.25, table d'hôte meal $5–$10. AE, MC, V. Daily 8am–midnight. QUÉBÉCOIS.

A popular all-bases place for meals or just coffee and cake, the café's name comes from a story of a beautiful maiden who would run ("la coureuse") along the river's shores ("des grèves"), tempting fishermen and mariners who tried to capture her. Copious portions are the rule, of items including pastas, chicken, steak, seafood, vegetarian dishes, kebabs, a cheese plate with fresh fruit, and fish chowder. The cheerful hostess and her staff speak little English, so just point. The painted plank walls provide a venue for changing exhibitions of works by local artists, none of whom challenge Wyeth or Matisse. The upstairs bar gets lively with local musicians on Thursday evenings.

KAMOURASKA

A bit farther up the coast along Route 132 is Kamouraska, 65 kilometers (40 miles) east of St-Jean-Port-Joli. One of the southern shore's oldest settlements, it has a modest museum, a number of old houses, riverbank panoramas, and a couple of bed-and-breakfasts.

Flight of the Bone-Headed Goose

Every spring and fall, thousands of snow geese stop for a while along the shores of the St. Lawrence on their journeys between their winter habitat in coastal Virginia and summer vacations on Baffin Island beyond the Arctic Circle. All white with black feathers on the trailing edges of their wings, the big birds settle down for a few weeks, periodically lifting in dense, screeching, flapping clouds, only to land in a milling cacophony a few hundred yards away. Since they are a protected species, hunting of them is severely restricted.

They are always welcome at Cape Tourmente, a national wildfowl preserve near Mount Ste-Anne, not far north of Québec City. But farmers on the south shore, especially around Kamouraska and L'islet-sur-Mer, are rarely as enthusiastic about the semi-annual event. Some of them erect flat plywood cutouts picturing men in yellow fatigues holding shotguns at the ready. It seems unlikely that such a patently unrealistic ruse would discourage a single gullible bird. But in fact, the flocks appear to land only in fields unprotected by the faux hunters. They're beautiful creatures, but with the intelligence quotients of cantaloupes.

Ordinarily, it will not long detain the average traveler. But during the spring and fall migratory seasons, the fields around Kamouraska host uncountable thousands of snow geese, a beautiful sight.

To cross the river (in order to return through the Charlevoix region to Québec City), drive upriver a bit farther and take the car-ferry from Rivière-du-Loup to St-Simeon, on the northern shore. Rivière-du-Loup is the region's commercial, governmental, and educational hub with a number of motels and restaurants for those who choose to spend the night or get there too late for the ferry.

Follow Highway 132 through the town and follow the signs for the ferry landing. For the latest information on fares and departure times, call ☎ 418/862-5094 for recorded information in French, then English. Boarding is on a first-come, first-served basis; no reservations. The trip takes 65–75 minutes and food is served on board. For additional details, see page 273.

Index

MONTRÉAL

Accommodations, 49–64
    Ayer's Cliff, 187–88
    Best bets for, 50–52
    Bromont, 180
    for children, 51, 61
    downtown, 52–62
    Knowlton, 181
    Magog, 184
    Mont-Gabriel, 160
    Mont-Orford, 182–83
    Mont-Tremblant, 172–76
    North Hatley, 186–87
    Old Montréal, 62–64
    Plateau Mont-Royal, 64
    Ste-Adèle, 161–63
    Ste-Agathe-des-Monts, 169
    St-Faustin, 170
    St-Sauveur-des-Monts, 158–59
    Sherbrooke, 188
    Val-David, 167
    Val-Morin, 166
    Ville d'Estérel, 164–65
Addresses, locating, 36–37
After dark, 141–53
Airports, 29, 34
Air travel, 29–30, 34
American Express, 43
Amusement Park, La Ronde, 103
Angrignon Park, 109
Antiques, shopping for, 126, 133–34
Architecture museum, 104–5, 135
Arriving in Montréal, 34–35
Art museums
    Musée d'Art Contemporain de
        Montréal, 97–98
    Musée des Arts Decoratifs de
        Montréal, 102
    Musée des Beaux-Arts, 90–92, 123
    Musée Marc-Aurèle Fortin, 105,
        118
Arts and crafts, shopping for, 126,
    134–35, 166
ATMs (automated teller machines),
    22–23
Auberge de la Fontaine, 64
Auberge Hatley Inn (North Hatley),
    186
Auberge Ripplecove (Ayer's Cliff),
    187–88
Ayer's Cliff, 187–88

Ballet, 143
Bank of Montréal Museum, 105, 116
Bars, 150–52
Baseball, 108
Basilique Notre-Dame, 93–94, 115
Bateau-mouche, 106
Beaver Club, The, 70–71
Beaver Lake, 130
Bed-and-breakfasts, 49, 51, 163
Beebe Plain, 189
Benedictine Abbey of Saint-Benoît-du-
    Lac, 184
Bicycling, 109, 183
    La Tour d l'Île de Montréal, 25
    the Laurentians, 166, 168
Biodôme de Montréal, 95
Blue Bonnets Racetrack, 108
Blues, 148–49
Boating
    the Laurentians, 161, 168–69,
        171, 172
    Magog, 183
Boat cruises, 106–7
Books, recommended, 16
Bookstores, 43–44, 125, 127, 135,
    181
Boulevard René-Lévesque, 119
Boulevard St-Laurent, 36, 39,
    126–27
Bromont, 179–80
Buses, 41
    to Montréal, 31, 35
    tours, 107
Business hours, 44, 133

Cafés, 150–52
    Calèches, 107
Calendar of events, 24–27
Cameras and film, 45–46
Cars and driving, 41–43
    to Montréal, 31–32, 35
    parking, 43, 67
    rentals, 41–42
Cartier, George-Etienne, 93, 100
Cartier, Jacques, 4, 6–7, 106
Casa de Matéo, 77
Casino, 153
Cathédrale-Basilique Marie-Reine-
    du-Monde, 97, 119–20
Cathédrale Christ Church, 97, 122

Centaur Theatre, 116, 142
Centre Canadien d'Architecture,
104–5, 135
Centre d'Arts Orford, 181
Centre d'Histoire de Montréal, 105,
117–18
Chalet Lookout, 130–31
Château Ramezay, 98–99, 114
Chez Schwartz Charcuterie Hébraïque
de Montréal, 83, 127
Children
accommodations, 51, 61
restaurants, 67–68, 78
sightseeing, 103–4
travel tips, 28
Chinatown, 40
Churches and cathedrals
Basilique Notre-Dame, 93–94, 115
Cathédrale-Basilique Marie-Reine-
du-Monde, 97, 119–20
Cathédrale Christ Church, 97, 122
Eglise Notre-Dame-de-Bonsecours,
99, 111
Oratoire St-Joseph, 101
Cirque du Soleil, 141, 145–46
City Hall, 99, 114
Classical music, 17, 143–44
Claude Postel, 76–77
Climate, 24
Clothing stores, 124, 135–37
Club Tremblant (Mont-Tremblant),
172–73
Coffee and teas, shopping for, 137
Comedy, 146
Just for Laughs Festival, 26, 146
Musée Juste Pour Rire, 89
Concert halls, 144–45
Consulates, 44
Cost of everyday items, 22
Credit cards, 22
Cross-country skiing
Granby, 179
Lake Massawippi, 185
Magog, 183
Parc du Mont-Royal, 93, 109
Val-David, 166
Cuisine, 2, 15–16, 65–66
restaurants by, 69–70
Currency and exchange, 20, 21–22,
44, 133
Customs regulations, 20–21

Dance, 143
International Festival of New Dance,
27, 143
Dance clubs, 149–50
Department stores, 137–38
Disabled travelers, 27

Documents for entry into Canada,
19
Dorchester Square, 119
Downtown, 37
accommodations, 52–62
restaurants, 70–76, 123
sightseeing, 89–93, 97–98
walking tour, 118–24
Drugstores, 44
Dunham, 182
Dutoit, Charles, 144

Edifice Aldred, 116
Edifice New York Life Insurance,
116
Eglise Notre-Dame-de-Bonsecours,
99, 111
Emergencies, 44
Entertainment, 141–53
Entry into Canada, requirements for,
19
Estérel, 164–65
Estrie Region, the, 177–89, 194
tourist information, 179
traveling to, 178–79
Excursion areas, 154–89

Factory outlets, in the Estrie Region,
179–80
Families, tips for, 28. *See also* Children
Famous and historical figures, 10–13.
See also specific figures
Far Hills Inn (Val-Morin), 166
Fast facts, 43–47
Festivals, 24–27, 141, 155, 166, 180,
183, 188
Film, 16–17
International Festival of New
Cinema and Video, 25
movie theaters, 153
World Film Festival, 27
Fireworks Competition, Benson &
Hedges International, 26, 103
Flea markets, 139, 180
Folk music, 146–47
Fortin, Marc-Aurèle, 105, 118
Franklin, Benjamin, 6, 98, 112, 114

Gambling, 153
Gay men and lesbian travelers, 28, 40,
44, 48, 152–53
Georgeville, 184–85
Gift shops, 138–39
Granby, 179
Gray Rocks (Mont-Tremblant), 173

Harness-racing, 108
Hiking, 109, 181

Historical and cultural museums
Centre d'Histoire de Montréal, 105, 117–18
Musée Colby Curtis (Stanstead Plain), 189
Musée David M. Stewart, 105–6
Musée de la Banque de Montréal, 105, 116
Musée des Hospitalières de l' Hôtel-Dieu, 100
Musée Historique du Comté de Brome (Knowlton), 180–81
Musée Juste Pour Rire, 89
Musée McCord, 89–90, 124
Musée Village de Séraphin (Ste-Adèle), 161
Museum of Archeology and History, 94–95, 117
Redpath Museum, 98, 123
History, 3–9
Hockey, 108
roller, 108–9
Holidays, 24
Hôpital des Soeurs Grises, 118
Horse-drawn carriage tours, 107
Hospitals, 44
Hôtel de Ville, 99, 114
Hotel Rasco, 112
Hotel Vogue, 50, 52–53

Ice skating, 130, 183
Île Ste-Hélène, 40–41
IMAX Theatre, 103, 153
Information sources. See Telephone numbers, useful; Tourist information
Insectarium, 96, 103
Inter-Continental Montréal, 62–63
Itineraries, 87–88

Jardin Botanique, 95–96
Jazz, 2, 148–49
International Jazz Festival, 26, 148
Jogging, 109
John the Baptist, Saint, 25–26
Knowlton, 180–81
La Biosphère, 101–2

Lachine Rapids of St. Lawrence River, 6–7, 107
Lake Massawippi, 185
La Marée, 76
Lambert, Phyllis, 11, 104
Language, politics of, 8, 13–15
La Ronde Amusement Park, 103
Late night restaurants, 68, 85–86
Laurentians, the, 4, 154–77
tourist information, 156
traveling to, 155–56

Layout of Montréal, 36
L'Eau à la Bouche (Ste-Adèle), 1 63–64
Les Grands Ballets Canadiens, 143
Le Taj, 74
Le Village du Père Noël (Val-David), 167
Le Westin Mont-Royal, 54–56
L'Express, 81–82
Lieu Historique Sir George-Etienne Cartier, 100
Liquor, 16. See also Wine and vineyards
Liquor laws, 45

McCord Museum of Canadian History, 89–90, 124
McGill University, 108, 123
Magog, 178, 183–84
Maison Calvet, 112
Maisonneuve, Paul de Chomedey de, 7, 115, 131
Mance, Jeanne, 7, 100
Manoir Hovey (North Hatley), 186–87
Marché Bonsecours, 100, 112
Markets, 139, 180
Metro, 41
Money, 21–23
Mont-Blanc, 170
Mont-Gabriel, 159–60
Mont-Orford, 177, 181–83
Montréal Canadiens, 108
Montréal Expos, 108
Montréal Symphony, 17, 144
Mont-Royal, 4, 7, 92, 109. See also Parc du Mont-Royal
walking tour, 127–31
Mont-Tremblant, 154, 170–77
accommodations, 172–76
restaurants, 176–77
Movie theaters, 153
Mulroney, Brian, 11–12, 14
Musée d'Art Contemporain de Montréal, 97–98
Musée David M. Stewart, 105–6
Musée de la Banque de Montréal, 105, 116
Musée des Arts Decoratifs de Montréal, 102
Musée des Beaux-Arts, 90–92, 123
Musée des Hospitalières de l'Hôtel-Dieu, 100
Musée Historique du Comté de Brome (Knowlton), 180–81
Musée Juste Pour Rire, 89
Musée Marc-Aurèle Fortin, 105, 118
Musée McCord, 89–90, 124

Musée Village de Séraphin
(Ste-Adèle), 161
Museum of Archeology and
History (Pointe-à-Callière),
94–95, 117
Museums. *See also* Art museums;
Historical and cultural museums
Montréal Museums Pass, 87
shopping at, 132, 138–39
Music, 124. *See also* Jazz
blues, 148–49
classical and opera, 143–44
Festival Orford, 181–82
folk/rock/pop, 146–47
Music Competition, 25
recordings, 17
shopping for, 139
Mystic, 178

Native Americans, 6, 7, 115, 183
Neighborhoods, 37–41. *See also
specific neighborhoods*
Networks and resources, 48
Nightlife, 141–53
North Hatley, 185–87
Notre-Dame-des-Neiges Cemetery,
130

Ogilvy, 122, 138
Old Court House, 115
Old Customs House, 117
Old Montréal, 2, 7, 36, 38
accommodations, 62–64
nightlife, 142
restaurants, 76–79, 113, 117, 118
sightseeing, 93–95, 98–100
walking tour, 111–18
Old Port, 94, 118
Olmsted Road (Parc Mont-Royal),
128
Olympic Stadium, 96–97, 108
Opera, 143–44

Package tours, 32–33
Parc du Mont-Royal, 40, 92–93,
128–31
cross-country skiing in, 93, 109
Parc Lafontaine, 100–101
Parks
Angrignon Park, 109
Mont Orford Provincial Park,
181
Parc du Mont-Royal, 40, 92–93,
109, 128–31
Parc Lafontaine, 100–101
Pastry shops, 84–85
Performing arts, 142–46
Peterson, Oscar, 12, 17
Picnicking, 86, 129–30

Place d'Armes, 115–16
Place des Arts, 144
Place Jacques-Cartier, 2, 94, 112
Place Vauquelin, 115
Place Ville-Marie, 122
Planetarium de Montréal, 103–4
Planning and preparing for your trip,
18–33
Plateau Mont-Royal, 39
accommodations, 64
nightlife, 142
restaurants, 79–84
sightseeing, 100–101
walking tour, 124–27
Pointe-à-Callière (Museum of
Archeology and History), 94–95,
117
Police, 46
Post office, 46
Puppet theater, 104

Recordings, 17
Redpath Museum, 98, 123
Restaurants, 2, 16, 65–86
best bets for, 67–69
for children, 67–68, 78
by cuisine, 69–70
downtown, 70–76, 123
Georgeville, 185
Mont-Tremblant, 176–77
North Hatley, 186–87
Old Montréal, 76–79, 113, 117,
118
Plateau Mont-Royal, 79–84
Ste-Adèle, 163–64
Ste-Agathe-des-Monts, 169–70
Ste-Marguerite, 165
St-Sauveur-des-Monts, 159
Sherbrooke, 189
Val-David, 167–68
Ritz-Carlton Kempinski Montréal, 50,
53, 151
Rock Island, 189
Rock music, 146–47
Roller hockey, 108–9
Rougemont, 178
Rue Crescent, 38, 122, 142
Rue Duluth, 39, 126
Rue Prince-Arthur, 39, 127
Rue St-Denis, 38–39, 69, 126,
150–51
Running, 109

Safdie, Moshe, 12, 92, 226
Safety, 46
Sailors' Church, 99, 111
St-Césaire, 178
Ste-Adèle, 160–64
accommodations, 161–63

St-Césaire (*cont.*)
  restaurants, 163–64
  sightseeing, 161
Ste-Agathe-des-Monts, 168–70
Ste-Marguerite, 164, 165
St-Faustin, 170
St-Jovite, 170–77
St-Lambert Lock, St. Lawrence
    Seaway, 102–3, 109
St. Lawrence River, 4, 6–7, 36, 40, 95,
    102
  cruises, 106–7
St-Paul-d'Abbotsford, 178
St-Sauveur-des-Monts, 157–59
Santa Claus' home, in Val-David, 167
Sawatdee, 73–74
Senior citizen travelers, 27–28
Separatist movement, 8–9, 13–15
Sherbrooke, 177, 188–89
Shopping, 2, 132–40
  Plateau Mont-Royal, 124–27
Sightseeing, 87–107. *See also* Walking
    tours
Single travelers, 28
Skating, 109
Skiing, in the Laurentians, 154.
    See also Cross country skiing
  Mont-Blanc, 170
  Mont-Gabriel, 159–60
  Mont-Orford, 181
  Mont-Tremblant, 171–72
  Ste-Adèle, 161
  St-Sauveur-des-Monts, 158
  tours, 33
Smith House (Parc Mont-Royal), 130
Snow Festival (La Fete des Neiges),
    24–25
S.O.S. Labyrinthe, 104
Special events, 24–27, 141, 166, 180,
    183, 188
Spectrum de Montréal, 145
Sports, 108–9. *See also* Skiing
Stanbridge East, 178
Stanstead Plain, 189
Student travelers, 29, 48
Subway, 41
Sutton, 181
  Swimming, 109–10

Taxes, 46–47, 50, 133
Taxis, 41
Telephone, 47
Telephone numbers, useful, 47
  hotlines, 45

Temperatures, average monthly, 24
Theater, 141, 142–43
  Festival de Théâtre des Amériques,
    141, 142
  puppet, 104
Tipping, 47
Toqué, 79–80
Tourist information, 18–19, 35–36,
    106, 115, 119
  the Estrie Region, 179
  the Laurentians, 156
Tours
  by boat, 106–7
  by bus, 107
  package, 32–33
Train travel, 30, 34–35
Transportation, 41–43, 47
Traveling
  to the Estrie Region, 178–79
  to the Laurentians, 155–56
  to Montréal, 29–32, 34–35
  Underground City, 37–38, 139–40

Val-David, 165, 166–68
Val-Morin, 165, 166–68
Vieille Douane, 117
Vieux-Montréal. *See* Old Montréal
Vieux Palais de Justice, 115
Vieux-Port, 94, 118
Vieux Séminaire de St-Sulpice, 116
Ville d'Estérel, 164–65
  Visitor information, 18–19, 35–36,
    106, 115, 119

Walking tours
  downtown, 118–24
  Mont-Royal, 127–31
  Old Montréal, 111–18
  organized, 108
  Plateau Mont-Royal, 124–27
Weather, 24
Wine and vineyards
  the Estrie Region, 182
  shopping for, 140
  Wine Festival, 155
Wolfe, James, 5
  Women travelers, 48

YMCA/YWCA, 61–62
  Youville Stables, 117

Zoo, Granby, 179

QUÉBEC CITY

Accommodations, 200–211
  Baie-St-Paul, 274–75
  best bets for, 201–2
  for children, 203
  Lower Town, 210–11
  Montmagny, 279
  Murray Bay, 277
  on or near the Grande-Allée,
      207–10
  Ste-Anne-de-Beaupré, 272
  Ste-Laurent, 266
  Ste-Pétronille, 266
  St-Irénée, 275
  St-Jean-Port-Joli, 281–82
  Upper Town, 202–7
Addresses, locating, 193
After dark, 257–62
Agora, 258
Airport, Jean-Lesage International,
    191
Air travel, 29–30, 191
American Express, 196
Anne, Saint, 270, 271
Antiques, shopping for, 250, 252
Arriving in Québec City, 191–92
Art museums
  historical and cultural museums, 231
  Le Centre d'Exposition
      (Baie-St-Paul), 274
  Musée de Charlevoix
      (Pointe-au-Pic), 276
  Musée des Anciens Canadiens
      (St-Jean-Port-Joli), 281
  Musée du Québec, 228–29
Arts and crafts, shopping for, 251,
    253, 268, 274, 280–81
ATMs (automated teller machines),
    22–23
Auberge La Goéliche (Ste-Pétronille),
    265, 266
Auberge St-Antoine, 201, 210
  Auditoriums, 258, 261

Baie-St-Paul, 273, 274–75
Bars, 260–62
Basilique-cathédrale Notre-Dame,
    229–30, 242, 262
Basse-Ville. See Lower Town
Bateau-mouche, 235, 262
Battlefields Park, 3, 229, 234, 236
Bernier, Elzéar, 279–80
Bicycling, 196, 264
Birdwatching, 283
Blues, 259
Boat travel and cruises, 235, 262
  Lévis Ferry, 3, 233
Books, recommended, 16
Bookstores, 196, 250, 254

Bourgault brothers, 280, 281
Breakneck Stairs, 245
Buses
  to Québec City, 31, 191
  tours, 234
Business hours, 196, 252

Cabaret, 258
Cafés, 3, 260–62
Calèches, 233, 234–35
Calendar of events, 24–27
Cap-à-l'Aigle (La Malbaie), 276–77
Cape Diamond, 4, 5, 191, 193, 225
Cape Tourmente, 283
Carnaval d'Hiver, 25, 243, 244, 257
Cars and driving, 195–96
  parking, 195–96
  to Québec City, 31, 32, 191–92
  rentals, 195
Casino de Charlevoix (Pointe-au-Pic),
    276
Centre d'Interpretation de la Vie
    Urbaine, 230, 242
Champlain, Samuel de, 4, 5, 232, 239,
    269–70
Chapelle/Musée des Ursulines, 231,
    243
Charlevoix, 273–77
  tourist information, 273–74
  traveling to, 273
Château Frontenac, 201–2, 203, 225,
    239
Chevalier House, 232, 246
Children
  accommodations, 203
  restaurants, 220
  sightseeing, 233–34
  travel tips, 28
Christmas items, shopping for, 254
Churches and cathedrals
  Anglican Cathedral of the Holy
      Trinity, 243
  Basilique-cathédrale Notre-Dame,
      229–30, 242, 262
  Chapelle/Musée des Ursulines,
      231, 243
  Church of Notre-Dame-des-
      Victoires, 228, 248
  Church of Ste-Anne-de-Beaupré,
      271
  Church of Ste-Laurent, 267
  Church of St-Jean, 267
  Church of St-Jean-Port-Joli, 281
  Notre-Dame Congregation
      (Ste-Famille), 268
Citadel, The, 225, 233, 244
City Hall, 242
Classical music, 257–58

Climate, 24, 198
Clothing stores, 254–55
Concert halls, 258, 261
Consulate, 196
Cost of everyday items, 23
Cuisine, 15–16, 212, 217
  restaurants by, 214
Currency and exchange, 20, 21–22,
  196–97
  Customs regulations, 20–21

Dance clubs, 260
Department store, 255
Disabled travelers, 27
Documents for entry into Canada,
  19
Dogsledding, 236
Domaine Forget (St-Irénée), 275

Emergencies, 197
Entertainment, 257–62
Entry into Canada, requirements for,
  19
Escalier Casse-Cou, 245
Excursion areas, 263–83
Explore Sound and Light Show, 232

Factory outlets, 272
Families, tips for, 28. *See also* Children
Famous and historical figures, 10–13.
  See also specific figures
Farmers' market, 250
Fast facts, 196–98
Festivals, 24–27, 257, 275
Film, 17
  movie theaters, 262
Fishing, 268
Folk music, 259–60
Food, shopping for, 223, 255–56, 268
Fruit orchards, 263, 279
Funicular, 3, 195, 233, 245

Gay men and lesbian travelers, 28,
  199, 262
Gift shops, 256
Glass blowing, 245–46
Governors' Park, 237–38
Grande-Allée, 193–94, 245
  accommodations, 207–10
  cafés, 3, 260
  restaurants, 218–20
  sightseeing, 228–29, 233
Grand Théâtre de Québec, 258, 261
Grosse Île (Montmagny), 278

Harness racing, 236
Haute-Ville. *See* Upper Town
Hilton International Québec, 207–8
Hippodrome, 236

Historical and cultural museums
  Explore Sound and Light Show, 232
  Maison Chevalier, 232
  Mauvide-Genest Manor (St-Jean),
    267
  Musée de la Civilisation, 225–28,
    233, 248–49
  Musée de l'Amerique Française, 231
  Musée du Fort, 230
  Musée Maritime Bernier
    (L'islet-sur-Mer), 280
  Urban Life Interpretation Center,
    230, 242
  Vieux-Port Interpretation Center,
    232–33, 249–50
History, 3–9
Holidays, 24
Horse-drawn carriage tours, 233,
  234–35
Hôtel-de-Ville, 242
Hôtel du Parlement, 233, 244–45
Hunting, 279

Ice skating, 236
Ile d'Orléans, 263–69
  tourist information, 264
  traveling to, 263–64
Information sources. *See* Telephone
  numbers, useful; Visitor
  information
Itineraries, 224–25

Jazz, 259
Jean-Lesage International Airport,
  191
John the Baptist, Saint, 25–26

Kamouraska, 282–83

La Citadelle, 225, 233, 244
Language, politics of, 8, 13–14, 194
  La Pinsonnière (Murray Bay), 277
Laurie Raphaël, 213, 220
Layout of Québec City, 192–93
Le Café du Monde, 221–22, 248
Le Centre d'Exposition (Baie-St-Paul),
  274
Le Graffiti, 219
Le Marie-Clarisse, 214, 222
Le Saint-Amour, 213, 215
Lévis Ferry, 3, 233
Lighthouse, Pointe à la Renommé,
  246
Liquor-stores, 197, 248, 256
L'islet-sur-Mer, 279–80
Lower Town, 5, 191, 192, 193
  accommodations, 210–11
  restaurants, 220–22, 248, 250
  shopping, 251, 252

sightseeing, 225–28, 232–33
walking tour, 245–50
Maison Chevalier, 232, 246
Maison Jacquet, 238
Maison Kent, 238
Maison Louis Jolliet, 246
Maison Maillou, 239
Marché du Vieux-Port, 250
Mauvide-Genest Manor (St-Jean), 267
Medieval Festival, Québec, 26–27
Ministry of Finance, 239
Money, 20, 21–23
Montcalm, Louis Joseph, marquis de, 5, 229, 230, 231, 237–38, 243
Monte Ste-Anne, 272–73
Montmagny, 278–79
Montmorency Falls, 234, 269–70
Movie theaters, 262
Murray Bay, 275–77
Musée de Charlevoix (Pointe-au-Pic), 276
Musée de Cire Grévin, 230–31, 233
Musée de la Civilisation, 225–28, 233, 248–49
Musée de l'Amerique Française, 231
Musée des Anciens Canadiens (St-Jean-Port-Joli), 281
Musée du Fort, 230
Musée du Québec, 228–29
Musée Maritime Bernier (L'islet-sur-Mer), 280
Museums. *See* Art museums; Historical and cultural museums; *and specific museums*
Music
classical and opera, 257–58
folk, 259–60
jazz and blues, 259
rock, 258–59

Native Americans, 5, 244
Naturalium, 249
Neighborhoods, 193–94. *See also specific neighborhoods*
Networks and resources, 198–99
Nightlife, 257–62

Opera, 257–58

Package tours, 32–33
Panoramas, 191
Parc de Champs de Bataille Interpretation Centre, 3, 229, 234, 236
Parc de la Jacques-Cartier, 236
Parc de l'Esplanade, 243–44
Parc des Gouverneurs, 237–38
Parc du Porche, 223
Parc Maritime de St-Laurent, 267

Parks
Battlefields Park, 3, 229, 234, 236
Governors' Park, 237–38
Parc de la Jacques-Cartier, 236
Parc de l'Esplanade, 243–44
Parc du Porche, 223
Parc Maritime de St-Laurent, 267
Performing arts, 257–58
Place d'Armes, 239
Place de Paris, 248
Place Royale, 193, 228, 248
Plains of Abraham, 5, 225, 230, 232, 234, 270
Planning and preparing for your trip, 18–32
Pointe-à-Carcy, 249
Pointe à la Renommé Lighthouse, 246
Pointe-au-Pic, 275–77
Police, 198
Post office, 198
Promenade des Gouverneurs, 238

Québec Medieval Festival, 26–27
Québec Museum, 228–29
Recreational activities, 236, 273
Restaurants, 3, 16, 212–23
best bets for, 213–14
for children, 220
by cuisine, 214
Lower Town, 220–22, 248, 250
Montmagny, 279
on or near the Grande-Allée, 218–20
Ste-Anne-de-Beaupré, 272
Ste-Famille, 269
Ste-Laurent, 267
St-François, 268
St-Jean-Port-Joli, 282
Upper Town, 215–18, 238, 240, 245
Restrooms, 198
Rock music, 258–59
Royal Battery, 247–48
Rue du Petit-Champlain, 246
Rue du Trésor, 241

Safety, 198
Ste-Anne-de-Beaupré, 270–72
tourist information, 271
traveling to, 270–71
Ste-Famille (Ile d'Orléans), 268–69
Ste-Laurent (Île d'Orléans), 266–67
Ste-Pétronille (Île d'Orléans), 264–66
St-François (Île d'Orléans), 268
St-Irénée, 275
St-Jean (Île d'Orléans), 267
St-Jean-Port-Joli, 280–82

St. Lawrence River, 3, 4, 190, 268, 270, 272
  cruises, 235, 262
  southern bank, towns along, 278–83
St-Pierre (Île d'Orléans), 269
Seigneurie des Aulnaies (St-Roch-des-Aulnaies), 281
Séminare de Québec, 242
Senior citizen travelers, 27–28, 199
Separatist movement, 8–9, 13–14, 194
  Serge Bruyère, 215
Shopping, 251–56
  best buys, 251–52
Sightseeing, 224–34. *See also* Walking tours
Single travelers, 28
Skiing, 236, 268, 273
Snow geese, 283
Sound-and-light shows, 230, 232, 262
Southern Bank, 278–83
Special events, 24–27, 257, 275
Sports, 235–36, 273
Student travelers, 29, 198–99
Summer Festival, 26, 257

Taxes, 252
Taxis, 195
Telephone numbers, useful, 198
  concert and performance halls, 261
Temperatures, average monthly, 24
Terrasse Dufferin, 3, 5, 238, 262
Tipping, 198
Tourist information, 18–19, 192, 228, 243
  Charlevoix, 273–74
  Ile d'Orléans, 264
  Montmorency Falls, 270
  Ste-Anne-de-Beaupré, 271
Tours
  by boat, 235
  by bus, 234
  by horse-drawn carriage, 233, 234–35

of Île d'Orléans, 264
  to Montmorency Falls, 270
  package, 32–33
  walking, 235
Train travel, 30–31, 191
Transportation, 194–96, 198
Traveling
  to Charlevoix, 273
  to Île d'Orléans, 263–64
  to Monte Ste-Anne, 272
  to Montmorency Falls, 270
  to Québec City, 29–32, 191–92
  to Ste-Anne-de-Beaupré, 270–71

Upper Town, 191, 192, 193
  accommodations, 202–7
  restaurants, 215–18, 238, 240, 245
  shopping, 251, 252
  sightseeing, 225, 229–31
  walking tour, 237–45
Urban Life Interpretation Center, 230
Ursuline Convent, 231, 243

Vieux-Port, 249
Vieux-Port Interpretation Center, 232–33, 249–50
Visitor information, 18–19, 192, 228, 243

Walking tours
  Lower Town, 245–50
  organized, 235
  Upper Town, 237–45
Water park, 234
Wax Museum, 230–31, 233
Weather, 24, 198
Wines, shopping for, 197, 248, 256
Winter Carnival, 25, 243, 244, 257
Wolfe, James, 5, 229, 230, 237–38, 270
Women travelers, 199
Woodcarving, in St-Jean-Port-Joli, 280–81

Now Save Money on All Your Travels by Joining

Frommer's

T R A V E L   B O O K   C L U B

The Advantages of Membership:

1. Your choice of any **TWO FREE BOOKS.**

2. Your own subscription to the **TRIPS & TRAVEL** quarterly newsletter, where you'll discover the best buys in travel, the hottest vacation spots, the latest travel trends, world-class events and festivals, and much more.

3. A **30% DISCOUNT** on any additional books you order through the club.

4. **DOMESTIC TRIP-ROUTING KITS** (available for a small additional fee). We'll send you a detailed map highlighting the most direct or scenic route to your destination, anywhere in North America.

Here's all you have to do to join:

Send in your annual membership fee of $25.00 ($35.00 Canada/Foreign) with your name, address, and selections on the form below. Or call 815/734-1104 to use your credit card.

Send all orders to:

FROMMER'S TRAVEL BOOK CLUB
P.O. Box 473 • Mt. Morris, IL 61054-0473 • ☎ 815/734-1104

YES! I want to take advantage of this opportunity to join Frommer's Travel Book Club.

[ ] My check for $25.00 ($35.00 for Canadian or foreign orders) is enclosed.
    All orders must be prepaid in U.S. funds only. Please make checks payable to Frommer's Travel Book Club.
[ ] Please charge my credit card: [ ] Visa or [ ] Mastercard

   Credit card number: _____

   Expiration date: ___ / ___ / ___

   Signature: _____

   Or call 815/734-1104 to use your credit card by phone.

Name: _____

Address: _____

City: _____ State: _____ Zip code: _____

Phone number (in case we have a question regarding your order): _____

Please indicate your choices for TWO FREE books (*see following pages*):

   Book 1 - Code: _____ Title: _____

   Book 2 - Code: _____ Title: _____

For information on ordering additional titles, see your first issue of the *Trips & Travel* newsletter.

Allow 4–6 weeks for delivery for all items. Prices of books, membership fee, and publication dates are subject to change without notice. All orders are subject to acceptance and availability.   AC1

The following Frommer's guides are available from your favorite bookstore, or you can use the order form on the preceding page to request them as part of your membership in Frommer's Travel Book Club.

FROMMER'S COMPLETE TRAVEL GUIDES

(Comprehensive guides to sightseeing, dining and accommodations, with selections in all price ranges—from deluxe to budget)

Acapulco/Ixtapa/Taxco,		Italy '96 (avail. 11/95)	C183
2nd Ed.	C157	Jamaica/Barbados, 2nd Ed.	C149
Alaska '94-'95	C131	Japan '94-'95	C144
Arizona '95	C166	Maui, 1st Ed.	C153
Australia '94-'95	C147	Nepal, 3rd Ed. (avail. 11/95)	C184
Austria, 6th Ed.	C162	New England '95	C165
Bahamas '96 (avail. 8/95)	C172	New Mexico, 3rd Ed.	C167
Belgium/Holland/Luxembourg,		New York State, 4th Ed.	C133
4th Ed.	C170	Northwest, 5th Ed.	C140
Bermuda '96 (avail. 8/95)	C174	Portugal '94-'95	C141
California '95	C164	Puerto Rico '95-'96	C151
Canada '94-'95	C145	Puerto Vallarta/Manzanillo/	
Caribbean '96 (avail. 9/95)	C173	Guadalajara, 2nd Ed.	C135
Carolinas/Georgia, 2nd Ed.	C128	Scandinavia, 16th Ed.	C169
Colorado '96 (avail. 11/95)	C179	Scotland '94-'95	C146
Costa Rica, 1st Ed.	C161	South Pacific '94-'95	C138
Cruises '95-'96	C150	Spain, 16th Ed.	C163
Delaware/Maryland '94-'95	C136	Switzerland, 7th Ed.	
England '96 (avail. 10/95)	C180	(avail. 9/95)	C177
Florida '96 (avail. 9/95)	C181	Thailand, 2nd Ed.	C154
France '96 (avail. 11/95)	C182	U.S.A., 4th Ed.	C156
Germany '96 (avail. 9/95)	C176	Virgin Islands, 3rd Ed.	
Honolulu/Waikiki/Oahu,		(avail. 8/95)	C175
4th Ed. (avail. 10/95)	C178	Virginia '94-'95	C142
Ireland, 1st Ed.	C168	Yucatán '95-'96	C155

FROMMER'S $-A-DAY GUIDES

(Dream Vacations at Down-to-Earth Prices)

Australia on $45 '95-'96	D122	Ireland on $45 '94-'95	D118
Berlin from $50, 3rd Ed.		Israel on $45, 15th Ed.	D130
(avail. 10/95)	D137	London from $55 '96	
Caribbean from $60, 1st Ed.		(avail. 11/95)	D136
(avail. 9/95)	D133	Madrid on $50 '94-'95	D119
Costa Rica/Guatemala/Belize		Mexico from $35 '96	
on $35, 3rd Ed.	D126	(avail. 10/95)	D135
Eastern Europe on $30,		New York on $70 '94-'95	D121
5th Ed.	D129	New Zealand from $45,	
England from $50 '96		6th Ed.	D132
(avail. 11/95)	D138	Paris on $45 '94-'95	D117
Europe from $50 '96		South America on $40,	
(avail. 10/95)	D139	16th Ed.	D123
Greece from $45, 6th Ed.	D131	Washington, D.C. on	
Hawaii from $60 '96		$50 '94-'95	D120
(avail. 9/95)	D134		

FROMMER'S COMPLETE CITY GUIDES

(Comprehensive guides to sightseeing, dining, and accommodations in all price ranges)

Amsterdam, 8th Ed.	S176	Miami '95-'96	S149
Athens, 10th Ed.	S174	Minneapolis/St. Paul, 4th Ed.	S159
Atlanta & the Summer Olympic		Montréal/Québec City '95	S166
Games '96 (avail. 11/95)	S181	Nashville/Memphis, 1st Ed.	S141
Atlantic City/Cape May,		New Orleans '96 (avail. 10/95)	S182
5th Ed.	S130	New York City '96 (avail. 11/95)	S183
Bangkok, 2nd Ed.	S147	Paris '96 (avail. 9/95)	S180
Barcelona '93-'94	S115	Philadelphia, 8th Ed.	S167
Berlin, 3rd Ed.	S162	Prague, 1st Ed.	S143
Boston '95	S160	Rome, 10th Ed.	S168
Budapest, 1st Ed.	S139	St. Louis/Kansas City, 2nd Ed.	S127
Chicago '95	S169	San Antonio/Austin, 1st Ed.	S177
Denver/Boulder/		San Diego '95	S158
Colorado Springs, 3rd Ed.	S154	San Francisco '96 (avail. 10/95)	S184
Disney World/Orlando '96		Santa Fe/Taos/	
(avail. 9/95)	S178	Albuquerque '95	S172
Dublin, 2nd Ed.	S157	Seattle/Portland '94-'95	S137
Hong Kong '94-'95	S140	Sydney, 4th Ed.	S171
Las Vegas '95	S163	Tampa/St. Petersburg, 3rd Ed.	S146
London '96 (avail. 9/95)	S179	Tokyo '94-'95	S144
Los Angeles '95	S164	Toronto, 3rd Ed.	S173
Madrid/Costa del Sol, 2nd Ed.	S165	Vancouver/Victoria '94-'95	S142
Mexico City, 1st Ed.	S175	Washington, D.C. '95	S153

FROMMER'S FAMILY GUIDES

(Guides to family-friendly hotels, restaurants, activities, and attractions)

California with Kids	F105	San Francisco with Kids	F104
Los Angeles with Kids	F103	Washington, D.C. with Kids	F102
New York City with Kids	F101		

FROMMER'S WALKING TOURS

(Memorable strolls through colorful and historic neighborhoods, accompanied by detailed directions and maps)

Berlin	W100	San Francisco, 2nd Ed.	W115
Chicago	W107	Spain's Favorite Cities	
England's Favorite Cities	W108	(avail. 9/95)	W116
London, 2nd Ed.	W111	Tokyo	W109
Montréal/Québec City	W106	Venice	W110
New York, 2nd Ed.	W113	Washington, D.C., 2nd Ed.	W114
Paris, 2nd Ed.	W112		

FROMMER'S AMERICA ON WHEELS

(Guides for travelers who are exploring the U.S.A. by car, featuring a brand-new rating system for accommodations and full-color road maps)

Arizona/New Mexico	A100	Florida	A102
California/Nevada	A101	Mid-Atlantic	A103

FROMMER'S SPECIAL-INTEREST TITLES

Arthur Frommer's Branson!	P107	Frommer's Where to	
Arthur Frommer's New World		Stay U.S.A., 11th Ed.	P102
of Travel (avail. 11/95)	P112	National Park Guide, 29th Ed.	P106
Frommer's Caribbean		USA Today Golf	
Hideaways (avail. 9/95)	P110	Tournament Guide	P113
Frommer's America's 100		USA Today Minor League	
Best-Loved State Parks	P109	Baseball Book	P111

FROMMER'S BEST BEACH VACATIONS
(The top places to sun, stroll, shop, stay, play, party, and swim—with each beach rated for beauty, swimming, sand, and amenities)

California (avail. 10/95)	G100	Hawaii (avail. 10/95)	G102
Florida (avail. 10/95)	G101		

FROMMER'S BED & BREAKFAST GUIDES
(Selective guides with four-color photos and full descriptions of the best inns in each region)

California	B100	Hawaii	B105
Caribbean	B101	Pacific Northwest	B106
East Coast	B102	Rockies	B107
Eastern United States	B103	Southwest	B108
Great American Cities	B104		

FROMMER'S IRREVERENT GUIDES
(Wickedly honest guides for sophisticated travelers and those who want to be)

Chicago (avail. 11/95)	I100	New Orleans (avail. 11/95)	I103
London (avail. 11/95)	I101	San Francisco (avail. 11/95)	I104
Manhattan (avail. 11/95)	I102	Virgin Islands (avail. 11/95)	I105

FROMMER'S DRIVING TOURS
(Four-color photos and detailed maps outlining spectacular scenic driving routes)

Australia	Y100	Italy	Y108
Austria	Y101	Mexico	Y109
Britain	Y102	Scandinavia	Y110
Canada	Y103	Scotland	Y111
Florida	Y104	Spain	Y112
France	Y105	Switzerland	Y113
Germany	Y106	U.S.A.	Y114
Ireland	Y107		

FROMMER'S BORN TO SHOP
(The ultimate travel guides for discriminating shoppers—from cut-rate to couture)

Hong Kong (avail. 11/95)	Z100	London (avail. 11/95)	Z101